More Praise for *Black Tudors*

'The book is based on impeccable research in a rich array of sources. But Dr Kaufmann wears her learning lightly and tells a series of fascinating stories with an elegance and wit that should appeal to many readers.'

Dr Clive Holmes, Emeritus Fellow and Lecturer in History, Lady Margaret Hall, University of Oxford

'Miranda Kaufmann's *Black Tudors*, grounded in extensive and impeccable archival research, presents an evocative and convincing picture of the lives of real men and women of black African descent in Renaissance England. Concentrating on ten strikingly varied individuals – from a royal trumpeter to a silk-weaver – Kaufmann persuasively argues that Africans who came to England in this era were able to find a meaningful place in English society, not only in London, Southampton and Bristol but also in rural areas. Drawing on parish records, legal cases, letters, visual images and her broad knowledge of Tudor-era economic history and global mercantile expansion, she dispels the myth that the black Britons of this era existed only at the very upper or lower margins of society. Each of her ten individuals, who are cleverly linked to the records of many others, is vividly brought to life through a discussion of their goals, their labour and their vicissitudes, and set within the complex social, political, economic and religious history of the period. The book is a brilliant example of how to use the most detailed kind of archival data to present a broadly accessible picture of the past, and one which has enormous relevance to the present controversies about immigration and diversity.'

Paul Kaplan, Professor of Art History, State University of New York

'Who knew that a diver from West Africa worked to salvage Henry VIII's flagship the *Mary Rose*? Based on a wealth of original research, Miranda Kaufmann's *Black Tudors* restores the black presence to sixteenth- and seventeenth-century England in all its lively detail. Africans lived and worked not as slaves but as independent agents, from mariners to silk weavers, women and men, prince and prostitute. *Black Tudors* challenges assumptions about ethnic identity and racism in Tudor England. It will be required reading for anyone interested in new directions in Tudor history.'

Dr John Cooper, Senior Lecturer in History, University of York, and author of *The Queen's Agent*

BLACK TUDORS

THE UNTOLD STORY

MIRANDA KAUFMANN

ONEWORLD

A Oneworld Book

First published by Oneworld Publications, 2017

ISBN 978-1-78607-184-2
eISBN 978-1-78607-185-9

Typeset in Minion Pro by Palimpsest Book Production Ltd, Falkirk, Stirlingshire

Printed and bound in Great Britain by Clays Ltd, St Ives plc

Oneworld Publications
10 Bloomsbury Street
London WC1B 3SR
England

Stay up to date with the latest books,
special offers, and exclusive content from
Oneworld with our monthly newsletter

Sign up on our website
oneworld-publications.com

MIX
Paper from
responsible sources
FSC® C018072

For my husband Olivier, my shelter from the storm.

My lover is an olive tree whose roots grow by the sea.

Jeanette Winterson

Contents

Introduction

IN APRIL 1645 Sir John Wynter burnt his home to the ground rather than see it fall into Parliamentary hands. White Cross Manor, built at the zenith of the Tudor age, had been destroyed by the Civil War that marked the nadir of the following century. The Wynter family featured the sorts of characters that traditionally appear in Tudor history books: Sir William Wynter commanded the *Vanguard* in the fight against the Spanish Armada and his son, Sir Edward, sailed with Sir Francis Drake. The Reformation unleashed by Henry VIII had forced the family to practise their Catholic faith in secret. But White Cross Manor was also the scene of an unknown episode of Tudor history. For it was there, in the last decade of Elizabeth I's reign, that a Black Tudor, known as Edward Swarthye, alias 'Negro', whipped an Englishman named John Guye.

Despite the insatiable appetite for all things Tudor, from raunchy television series to bath ducks modelled as Henry VIII and Anne Boleyn, the existence of the Black Tudors is little known. The popular concept, as dramatised in the Opening Ceremony of the London Olympics in 2012, is that people of African origin first arrived in England when the *Empire Windrush* docked at Tilbury in 1948. It's quite a jolt to consider that there could have been Africans in the crowd gathered at those very same docks when Elizabeth I galvanised her troops to face the Spanish Armada three hundred and sixty years earlier. There were Africans present at the royal courts of Henry VII, Henry VIII, Elizabeth I and James I, and in the households of famous Tudors including Robert Dudley (Earl of Leicester), Sir Walter Ralegh, Sir Francis Drake, William Cecil (Lord Burghley) and his son, Robert; and across England from Hull to Truro. Black Tudors played fascinating roles in the famous stories of the *Mary Rose* and the *Golden Hinde*, as well as in a host of other untold stories, like the whipping at White Cross Manor.

Once people learn of the presence of Africans in Tudor England, they often assume their experience was one of enslavement and racial discrimination. This attitude is neatly summarized by the only three entries in the *Guardian* Black history timeline for the period: '1562: First English slave trade expedition', '1596: Elizabeth I expels Africans' and '1604: Shakespeare and Othello'.[1] It is true that John Hawkins masterminded the first English transatlantic slaving voyages in the 1560s, but he was, in an awful sense, ahead of his time. After his final voyage returned in disarray in 1569, the English did not take up the trade again in earnest until the 1640s. Elizabeth I did not 'expel' Africans from England in 1596; rather her Privy Council issued a limited licence to an unscrupulous merchant named Caspar Van Senden, who was only allowed to transport individuals out of England with their masters' consent: a consent that he utterly failed to obtain.[2] And although much has been written on the question of racism in Shakespeare's *Othello*, we mustn't forget that it was a work of fiction designed to entertain, and so must be set alongside archival evidence of how Africans were treated in England's churches, households and law courts.

The misconceptions surrounding the status of Black Tudors are part of a wider impression that any African living outside Africa before the mid-nineteenth century, be it in Europe or the Americas, must have been enslaved. When most of us think of a slave, the image that appears in our minds is of an African. There is more than enough visual material to draw upon, from films such as *12 Years a Slave* and television series such as *Roots*, to the exhibits at museums such as the *International Slavery Museum* in Liverpool and the 'London, Sugar and Slavery' gallery at *Museum of London, Docklands*.[3] Often the first and only mention of Africa in the school curriculum is when children are taught about the slave trade. They see Africans reduced to one of a series of commodities traded in a triangle, packed into ships in chains. Equal attention is not given to the extensive history of Africa before the Europeans arrived there and to examples of collaboration between Europeans and Africans, or to the free Africans living in Europe.

Not all slaves were African. The word 'slave' itself comes from 'Slav', referring to the Slavonic peoples of Eastern Europe, who were enslaved in great numbers by the Holy Roman Emperor Otto the Great and his successors from the tenth century onwards.[4] And more than a million white Europeans were enslaved in North Africa between 1530 and 1780, having been captured from the shores of England, Ireland, France, Spain and Portugal by the Barbary pirates.[5]

Contemporary concerns naturally shape the questions we ask about our past. It is difficult for us in the twenty-first century to push aside the nationalist myth of the Tudors created by nineteenth-century imperialists and imagine an England before the emergence of the British Empire. Tudor England was a small, relatively weak kingdom on the edge of Europe, which had not yet experienced the full horrors of the transatlantic slave trade and colonial plantation slavery. These abominations, alongside the imperialism and scientific racism that followed, cast their shadows across almost every discussion of the history of Africans in Britain. Today, immigration and the question of whether institutional racism is endemic to society bedevil political discourse. These issues may be the source of our questions, but they cannot be allowed to shape our conclusions about the past.

The answers are complex, but the questions that most commonly spring to mind about the Black Tudors are simple: why and how did they come to England? How were they treated? What were their lives like?

To understand how and why Africans came to England, we must look to the dramatic developments going on in the wider world. In a century dominated by the Spanish and Portuguese, England was small fry on the global stage. Following Columbus's discovery of the Americas in 1492, the Iberian powers carved up the world between them in the Treaty of Tordesillas in 1494. Spain laid claim to the New World of South America and the Caribbean, while

Portugal looked to Africa and the East Indies. Their empires were united from 1580 under the rule of Philip II. Strangely enough, it was the death of the young Portuguese King, Don Sebastian, on *African* soil, at the Battle of Alcazar in 1578, that allowed Philip of Spain to annex the Portuguese crown and become the dreaded 'universal monarch', establishing a global dominion 'on which the sun never set'.

The Portuguese had been the first Europeans to visit Africa, *en route* to India, in the fifteenth century. They brought the first enslaved Africans to Europe in 1444.[6] From then, a substantial black population developed across southern Europe, with smaller numbers appearing in the more northerly parts of the continent. By 1502 the transatlantic slave trade had begun, and over the next century more than 370,000 Africans would be transported to the Spanish Americas.[7] With people of African origin scattered across the early modern world, Black Tudors could arrive in England not only directly from Africa, but also from Europe, the Americas and places in between. The fact that they had often travelled through the Iberian world is reflected in names such as Catalina or Diego.

Understanding the world of the Black Tudors means becoming familiar with the sixteenth-century mind-set and its ideas about religion, politics, life and death, so very different from our own. When the Black Tudors encountered Tudor Englishmen, they found a people who, though certainly xenophobic on occasion, were deeply curious about the world beyond the seas. Most English men and women knew little or nothing of the world beyond their parish boundary. A 'stranger' was simply someone from outside the parish. Tudors were far more likely to judge a new acquaintance by his or her religion and social class than by where they were born or the colour of their skin, though these categories did on occasion intersect.

How Africans were treated by the church tells us a lot about where they stood in Tudor England. This was a deeply religious society, in which life after death was no abstract ideal but the foundation of daily life. Death was impossible to ignore; high child mortality rates and a range of gruesome, incurable diseases conspired to impose an average life expectancy at birth of just thirty-eight years.[8] Was a Black Tudor's acceptance into a parish community through the rituals of baptism, marriage and burial an effacement of African identity, or was the promise of eternal life the greatest gift a Christian society could bestow?

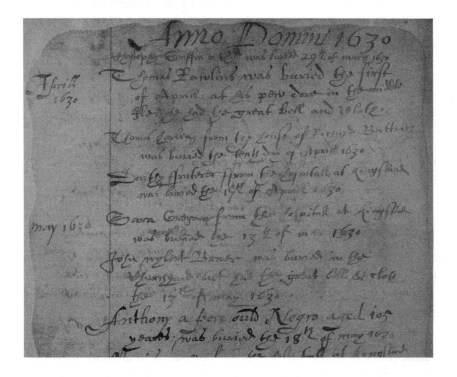

Many of the hundreds of Africans in Tudor England are only recorded in tantalizing one-liners, such as this 1630 burial record for 'Anthony a pore ould Negro aged 105', from the parish register of St Augustine's Church, Hackney.

Social class governed society. Everyone, from the King (who ruled by divine right), through the aristocracy, to the gentry, yeomen and husbandmen, down to the lowliest vagrant, occupied a particular place in the 'Great Chain of Being'. When Africans arrived in England as ambassadors, they were treated as such, but when they arrived aboard a captured ship, they found themselves at the bottom of the pile. Those who had skills, such as musicians, sailors or craftsmen, fared better. In many ways, their lives were no worse than those of the vast majority of Tudors: 'nasty, brutish and short', but this was the result of having no social standing, not of having dark skin.[9]

In 1772, Lord Chief Justice Mansfield heard the landmark case of James Somerset, an African whose former master wished to transport him forcibly to Jamaica for sale. One of the lawyers defending him cited as precedent a court ruling from 1569. In the same year that Hawkins's final slaving venture returned, it had been pronounced that 'England was too pure an air for a slave to breathe in'. Somerset's lawyer argued that 'the plain inference from it is, that the slave was become free by his arrival in England'.[10] The idea that setting foot on English soil conferred freedom was so widespread in the Tudor period that it reached the ears of Juan Gelofe, a forty-year-old Wolof from West Africa, enslaved in a Mexican silver mine belonging to one Francisco Ginoves. In 1572 he told an English sailor named William Collins that England 'must be a good country as there were no slaves there'.[11] His conclusion, like the knowledge that Edward Swarthye whipped John Guye in Elizabethan Gloucestershire, confounds modern assumptions about the lives of Africans in Tudor England.

For all who thought they knew the Tudors, it is time to think again . . .

I

John Blanke,
the Trumpeter

He gripped the horse tightly with his thighs, steadying her against the shock of the trumpet's blast. It had taken a while to master the art of playing the trumpet on horseback but now he was doing just that, as one of the King's trumpeters at the Westminster Tournament. King Henry had decreed two days of jousting to celebrate the birth of a son to his wife, Katherine of Aragon. He had also commissioned the heraldic artists of the College of Arms to record the proceedings on vellum. As Blanke watched the King charge towards his opponent, he considered that the artists might need to use a bit of licence when they recorded the scene for posterity. Best to show the King in some feat of great chivalric prowess, such as breaking a lance on the helm. It didn't really matter whether it had actually happened. He wondered how he would appear in the vellum roll – on horseback amongst the other trumpeters, of course, dressed in the royal livery of yellow halved with grey. The artists would enjoy painting the brightly coloured tasselled banners, with their quartered fleur-de-lys and lions, hanging from their trumpets. The instruments themselves would be flecked with gold. But would they remember his turban, which set him apart from his bareheaded companions? And how would they depict his dark skin? It was not a pigment they would be accustomed to using. Indeed, it might be the first time anyone had painted a Black Tudor.

THE TWO IMAGES of John Blanke in the 60-foot-long vellum manuscript known as the *Westminster Tournament Roll* comprise the only identifiable portrait of an African in Tudor England.¹ It's the most popular image of all those kept in the vast collection of the College of Arms and it shows that Africans were present in England from the earliest years of the sixteenth century. Seeing him for the first time provokes a visceral reaction: often surprise, followed closely by curiosity. His presence at the Tudor court raises as many, if not more, questions than it answers. Was he the only African in England at this time? What brought him to London? What were the circumstances of his arrival, decades before the English began engaging in direct trade with Africa, or in the slave trade? How much about his origin or religious beliefs can we deduce from the fact that he wears a turban? His striking image is regularly used to demonstrate that Africans were present in Tudor times, without much further interrogation of his story, or the existence of any contemporaries.

Histories of the early Tudor period, when England was just emerging from the shadow cast by the Wars of the Roses, are often focused on domestic politics, or relations with other European powers. John Blanke forces us to consider the country's relationship with the wider world. In the early sixteenth century England did not have strong, direct links with the world beyond Europe. The Englishmen John Tintam and William Fabian had contemplated a voyage to Guinea in 1481 but the Portuguese complained to Edward IV about the intrusion into João II's imperial dominion, and the expedition was abandoned. In 1497, Henry VII commissioned the Italian explorer John Cabot's voyage to America, yet few Englishmen came forward to follow in his footsteps.²

Any connections with Africa, Asia and the Americas were mediated through southern Europe. In 1535, Andrew Boorde sent Thomas Cromwell 'seeds of rhubarb' from Catalonia, explaining that they came 'out of Barbary' and were considered 'a great treasure' or delicacy by the Catalans.³ Africans themselves tended to arrive in England via Portugal, Spain or Italy.

John Blanke is described as 'black' and depicted with dark skin and wearing a turban in the *Westminster Tournament Roll*, but that is the extent of our knowledge as to his origin. Given his youthful appearance in the *Roll*, and the extent of the African diaspora in the early years of the sixteenth century, we can posit that he was born in North or West Africa, or in southern Europe to African parents, in the late fifteenth century. The turban suggests an Islamic heritage, and its relatively flat shape is reminiscent of North African or Andalusian styles. That said, Henry VIII enjoyed dressing himself and his courtiers in Turkish or Moorish fashion and may also have chosen to dress John Blanke in this way.[4] As musical knowledge was often passed, like any trade, from father to son, John Blanke probably came from a musical family.[5]

The first record of wages being paid to 'John Blanke the blacke Trumpet' dates from December 1507.[6] One wonders how his name was coined, and whether it was thought humorous to use the French word '*blanc*', in the same spirit that Robin Hood's tall friend was called Little John. It seems to have been a joke with wide appeal: an African slave named 'Juan Blanco' appeared in Granada in 1565.[7] Blanke was paid 20 shillings (at a rate of 8d a day) for his work that December and he continued to receive monthly payments of the same amount through the following year.[8] His annual wage of £12 was twice that of an agricultural labourer and three times the average servant's wage.[9] Blanke joined a group of seven existing trumpeters retained by Henry VII. A position at court was the best any musician could hope for; it brought high status and a regular wage, as well as board, lodging and a clothing allowance.

Music echoed through the corridors of Tudor palaces. No architect of the time would have countenanced designing a Great Hall without a minstrels' gallery. The Crown employed a man whose sole purpose was to marshal the court musicians, ensuring they were in the right place at the right time, prepared to entertain the King and his household with their 'blowings and pipings' at 'meats and suppers'.[10] Trumpeters played a vital part in royal entries, tournaments, funerals, executions, banquets, weddings, coronations, battles and sea voyages, as well as the annual grand festivities over Christmas and New Year. They were required to 'blow the court to supper' and to make music 'at the king's pleasure'. They heralded the King's arrival: 'The King's coming, I know by his trumpets,' Lavatch says in *All's Well That Ends Well*. Henry VII even commissioned a pair of stone trumpeters to stand either side of the gateway leading to the inner court at Richmond Palace. At the wedding of Katherine of Aragon and Prince Arthur in 1501, the largest court festival of the first Henry Tudor's reign, the trumpeters were ordered to 'blow continually' from the moment the Spanish princess left her lodgings until she reached the altar. After the ceremony, the court travelled down the Thames to Greenwich by boat. Their journey was accompanied by the music of a host of instruments, including 'the most goodly and pleasant mirth of trumpets'. The sound of all this on the water was unlike anything that had ever been heard before.[11]

It is unlikely that court trumpeters at this time could read music, but some might have read plainsong and other unmeasured notation, such as the fashionable *basse danse* tunes. They could play quite intricate pieces: the double-curved instruments John Blanke and his fellows are shown playing in the Westminster Tournament Roll, now known as cavalry trumpets, were able to do much more than the straight *busine* designed for military-style fanfares.[12] The craft of trumpet-making was well established in the City of London, centred near the Guildhall in a road now known as 'Trump Street'.[13]

Trumpets have been used to mark power, status, military might and even divine power in civilisations across the world. The walls of Jericho tumbled down at the sound of trumpets. The Jewish New Year, Rosh Hashanah, is also known as the Feast of the Trumpets, because the Torah stipulates the day should be marked with trumpet fanfares.[14] Silver and bronze trumpets inscribed with the names of military gods were found in the tomb of King Tutankhamen. In some northern Nigerian kingdoms, the capture of the royal trumpets effectively signalled a *coup d'état*, while on the South Pacific island of Rarotonga, the word for a conch-shell trumpet is the same as that used for a chief, ruler or priest.[15]

As symbols of royal authority, trumpeters sometimes served as messengers or envoys, roles that could lead them into dangerous territory. When Francis I sent a royal trumpeter to impose order on the rioting students of Paris in 1518, they broke his instrument and cut off his horse's ears. Worse, in 1538, when the Prince of Parma, general of the Spanish troops, sent his trumpeter as a messenger to Ypres while he held it under siege, the captains and magistrates of the town burnt the letter and hanged the trumpeter. Because trumpeters acted as messengers, they were supposed to enjoy diplomatic immunity, allowing them free passage through foreign, and often enemy, territory. This left them open to suspicion of espionage: in 1560, the Duke of Norfolk wrote to William Cecil that a Scottish trumpeter had arrived with letters, but 'more to spy than otherwise'.[16]

The court musicians of Europe were highly cosmopolitan, hailing predominantly from Flanders, France and Italy. Henry VII's court was no exception. The marshal of his trumpeters, Peter de Casa Nova, was Italian.[17] German drummers, the Prince of Castile's taberet, a French organ player, Dutch and French minstrels and some musicians simply described as 'strange' all played for the King.[18] Henry had spent much of his youth at the court of Duke Francis of Brittany, and some time in France, so no doubt he continued to enjoy the familiar continental style of entertainment. More importantly, it was fashionable and prestigious to employ an international troupe of musicians.[19]

African musicians had been playing for European monarchs and nobility since at least the twelfth century, in a tradition that owed much to medieval Islamic courts from Spain to Syria. In 1194, turbaned black trumpeters accompanied the Holy Roman Emperor Henry VI on his triumphal entry into Palermo in Sicily.[20] In Renaissance Italy, trumpeters worked on board royal ships. Martino, a 'black slave', was purchased by Ferdinand, King of Naples, in 1470, to play on the royal ship *Barcha*. An African trumpeter travelled with Cosimo I de' Medici of Florence on his galley in 1555. In Portugal ten black musicians played the *charamela* (a wind-instrument) at the court of Teodosio I, Duke of Bragança.[21]

Closer to home, James IV of Scotland employed a Moorish drummer in the early years of the sixteenth century. This musician, who is known only as the 'More taubronar', not only played the tabor drum but was something of a choreographer. He devised a dance with twelve performers in black and white costumes for the 1505 Shrove Tuesday celebrations at the Scottish court. This may have been a boisterous event, resulting in some wear and tear to his instrument, because the following month he was given 28 shillings 'to pay for the painting of his taubroun'.[22]

The ubiquitous presence of black musicians at European courts is echoed in the artwork of the time: a dark-skinned trumpeter in French livery appears in a tapestry depicting part of the festivities at the Field of the Cloth of Gold in 1520.[23] A group of African boys making music with a variety of wind and brass instruments, including a trombone, are featured in *The Engagement of St Ursula and Prince Etherius*, commissioned in 1522 by Eleanor, Queen of Portugal, to adorn the St Auta altarpiece in the Convent of Madre de Deus, in Lisbon.[24]

When John Blanke arrived, England was a relatively weak kingdom on the edge of Europe. Henry VII was still trying to cement the legitimacy of his new Tudor dynasty. Like the marriage he negotiated between his son Arthur and the Spanish Infanta, emulating other European rulers by employing an African musician at court was a way of enhancing his prestige on the European stage.

There is no record of exactly how John Blanke came to be working as a trumpeter at the Tudor court. However, trumpeters were the most mobile of musicians, used as messengers and required for diplomatic exchanges and ceremonial affairs. They accompanied rulers and their representatives on foreign journeys, giving them the opportunity to jump ship and remain as a permanent employee in the court they were visiting. So it proved for John de Cecil, a Spaniard who played for Archduke Philip the Handsome in Brussels in the 1490s. By 1496, he had returned to Spain, and was chosen to accompany Katherine of Aragon to England for her marriage in 1501. In January 1502 he was issued with a banner in England and began to receive a monthly wage of 20 shillings from Henry VII, the same rate at which the King was to pay John Blanke. De Cecil continued to travel around Europe. In 1511, he accompanied Lord Darcy on a diplomatic mission to the court of Ferdinand of Aragon, while in 1514 he attended Henry's younger sister Mary on her journey to become Queen of France. He does not appear in the English records after that date, which suggests he found permanent employment in the French court.[25]

Like John de Cecil, John Blanke may well have arrived in England with Katherine of Aragon in 1501. She certainly brought a group of trumpeters with her; Henry VII's Treasurer of the Chamber paid a reward of £4 to '9 trumpets of Spain' shortly after her arrival. In January 1502, a reward of 20 shillings was paid to 'the new trumpet,' who remains anonymous.[26]

It was certainly possible that one of Katherine's trumpeters was African and skilled enough to attract the attention of Henry VII. Music thrived at the Spanish court of Ferdinand and Isabella and the number of musicians employed increased dramatically during their reign. Princess Katherine and her siblings were taught music by the famous composer Juan de Anchieta in the royal chapel, and each had their own troupe of household musicians.[27]

By this time, growing numbers of Africans were living in Spain; a consequence of the growing Spanish empire. This was a newly arrived population, in contrast to the North African Moors who had ruled parts of Spain since the eighth century. Between 1441 and 1521, an estimated 156,000 Africans arrived in Spain, Portugal and the Atlantic islands, mostly from the modern-day West African nations of Guinea-Bissau, Guinea-Conakry, Senegal, the Gambia and parts of Mali and Burkina Faso. By 1550, they made up 7.5% of the population of Seville and in 1574 Melchor de Santa Cruz described the city as a 'giant chessboard containing an equal number of white and black chessmen'. But while some gained their freedom, most were enslaved.[28]

Seville was one of the regular haunts of the peripatetic Spanish court, which travelled between the principal cities of the kingdoms of Castile (Seville, Valladolid, Toledo and after 1492, Granada), and of Aragon (Barcelona, Zaragoza and Valencia).[29] Katherine's mother, Isabella of Castile, and her husband, Ferdinand of Aragon, had at least one African in their entourage in the early years of their reign: in the summer of 1475 a black slave was amongst those who died of thirst while they travelled around Castile.[30] Not all royal slaves were African; people of many ethnicities were enslaved in Spain at this time. Indeed, one of the two individuals enslaved in the Spanish household of Katherine of Aragon was a native Guanche from the recently colonised Canary Islands. A slightly later African presence at the Spanish court was depicted by the German artist Christoph Weiditz in 1529. When he accompanied Charles V through Aragon and Catalonia that summer, he included a picture of an attendant African drummer amongst his sketches of the progress.[31] As Africans were increasingly present in royal and aristocratic households across Europe, especially in the Italian states, Spain and Portugal, it's easy to imagine that one of the trumpeters Katherine of Aragon brought to England in 1501 was of African origin.[32]

There was some debate between Katherine's parents and her future father-in-law as to how large a household she might be allowed to bring with her to her new home. Ferdinand and Isabella wrote to Henry VII in October 1500 with a list of fifty-eight names. The list did not include John Blanke but did mention 'two slaves to attend on the maids of honour'. Henry, no doubt considering the cost of feeding and clothing all these Spaniards, insisted the future Queen of England would be better served by a more modest household of some twenty people of English stock. When Katherine disembarked in Plymouth on 1 October 1501, her entourage numbered close to sixty.[33] Her new father-in-law's advice had evidently fallen on deaf ears.

The journey across Spain to the Atlantic port of La Coruña had begun from Granada, where Ferdinand and Isabella had been obliged to go to deal with the revolt of the Moors of Ronda. The Moorish kingdom of Granada had only submitted to Spanish rule in 1492 and the aftershocks were still being felt. The princess's retinue would have been used to travelling with the court around Castile and Aragon but many would be unfamiliar with the most northerly reaches of the peninsula, and would have been glad of the opportunity to call *en route* at the shrine of Santiago de Compostela in Galicia. They would have been considerably less enamoured of what, for most of them, would have been their first sea voyage. The weather was so bad the first time they set sail from La Coruña that they were forced to return to port. They finally made landfall in Plymouth, then continued the journey to London by road. King Henry and Prince Arthur met them at Dogmersfield in Hampshire on 6 November and the travellers reached the capital a week later.[34]

Thomas More witnessed Katherine's entry into London. In a letter to his friend, John Holt, he described her retinue as '*laceri, nudipedes pigmei Ethiopes*' (hunchbacked, barefoot Ethiopian pigmies). It would be tempting to take this description as confirmation that some were African but it smacks of rhetorical exaggeration. Just as the ladies are thought to have been wearing sandals, and so appeared to be barefoot, More was most likely commenting on the darker features of the Spaniards rather than recording their true ethnicity. Other accounts only mention that the Spanish women were 'not of the fairest'.[35]

One woman who accompanied Katherine probably was dark-skinned. Catalina, born in Motril, Granada, was presumably from a Moorish Muslim family, though she would have had to convert to Christianity to become part of Katherine's household. In all likelihood, she was one of the two 'slaves to attend on the maids of honour' listed in Katherine's entourage in 1500. It was her duty to 'make the Queen's bed and attend to other secret or private services of her Highness's chamber'. She was in attendance on both of Katherine's wedding nights, in 1501 and 1509, making her a sought-after witness when Henry VIII began divorce proceedings and the question of whether the first marriage, to Arthur, had been consummated became a live issue. Catalina was one of a handful of people who knew the answer. By this time, she had gone back to Spain, where she married a Moorish crossbow-maker named Oviedo. After his death, she returned to her native Motril with their two daughters.[36]

While Ferdinand and Isabella may have considered the people they chose to wait on their daughter's maids of honour as 'slaves', this was not a recognised status in England. Henry VII had made the distinction clear earlier in his reign, when he set free Pero Alvarez, an African man who had come to England from Portugal. This act of manumission, and its validity in his kingdom, was confirmed by King João II of Portugal in 1490.[37] When the question arose in an English court of law in 1569, it was resolved 'that England has too pure an Air for Slaves to breathe in.' As William Harrison put it, in his *Description of England* some twenty years later:

As for slaves and bondmen, we have none; nay such is the privilege of our country by the especial grace of God and bounty of our princes, that if any come hither from other realms, so soon as they set foot on land they become as free in condition as their masters, whereby all note of servile bondage is utterly removed from them.[38]

Although Harrison's text is designed to show England in the best possible light, there is a ring of truth to his theory. It is echoed in many of the experiences of Africans in England, as well as in the absence of legislation establishing the status of slavery under English law. Parliament never issued any law codes delineating slavery to compare with the Portuguese *Ordenações Manuelinas* (1481–1514), the Dutch *East India Ordinances* (1622), France's *Code Noir* (1685) or the codes that appeared in Virginia and other American states from the 1670s.[39] Of course, the absence of a written law would not make it impossible for Africans to be treated as slaves in practice.[40] If they were referred to as slaves, bought and sold, subjected to brutal whippings and other harsh physical punishments, and did not receive any payment or other compensation for their labour, it would be fair to conclude that they were enslaved. But we know John Blanke was paid wages like the rest of the court musicians. Catalina was later described as '*esclava que fue*', literally the 'slave that was', suggesting she had been enslaved in Spain, but became free in England.[41]

The status of John Blanke, Catalina and any other Africans in Katherine's retinue was certainly better in England than in Spain, where African slaves were sold on the Cathedral steps in Seville, alongside goods such as tapestries and jewellery.[42] John Blanke's musical skills earned him a decent wage at the Tudor court, and in England he was free. Or, at least, freer. His status was as much dictated by his class as his colour; very few Englishmen could be said to be truly 'free' in this period. Some, known as 'villeins', were still legally unfree. Villeins were men bound either to a personal lord or to work on a manor: a feudal legacy. In 1485, at least four hundred manors in thirty English and Welsh counties still had villeins. By the 1560s, this figure had fallen to one hundred manors in twenty-one counties.[43] Villeins were in the minority but far more English people were severely limited by their circumstances. Two-fifths of the rural population and between a half and two-thirds of those in cities were in service, working in husbandry, or as apprentices or domestics.[44] That said, other servants could move around more freely and had families to support them in times of trouble. John Blanke did not have that luxury.

In Spain, Blanke would have been one of many Africans, but in Henry's England he would rarely encounter a fellow countryman. Only a handful of Africans appear in the records before the age of Elizabeth: Pero Alvarez met Henry VII in the late 1480s; in 1522, Peter Blackmore, 'a moren borne', was listed among 'bill men' ready to fight in St Petrock, Exeter; and one 'Thomas Bull, niger' was buried in Eydon, Northamptonshire in 1545. As we will see in the next chapter, Jacques Francis, born off the Guinea coast, was living in Southampton in the late 1540s. At least one 'blakemor' was among the entourage of Philip II when he came to London to marry Mary Tudor in 1554, and chroniclers relate that an African needlemaker operated in Cheapside during her reign.[45] The paucity of records can partly be explained by the fact that it only became compulsory for parishes to keep registers of baptisms, marriages and burials in 1538, and few survive from before 1558. Although some Africans might have come to England unrecorded in this period, it is safe to say that there were far fewer in England than in southern Europe.

More Africans were recorded in Scotland than in England in the first half of the sixteenth century. The drummer who played for James IV was one of at least seven Africans, male and female, living at or visiting the Scottish court. Some we know by name: Peter the Moor, present in 1501 and 1504, was paid a pension by the King and travelled to France and back, as well as journeying around Scotland with the court. Perhaps John Blanke heard about him from the trumpeters at the English court who accompanied Margaret Tudor to Edinburgh for her marriage in 1503? Margaret and Elene (or Helenor), probably the 'More lasses' who arrived in 1504, formed part of the household of Margaret Stewart, James IV's illegitimate daughter. They were well looked after and regularly

provided with new clothes and shoes.[46] Others are recorded without
a name. On St Valentine's Day in 1506, a nurse brought 'the Moor's
bairn [child]' to show the King. Two 'blak More freirs' (friars) were
James IV's guests at court in 1508. In 1512, an African servant of
Andrew Forman, Bishop of Moray, was paid a reward of 14 shillings
for bringing a present to the king. Mary of Guise distributed bread
to 'moors' at Stirling Castle each day throughout 1549,[47] and in
March of that year she received a letter from Lady Home recommending a 'Mour' who was billeted at Hume Castle, Berwickshire,
as being 'as sharp a man as rides'.[48]

The position of members of Katherine's household in England
soon became precarious. Just five months after her marriage to
Prince Arthur at St Paul's Cathedral, he was dead. The widowed
Katherine became a pawn in the game of diplomacy played out by
the rulers of Europe, and her household suffered. As Henry and
Ferdinand squabbled over her dowry, Katherine was forced to sell
or pawn some of her possessions to feed herself and her household.
In 1506, she complained that she had only been able to buy two
new dresses since her arrival in England five years earlier. After
arriving to replace the unsatisfactory ambassador González De
Puebla in 1508, Don Gutierre Gómez de Fuensalida reported to
the Spanish King that 'never was such cruelty inflicted on a captive
in the lands of the Moors as the princess is subjected to here'.[49] His
choice of simile is striking. Certainly, in these years, Katherine was
hardly in a position to employ a trumpeter, and so, if he had not
already done so, this would have been the time for John Blanke to
transfer to the royal household.

Although the consensus is that John Blanke arrived in
England with Katherine of Aragon, there is another possibility.
On 15 January 1506, Katherine's sister Juana of Castile and her
husband Philip the Handsome were shipwrecked on the Dorset
coast while *en route* to Spain from the Netherlands to claim the
throne of Castile following the death of Queen Isabella. This
left the royal couple in the hands of Henry VII, who detained
them until April while he wrung various political concessions
from Philip.[50] Two musicians arrived at the Tudor court in this
way; a minstrel named Bartram Brewer and a lute and viol

player named Matthew de Weldre, so it is not unthinkable that Blanke also came via the Burgundian court.[51]

In April 1509 Henry VII died. John Blanke, and the other court servants, were issued with new black outfits for the funeral.[52] They followed the cortège over two days as it proceeded from Richmond to St Paul's Cathedral then onwards to Westminster Abbey, where the first Tudor king was laid to rest beside his queen, Elizabeth of York, who had died in childbirth in 1503. The trumpeters passed through the City of London, behind the sword bearer and vice-chamberlain of London, the Masters of the Bridge House and the King's messengers. After the trumpeters came the 'Florentines, Venetians, Portingals, Spaniards, Frenchmen, and Easterlings'.[53] They were near the front of a very long line of dignitaries, gentlemen and courtiers. The streets of London were packed with onlookers, with representatives of all the City Guilds and Companies prominent among them.[54] John Blanke was at the centre of a great royal spectacle.

A few weeks later, this time sporting a scarlet livery, John Blanke played at the joint coronation of Henry VIII and his new Queen, Katherine.[55] Scarlet cloth was reserved for the higher-ranking royal servants, those at the level of yeoman usher and above, while yeomen, grooms and pages wore red. Ideas about the fabric and colour of clothes reflecting status had existed since at least 46 BCE, when Julius Caesar restricted the use of the colour purple. England's first sumptuary law appeared during the reign of Edward III, and two hundred years later Henry VIII was also keen to regulate dress, passing four 'Acts of Apparel' between 1510 and 1533.[56] John Blanke was given 4½ yards of scarlet, above the average gift of 3 yards, which he presumably used to make a gown and a hood.

The coronation ceremonies stretched over three days. On Friday, Henry held vigil at the Tower of London, on Saturday the court proceeded from the Tower to the Palace of Westminster and on Sunday, which was Midsummer's Day, the royal couple walked from the palace to Westminster Abbey to be crowned. There followed a grand banquet where 'at the bringing of the first course, the trumpets blew up' and a tournament, where 'the trumpets blew to the field the fresh young gallants'.[57]

Henry VIII was still a teenager when he came to the throne, and his youth and vigour brought a new atmosphere of gaiety and exuberance to court life. The early years of his reign were filled with festivities, tournaments, banquets, 'disguisings', dancing and other revelry. In January 1510, he and eleven nobles, disguised as Robin Hood and his men, burst into the Queen's chamber where they danced and 'made pastime' with Katherine and her ladies. In February, during the Shrovetide celebrations, he and the Earl of Essex appeared dressed 'after the Turkey fashion' with torchbearers dressed 'like Moriscos, their faces black'. Some of the ladies dressed as Egyptians, their faces, necks, arms and hands painted black so that they 'seemed to be nygrost [negroes] or blacke Mores'.[58] The services of his trumpet players were in constant demand. In the first year of his reign, Henry increased the number of royal trumpeters to fifteen.[59]

The King loved music. He employed more than fifty musicians, and he himself played the organ, the lute, the virginal and the recorder. He even enjoyed sight-reading songs with his courtiers. The Venetian ambassadors heard the King play and sing for them when they visited in May 1517. Henry was also an amateur composer. Although there is no evidence that he wrote 'Greensleeves', he did write other songs, such as 'Pastime with good company', 'Helas Madame', motets and masses.[60] An inventory compiled towards the end of his reign shows that he owned an unusually large variety of richly decorated musical instruments. His court supported musicians and poets including Skelton, Wyatt, Robert Fairfax, William Cornish, John Heywood and the Earl of Surrey.[61] Music-making at court was such that, while visiting Thomas More in 1509, the Dutch theologian Erasmus remarked that 'the English challenge the prerogative of having the most handsome women, of being the most accomplished in the skill of music, and of keeping the best tables'.

Henry was not above recruiting from abroad to ensure he had the best musicians around him. In 1516 he poached Dionysius Memo, formerly the organist at San Marco in Venice, who became a firm favourite, not least in the eyes of the young Princess Mary. The Venetian ambassador reported that he 'played . . . to the incredible admiration and pleasure of everybody, and especially of his Majesty, who is extremely skilled in Music'. Another organist, Benedictus de Opitiis, arrived from Antwerp the same year. Not all foreign musicians found favour, however. Zuan da Leze, a harpsichordist from Cyprus, was so disappointed with his reception at court in 1525 that he hanged himself.[62]

The start of a new reign was a time of fluctuating fortunes. For some, like the unpopular royal councillors Richard Empson and Edmund Dudley, it signalled a trip to the Tower and, ultimately, death. For others, it was an opportunity for swift promotion. One of Blanke's fellow trumpeters, the Italian Dominic Justinian, had recently died, and Blanke took the chance to petition the new King for a pay rise.[63] The petition survives amongst a pile of similar documents from the early years of Henry's reign. Although it was written by a clerk and is somewhat formulaic, it is the closest we get to hearing John Blanke's own voice echoing through the centuries:

> To the King, our sovereign Lord,
>   In most humble wise beseecheth your highness, your true and faithful servant John Bla[n]ke, one of your trumpets. That whereas his wage now and as yet is not sufficient to maintain and keep him to do your Grace like service as other your trumpets do. It may therefore please your highness in consideration of the true & faithful service which your servant daily doeth unto your Grace and so during his life intendeth to do, to give and grant unto him the same room [position] of Trumpet which Dominic deceased late had, to have and enjoy the said room to your said servant from the first day of December last passed during your most gracious pleasure, with the wage of 16d by the day. And that this bill signed with your most gracious hand may be sufficient warrant and discharge unto John Heron treasurer of your Chamber for the payment of the said wage accordingly. And he shall daily pray to God for the preservation of your most noble and royal estate long to endure.[64]

Reading between stock phrases such as 'true and faithful servant', the petition shows that Blanke was ambitious and keen to grasp the opportunity for promotion that the death of his fellow trumpeter provided. There also seems to be some rivalry with the other trumpeters: he wants to live in the same style as his peers and claims that his previous wage of 8d a day was insufficient for this. As we know, he was not the only trumpeter paid at this rate. John de Cecil was paid the same in 1502, and other trumpeters were still being hired at the rate of 8d a day in the 1540s. Many of the payments to trumpeters were made to them as a group, so it is not possible to be sure how much each individual received. If the payments were split equally, then the main group of trumpeters were each receiving 16d a day. However, from December 1509 to July 1512, a group of four to six additional trumpeters were each being paid at a rate of 12d a day.[65] So wages varied, depending on experience, skill or length of service. On this basis, having been at court for at least two years, Blanke could justify a rise.

What did Blanke want, or need, that 8d a day would not cover? Like other court servants, he had his livery, board and lodging paid for by the King. However, when the court travelled, servants often had to pay for their own accommodation and transport. In 1518, the poet William Cornish made 'a merry supplication unto the King's grace for a bucket of hay and a horse loft' in which to lodge while the court was at Abingdon. Like Cornish, Blanke may also have been responsible for keeping his own horse, which might cost him some five shillings a week.[66] Perhaps Blanke wanted to buy more expensive clothing; like actors, minstrels were exempted from the Acts of Apparel that forbade people to wear clothes above their station.[67]

The phrase that suggests that the King's signature will suffice to grant the rise was standard for these petitions and was designed to minimise the amount of time and effort required from the King in response. Blanke's petition obviously hit the right note, as his request was granted. It was clearly not too much to ask from a musical king who was hiring new instrumentalists. The trumpeter's wage had doubled.

* * *

On New Year's Day, 1511, word spread around Richmond Palace that Katherine of Aragon had given birth to a prince. Thanks were given to God for providing England with a male heir, bonfires were lit and free wine was distributed to 'such as would take thereof, in certain streets in London'.⁶⁸ But John Blanke and his fellow trumpeters couldn't spend too much time celebrating; they were soon hard at work. The arrival of a male heir to the throne required a series of official ceremonies and festivities in which their services would be vital.

At his baptism on 5 January, the boy was named Henry, like his father and grandfather. Louis XII of France and Margaret of Savoy were named as godparents, alongside William Warham, Archbishop of Canterbury, Thomas Howard, Earl of Surrey and Katherine, Countess of Devon, one of the younger daughters of Edward IV. The ceremony was attended by ambassadors from the Pope, France, Spain and Venice, who afterwards visited and congratulated the Queen before writing dispatches to their sovereigns.⁶⁹

The same day, a letter arrived, purportedly from the Queen *Noble Renown* of the realm of *Coeur Noble*. News of the birth gave her 'the most Joye and comfort' and in honour of the young prince's arrival, she would send four Challengers from her kingdom to 'accomplish certain feats of Arms'. They would take on all comers at Candlemas next. The letter, known as the Westminster Challenge, was typical of the allegorical, romantic documents that were produced at this time to announce a forthcoming jousting event.⁷⁰

The Westminster Tournament was held in February. The two days of jousting, pageantry and merry-making were particularly onerous for the King's trumpeters, who were called upon to sound fanfares, retreats and more from dawn till dusk. They were amply rewarded for their labours, receiving ten times their usual day's pay for their services.

Henry, 'being lusty, young, and courageous, greatly delighted in feats of chivalry', and particularly favoured jousts, where he could parade his sporting prowess.⁷¹ Taking part in this violent competition was dangerous: King Henri II of France was fatally injured during a tournament in 1559 and Henry VIII himself suffered some nasty blows later in his jousting career, notably on one occasion in 1524, when he forgot to lower his visor. As well as showcasing the King's virility and bravery, the military spectacle broadcast loud and clear the message that England was a power to be reckoned with. The Westminster Tournament of February 1511 was by far the most splendid of these events. *The Great Chronicle of London* concluded that the two-day event was the most 'excelling joust' England had ever seen.[72] The King cut a resplendent figure in his rich costume, but the cost of the festivities exceeded all others in living memory.

The entire event, carefully accounted for by Richard Gibson, Master of the Revels, cost nearly £4,400.[73] This was a staggering amount; almost two hundred times John Blanke's annual wage. Ostensibly a celebration of the birth of a prince, the Tournament was part of a larger agenda. Just as nations today use major sporting events such as the Olympics or the World Cup as promotional vehicles, Henry saw this tournament as an opportunity to make his mark on the European scene. It was designed to match, even excel, the most extravagant displays from the time of Philip the Good, Duke of Burgundy, or René d'Anjou. The tilting yard outside Westminster Hall, located roughly where Parliament Square is today, was transformed into a scene from a chivalric romance. The magnificent display would be reported to Europe's rulers by their ambassadors at the English court. The new King was, quite simply, buying European prestige.

On Wednesday 12 February, John Blanke rose early, donned his royal livery of yellow and grey and carefully wound his green and gold turban around his head.[74] He and the other trumpeters were going to have to work hard. The tournament was to begin with an elaborate ceremonial entry, and each arrival would require a fanfare from the fifteen trumpets. They would also play after the announcement of the rules, as a signal to the combatants to begin and again to announce the victory.

John Blanke was accustomed to court ceremonial and pageantry. But even he, a seasoned performer, would have been impressed when a great castle, made of gold paper, appeared before the crowds. An artificial forest, 26 feet long and 16 feet broad, built of hawthorn, oak, hazel, maple, birch, fern, broom and fir, enveloped the castle. The whole wheeled edifice was drawn into the tiltyard by a golden lion and a silver antelope, led by four 'wild men' in green silk. Like beauty queens in a modern-day carnival procession, ladies dressed in russet and blue damask rode each of these fantastic beasts, while perched high on the castle's ramparts, a maiden dressed in blue satin fashioned a garland of rosemary and other herbs for the Queen.

The trumpets sounded as each of the four costumed Challengers from the realm of *Coeur Noble* issued from the castle: Sir William Courtenay as *Bon Valour*, Sir Edward Neville as *Joyous Penser*, Sir Thomas Knyvet as *Valiant Desire* and finally the King himself as *Coeur Loyal*. Henry's choice of alias may seem unsuitable in light of his later marital history but it was entirely fitting in the optimistic early years of his reign.

Next, a dozen Answerers to the four knights' Challenge entered, to the accompaniment of trumpets and drums. Presided over by Thomas Wriothesley, the Garter King of Arms, both Challengers and Answerers signed their names on the Tournament Challenge in black ink. The Challenge was then hung in one of the artificial trees. This ritual, celebrated in the chivalric literature of the troubadours, followed the ceremonial of jousts traditional since the thirteenth century.[75]

The lords and ladies of the court looked on eagerly from the crowded stands as the jousts began. The Queen had the best seat in the house, or rather the best bed. Six weeks after giving birth, she was made comfortable on a large ornate couch, on a dais hung with cloth of gold.

There was no rest for the trumpeters. Each new champion entering the lists required a fanfare to announce his arrival. As Chaucer's Knight put it in his tale to the Canterbury pilgrims:

> Now the loud trumpets, and the clarion
> Ring out; and on the east side and the west
> In go the spears, couched firm for the attack,
> In go the spurs, sharp in the horse's side.
> We'll soon see who can joust, and who can ride![76]

Over two days, each of the four Challengers faced multiple opponents. The King himself entered the lists twenty-eight times. One chronicler recalls the 'lusty leaping, bouncing and mounting and flinging of the jolly and lusty four riders'.[77]

The second day brought further ceremonial, as there were new contenders to announce. Charles Brandon, the King's favourite jousting partner, arrived disguised as a hermit imprisoned in a tower, a 'long and full-grown beard reaching down to his saddle bow'. Led into the arena by a gaoler holding a large key, he petitioned the Queen for the right to joust. On receiving her blessing, he 'cast from him hastily his clothing, beard and hat, and showed himself in bright harness . . . smote his horse with the spurs and rode a lusty pace unto the tilt's end'. Other Answerers also came in disguise: Sir Thomas Boleyn and Henry Guildford, Marquess of Dorset, arrived as pilgrims from Santiago de Compostela, their black velvet costumes decorated with gold scallop shells.[78]

The scorecards, or 'jousting cheques', from the tournament survive: a sheaf of paper for each contestant with strange markings that record their performance. They show the King did well. He broke 12 lances and scored 9 attaints, or hits, on the body and one on the head. However, he did not break a lance on the helm, as he is depicted doing in the flattering central scene of the *Tournament Roll*. At the end of the first day, Queen Katherine awarded the prizes (worth 200 crowns each), to *Valiant Desire* (Sir Thomas Knyvet) on the Challengers' side and Richard Blount on the Answerers'. The second day's sport ended with prizes for *Coeur Loyal*, the King, for the Challengers and Edmund Howard for the answerers. As the winners were announced and the prizes collected, the trumpets, inevitably, sounded once more. The heralds then issued the cry '*a l'hostell*' to a final fanfare.[79] This signified the end of the day and invited the assembled company to proceed away from the field towards the hospitality that awaited them.

North of the border, tournaments at the Scottish court were being influenced by the African presence at James IV's court. In June 1507, the Scottish King disguised himself as a wild or black knight in 'the jousting of the wild knight for the black lady'. This 'black lady' was almost certainly one of the African women then present at court.

The entertainment was so popular that it was repeated again in May 1508, and inspired William Dunbar's poem to *Ane Blak Moir*. His description of the lady has been described as 'venomous', 'shocking' and 'uniquely bad'. These are modern reactions to his references to her 'thick lips', 'short cat nose' and 'mouth like an ape'. But these lines must be seen in the context of the Scottish tradition of '*flyting*', or poetic insult, which was equally rude to all its targets. Dunbar traded poetic insults with another court poet, whom he addressed as 'Cuntbitten craven Kennedy'. Kennedy in return called Dunbar an 'Ignorant elf, ape, owl irregular' and many worse things besides.

Having described the lady, Dunbar explains that:

> Who for her sake with spear and shield
> Fights most mightily in the field
> Shall kiss and embrace her
> And from thenceforth her love shall wield
> My lady with the thick lips
>
> And who in field receives shame
> And tarnishes his knightly name
> Shall come behind and kiss her hips
> And never to other comfort claim:
> My lady with the thick lips.[80]

The black lady played a central part in this spectacle, sitting in a 'chair triumphal' decorated with red Flemish taffeta, and taffeta 'flowers and pansies'. According to the Scottish chronicler Pitscottie, the tournament lasted forty days, and the black knight (James IV) was victorious throughout. One wonders whether he did indeed kiss the black lady in the way that Dunbar describes. Once the jousting was over:

> The king caused to make a great triumph and banquet in Holyrood House which lasted the space of three days, beginning at 9 in the morning and lasting till 9 at night . . . between every course there was a farce or play, some spoken, some necromancy, which caused men to see things appear which were

not. And so at the . . . play upon the third day there came a cloud out of the roof of the hall, as appeared to men, which opened and collected up the black lady in the presence of them all that she was no more seen, but this was done by the art of necromancy for the king's pleasure [by] one called Bishop Andrew Forman who was a magician and served the king at such times for his pastime and pleasure.[81]

The Westminster Tournament was also followed by a banquet, held in the White Hall. The resident ambassadors were guests of honour and lavish entertainments were staged to impress them. These took the form of 'disguisings', a sort of fancy-dress pageant; a forerunner of the masque. That night's theatrics, entitled *The Golden Arber in the Archyard of Pleasure*, began with John Blanke and the other trumpeters welcoming the arrival of the extravagant pageant car. It held a 'golden arbour' of trees and flowers, and was inhabited by six ladies and six lords. The edifice was so heavy that it had fallen through the floor at the Bishop of Hereford's palace during rehearsals. The twelve performers, the King and a bevy of courtiers, wore the Tudor colours of white and green, their costumes adorned with the letters 'H' and 'K' in yellow. In a flash of bawdy humour, Knyvet (*Valiant Desire*) sported the word 'Desyr' in gold on his codpiece.[82]

When the pageant car was put to one side to accommodate the ensuing dancing, the 'rude people' suddenly ran towards it, each wanting a piece of its costly decoration: the car was completely torn to pieces. The King was in danger of a similar fate when, later in the evening, the ladies, gentlewomen and ambassadors were encouraged to pluck the gold letters from his person 'in token of liberality'. Things got out of hand, and the rest of the crowd joined in, stripping him and his companions down to their hose and doublets. Even the ladies were 'spoyled', and the King's guard had to be called in to fend off the ravening crowd. The King retired to his chamber with the Queen and her ladies, where 'all these hurts were turned to laughing and game', and so the night ended with 'mirth and gladness'.[83] After two long days, John Blanke and the attendant trumpeters were finally able to retire.

A mere ten days later, on 22 February 1511, the infant Prince Henry died. He had lived for only 53 days. The Queen, 'like a natural woman, made much lamentation'. Henry played tennis and dice to distract himself, and by the end of April had issued a new Challenge for jousting in May. When this failed to prove distraction enough, he set about making preparations to declare war against Louis XII of France.'[84]

John Blanke soon had his own cause for celebration; he married in January 1512. We do not know whom he married, but it seems probable, given the dearth of Africans in England at this time, that she was an Englishwoman. To marry in a Catholic ceremony, both parties had to have been baptised. Hence, while he may have been born into a Muslim family in North Africa or Spain, and despite the turban he wore at the Westminster Tournament the year before, by 1512 John Blanke was a Christian, at least on paper.

The court had spent Christmas and New Year at Greenwich Palace, built by Henry VII on the site of today's Old Royal Naval College. Henry VIII was born there and it was the younger King's favourite residence until the rebuilding of Whitehall in the early 1530s. The Palace had its own chapel, at the eastern end of the complex, but this was mostly used by aristocrats and so is unlikely to have been the site of the Blanke wedding. Men of the trumpeter's status were more often married at the local parish church of St Nicholas.[85]

Henry VIII himself footed the bill for John Blanke's wedding outfit. At Greenwich, on 14 January, the King ordered a gown of violet cloth, and also a bonnet and a hat, which was 'to be taken of our gift against' the marriage of 'our trumpeter'.[86] Gifts of clothing were a common wedding present, and violet was a popular colour for the cloth.[87] On the same day that he authorised the gift to John Blanke, the King also signed a warrant in favour of Richard Mayre, a yeoman of the Ewery; he was to receive 'for his wedding apparel, a gown cloth of violet containing four broad yards and as much black Irish lamb as will suffice to fur the same, also tawny chamlet for a jacket, and for his wife three broad yards of violet cloth for her gown'.[88] This was a more substantial gift. Mayre was in charge of the Ewer, a vessel which carried water, as well as all the royal napkins and basins, and so was responsible for washing the hands of the King and his guests, and shaving the King every morning. This was a position of great responsibility, with personal access to the King, hence the larger gift. Other servants received similar or lesser gifts to Blanke. William Toke, page of the laundry, received a gown, jacket, doublet and a bonnet at the time of his marriage, while John Hethe, yeoman almoner of the King's chamber, was given broadcloth for a gown before his wedding.[89]

The record of John Blanke's wedding present is the last mention of him in the royal records. Although his petition had stated that he intended to serve the King for the rest of his life, he is not named in the next full list of trumpeters dated 31 January 1514.[90] People at court came and went, of course, and musicians in particular frequently exchanged one European royal master for another. It is also possible that Blanke's marriage heralded a change of direction. It was not uncommon for court servants to marry a widow and take on her former husband's trade in the City.[91] A more morbid conclusion is that Blanke's court career ended with his death. He could have perished in the fire that consumed the living quarters of the palace of Westminster in 1512, or he might have met his death at either the Battle of the Spurs in France or the Battle of Flodden against the Scots the following year.[92]

The trend for employing Africans at royal courts continued after John Blanke's time, both in England and across Europe. As well as making music, they also worked in the stables and the kitchens. Others went on to greater things, such as João de Sa Panasco , who began as a court jester in Lisbon, went on to become a gentleman of the household, King's valet, a soldier who partic-ipated in Charles V's campaign in North Africa in 1535 and finally a member of the prestigious Order of Santiago. At the English court, Elizabeth I paid for an outfit in white taffeta with gold and silver detailing for a 'little blackamore' in 1575.[93] Anthony Vause, a 'black-more' trumpeter, was employed at the Tower of London by James I in 1618. Both King James's wife, Anne of Denmark, and his son, Charles I, appear in paintings in which their horses are attended to by African grooms.[94]

John Blanke was not the last African to serve King Henry VIII.

As a French diplomat remarked to his English counterpart in the summer of 1545: 'King's hearts are in God's hand and he turns them as pleases him from peace to war and from war to peace'.[95] During his final war with France, instead of a skilled musician King Henry required the services of a man versed in an art that was at this time little practised by Europeans, but which people from West Africa were taught from birth: swimming and diving.

Jacques Francis,
the Salvage Diver

Jacques plunged into the sea, and the cold engulfed him. It was so different to the warm waters where he'd learnt to swim and dive as a child. He took a series of deep breaths, allowing his lungs to inflate with air and take precious oxygen into his blood, and dived beneath the waves. As he reached the depths, he began to make out the shape of the wreck through the murky water. He had heard the tale of how this proud warship had met her doom. The men of the town didn't agree on exactly what had caused her to sink, but they well recalled the spectacle of her quick, cruel disappearance beneath the waves. The screams of the drowning men were loud enough to reach the shore. Their skeletons would be waiting for him among the sunken timbers. Hundreds of onlookers, including King Henry himself, had watched, helpless, as the ship went down. The Mary Rose; that was what they called her. And now that splendid ship lay lifeless before him in the water. Her side was studded with guns of iron and bronze, the latter marked with the royal crest. That was why he was here, why the King had hired his master: to salvage the expensive weaponry. The Venetian could not dive this deep himself and so he'd found Jacques, and the other divers in his team, and brought them to this cold island to perform a miracle for the English King.

FEW OF US know that there were attempts to salvage the *Mary Rose* in the Tudor period, still fewer that some of the men qualified to undertake the job came from Africa. How did they manage to retrieve objects from the sea floor centuries before the invention of modern diving equipment? Why was it that Africans were so skilled in diving when most Europeans couldn't even swim? How did Jacques Francis's expertise affect the way he was viewed and treated by Tudor society? Most of what we know about him comes from precious evidence preserved in the records of the High Court of Admiralty. Jacques was the very first known African to give testimony before an English court. But how would his words have been received? Yes, he was an eyewitness, but according to the prosecution he was also an infidel and a slave.

Jacques Francis was about eighteen when, in 1546, he began working for a Venetian named Peter Paulo Corsi. Corsi, who had been in Southampton since about 1539, was one of a considerable, though dwindling, number of Italians based in the port.[1] There had been a strong Venetian, Florentine and Genoese presence in Southampton in the medieval period. The merchants of these powerful city-states had come there since the thirteenth century to satisfy northern Italy's demand for English wool. The wool trade was central to the English economy, its importance symbolised by the fact that, since the reign of Edward III, the Lord Chancellor sat on the Woolsack in the House of Lords, as the Lord Speaker does today. As the geographer Richard Hakluyt put it in 1584: 'for certain hundreds [of] years . . . by the peculiar commodities of wools, and of later years by clothing of the same . . . [England] raised itself from meaner state to greater wealth and much higher honour might and power than before'. Southampton was also the chief centre for the export of Cornish tin, since Henry VII had established a staple, or exclusive market, for metals there in 1492. But by the 1540s the port was in a terminal decline brought on by the increasing dominance of the capital, with fewer and fewer Italian visitors.[2]

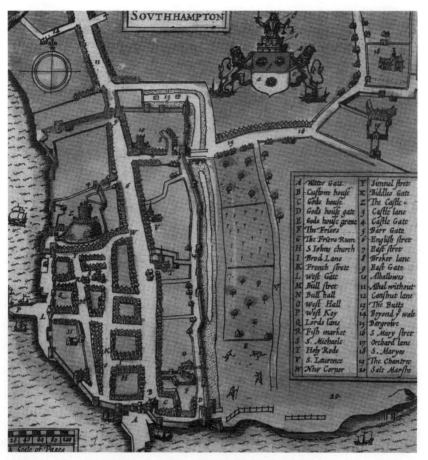

SOVTHHAMPTON

A	Water Gate	Y	Simnel ſtret
B	Cuſtome houſe	X	Biddles Gate
C	Gods houſe	Z	The Caſtle
D	Gods houſe gate	3	Caſtle lane
E	Gods houſe grene	4	Caſtle Gate
F	The Friers	5	Barr Gate
G	The Friers Rum	6	Engliſh ſtret
H	S Johns church	7	Eaſt ſtret
I	Brod Lane	8	Broker lane
K	French ſtrete	9	Baſt Gate
L	Weſt Gate	10	Alhallowes
M	Bull ſtret	11	Alhal without
N	Bull hall	12	Canſhut lane
O	Weſt Hall	13	The Butts
P	Weſt Key	14	Beyond y wale
Q	Lords lane	15	Bargrowe
R	Fyſh market	16	S Mary ſtret
S	S. Michaels	17	Orchard lane
T	Holy Rode	18	S. Maryes
V	S. Laurence	19	The Chantrie
W	New Corner	20	Salt Marſhe

John Speed's map of Southampton in 1611.

Like John Blanke, Jacques Francis arrived in England before regular, direct trade with Africa began. Francis was born in the 1520s, on an island off the coast of the part of West Africa known to the Tudors as 'Guinea'. We do not know the exact route by which he came to Southampton. Corsi may have hired him directly from Africa through a Portuguese intermediary, or perhaps they met in Corsi's home city, Venice. After Spain and Portugal, the next largest African population in Europe was in the collection of states that today make up modern Italy, of which Milan, Naples and Sicily were ruled from Madrid after 1535. Most came via Portugal, the country that initiated the import of Africans into Europe in the

1440s; the trade partly financed by Italian investors. The largest numbers of Africans were in the south, especially in Sicily, but in the sixteenth century there was a growing presence in the northern cities of Mantua, Milan, Ferrara and Corsi's Venice. This was where Isabella d'Este, Marchesa of Mantua, sent her agent in 1491 when she was looking for a girl 'as black as possible' to serve her. The presence of enslaved Africans in Venice was certainly a truism by Shakespeare's time: in *The Merchant of Venice* (c. 1596–1598) Shylock tells the Venetians:

> You have among you many a purchased slave,
> Which, like your asses and your dogs and mules,
> You use in abject and in slavish parts,
> Because you bought them.

And of course, Othello was employed by the Venetian state.

Although most Africans had arrived as slaves, some were manumitted and found employment. It was not uncommon to spot a free African in command of a gondola, gliding along the Grand Canal beneath the Rialto Bridge. The first hereditary Duke of Florence, Alessandro de' Medici (d. 1537), was said to be the son of an African woman, named either Simunetta or Anna, who may have been a former slave.[3]

At least one African had come to Southampton from Italy before Jacques Francis's arrival. In 1491, Richard Hortensell, beadle of God's House hospital, was fined for his involvement in a fight with 'a black man that was a taboryn in the galley of [South]Hampton'. This galley, a low ship powered chiefly by oars and favoured in piracy and war, was probably part of the Florentine or Venetian state fleet, as both used Southampton as their English base at that time.[4] The 'taboryn' was a drummer, a musician like the Scottish 'More taubronar' or John Blanke, who would usually play alongside a piper, setting a beat for revellers to dance or, to in this case, keeping time for the strokes of the oarsmen.

In the summer of 1545, England was under attack. Two hundred and thirty-five ships bearing 30,000 Frenchmen spoiling for a fight were on their way across the Channel.[5] Two years before his death, King Henry VIII was once again at war with the foe of his youth. His navy gathered at Portsmouth and set sail on a calm, sunny July day; the *Mary Rose* one of the vessels leading the fleet. Henry had built this four-masted, 400-ton battleship in the first years of his reign and she had given good service, particularly in the sack of Brest in 1512, on the eve of the better-known 1513 victories at Flodden and the Battle of the Spurs. After an extensive refit in 1536, the ship was ready to attack the French once more. Loaded with ninety-one guns and packed with some five hundred men, she set out to meet the enemy in what was to become known – before being largely forgotten – as the Battle of the Solent. Yet, before she was able to engage the French, in fact while she was still in full view of the harbour, the *Mary Rose* sank. As Jacques Francis would have heard from those recounting the tale, the piercing cries of the drowning men echoed across the water to the shore. Fewer than thirty men survived.

The lack of wind had lulled the crew into a false sense of security. The sea was so calm that no one thought it necessary to close the gun ports before setting sail. When the wind suddenly picked up and the *Mary Rose* attempted to tack, water poured into the open gun ports. Once the ship began to heel, the heavy cannonballs and ballast slid to the starboard side and gravity did the rest. The last recorded words of the ship's commander, Sir George Carew, which he called out to his uncle, Sir Gawen Carew, close by on the *Matthew Gonson*, were 'I have the sort of knaves I cannot rule'. But the disaster was hardly the fault of the crew. From his vantage point on top of Southsea Castle, Henry VIII could only look on in horror as the ship where he had dined earlier that day keeled over and sank before his eyes and comfort Lady Carew, who fell into a faint as she watched her husband sink to his certain death, along with most of his crew.

Most Tudor sailors did not know how to swim. It was thought unlucky, and of little use, as ships were not in the habit of changing course to rescue those who fell overboard; better to drown quickly. Those aboard the *Mary Rose* had the extra impediment of the anti-boarding nets, which now kept the sailors in, instead of keeping the enemy out.

The loss of the *Mary Rose* was not a unique disaster. Just two weeks earlier, the French flagship the *Carraquon* had also sunk. If the English Achilles' heel was the changeable weather, the French weakness was their stomachs. Before leaving Le Havre, the French King, Francis I, and his men, together with the ladies of the court, had eaten well over the course of several hours aboard the flagship. Late in the afternoon, a fire broke out in the galley. It spread rapidly to the gun deck, where the heat caused the loaded guns to explode, bombarding the surrounding vessels. The *Carraquon* took several down with her. In an almost farcical turn of events, the ship that Admiral D'Annebault chose as a replacement, *La Maitresse*, also sank before she reached the Solent.

As sinking ships were not altogether uncommon, there were men who specialised in recovering them. Despite the continuing threat of French invasion, Henry VIII lost no time in ordering that the *Mary Rose* be brought back up. The ship itself was valuable, but it was the loss of the guns that would be most costly. In 1552, it was estimated that the ordnance lost on the *Mary Rose* was worth £1,723; about £2 million today.[6]

A group of Venetian salvage operators, led by Petre de Andreas and Symonde de Maryne, were deployed in August 1545. Their team comprised thirty-one Venetians, one of whom was a carpenter, with some sixty English sailors supporting them. They required plenty of equipment: fifty pulleys, sixty ballast baskets, 40 lb of tallow, or animal fat, 'a great quantity of cordage of all sorts' and two large ships, the *Samson* and the *Jesus of Lubeck*, which were to be spared from the King's fighting force.* The plan was to heave the *Mary Rose* upright by pulling on her masts, then run cables from the two larger ships under the hull and pull them taut, thus raising the vessel from the sea bed to a level where she could then be pumped out and floated. Despite early optimism, the wreck proved beyond their expertise, and having broken the *Mary Rose*'s mast they called it a day. The fact that 35,904 pints of beer were consumed by the salvage team in less than a month – an expense duly billed to the crown

---

* The latter ship was to be put to entirely different work in the 1560s, when Elizabeth I lent it to John Hawkins for his slaving expeditions.

– cannot have helped. While the Tudors avoided drinking water for fear of disease, and it was considered normal for a man to drink up to eight pints of weak beer a day, the team had each consumed more than fourteen pints a day while working on the project![7]

Nonetheless, the ordnance was too precious to be left on the ocean floor and, once the French threat had receded, a smaller salvage operation began. Lord Admiral John Dudley, Viscount Lisle, hired Peter Paulo Corsi to bring up as much of the *Mary Rose*'s valuable weaponry as possible. Corsi duly 'caused certain instruments to be made for the only intent and purpose' to retrieve 'certain gear' out of the *Mary Rose*.[8] As well as equipment, the job required specialist divers. He assembled a team of eight men, including Jacques Francis, John Iko and George Blacke. Iko and Blacke may also have been of African origin, given their names and their diving skills.

Corsi was now on the royal pay roll. In 1547, Edward Vaughan, Captain at Portsmouth, was reimbursed by the Treasurer for Marine Causes for £37 11s 5d he'd paid Corsi for the recovery of 'certain anchors and ordnance out of the *Mary Rose*'. The register of the Privy Council records further payments made to Corsi: £20 via Sir John Williams on 17 May 1547 and £50 by 'Mr Carew' on 3 August 1549. This was not of course the George Carew who drowned in the *Mary Rose*, but Sir Wymond Carew, Treasurer of the First Fruits and Tenths. The money Carew paid to Corsi had been 'imprest of the relief of spirituality', that is, it came from a clerical tax revenue that had previously enriched the Pope, but was redirected into the royal coffers by Thomas Cromwell in 1534. The total cost of the salvage attempts over four years, from 1545 when the *Mary Rose* sank until 1549 when Carew made the final payment, amounted to nearly £560. About a fifth of that was paid to Corsi, who, with his team, had succeeded in taking 'certain guns out of the ship drowned'.[9]

The *Mary Rose* was not the only wreck Jacques Francis and Corsi's team worked on during this period. On St Martin's Day, 11 November 1546, the *Sancta Maria and Sanctus Edwardus* suffered a 'great mischance'. She had set sail from Southampton bound for the Italian ports of Livorno, Messina and Venice laden with the typical exports of woollen clothing, kerseys (woollen cloth) and Cornish tin, plus cottons, leather and lead. Before she left Southampton Water, a fire broke out on board and the ship sank some two miles from shore.[10]

The *Sancta Maria and Sanctus Edwardus* belonged to Francesco Bernardi of Venice, but she was carrying merchandise belonging to various prominent Italian merchants. One was Domenico Erizzo, who had been elected consul of the Venetians in London in 1533. The Florentine Bartholomew Fortini, who made a fortune supplying the King with saltpetre and brimstone for the royal arsenal, also had goods on board. Another, Niccolo de Marini, came from a large mercantile family with business interests in Southampton. He was born in West Hall, one of the town's largest mansions, in 1509, but went back to Genoa as a boy and grew up there before returning to his birthplace in 1526, aged 17.[11] A fourth, Angelo de Milanes, was originally from Florence. These men were all anxious to recoup what they could of the goods lost when the ship went down.

Nothing could be done in the immediate aftermath of the shipwreck, due to the weather. Diving was a seasonal business; Francis himself said that the month of May was the best time for salvage work, while Erizzo commented that winter 'was ever too cold and out of fashion and season'.[12] The merchants hired Peter Paulo Corsi and his team to bring up the lost goods the following summer. For the months of July, August and September 1547 they were paid 2s 4d a day, and the cost of their 'victualling', that is their food and drink, was also covered. These meals, which included the luxury of meat, were taken at the Dolphin Inn, the principal inn of the town, which is still in business today.

As the summer drew to an end, a lack of results caused relations with their employers to sour. Around Michaelmas (29 September), Corsi was detained and taken before the Mayor of Southampton, Thomas Beckingham. He was accused by two of the merchants, Domenico Erizzo and Bartholomew Fortini, of stealing their goods from the wreck of the *Sancta Maria and Sanctus Edwardus*. It was alleged that Corsi and his team went 'craftily in the night time' and stole two pieces of tin worth at least £20 together out of the wreck, one belonging to Erizzo and the other to Fortini. Corsi had, they claimed, then stashed one piece of tin under a bed in one Mr Pope's house in Gosport, near Portsmouth. The whereabouts of the tin was reported to Niccolo de Marini, the Genoese merchant who had also lost goods aboard the ship, and he sent a servant to retrieve it. 'After many words' with Mr Pope, the servant found the piece of tin and carried it to the house of Edward Vaughan, the Captain of Portsmouth. Vaughan was, of course, already acquainted with Corsi, having paid him on the government's behalf for his labours on the *Mary Rose*. It seems he had developed a rapport with the diving operator, because when Corsi claimed he'd simply found the tin on the seabed, away from the wreck, Vaughan took him at his word.

In an act so brazen as to verge on utter recklessness, Corsi then took one piece of tin to the Florentine merchant Angelo de Milanes's house, to see if he could get a reward for it. Milanes restored the tin to its rightful owner, Fortini, who offered Corsi a finder's fee of 20s. Corsi complained that this was not enough, so Fortini and Erizzo joined forces to have him arrested. It transpired that he had in his possession a second piece of tin marked with Erizzo's initials, 'DE', and the Mayor of Southampton ordered him to return it immediately to its rightful owner.

When confronted with his crime, Corsi did not deny it. He only averred that his wages were too little for him and his servants, and so he felt justified in keeping some of the salvaged goods for himself. He was later overheard at the Dolphin tavern exclaiming that if he had taken two or three pieces more of tin, it still would not have been enough.

Corsi was not detained long. Mayor Thomas Beckingham recalled he was 'still at his liberty and not stopped one day'.[13] It was Angelo de Milanes, of all people, who secured Corsi's freedom. Vouching for a suspected thief suggests Corsi's salvaging services were simply indispensable.

Soon afterwards, Corsi, fearing that he would be further troubled in Southampton for stealing the tin, came to London and obtained letters missive addressed to the Mayor of Southampton from Thomas

Seymour, the Lord Admiral, which stated that he 'should not be any time troubled, but permitted to pass quietly, without vexation'.[14] His work for the crown in salvaging the *Mary Rose* took precedence over any other considerations; he must be free to continue.

Erizzo was clearly not satisfied by how things had gone in Southampton. He may have had his tin returned, but Corsi had evaded any serious punishment. In December 1547, the Venetian merchant took his case to the High Court of Admiralty, which met in St Margaret's Hill, London, south of the river, close to today's Borough Market. The case rumbled on for two years, and many men gave testimony: merchants and sailors from Southampton, Venice and Florence, and from other parts of England, such as London and Devon.

Jacques Francis testified on Wednesday 8 February 1548.[15] He did not speak English very well, and so the court appointed an interpreter named John Tyrart to translate his words. What language did they converse in? Francis would have needed some means of communicating with his fellow divers and their Venetian master. Given the Portuguese presence in West Africa, Francis may well have spoken their language, albeit in some pidgin form, intermingled with his mother tongue.[16] The court record gives no further information about Tyrart, but there was a vintner or wine merchant of that name living in Blackfriars, London, in 1554.[17] Maybe Tyrart had picked up some Portuguese whilst importing wine? It was not unusual for merchants to act as interpreters for the court, usually as an informal favour to someone they knew who was involved in the case.[18]

Through Tyrart, Francis explained that he was a member of Corsi's household, and that he had known the Venetian for two years. He stated that he was about twenty years old and had been born in 'Insula de Guinea' or an island of Guinea. This could refer to any one of the large number of tiny islands off the West African coast, including the Cape Verde Islands, Fernando Po, São Tomé and Príncipe. The most likely candidate is Arguin (off Mauritania), where the Portuguese had built their first African trading fort. The island's treacherous waters wrecked many ships, making it a plausible birthplace and training ground for a salvage diver.[19] Francis had known

Erizzo for about seven months, since the team had been hired to dive the *Sancta Maria and Sanctus Edwardus* wreck the previous July. The fact that he, of all of Corsi's team of divers, was singled out to give testimony suggests that he was the most senior.[20]

Francis did his best to defend his master from the accusations levelled against him. According to his evidence, the team 'chanced to find in the sea at the Needles' two hundred blocks of tin, a bell and some lead. The Needles, a series of rocks just off the most westerly tip of the Isle of Wight, was the site of many shipwrecks, and so a plausible location for such a discovery. They had, Francis claimed, found these items around Easter 1547, a few months before Corsi was commissioned to dive the *Sancta Maria and Sanctus Edwardus*. He also attested that Erizzo had caused his master to be detained for the whole month of May, to Corsi's great cost. He had spent 300 crowns on the 'instruments and vittles' required to bring up the goods he had discovered, which subsequently went unused during the best time of year for diving work, and £700 worth of treasure remained on the seabed. Francis was adamant that Corsi had been falsely accused. Perhaps Francis and Corsi thought that if they could show that Erizzo had arrested him under false pretences, they might have a compensation claim against him. Francis's assertion that Corsi had been detained throughout May 1547 is in complete contradiction of the accounts given by a host of other witnesses, who all said he was arrested for no more than a day or two at the end of September. Could Francis have tried to backdate and extend the length of the arrest to make it seem as if Corsi had really suffered at the merchants' hands?

Jacques Francis's testimony demonstrates how good a diver he was. He was able to stay deep underwater long enough to 'handle and see . . . [the tin, a bell and the lead] being there perished and forsaken'. To salvage heavy objects from the seabed, Francis must have mastered the art of free diving; that is, diving without any breathing apparatus. Still practised today, this requires years of training from an early age to develop the necessary lung capacity and mental strength, and to learn how to equalise the pressure in one's ears, and breathe effectively.[21]

One can paint a vivid picture of Francis as a child growing up on a West African island, learning to swim and dive from his parents and friends. The people of that region were said to be 'the most expert swimmers in the world', as Robert Baker and eight other Englishmen found when they were saved from a shipwreck on the Gold Coast in 1568. They used their diving ability to gather valuable currency: in Kongo, women dived for cowrie shells, while gold was brought up from the Ankobra riverbed in modern Ghana. Their aquatic skills could also be used for nefarious purposes. While on the coast of modern-day Liberia between 1599 and 1600, Johann von Lübelfing, a German soldier in Dutch employ, witnessed a theft by an adept African diver:

> They can swim below the water like a fish, as they proved there. One of them, who had a pewter tankard of beer in his hand and a soldier's helmet on his head, jumped into the water with them and swam thus a great distance underwater; then he re-emerged and jumped into his little boat, which his companion had to bring to him. Thus he got away with the helmet and tankard, and no-one could overtake him.[22]

Francis's swimming and diving would have been equally impressive to the people of Southampton, as they were not skills known to the average Englishman, even sailors and port-dwellers. When Everard Digby published a treatise on the art of swimming in 1587, he had to illustrate it heavily to demonstrate the necessary strokes. Swimming was generally considered dangerous. 'Perilous Pond', north of Bunhill Fields in London, got its name because so many people drowned there. The Vice-Chancellor of Cambridge forbade his scholars from swimming there in 1571 with penalties including whipping, fines, being set in the stocks and expulsion for those caught twice. In his youth, the diplomat and writer Lord Edward Herbert of Cherbury's mother made him promise never to swim, for 'she had heard of more drowned than saved by it'.[23] Even if one didn't drown, immersing oneself in water was generally viewed with suspicion. The royal physician Andrew Boorde wrote that bathing 'allowed the venomous airs to enter and destroyeth the lively spirits in man and enfeebleth the body'.[24]

As most Renaissance Europeans were unable to swim, the free-diving skills of Africans such as Francis were admired and prized across Europe and the Atlantic world. A 1500 painting by Gentile Bellini, *Miracle of the Cross at the Bridge of San Lorenzo*, shows an African about to jump into a Venetian canal. In Genoa, Cardinal Bandinello Sauli employed an African as a swimming and diving instructor.[25] Ferdinando I de Medici was saved from drowning in the River Arno in 1588 by 'a negro of his, a very notable swimmer'.[26] When Richard Hawkins visited the Spanish pearl fishery at La Margarita, off the north-eastern coast of Venezuela, in 1593, he observed that the Africans deployed there were 'expert swimmers, and great divers', who over time and with 'continual practice' had 'learned to hold their breath long underwater, for the better achieving their work.' Pieter de Marees, a Dutchman who travelled to the Gold Coast in 1602, noted that Venezuelan slaveholders sought men from that specific area to employ as pearl divers as they were 'very fast swimmers and can keep themselves underwater for a long time. They can dive amazingly far, no less deep, and can see underwater.'[27]

As well as diving for pearls, Africans were also employed in salvage operations. In September 1622, twenty-eight Spanish ships were wrecked by a hurricane the day after they left Havana. Twenty enslaved divers were sent to recover the silver and other goods aboard. Their master, Francisco Núñez Melián, inspired them in their work by promising freedom to the first man to discover a wreck. In due course, one of them found the remains of the *Santa Margarita*, and was set free. The English were also beginning to exploit this expertise: on Edward Fenton's abortive 1582 voyage to the East Indies, it was a 'Negro' who dived to retrieve the *Edward*'s lost anchor and cables. In 1622, two black indentured servants were paid for salvage operations on an English ship that was lost near Bermuda. The association became axiomatic. In George Chapman's 1596 play *The Blind Beggar of Alexandria*, a character named Aegiale says he will 'Moor-like, learn to swim and dive/ into the bottom of the sea'.[28]

In the course of Corsi's trial, some called to testify spoke of the Venetian himself diving into the water. John Westcott, a London merchant, said he saw him 'dive under the water with certain instruments', while William Mussen, a sailor aboard Westcott's ship, said he saw him 'in the water'. Could he too have mastered the art of free diving or was he merely able to swim, enabling him to help collect the recovered goods when they reached the surface? A Venetian was certainly more likely to be able to dive than an Englishman; we know that Greeks and Southern Italians were diving for sponges in this period. Corsi may have been able to dive to about 25 to 30 feet. This is the threshold at which divers need to equalise the pressure in their ears. Failure to do this is very painful, and can result in ruptured eardrums and damaged sinuses, manifested as bleeding from ears, nose, and even the eyes. Francis would have known how to equalise and so was able to dive as deep as 90 feet. If Corsi's diving team was structured in a similar way to that of the Spanish pearl diving teams, then we can imagine the Venetian as the *patron*, or owner of the boat, who employed a team of half-a-dozen divers led by an African expert. Clearly such men had to be treated well. If you wanted someone to be able to dive regularly, he had to be kept in peak physical condition.[29] In this context, Corsi's purchase of meat and drink at the Dolphin was a necessary investment in his skilled employees.

What were the 'certain instruments' that Corsi's team used? Leonardo da Vinci had designed various underwater breathing devices for the Venetian State in the early sixteenth century, one of which he claimed would allow a man to stay submerged for four hours. But, fearful of the 'evil nature of man', he refused to test or even reveal his designs, in case they were used 'as a means of murder at the bottom of the sea, by breaking the bottoms of ships and sinking them altogether with the men in them'.[30] The development of modern diving equipment only began in the nineteenth century. In 1818 a young diver named John Deane was present when a fire broke out at a farmhouse near Whitstable in Kent. He seized a helmet from an old suit of armour and used a pump and hose to supply it with oxygen while he saved the horses from a burning barn. He and his brother Charles Anthony patented his invention and later developed it into a diving helmet. In 1836 they would use their invention to rediscover the wreck of the *Mary Rose*.[31]

One useful piece of equipment available to Corsi's team, at least in a rudimentary form, was the diving bell. This captured a pocket of air as the divers descended, allowing them to breathe from this reserve at certain intervals instead of returning to the surface. Guglielmo de Lorena and Francesco de Marchi had deployed such a device in 1535 to explore and retrieve items from Caligula's pleasure barges, submerged in Lake Nemi near Rome.[32] As well as the diving bell, divers used a technique where they tied two large stones together with cord and slung them over their shoulder as they entered the water. This weighed them down sufficiently to reach the depths, and could be discarded when they wanted to return to the surface. As divers came up and down several times in a session, they required a good store of such stones and cord in their boat. Regular diving from an early age would naturally improve their ability to see underwater. Glass or bamboo goggles were available, although these became less useful at greater depths as the water pressure pressed them painfully against the face.[33]

The testimony of Domenico Paza, a 31-year-old from Verona who found himself aboard Corsi's salvaging boat, provides us with an insight into how Francis and his team brought the tin to the surface. Corsi had tied a rope around a piece of tin, Paza had given it a tug and the rope had broken. The angry Corsi chastised Paza for having 'done ill to meddle with that which [he] had taken in hand'.[34]

Three of the fifteen witnesses in the case questioned Francis's testimony when they were recalled to give further evidence in late May and early June 1549. Antonio de Nicolao, a 32-year-old Venetian sailor resident in Southampton, declared Francis was 'a morisco, born where they are not christened, and slave to the said Peter Paulo [Corsi]', and that 'no credit nor faith ought to be given to his sayings, as in other strange [foreign] Christian countries it is to no such slave given'. Niccolo de Marini, the Genoese merchant who had lost goods aboard the sunken ship, pronounced Francis 'a morisco . . . [who] had been for the space of three years slave and bondman to the said Peter Paulo and an infidel born, and so is commonly reputed and taken of all men knowing him'. At the end of his testimony he emphasised that 'no faith ought to be given to the sayings of the same Blackemore for that he is slave to the same Peter [Corsi] and an infidel born'. Finally, Domenico Milanes, factor to (and possibly a relative of) fellow Florentine, Angelo de Milanes, said Francis was 'a gynno [Guinean] born where they are not christened and hath been for these two years slave and bondman to the said Peter Paulo [Corsi] wherefore he thinks that no credit should be given to his sayings or depositions'.[35] These three statements are so similar that they sound like they had been planned in advance; that the men got together and discussed how to pour doubt on Francis's unhelpful testimony. There are three interesting issues here: first, what was Francis's geographical origin, second, what was his religious status and finally, was he enslaved?

Unfortunately, the description of Francis as a 'morisco' doesn't give us any further information about precisely where he came from. The term was only rarely used to describe individuals in Tudor England but it occasionally appeared as a place name. Thomas Elyot, discussing the Roman occupation of North Africa in his *Book named the Gouernour* (1531), commented that Roman 'Numidia, Libya, & such other countries, now be called Barbary & Morisco'.[36] 'Morisco' was also used to signify Morocco in a 1597 London parish register, as we shall see in Chapter Six. However, Francis himself testified that he was born on an island off the coast of Guinea, not Morocco.

The term 'morisco' might also have had some religious significance. It was used by the Spanish to describe Moorish converts to Christianity, of which there had been many since the Spanish retook Granada in 1492. In the description of 'Robert Tego, a Morisco, servant with Thomas Castlyn', who was living in Vintry Ward, London, in 1567, this is the meaning that makes most sense.[37] 'Castlyn' suggests 'Castilian', so Tego was probably a Moorish convert to Christianity, brought from Spain to England by his master. Jacques Francis was allegedly 'an infidel', born 'where they are not christened'. Certainly there was a substantial Muslim population in West Africa around the time of his birth. But the term 'morisco', together with his 'Christian' name, suggests that Francis had subsequently been baptised. Quite apart from anything else, the High Court of Admiralty would not have accepted his testimony were he were unable to convince it of his Christian status and swear an oath on the Bible to tell the truth.

There was no reason why Corsi or another European he had met *en route* to Southampton could not have arranged for Francis to be baptised. The Bible tells of 'a man of Ethiopia', treasurer to Queen Candace, who was converted and baptised by Philip on the road to Jerusalem. This example was followed by Europeans throughout the Renaissance period. In 1520, Pope Leo X baptised the writer Al-Hasan ibn Muhammad al-Wazzan al-Fasi, naming him Leo Africanus. Eighty years later, Africanus's English translator, John Pory, was so impressed with Portuguese missionary work in Kongo and Angola that he wrote of the 'exceeding glory', with which they had 'no less advanced the honour of their own nation, than the propagating of the Christian faith'.[38]

So Francis was presumably a Christian by 1549, and the three witnesses were ignoring this in their efforts to discredit the testimony of the only witness who supported Corsi's side of the argument. It is interesting to consider that Francis might have been born into a Muslim family and later converted either by Corsi or one of his countrymen. He would then have been a Catholic, a status that would become increasingly troublesome for him in Reformation England. With the succession of the young Edward VI in 1547 came evangelical Protestantism and the first Book of Common Prayer in English, use of which was enforced under the Act of Uniformity from 9 June 1549.[39]

What of the assertion that Francis was a slave? Antonio de Nicolao claimed that Corsi had offered to sell his lead diver to anybody who wanted to buy him, but none of the people of Southampton stepped forward to buy him that day. Such a transaction would of course have been illegal. In his testimony, de Marini insisted Francis was 'commonly reputed' to be a slave and taken as such by all who knew him. Even if this were true, it doesn't change the fact that it was not legally possible to be enslaved under English Common Law. This was in stark contrast to the laws the Italians were familiar with at home. In Venice, the Senate had decreed in 1489 that anyone who killed a runaway 'Ethiopian or saracen' slave would be immune from prosecution for murder.[40] We can sense Antonio de Nicolao's confusion in his pains to point out to the court that 'in other strange countries' the right to testify 'is to no such slaves given'. However, Francis was not a slave in England.

This clash of jurisdictions is a common theme when members of foreign merchants' households appear in English courts. When the Venetian Filippo Cini tried to sell his servant Maria Moriana to a Genoese merchant for £20 in Southampton in the 1470s, she protested her freedom. Not to be thwarted, Cini made her sign a document she was unable to read, certifying that she owed him £20, before having her thrown into prison. She petitioned the Lord Chancellor, asking him to redress this gross injustice, but his response does not survive. Cini thought that he could treat Maria as a slave in England, as he could at home in Italy, but she was aware that he could not. More than a century later, Hector Nunes, a Portuguese physician and *converso* (the name given to former Jews ostensibly converted to Christianity), also appeared to believe the laws on slavery were the same in England as in his native land. He had illegally purchased an 'Ethiopian Negar' from a Cornish mariner in 1587, but was soon afterwards forced to acknowledge that the Common Law of England did not allow him to compel the man to 'tarry and serve' him.[41]

Although slavery was illegal, it may still have been practised, especially in foreign households, where they were used to other customs. In 1537 Diego Sanchez, a Spaniard living in the parish of St Benet's in the City of London, named 'Johan [Joan] my slave' in his will. She may not have been of African origin, as her ethnicity is not mentioned, and, as we've seen, Africans were not the only peoples to be enslaved in Europe. Sanchez left instructions that Johan should serve his wife, Eleanor de la Palma, for two years after his death, after which time she would be freed, and given clothes and four ducats of gold. Johan's two daughters, Agnes and Mary, who had been fathered by Sanchez, were left a dowry on their marriages of 10,000 maravedis each.* This was to be paid in

---

* Approximately £6 18s 10d. Maravedis were Spanish copper coins worth one sixth of a penny.

'household stuff', which would be 'a remembrance to them to pray for me'.[42] Sanchez does not appear to have lived very long in London, where he says he is living 'at this present time', and he makes his provisions 'if God do take me out of this present life in this Realm of England'. He also had the will written in Spanish so his heirs and friends could read it. It appears Sanchez brought Johan with him from Spain, and continued to treat her as a slave in England. Nothing existed in English law that could have compelled Johan to continue to serve Sanchez's wife after he'd died, but she may have done so. She is the only person known to be described as a slave in a Tudor will, no doubt because the will was made by a Spaniard resident in London. As we shall see in Chapter Ten, when Englishmen and women mentioned Africans in their wills, they appeared not as slaves, but as beneficiaries.

One strong indicator that Jacques Francis was not enslaved is that various witnesses in the High Court of Admiralty case make reference to him being paid wages. Antonio de Nicolao described Francis and the other divers as 'poor labouring men . . . seeking their living about in sundry places where they may get it having but little of their own'.[43] This description does not sound like that of enslaved men. The men, though poor, seem to have had the freedom to work for whom they pleased. Nicolao himself had observed them doing other work during the times of the year when the weather prohibited diving. Perhaps they worked in the docks, loading and unloading goods? Even if Francis had 'little of his own', the possession of anything at all, and more importantly, the fact that he was earning his living, shows that he was not enslaved.

Domenico Erizzo testified that in October and November 1547 he had seen Corsi 'walk up and down in the street . . . in a long gown being in variance with a servant of his for that he denied to pay his wages'.[44] This is further evidence that Francis and the other divers were, at least in theory, receiving wages. Corsi had told the mayor of Southampton that he had stolen the tin because the wages he and his servants were being paid were too low. This raises the possibility that the fight in the street was because his servants wanted more money and he was driven to the theft to satisfy their demands. Our interpretation depends on how we imagine the balance of power between Corsi and his divers. Given their unrivalled skills, Corsi's team were actually in a pretty strong negotiating position should they have wished to make demands of their master; he would find it difficult to replace them.

Others might have regarded him as a slave, but how did Francis see himself? He gave evidence 'of his own free will'. According to John Tyrart, the court interpreter, Francis asserted that he was a '*famulus*' to the Venetian. *Famulus* meant a servant or attendant, a member of someone's entourage or household, in contrast to *servus,* meaning slave.[45] Tyrart, and by extension, the court, accepted and recorded this term when Francis used it to identify himself. While Francis may not have had a clear idea of his status in England before the court case, the experience of testifying showed him that he was considered free in the eyes of the law. It's quite possible that this understanding began to dawn on him the day that Corsi offered to sell him in Southampton and got no response.

That Francis was allowed to testify in an English court of law is powerful evidence that he was not considered a slave. Enslaved or unfree people have been prevented from testifying throughout history, partly due to the concern that they would be forced by their circumstances to say whatever their masters told them to say. Roman law stated that slaves could not give evidence unless it was taken under torture. The villeins or serfs of medieval England could not give evidence in court. As late as the 1530s, the Duke of Suffolk was brought before the Court of Chancery to represent one of his villeins from his Suffolk manor of Frostenden, the man not being allowed to speak for himself. In the early years of the American colonies Africans were able to give testimony, but once their slave status was confirmed this right was removed. In 1732, the state of Virginia declared that black men and women 'are people of such base and corrupt natures that their testimony cannot be certainly depended on'.[46]

Yet English courts were to depend on the testimony of Africans on more than one occasion in the century following Francis's appearance. As we shall see in Chapter Four, Edward Swarthye, like Francis, gave evidence in support of his employer. But not all

African witnesses did. In 1609 the pirate William Longcastle, 'a man of evil fame and little or no substance', was put on trial in the High Court of Admiralty. His alleged crime was seizing the *Susan*, of Bristol, off the coast of Morocco. According to the prosecution, Longcastle had come alongside the *Susan* as she lay close to the port of Safi and invited most of her crew aboard his ship, the *Ulysses*, 'to banquet and revel'. While they were being entertained, he captured the ship and made off with her to the West Indies. But the main witness to the crime, Captain Anthony Wye, master of the *Susan*, was absent at sea when the case came to trial and so it looked as if Longcastle would be acquitted.

However, Longcastle had made a fatal error. He had, in his 'rashness to surprise and haste to get off', left an African boy behind at the scene of the crime. Wye took the boy back to England with him, where he left him at the home of a London merchant, Richard Hall, the owner of Longcastle's ship, the *Ulysses*. The boy was brought into court and convincingly testified against Longcastle. The pirate, in words that strongly echo the complaints of the Italian merchants in 1549, begged the judges to 'let the tongue of a Christian and not of a Pagan cut off my life'. It was a plea made in vain, for Longcastle had compounded his error in leaving the boy behind by having had him christened: 'The Court resolved, that where he desired to have the oath of a Christian, [he] himself, & the *Moore* had confessed he had made him one'. The boy might have been purchased as a slave abroad, but in England he was free and as a Christian he could testify against his former master. Longcastle and his accomplices were found guilty and sentenced to death. They were executed at Wapping in December 1609.[47]

In accusing Francis of being an infidel and a slave the Italians were being disingenuous. They attacked him, not because of his heritage but because his evidence in his master's defence went against their interests. However vitriolic and xenophobic the Italians' words about Francis were, we must remember they were said in court in a failed attempt to discredit him, and he was not the only witness whose testimony was questioned in this way. In March 1549 an agent of Domenico Erizzo asked the court to disregard the testimony of four others: John Westcott, William

Mussen, John Iko and George Blacke. Not only did he accuse them of being unfit witnesses, partial to Corsi, but he also asserted that they were 'unhealthy, of capricious opinions, living corrupted lives, poor and needy vagabonds'. The list goes on, as if the lawyers were reeling off every conceivable objection to a witness. Most striking are the accusations that these men were 'vagabonds, wandering through different places and kingdoms all over the world', who were 'without faith, infidels and pagans, by no means professing the Christian religion'.[48] The latter strongly echoes the accusation made against Jacques Francis and yet his name is not listed in this document. The objections do, however, confirm our suspicions that Iko and Blacke, like Francis, had learnt their diving skills in their native Africa. It is odd that two Englishmen – Westcott, originally from Barnstaple in Devon, and Mussen, a Warwickshire man – are listed alongside the divers, as their accounts supported Erizzo's own. It may simply be that the objections against all four men were simply lumped together in one document to minimise the cost of the paperwork.

We do not know whether Francis's testimony was enough to exonerate his master, as the verdict does not survive. In any case, it wasn't long before Corsi found himself imprisoned for a different offence. In September 1549, Henry Fitzalan, Earl of Arundel, persuaded Corsi to leave Portsmouth to 'take certain of his stuff out of the sea'. Corsi and his team duly set off for Arundel Castle, some thirty miles east along the coast. The Duke of Somerset regarded this as Corsi abandoning his work on the *Mary Rose* and had him committed to the Tower. Corsi was examined by Sir Edward Wotton, who had been on the Privy Council since 1547. Wotton clearly found fault, as Corsi remained incarcerated for the next six months. He was finally released on 26 March 1550, without having to pay any fees for his imprisonment.[49] This was a boon as prisoners usually faced a bill for board and lodging.

After his stint in the Tower, Corsi may no longer have been in a position to employ Jacques Francis. Yet his team's services had been called upon by the King, Erizzo and his fellow merchants, and the Earl of Arundel in quick succession. With such high demand for salvage expertise, surely Francis could name his price? The *Sancta*

Maria and Sanctus Edwardus case had made him enemies amongst the merchant population of Southampton, and even London. That said, his loyalty to his master should have recommended him to other employers. He might even have had international employment prospects. In 1569 Francisco Gonzales, a free African diver living in Seville, requested a licence to travel with his wife to Veracruz in New Spain, where he intended to continue plying his trade.[50] Such journeys would have been fraught with dangers, not least the very real threat of enslavement, so it would hardly be surprising if Francis had chosen to remain in England.

Jacques Francis was not the last African to live in Southampton in the Tudor era. By the end of the sixteenth century, a number of Africans were living in the households of English merchants and townspeople. We know this because they were subject to an 'alien' poll tax of 8d a head, levied on any foreigner living in England. The tax returns for Southampton show that between 1594 and 1611 there were as many as ten Africans resident, in twelve different households, the majority of which were those of wealthy merchants, within the parishes of Holy Rood, St Laurence, St Michael and St John. Four of the men with African servants served as Mayor of Southampton, two were members of Parliament and two had connections with the Dolphin Inn: John Sedgewick was the innkeeper in the 1580s, while John Jeffrey had become the owner before 1611. Three of the Africans were recorded by name: Joane, maid to Lawrence and Mary Groce; Maudlin, who lived in the household of John Andrews; and Michael, servant to Mayor Thomas Holmes. In July 1591, Michael and another African, servant to Thomas Heaton, were accused of theft by an alehouse keeper, Dennis Edwards. They were sent to prison on suspicion of cutting and stealing a cable from his ship. No further charge was made against them, and they were 'punished in the stocks and so freed', despite protesting their innocence.[51]

As the numbers of Italian merchants in Southampton dwindled, English merchants began to take over the long-distance trades, traversing the seas as never before. From 1558 there was regular trade with Morocco, and from 1530 voyages began to venture further down the coast of West Africa, and across the Atlantic to South America and the Caribbean. This brought more Africans to English shores. Where before they came via southern Europe, they now began to travel directly from Africa and the Atlantic world as a result of English privateering, which is why Africans begin to appear in Southampton records again in the 1590s. One Englishman who made a career of seizing Spanish ships and raiding Spanish ports around the world was Sir Francis Drake. His exploits are well known, but few know the role played by Africans in his successes against the Spanish, or that some returned to England with him. Diego, who was to meet Drake in Panama, was one such man . . .

3

Diego,
the Circumnavigator

Diego ran headlong through the gunshot towards the boats on the beach. 'Are you Captain Drake's?' he cried. He had to get on board. He had heard there were no slaves in England and if he joined the English they might take him there. He knew some of their countrymen traded in slaves, but he was willing to stake everything on this chance of freedom. Nothing could be worse than staying with his Spanish master. He could not join the runaway slaves in the mountains. He had betrayed them once too often. Francis Drake was his only hope. 'I must join you,' he shouted, 'let me aboard.' A bullet whistled past his head in answer. 'I have important information. You are in great danger!' Again they shot at him. 'Listen! If you don't take me aboard you will all die.' They fired at him once more. 'There isn't much time. Let me aboard!' At last they relented, and as his feet hit the deck he felt elated. A handful of English sailors pressed around him. They demanded to know what he had to say. 'You must send word to your Captain,' he said breathlessly. 'He must retreat. If you do not depart before daybreak you face certain death.' A few men were dispatched to warn Drake and his raiding party. Diego sank to the deck in relief.

THE FIRST ENSLAVED Africans arrived in the Spanish colonies within a decade of Columbus's 1492 voyage. From the beginning, they resisted: one of the Africans brought to

Hispaniola in 1502 managed to escape to the mountains. He became the first of many *Cimarrons*: the name given to those who escaped their Spanish masters and established settlements in the hinterland.[1] By the time Englishmen such as Francis Drake arrived more than half a century later, there were many Africans, both enslaved and free, living in Spanish America. Drake had participated in some of John Hawkins's slaving voyages in the 1560s, so why didn't he attempt to enslave Diego when their paths crossed?

Francis Drake had heard tales of Africa and Africans from an early age. He grew up in the Plymouth household of his kinsman William Hawkins, alongside his sons William and John. William Hawkins senior, 'a man for his wisdom, value, experience and skill in sea causes much esteemed and beloved of King Henry the Eighth', was a pioneer of trade to Guinea and Brazil in the 1530s. He returned from these voyages with cargoes of Brazil wood, 'elephants' teeth' (ivory), 'grains of paradise' (meleguetta pepper, a much-prized spice) and no doubt some tall tales. His son, John Hawkins, initiated the English slave trade in 1562, having heard from merchants in the Canary Islands that 'Negroes were very good merchandise in Hispaniola, and that store of negroes might easily be had upon the coast of Guinea'. Over the next decade, Hawkins would be responsible for the transportation of an estimated 1,500 enslaved Africans across the Atlantic.[2] Drake encountered the harsh realities of this trade at close quarters, as he sailed on John Lovell's slaving voyage in 1566–7 – a venture sponsored by Hawkins – and went on to serve as Captain of the *Judith* on the last of Hawkins's slaving ventures the following year.[3]

Initially, the Spanish used Native Americans as a labour force in their colonies, but the importation of African labour became increasingly practical and desirable as the local population succumbed to Old World diseases, and writers such as Bartholomé de las Casas objected to their enslavement.[4] The first enslaved Africans brought across the Atlantic arrived in Hispaniola in 1502. By 1619, the year the first enslaved Africans arrived in Virginia, more than 370,000 individuals had already been transported to the Spanish Americas from Africa.[5] Later, once the British dominated the transatlantic slave trade, they were responsible for wrenching more than three million Africans from their homelands over the course of the long eighteenth century.[6] Sickeningly, the uncertainty about the exact figure is in part due to the discrepancy between numbers embarked and numbers disembarked: a stark statistical reminder of how many died in the crossing. But in the Tudor era, the English had not yet taken to this abhorrent trade in earnest; not due to any superior moral feeling, but simply because they did not have any colonies of their own to provide markets for enslaved Africans. Hawkins was the only English merchant to attempt the trade before the 1640s, and he was an interloper, selling to the Spanish Caribbean.

The Spaniards did not take kindly to Hawkins's efforts. They caught up with him in September 1568, off the coast of Mexico at San Juan de Ulúa; in the ensuing battle the English lost five of their seven ships. This was such a disaster, both personal and financial, that it put Hawkins and his countrymen off the trade in slaves for the next seventy years.[7] So many provisions were lost in the fray that Hawkins was forced to put almost one hundred of the men from his ship, the *Minion*, ashore on the beach near Tampico, abandoning them to the mercy of the Mexican Inquisition.[8] He asked Drake to take some of them home on the other surviving ship, the *Judith*. But, as Hawkins later complained, Drake 'forsook us in our great misery', and set off for England on his own. The events at San Juan de Ulúa left Drake hungry for revenge.[9] He began a series of raids on the Spanish colonies, plundering ports and seizing ships. It was during one of these attacks, in the summer of 1572, that he met Diego.

Diego lived in Nombre de Dios, a small unfortified town of some one hundred and fifty to two hundred houses on the Atlantic coast of Panama. He was enslaved in the household of Captain Gonzalo de Palma, the High Admiral and Captain General of the town.[10] Like most Africans brought to the Caribbean by the Spanish at this time, he was probably from Senegambia, the region of West Africa that lay between the Senegal and Gambia rivers. Prisoners of war, they were sold to Portuguese and Spanish merchants, and shipped across the Atlantic. Some were employed in rural areas on farms, sugar plantations and in silver and gold mines. Those who lived in ports, towns and cities worked in every conceivable service role: dockworkers, cooks, carpenters, seam-stresses, cobblers, blacksmiths and laundresses, to name a few. Indeed, one Spanish official noted that 'we cannot live without black people; it is they who are the labourers, and no Spanish person will work here.'[11]

Nombre de Dios was where the Spanish treasure fleet docked every year to collect silver that had been brought from Peru. The treasure first travelled by ship from Lima to Panama City, on the Pacific coast, and was then carried across the isthmus of Panama by mule-train to Nombre de Dios, whence it was shipped to Seville.[12]

At three o'clock in the morning of 29 July 1572, under a bright moon, Drake and his men attacked the town.[13] By the shore, twelve men waited aboard four pinnaces; smaller, lighter vessels, so named because they were originally made of pine: the *Lion*, the *Minion*, the *Bear* and a fourth unnamed vessel, to ensure a safe retreat. Out of the darkness, a figure appeared on the shore:

> one Diego, a negro . . . came and called to our pinnaces to know whether they were Captain Drake's? And upon answer received continued entreating to be taken on board, though he had first three or four shot made at him, until at length they fetched him.

Diego warned the English that their raiding party was in great danger. The town was full of people. What's more, about eight days earlier, the King had sent some one hundred and fifty soldiers to guard Nombre de Dios against the Cimarrons. This wasn't actually true; Spanish sources show that no reinforcements were sent to the town until after news of Drake's attack.[14] Diego must have been exaggerating the danger in order to persuade the English to leave the port, with him aboard, forthwith. But they believed him, and sent some men to warn those ashore. His information 'agreed with the report of the Negroes' whom they had taken at the Isle of Pines a week earlier; the English routinely interrogated Africans they encountered to gain intelligence of this kind. This particular group had been set ashore on the mainland so 'that they might perhaps join themselves to their countrymen the Cimarrons, and gain their liberty'. But Drake took care to leave them far enough from the town that they could not warn the Spanish of his approach.[15]

The main account of the adventure, *Sir Francis Drake Revived*, compiled for Drake by the preacher Philip Nichols in 1593 from the notes of Drake himself and some of his crew, takes pains to portray Diego as insisting on being taken aboard but this impression is contradicted by a Portuguese pilot who met the African some years later. He reported that Diego had been taken prisoner by Drake from a frigate near Nombre de Dios.[16]

It is not unthinkable that an African might want to join the English at this time. In 1572, there were no English colonies. Those who boarded English ships would, if they survived the considerable dangers of the voyage, be taken to England, where rumour had it that all men were free; something spoken of across the Atlantic world. It was in the same year that Diego joined Drake that the Wolof Juan Gelofe and the English sailor William Collins had their conversation in a Mexican silver mine. In response to Gelofe's comment that there were no slaves in England, Collins confirmed 'it was true, that there they were all freemen'.[17] Spanish officials sang the same tune: in 1586 Pedro de Arana wrote to the Spanish House of Trade from Havana, commenting that in Drake's country 'negro labourers' were free. Diogo, an African taken to England by an English pirate in 1614, later reported to the Portuguese Inquisition that when he laid foot on English soil, 'he immediately became free, because in that Reign nobody is a slave.'[18] Such talk might well have reached Diego's ears, and encouraged him to seek out Drake's ships.

The Nombre de Dios raiding party did not meet with much resistance, but neither did it meet with much treasure. The Spanish fleet had already been and gone that summer. In *Sir Francis Drake Revived*, Nichols claimed that there was 'a huge heap of silver' in the Governor's House and 'more gold and jewels than all our four pinnaces could carry' in the King's Treasure House. The English would have made off with these riches if

Drake had not suddenly fainted from loss of blood following a leg wound.[19] Faced with losing their leader or the treasure, Drake's men supposedly chose loyalty over silver and gold. This fabrication was far less embarrassing than admitting that they'd simply got their timing wrong.

In the aftermath of their failed raid, Diego was able to offer the English new hope. He knew how they could get their hands on enough gold and silver to assuage the sting of defeat. This was tempting enough to allow the English to disregard the fact that Diego had seriously exaggerated how many soldiers were guarding Nombre de Dios. Diego proposed that the English seek out the escaped Africans who had been attacking Nombre de Dios. They had set up their own settlements, known as *palenques*, in the mountainous hinterland, often intermarrying with native peoples. The Cimarron community in Panama was well established by the time Drake arrived. They had three main *palenques*, one near the future town of Portobello, one in the mountains of the Cerro de Cabra near Panama City and a third some fifty miles southeast of the city.[20] Such runaway communities developed across the Spanish Americas from the earliest years of the Empire.[21] One Spanish bishop complained in 1571 that three hundred of the thousand Africans who arrived in the area annually escaped 'to the wilds', while another official estimated that there were 3,000 Cimarrons in the area by May 1573. The Cimarrons had regularly attacked Spanish settlements for fifty years or so, partly to liberate enslaved Africans to augment their numbers, partly to seize supplies, food and wine. Spanish attempts to hunt them down were treated with contempt. Informed that one Esteban de Trexo was on his way to find them in 1570, they erected a gallows beside the road he was to take and hung knives from it, signalling that they would hang de Trexo and decapitate his men.[22]

Diego, a canny operator, volunteered to help the English make contact with the Cimarrons, amongst whom, he assured them, Drake's name was 'most precious and highly honoured'. It was a case of my enemy's enemy is my friend. There was just one small problem: Diego told the English that he had betrayed the runaways so many times that they would kill him if they set eyes upon him again. However, if Drake promised to protect him, he would 'adventure his life'.[23]

What sort of betrayals was Diego talking about? He knew where the Cimarrons lived, and what they thought of Drake, but he was not at this time living as part of the Cimarron community. One can only imagine that on one or more occasion he had fled de Palma's household to join the Cimarrons, but then had the misfortune to be recaptured by the Spanish and forced to reveal their whereabouts and plans. Such a life cannot have been easy. No wonder he was willing to chance joining the English in the hope of finding a way out.

Diego's offer to lead the English to the Cimarrons was not immediately taken up. The English returned to the refuge on the Isle of Pines that they called Port Plenty, where they had left the rest of their ships, then sailed on to Cartagena, in modern-day Colombia.[24] However, it became clear that news of Drake's presence in the area had spread. The element of surprise lost, they decided to lie low for a while, and retreated to a quiet spot in the Sound of Darien. This was an area Diego knew, and he helped set up the camp there, assisting in the erection of lodging houses and a building for public meetings. His experience in local methods of building proved useful again a few weeks later, when the English returned to Port Plenty. There, they built a number of storehouses to protect themselves from attack, some on islands and some on the mainland, separated by distances of thirty or sixty miles, so that if any were taken, there would be others to fall back on. Diego's talents were of great help. He had, the English observed, a 'special skill in the speedy erection of such houses'.

Diego led Drake's brother John to the Cimarrons. His earlier fears, perhaps exaggerated for effect, that they might kill him on sight, had dissipated. Instead, he facilitated a successful negotiation with the Cimarron leader, Pedro. They agreed to meet again the next day, 14 September, at a river halfway between the two camps. As security, two Englishmen were left behind, in exchange for two Cimarrons, who returned with the English to Port Plenty.

When these two Africans arrived in the English camp they

confirmed what Diego had originally reported. They told Drake that the Cimarrons were delighted at his arrival. They knew he was a great enemy of the Spaniards, and had heard tell not only of his recent attack on Nombre de Dios, but also of his previous raiding voyages. They would do their utmost to assist him in any enterprise he had in mind against their mutual foe.

The alliance that Diego had inspired was taking shape. Drake resolved to set out with his brother and the two Cimarron emissaries that very evening to meet his new allies. The rest of the fleet was to follow the next morning. When they met, the English offered the Cimarrons entertainment and 'received good testimonies of their joy and good will towards us'. This was all well and good, but, as Diego knew, the English wanted more than friendship. Drake cut to the chase. He asked his guests 'what means they had to furnish him with gold and silver'. They answered apologetically that the stores of gold that they had taken from the Spaniards (out of spite rather than avarice) were not accessible. They kept this gold sunk at the bottom of various rivers, but the waters were now too high for them to retrieve it. If the English wanted to capture treasure from the Spanish, they explained, they would have to wait five months. Once the rainy season was over, the Spanish would set out across the isthmus from Panama City to Nombre de Dios with a mule-train laden with gold and silver. Of course, it was in the Cimarrons's interest not to hand over any treasure at this point. Far better to enlist the Englishmen's help in their next attack.[25]

The English felt it was worth waiting till spring for the opportunity to seize the treasure Diego had told them about under the expert guidance of the Cimarrons. Departing with two more of their new allies aboard, they agreed to a rendezvous at Rio Guana, where they would also meet another company of Cimarrons who lived in the mountains. After a few delays, they met again on 23 September and the next day the Cimarrons helped the English set up a new camp on an island in the Gulf of San Blas. Like Diego, they were expert builders. They built two large lodging houses and a 13-foot high fortress, which was named Fort Diego, after the author of the alliance.[26]

The autumn and winter passed, with a few largely unsuccessful attacks on other Spanish ports and ships, and various deaths, including those of Drake's two brothers, John and Joseph. One ship the English captured near Cartagena had five or six Africans on board, who were all set ashore, except for one 'young Negrito of three or four years old', of whom there is no further mention.[27] Over the weeks and months, Diego began to pick up a smattering of English. Any lingering fears he had that the Cimarrons wanted him dead abated. Indeed, bringing them new allies in their struggle against the old enemy may well have wiped the slate clean. All were focused on their shared goal, and they waited for the time to be right.

At the end of January, Cimarron scouts brought word that the Spanish fleet had arrived in Nombre de Dios. The allies began making plans for an attack on the mule-train that would soon be arriving. Pedro, the Cimarron leader, advised Drake and his company as to the weapons, food and clothing they would need for the expedition. In particular, he insisted that they take as many shoes as they could carry because they would be worn out by the gravel in the many stony rivers they would have to cross.

On Shrove Tuesday (3 February), thirty Cimarrons and eighteen Englishmen set off across the isthmus. It was a hard journey, and the better part of a fortnight passed before they caught sight of Panama City. Along the way, on 11 February, Pedro took Drake to a tall tree from which he could see both the Atlantic and the Pacific oceans. This was the first time an Englishman had set eyes on the Pacific. Drake was greatly inspired, and 'besought Almighty God of His goodness, to give him life and leave to sail once in an English ship, in that sea!' This wish would be granted in time, and when it was, Diego was by his side.

Without the Cimarrons, the expedition would not have been possible. Not only were they able to guide the party through the terrain they knew so well, but they also carried provisions, considerably lightening the Englishmen's load. They supplemented their supplies with animals hunted along the way, including an otter, which it took a little persuasion to induce Drake and his men to taste. Pedro showed no compunction in ridiculing Drake's reluctance, demanding of him: 'Are you a man of war, and in want; and yet doubt whether this be meat, that hath blood?'[28]

The Cimarrons erected lodgings or else led the English to camps they'd built before. At one point, the party stopped at a pleasant Cimarron town of some fifty-five houses where the English admired the 'fine and fitly' clothing of the inhabitants, 'made somewhat after the Spanish fashion'.[29] When an Englishman fainted from sickness or weariness, two Cimarrons carried him with ease for two miles or more. They were also excellent scouts. When they reached Panama City, a Cimarron was sent into the town to find out exactly when the mule train was going to depart. The chosen man had previously been enslaved in Panama, and, dressed in the usual clothing of a slave of that city, was able to pass unnoticed through its streets.

Once they had ascertained the movements of the train, the party split into two groups to lie in wait either side of the road. All wore white shirts over their clothing so they could identify each other 'in the pell mell in the night'. Within an hour, the ringing of the bells around the mules' necks could be heard. The treasure for which they had waited so long was almost within their grasp.[30]

Then, in a moment, all was lost. Robert Pike sprang forward, and before the Cimarron by his side was able to pull him down again, a Spaniard spotted his white shirt and galloped off to warn his countrymen. The bulk of the treasure train turned back, leaving only two horse-loads of silver to be seized in the ambush. The careful planning, the hard weeks of marching across the isthmus, had all been for nothing thanks to one man who had consumed so much *aqua vitae* without water that his excitement got the better of him. The disappointed party had no choice but to make their way back to Fort Diego by forced march, raiding the small Spanish settlement of Venta Chagre on the way, but finding little of value there.[31]

It took time for the men, 'strangely changed in countenance' by 'long fasting', 'sore travel' and worst of all the 'grief' of returning without the hoped-for gold and treasure, to regroup and gather their strength after this humiliating episode.[32] Towards the end of April they set out to ambush the Spanish treasure train once more. By this time they had also allied with some French corsairs led by Guillaume le Testu, who had come in search of Drake and his well-stocked storehouses. The Captain, a skilled cartographer from Le Havre, brought news of the horrific massacre of Huguenots orchestrated by Catherine de Medici on St Bartholomew's Day the previous summer. Both the French and the Cimarrons expressed some reluctance about working together, which was hardly surprising given that two years earlier another French pirate had relied on Cimarron help and been betrayed. Their guide, a man named Pedro Mandinga, had double-crossed them by warning the Spanish, who granted him his freedom in return. If this Pedro Mandinga was the same man as the Pedro who now led the Cimarrons allied with Drake, then the mutual suspicion is all the more understandable.[33] Drake did his best to reassure both parties, and they set their sights on besting their mutual enemy.

This time the plan was to set upon the mule train as it approached Nombre de Dios. The allies camped overnight a mile from the road, and awoke to the welcome sound of ringing bells. As the train got closer, they counted one hundred and ninety animals, each bearing 300 lbs of silver. When the attack came, the forty-five soldiers guarding the convoy were taken completely by surprise. One Cimarron was killed and le Testu 'sore wounded with hail-shot in the belly', before the Spanish retreated in search of reinforcements. The combined Cimarron, English and French force found themselves with more treasure than they were able to carry. They took what they could, burying the rest in land crabs' burrows, under fallen trees and in riverbeds. The injured French leader was left behind. He eventually died of his wounds and was decapitated by the Spaniards, who put his head on display in the marketplace of Nombre de Dios. Another Frenchman, who'd overloaded himself with treasure, got lost in the woods and was captured. The Spaniards tortured him until he revealed where the rest of the treasure had been hidden. Despite having to leave so much behind, the Cimarrons, the English and the French escaped with more than 150,000 pesos of gold and silver.[34] The voyage was made. Diego's promise had been fulfilled.

Drake invited Pedro and three of the 'chiefest' Cimarrons to choose anything they liked from the treasure haul to keep. But Pedro caught sight of a scimitar that had once belonged to Henri II of France. Drake had been given the curved sword the month before by his French ally, le Testu. Despite Drake's initial reluctance to part with the weapon, Pedro insisted on buying it from him for four pieces of gold. He, in turn, intended to present it to his King, 'who would make him a great man, even for this gift's sake'.[35] Before they left, the English tore their pinnaces to pieces and burnt them, so that the Cimarrons could have the ironwork. They had learnt that their allies valued iron above gold, skilfully using the metal to make four different types of arrow head: the smallest for hunting little animals, the largest for fighting Spaniards.

Parting from the Cimarrons with 'good love and liking' the English set sail for home. Diego went with them. It could be that he did not trust the Cimarrons to treat him well without Drake's protection, but he also had good reason to hope for a better life in England.

In 1588, Queen Elizabeth presented a remarkable jewel to Francis Drake. He wears it prominently, on a chain around his waist, in his 1591 portrait by Marcus Gheeraerts the Younger.[36] The successful alliance between the Cimarrons and the English casts new light on the symbolism of the Queen's gift. The so-called 'Drake Jewel' is a pendant, the lid of which has the bust of a black man, superimposed on a white figure, carved upon it in onyx stone. Inside is a miniature of Elizabeth by Nicholas Hilliard with a picture of a phoenix on the reverse. The meaning of the image of the African man that dominates this jewel has long been a subject of discussion. One explanation is that the nature of the onyx stone, with its black and white layers, made the 'blackamoor' a convenient emblem to carve from it. Another expert sees a black emperor, representing Saturn, an imperial ruler of the Golden Age. The woman in profile behind him is the imperial Virgin Astraea who will restore Saturn's reign. In light of what we know of Drake's alliance with the Cimarrons, a new interpretation emerges. The black and white busts symbolise how the forces of Englishmen and Africans united are powerful enough to liberate the world from the power of Spain. It was Drake's success in 1573 and the treasure he returned home with that first made his name and recommended him to his sovereign. This feat would not have been possible without the Cimarrons. And when Elizabeth gave Drake the jewel, in the aftermath of the defeat of the Armada, Spain was still their main adversary.[37]

It was hoped that the Cimarrons would continue to aid the English in their struggle. When Drake and Hawkins set out on their last voyage in 1596, they aspired to ally with the Cimarrons once more. However, when Sir Thomas Baskerville, who had become commander of the fleet after both Drake and Hawkins died *en route*, returned to England, he complained: 'as for those symerouns that were so much talked of before we left England I protest I heard not so much as the name of them in the Indies'. By this time, the political situation in Panama had changed and the Cimarrons sided with the Spanish against the English, who had not visited the region in any force for almost a decade, and could not be depended on to return.[38] And yet their reputation as potential allies lived on. Thomas Gage identified them as such in a narrative of his travels in the West Indies, first published in 1648, and in the plans for an invasion of the Spanish Caribbean that he submitted to Oliver Cromwell in 1654. The subsequent expedition failed to capture Hispaniola as planned, taking the lesser prize of Jamaica instead. Although the Cimarrons did nothing to help this so-called 'Western Design', they still featured positively in Sir William Davenant's *The History of Sir Francis Drake*, performed 'at the Cockpit in Drury Lane' in 1659. There, the audience heard the Cimarron King ask Drake to 'Instruct me how my Symerons and I/May help thee to afflict the Enemy.'[39]

Diego and Drake landed in Plymouth on 9 August 1573. It was a Sunday, and when the news reached the congregation of St Andrew's, they abandoned the service and flocked to the shore to welcome home the adventurers. Plymouth, a town of some 5,000 people, was one of Tudor England's most prominent ports, whence many of the most famous voyagers of the age set forth. The historian William Camden wrote in his *Britannia* of 1586 that 'the town is not very large, but its name and reputation is very great among all nations, and this not so much for the convenience of the harbour as for the valour and worth of the inhabitants'.[40]

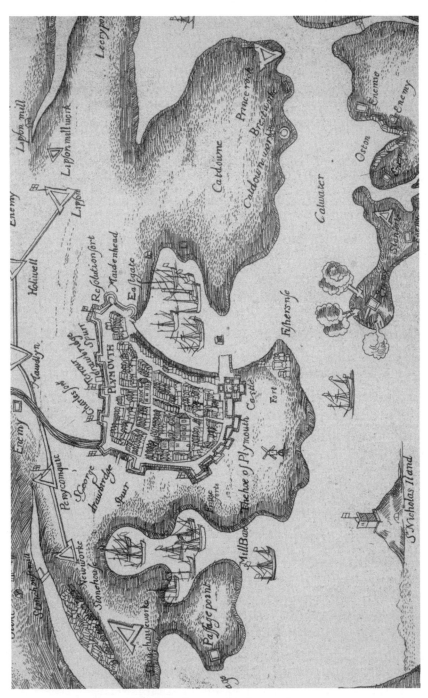

Wenceslas Hollar's map of Plymouth in 1645.

Diego was not the first African to arrive in Plymouth. John Blanke and Catalina of Motril may have landed there with Katherine of Aragon back in 1501. More recently, larger groups of Africans had arrived in the port on ships belonging to John Hawkins. A group of fifty or so that John Lovell had failed to sell in the Spanish Caribbean spent a few weeks in the town in September 1567, before taking ship with Hawkins on his third and final slaving voyage.[41] Clearly, they did not benefit from the general rule that all those who set foot on English soil became free, although the discrepancies in the numbers referred to by Hawkins's sailors suggest one or two managed to slip away and stay in England. Neither Lovell nor Hawkins attempted to sell Africans in Plymouth: there was no market for enslaved Africans there. When Hawkins returned from his final slaving voyage in January 1569, he brought seven Africans back to England with him. It is not known what became of these men, although 'Bastien a Blackmoore of Mr William Hawkins' who was buried at St Andrew's in December 1583, could conceivably have been one of them.[42]

There is no record of Diego's activities for the four years following his arrival in Plymouth in 1573. As he set sail with Drake again in 1577, it's probable that he remained in the sea captain's household. Using some of the riches he'd acquired in Panama, Drake purchased a prominent Plymouth townhouse with a garden, on the corner of Looe Street, close to the Guildhall. Perhaps Diego lived there, working for Drake and his wife Mary Newman, whom Drake had married at St Budeaux church, to the north-east of Plymouth, in 1569. Diego would not have been their only servant, now that Drake was a rich man. Another member of the household in these years was John Drake, Francis's young cousin, who would later sail with him.[43]

Diego may have accompanied Drake when he set off for Ireland in 1575. Walter Devereux, Earl of Essex, was attempting to colonise Ulster, a province he called 'the gall and misery of all evil men in Ireland'.[44] Essex enlisted Drake's help in his attack against Sorley Boy MacDonnell and his Scots mercenaries, who were based on Rathlin Island, off the north coast of Antrim. The island was heavily fortified and had long been thought a safe haven. Its Castle Bruce was named after Robert the Bruce, who had taken refuge there two centuries earlier. Now, Sorley Boy MacDonnell had sent the Scots' women and children there for safety. In July 1575, the English attacked and besieged the castle. Many were killed in the fierce fighting, but worse was to come. After the Scots surrendered, they began to make their way out of the castle, only for the English to set upon them. Two hundred men, women and children were massacred on the spot. Any who had managed to escape and hide in the island's caves were tracked down and killed in the days that followed. When it was all over, the total dead numbered some five hundred souls. Their deaths served little strategic purpose, as before the end of the year the English abandoned the island, having been forced to eat their own horses to stay alive.[45]

The voyage that would result in the first English circumnavigation of the globe was not conceived as a peaceful odyssey of geographical discovery. On the contrary, Drake would take every opportunity to harass the Spanish wherever he encountered them, just as he'd always done. The plan, which had never been attempted before, was to venture beyond the Caribbean, through the Straits of Magellan, and attack along the Pacific coast of South America. This strategy was the result of Drake's machinations with Sir Francis Walsingham. Drake had recently been introduced to the statesman, either by the Earl of Essex or his retainer, Thomas Doughty, who was to accompany Drake on the voyage. Investors in the enterprise included key members of the anti-Spanish lobby at court: Walsingham, the Earl of Leicester, Christopher Hatton, and the Queen herself.

Diego was one of about one hundred and seventy men who set sail with Drake from Plymouth on 15 November 1577. The fleet comprised five ships: Drake's *Pelican*; the *Elizabeth*, captained by John Wynter; the smaller *Marigold*; the provision ship *Swan* and the *Benedict*, a small pinnace.[46] Rather than reveal his true intentions, Drake told the crew that they were embarking on a trading voyage to Alexandria. It would have been hard to persuade men to take ship for a rampage around the world, with the very real dangers that entailed. Nonetheless, the more astute might have

Nicola van Sype's 1581 map shows Drake's circumnavigation route.

realised that Drake's past exploits and the presence of forty-one guns across the fleet made it unlikely that this was to be a peaceful trading expedition. Diego, given his previous experience of South America and proximity to Drake, may have known the truth.

On board the *Pelican*, Diego was Drake's personal manservant, preparing his clothing, serving his meals, and running errands. Diego's experience in long sea voyages would have recommended him as a crew member, and with Drake's command of the Spanish language less than strong, his fluency in Spanish and English would make him a useful interpreter when Spaniards or Spanish-speaking Portuguese were captured.[47] He could pass as a slave and spy on the Spanish, as one of the Cimarrons had in Panama City in 1573, and should Drake wish to ally with the Cimarrons, Diego could once again be the go-between.

Diego was not the only African sailor to work aboard a Tudor ship. Some joined English ships to replace crew that had died. In November 1582, off the coast of Sierra Leone, Captain Luke Warde bought four 'Negroes' from the Portuguese in return for some 'kersey [woollen cloth], pease and biscuit.' Warde had no moral qualms about buying Africans in this way, although one of the ministers on the voyage thought differently. Two of the men served on Warde's ship, the *Edward Bonaventure*, but on Friday 7 December, at the Bay of Good Comfort in Brazil, they escaped. Richard Madox, minister of the *Galleon Leicester*, wrote in his diary: 'Today those two Aethiopians whom Milo [Warde] had acquired with such burning eagerness took to their heels, and ours commended their flight'. It seems he disapproved of their acquisition, and was glad of their escape. The other two men, Massau and Zingo, served on the *Galleon Leicester*, but died before they reached England. The expedition's commander, Edward Fenton, recorded Zingo's death on Friday 7 June 1583.[48] Had these men not died or run away they would have returned to England with the potential to continue as sailors on future voyages. When Sir Walter Ralegh journeyed along the River Orinoco in Guiana in 1595, he had an African aboard, who he described as 'a proper young fellow'. Unfortunately, while swimming in the mouth of the river, he 'was in all our sights taken and devoured' by an alligator.[49]

Africans like Diego, who had formerly been enslaved by the Spanish, had language skills and local knowledge that proved very valuable to the English on their travels.[50] When Drake went ashore at Santiago in the Cape Verde Islands with seven hundred men in November 1585 he took an African as their guide. This man had come with them from England, but had formerly lived in Santiago, so was able to lead the English. Drake promised him that if they were able to capture his former master, then 'the Spaniard should be slave unto the Negro'. Whether or not this came to pass is not recorded.[51] George Clifford, Earl of Cumberland, used Africans as messengers. In 1586, at Rio de la Plata, he sent an African ashore with letters from the Portuguese held prisoner on the ship. Ten years later, in the Azores, he sent a Mozambican, bearing a flag of truce, to negotiate with the islanders.[52]

On Drake's circumnavigation voyage, Diego's skills as an interpreter proved particularly advantageous as the true nature of their mission became apparent. After an initial setback, when heavy storms forced Drake's fleet to seek shelter in Falmouth harbour for almost a month, they sailed south, catching sight of the coast of Morocco on Christmas Day 1577. Drake then began seizing Spanish and Portuguese shipping off the West African coast. The most significant of these attacks for our story came in January 1578 near the Cape Verde islands, when Drake captured the *Santa Maria*, a Portuguese vessel under the command of one Nuño de Silva. Unluckily for de Silva, he was an experienced pilot, well acquainted with the South American coastline. Drake decided to keep him aboard in order to exploit this expertise.[53]

As the voyage progressed, Diego and de Silva fell into conversation. Diego told de Silva about his adventures in Panama and how he had sent Francis's brother, John Drake, to meet the Cimarrons, whom de Silva described as 'the wild rebellious runaway negro slaves' when he later reported their conversation to the inquisitors in Mexico. It was de Silva who reported that Diego had been taken prisoner by Drake from a frigate near Nombre de Dios some seven or eight years earlier.[54] Maybe this was true, and Nichols had put an overly positive spin on events in *Sir Francis Drake Revived*. Then again, de Silva may have calculated that his interrogators would prefer to hear of a captured African, rather than one eager to escape. Or perhaps Diego felt it was easier to build a rapport with the Portuguese pilot if it appeared they were both on Drake's ship against their will.

Having crossed the Atlantic, the fleet reached Brazil in April 1578. As they travelled south along the coast they did battle with the Patagonian people that the Portuguese explorer Ferdinand Magellan had named 'Giants'. Magellan had become the first man to circumnavigate the globe in 1519–1522, and Drake's voyage followed in his wake in more ways than one. In the summer of 1578, Drake discovered the bones of the mutinous captains Magellan had executed at Port San Julian in southern Argentina. He then proceeded to have Captain Thomas Doughty, Essex's retainer, who he'd first met in Ireland, tried for mutiny in the same port; Doughty was found guilty and beheaded.

When the English attempted to cross the straits named after Magellan, their path was stormy. At times they feared for their lives, with good cause: eighty or more men were lost in the course of the crossing. The *Marigold* ran aground on 30 September, marooning its crew of twenty. Just over a week later, the *Elizabeth*, with fifty men aboard, was separated from the others. Her Captain, John Wynter, decided to turn back rather than sail on into the unknown. Another three pinnaces disappeared somewhere in the Straits. By the time Drake rounded Cape Horn in the *Pelican*, his was the only ship remaining. This was the moment when, according to Francis Fletcher, the ship's chaplain, he renamed the ship the *Golden Hinde*, after the personal crest of Christopher Hatton, Lord Chancellor of England, and one of the voyage's key sponsors.[55]

On 25 November 1578, just over a year after they had left Plymouth, Drake and his crew landed on Mocha Isle, off the coast of Chile. They were desperate for fresh water, firewood and food after their difficult passage across the straits. To their great delight, the inhabitants of the island gave them two sheep, chickens, Guinea wheat (maize) and fruits. Using sign language, the English asked for drinking water. Their hosts told them to return the next day. That night, the mutton and chicken were 'so sweet, that we longed for the day, that we might have more'.

The next morning, Diego, Drake and ten other men 'set out with joy' for the island. This time they were met not with friendship, but with a flurry of arrows 'so thick as gnats in the sun'. It seems that the day before, someone had foolishly used the Spanish word *agua* to ask for water. Overnight, the island people became convinced that the visitors were their mortal enemies. For the islanders were Araucanians, refugees from Arauco on the mainland, which they had abandoned after 'cruel and extreme dealing' from the Spaniards. As Diego was fluent in Spanish, he may have been the offender. Two men, Tom Brewer and Tom Flood, who had already gone ashore at the time of the ambush, were captured. Those remaining in the boat were 'enforced to be butts to every arrow', and, by some accounts, darts and stones as well.[56]

The fate of the two captured men, Brewer and Flood, is uncertain. The official account, *The World Encompassed by Sir Francis Drake* (1628), stated that they were 'suddenly slain', but Francis Fletcher's earlier notes on the voyage recorded a far more grisly fate. He claimed that when Drake's men returned, armed, to the island to try to recover the men, they saw them bound and lying on the ground. A crowd of 2,000 Araucanians was dancing wildly around them, while a few cut pieces of flesh from the Englishmen's bodies and tossed them in the air. The rest caught these 'gubbets' and 'like dogs devoured [them] in the most monstrous and unnatural manner . . . till they had picked their bones, life yet remaining in them'.[57] This episode reads like a typical account of the cannibalism supposedly practised by natives of South America and other distant lands, common to the travel literature of the time. And yet the detail is so vivid it is difficult to discount it entirely.

According to Richard Hawkins, Diego received more than twenty wounds in the Mocha Island attack.[58] However, Francis's cousin John recalled that 'the arrows did not enter the flesh deeply'.[59] In any case, he was not the only casualty: Drake was hit in the face and Great Nele the Dane died of his wounds within two days.[60] When the injured men returned to the ship, 'the horror of their bloody state wounded the hearts of all men to behold them'. They did not have much medical help. The chief surgeon was dead and the other was left behind in the *Elizabeth*. There was 'none left us but a boy, whose good will was more than any skill he had'.[61]

Even if there had been an experienced doctor to care for them, recovery was far from guaranteed. The Barber-Surgeon's chest found aboard the *Mary Rose* contains an impressive array of instruments that would be as useful for inflicting torture as effecting cures. William Clowes, a surgeon to Queen Elizabeth and her navy, included in his list of necessary equipment 'a sharp curved incision knife: for cutting skin and flesh', 'probes of silver, lead and tin, or wood for finding foreign bodies in deep wounds' and 'a dilator, with three prongs and an expanding mechanism to hold wounds open'. Surgery was well developed by this time but the same could not be said of Tudor understanding of the importance of hygiene and sterilisation; often the operation was a success but the patient died of shock or infection. In one of his medical textbooks, Clowes detailed the cure 'of a soldier being wounded with a poisoned arrow upon the coast of Brazil', in an incident not unlike the attack on Mocha Isle. The ship's surgeon was a man of 'fine skill' and 'great experience' who was familiar with such injuries, having 'travelled diverse times into those countries'. He cut a large incision around the wound, then filled it with 'hot Aeygptiacum' – a mixture of vinegar, honey and verdigris, the green rust that forms on copper – before covering it with a 'plaister of fine treacle'. But even this cutting-edge treatment, which Clowes recounted with approbation, did not save all who received it, and it is unlikely that the boy left aboard the *Golden Hinde* was up to speed with the latest cures.[62] *The World Encompassed* put the survival of the men injured at Mocha down to the grace of God, the 'diligent putting to of every man's help' and 'the very good advice of our Generall'.[63] Maybe Drake remembered his kinsman John Hawkins using a clove of garlic as a remedy for an arrow wound sustained whilst trying to capture Africans in Cape Verde a decade before.[64]

Despite his twenty wounds, Diego survived. Although the main text reporting the Mocha island incident reported that he died of his injuries, a marginal note adds that he died near the Indonesian Moluccas, islands which the *Golden Hinde* only reached twelve months later.[65] It's not clear how such wounds might take a year to kill a man, though the survival of the soldier who made it back from Brazil to consult William Clowes in 1591 shows it was possible for men to carry on for considerable lengths of time. It may be that one of his twenty wounds became infected and turned gangrenous, or he could have developed scurvy, which causes old wounds to reopen.[66]

Diego's survival until November 1579 is corroborated by the testimony of others who saw him aboard the *Golden Hinde* months after he was wounded at Mocha. Nuño de Silva testified that Diego, whom he mentioned by name, was still aboard when he left the ship at the Mexican port of Guatulco in April 1579. Drake's cousin listed an African 'they had brought with them from England' amongst those who set sail from Guatulco later that month.[67] Juan Pascual, another Portuguese pilot, also met Diego while a prisoner on the *Golden Hinde* in the first half of April 1579. He later testified that he'd met two 'negroes' on Drake's ship. One, clearly Diego, spoke Spanish and English, and 'everyone said that the Englishman had brought him from England'. The other was 'seized at sea'. Pascual also reported that one of these two men, though he could not recall which one, told him that they had 'made a contract with Francis Drake', meaning they were being paid wages, just like the rest of the crew.[68] This could only have been Diego, who had been with the ship from the outset.

Juan Pascual had joined the *Golden Hinde* from a Spanish ship Drake first encountered off the Pacific coast of Guatemala an hour before dawn on 4 April 1579. As the English approached, a Spaniard called out, asking for identification. Drake made one of his prisoners, Alonso Sanchez Colchero, answer in Spanish that this was Miguel Angel's ship from Peru. Thus deceived, it was quite a shock for the Spaniards when the English opened fire. The Spanish ship was unarmed, having set out on a trading voyage from Acapulco to Peru, and most of the men were still asleep when the English came aboard. The owner, Don Francisco de Zarate, was a member of the prestigious order of Santiago, and a cousin of the Duke of Medina Sidonia, one of Spain's most prominent noblemen, who would go on to command the Armada fleet in 1588. As one might expect, the first question Drake posed to this unfortunate gentleman once he had him in his cabin was 'How much silver and gold does your ship carry?' The answer was very little, but they were carrying porcelain, linen, taffeta and other silks, in abundance.[69] These were goods from the Philippines, so named in 1543 in honour of the future King Philip II of Spain.

Since 1565, the Spanish had conducted a regular trade between Manila and Acapulco, buying porcelain, spices, silks and other goods with their American silver.[70] Drake took what he pleased of this cargo, but spared Zarate and his ship. In gratitude, the Spaniard presented him with a golden falcon with an emerald embedded in its breast. William Camden later wrote that Zarate also gave Drake some 'faire Negroes' for sparing his ship, but contemporary accounts agree that Drake took an African man and a woman, 'a proper negro wench called Maria', without invitation.[71]

These two Africans were not the first to come aboard the *Golden Hinde* as she made her way north along the coast of South America. Who was the other African man that Juan Pascual met, the one who had been 'seized at sea'? He cannot have been the man taken from Zarate's ship with Maria, as Pascual had come from the same ship and so would have known him. Another African was taken from a ship in Arica, in northern Chile, on 5 February 1579, but a month later he expressed his desire to return to his master 'who was advanced in years' and Drake let him go, saying, 'Since thou wishest to go thou canst go with God's blessing, for I do not wish to take anyone with me against his will'. The second African Pascual referred to must have either have been the one taken from Gonzalo Alvarez's ship at Paita (north of Lima, in Peru) on 25 February 1579, or one of those taken from the ship of Benito Diaz Bravo, which Drake captured near Los Quijimes, Ecuador, three days later. Much to Drake's delight, the man who joined the *Golden Hinde* at Paita said he had been a Cimarron in Panama. Drake had fond memories of working with the Cimarrons and repeatedly asked the man whether his countrymen were now at peace or still embroiled in war with the Spanish.[72]

Juan Pascual reported that Diego and the other African man he met 'attended prayers' with the ship's company twice a day. By this time, Drake had taken the unusual step of officiating at these religious meetings, despite the presence on board of the ship's chaplain, Francis Fletcher. The meetings took place before lunch and before supper. Drake knelt on a cushion behind a table, read psalms and preached a sermon. The crew then sang together, accompanied by viols. The Catholic prisoners on board, with the exception of de Silva, withdrew to the prow of the ship during these ceremonies.[73] Diego's participation in the Protestant rituals signalled his allegiance, and possibly a true faith. Doubtless he would have been exposed to Catholicism while enslaved by the Spanish, but it would have been difficult to retain such beliefs, or at least to practise them, through four years in Protestant Plymouth. His experience can be likened to that of Chinano, a Turk baptised in London in 1586, who had been enslaved for twenty-five years before Drake liberated him from Cartagena. According to Meredith Hanmer, the vicar of St Leonard's Shoreditch, who preached a sermon at Chinano's christening, the Spaniards had failed to convert him to Catholicism. Chinano had been repelled by their cruelty and idolatry. It was only after he received 'love and kindness' from the 'good Christians' Francis Drake and William Hawkins that he was inspired to become a Protestant.[74] This account is obviously propaganda, but it certainly shows the English enthusiasm for making converts. Diego would have been strongly encouraged to share Drake's faith and it would have been politic for him to do so.

Juan Pascual and Diego shared further intriguing conversation. One day, at the prow of the ship, Diego 'inquired of [Pascual] secretly', 'Where is the port of Colima?' Pascual replied that it was beyond the Mexican region the Spaniards called New Galicia. 'I think that we are going thither', Diego revealed. 'Withdraw yourself from me. Do not let yourself be seen speaking to me.'[75] This exchange was reported by the royal licentiate of Guatemala, Valverde, in a letter to King Philip II in April 1579. At this stage, the Spaniards were desperate to know the route by which Drake would return to England. They had suffered numerous injuries at Drake's hands as he made his way up the western coast of South America, capturing unarmed Spanish merchant ships, plundering colonial ports and amassing huge amounts of treasure. The richest prize, taken in March off the coast of Ecuador, was the *Nuestra Señora de la Concepción* (nicknamed *Cacafuego*, 'fire-shitter'), which was carrying 362,000 pesos in silver and gold.[76]

At one point a fleet had set out to catch Drake, but turned back. The next attempt headed south to find him when he had in fact gone north.[77] In his letter, Valverde analysed Drake's four options. He could return the way he came, through the Straits of Magellan, but this would mean sailing back down a coastline full of angry Spaniards alert to his presence. He could continue north and try to find the mythical strait of Anian, a north-west passage some geographers believed separated North America from Asia, but Valverde reasoned this would be impossible 'because this is a strait which has never been navigated and is not known to exist'. Sailing west through the East Indies was a possibility, but this would be 'long and troublesome, as he would have to pilot and coast the entire world in order to return to England'. The final option was for Drake to cross back to the Atlantic overland via the isthmus of Panama, with the help of the Cimarrons. He could then, suggested another official, 'build launches and seize trading frigates so as to go with them to England.'[78]

Valverde believed that the presence of Diego 'who must be a chieftain amongst the negroes of [Panama]' under whose protection he could 'carry his booty by land', indicated that Drake had originally intended to take the overland route. But Drake would have learned from his captives that the Cimarrons had recently made peace with the Spanish authorities in Panama and that the area was well guarded.[79] Therefore, Valverde concluded, Drake would return by the Straits of Magellan. Seeking greater certainty, the Spaniards continued to interrogate anyone Drake left behind in an effort to discover his plans, hence their interest in Juan Pascual's conversation with Diego. If Drake were headed for Colima then he would be travelling to the north or west, rather than returning south or overland. Diego's whispers to Pascual, reported by a third party, can hardly have been prompted by a sense of loyalty to the Spanish. More probably, they were an attempt to spread misinformation, perhaps at Drake's direct request.

After releasing Zarate, Drake sailed on to the Mexican port of

Guatulco, which he raided in mid-April. Here, Drake abandoned Nuño de Silva, who had been with him since his capture near Cape Verde fifteen months before. The Portuguese pilot did not face a warm welcome from the Spanish authorities, who were suspicious that he had been rather too cooperative in Drake's endeavours and might even have converted to Lutheranism on the voyage. When pressed, de Silva reported that Drake aimed to sail home through the strait of Anian.[80]

On their arrival at Guatulco, the English found a court in session in the town hall. Three African men stood accused of plotting to set the town on fire. Drake took the judge, his officers and the defendants aboard his ship. The judge and his officials were released after he had written a letter commanding the townspeople not to resist the English. One of the three Africans wanted to stay in Mexico, and so he was set ashore, promptly fleeing into the woods 'to save himself'. The other two remained with Drake for the time being.[81] However, by the time Drake left Guatulco on 16 April only three African men remained aboard: Diego, the Cimarron from Paita and one of those taken from the Guatulco courtroom.[82]

There was also Maria, the 'proper negro wench' whom Drake had seized from Zarate's ship. The only description of Maria's time aboard the *Golden Hinde* states that she was 'gotten with child between the Captain and his men pirates'.[83] This brief mention in the anonymous narrative of the voyage preserved in the British Library's Harley manuscripts suggests that she served as a means, as some historians have callously commented, of easing the tedium of the sixty-eight-day voyage across the North Pacific.[84] It is just possible she was already pregnant when she joined the voyage. She was taken from Zarate's ship on 4 April 1579 and described in the anonymous account as 'very great' with child thirty-six weeks later.[85] Childbirth usually takes place at around forty weeks, and women rapidly gain weight in the third trimester, which begins in the twenty-ninth week of pregnancy.[86] So, Maria must have been between twenty-nine and forty weeks pregnant in mid-December. This means that the father could have been one of Zarate's crew, but, as the anonymous account asserts, the balance of probability is that the father was one of the sixty men aboard the *Golden Hinde* when Maria arrived. These were Drake himself, ten 'gentlemen adventurers', forty seamen, some boys and a few foreign sailors, Diego and the two other African men. At this stage in the voyage the surviving gentlemen included Drake's brother Thomas, his cousin John, John Hawkins's nephew William, Francis Fletcher the preacher who was nominated by Francis Walsingham, and John Doughty, brother of the captain executed at Port St Julian. We know little of the rest of the crew other than their names.

There was little privacy on the ship. The higher status men slept in the armoury; the seamen slept on the gun deck, a cramped, dark space with a low ceiling. Drake's was the only cabin. At Port St Julian, Drake is reported to have made a speech insisting that 'the Gentleman . . . haul and draw with the mariner, and the mariner with the Gentleman', but it seems unlikely that Maria would have been shared between the different social tiers of the crew.[87] Moreover, it is hard to imagine Drake, who took great care to assert his authority, sharing a woman with any of his men. Either she was his alone or he left her to the crew. One argument against Drake being the father of Maria's child is that there were no children from either of his two marriages. Infertility would not have prevented him from using Maria, of course, but it would mean that someone else was responsible for her pregnancy.

Whoever the father was, Drake, as the ship's captain, was ultimately to blame for how Maria was treated. His attitude towards her stands in stark contrast to his ostentatiously godly ways on the voyage, leading prayers twice a day. It was also quite at odds with his reported behaviour the year before at Cape Blanc, off the coast of Mauretania. There, he was offered 'a woman, a Moore (with her little babe hanging upon her dry dug [nipple], having scarce life in herself, much less milk to nourish her child), to be sold as a horse or a cow and calf by her side'. This, we are told, was a 'sort of merchandise' in which Drake 'would not deal'.[88] If so, his scruples had evolved since his earlier adventures with his cousin John Hawkins. Drake himself was aware that some of his actions were hypocritical, telling one of his Spanish prisoners that he must think him a 'devil who robs by day and prays by night', but he expressed no remorse for his treatment of Maria.[89]

Other English ships took African women aboard in this period. The log of the *Red Dragon* recounts a similar episode on the Guinea coast in 1586. After dinner on 30 October, the ship's captain led his men to a town at the lower point of the river. All the men of the town ran away 'and we took a Woman and brought her aboard'.[90] The entry records nothing more, save that this was a Sunday. More than one hundred years later, Captain Woodes Rogers did his best to defend himself from 'the censorious' when accounting for an experience strikingly similar to Maria's aboard his voyage.* In October 1709, an African woman aboard his ship 'was delivered of a Girl of a tawny Colour', though 'she had not been full 6 Months amongst us, so that the Child could belong to none of our Company'. 'Lewdness' was not countenanced aboard his ship and this woman and her companions had only been taken aboard 'because they spoke English and begged to be admitted for laundresses, cooks and seamstresses.'[91] One wonders if the innocent need protest so much.

The *Golden Hinde* sailed north along the American coast for six weeks. By early June, all aboard were suffering from the cold 'pinching and biting air', struggling through 'vile thick and stinking fogs' and 'congealed and frozen' rain. Their food seemed to freeze as soon as they took it from the fire and their hands were so numb that they were loath to bring them out from the shelter of their sleeves. They retreated southwards and finally found a protected bay in which to repair the damage the ship had sustained in the last few months. They stayed for some weeks, during which time they had friendly encounters with the native Miwok people. There is some debate about exactly where in California Drake sojourned, but wherever it was he nailed a plate of brass to a post before he left, laying claim to the territory in the name of Queen Elizabeth. This act of proto-imperialism, the first claim laid to American soil by an Englishman, was witnessed by Diego, Maria, and the two other African men still aboard. They may even have been the first

---

* On the same voyage, Captain Woodes Rogers rescued Alexander Selkirk – thought to be the inspiration for Robinson Crusoe.

Africans to set foot on North American soil in the company of Englishmen, some forty years before the first Africans arrived in Virginia.*

They then set out west across the Pacific, almost certainly following the charts Drake had seized from Alonso Sanchez Colchero in March, which detailed the trade route of the Manila galleons. They did not sight land again until the end of September, when they arrived at a place they named the 'Island of Thieves', now known as the Palau Islands. From there they sailed on to Mindanao in the Philippines, then through the Molucca passage in Indonesia, calling at Ternate and on towards Celebes.†

Diego died near the Moluccas, in early November 1579. As Richard Hawkins observed, he 'lived long after' he was wounded on Mocha Island nearly a year before. Hawkins mentions Diego in the same breath as the trumpeter John Brewer, also wounded at Mocha, who went on to serve as a pilot to Sir Thomas Cavendish in 1586. This has led some to conclude that Diego also made it back to England, but a year's survival seems long enough to explain Hawkins's comment.[92]

Whatever the exact cause of his death, Diego died a free man. He was Drake's 'man', his servant but not his slave. He had lived for four years as a free man in England and was paid wages on the circumnavigation voyage. He was not the first black circumnavigator, for there were Africans aboard Magellan's fleet when he made his voyage in 1519–1522.[93] In any case, Diego did not make it all the way around the world. Nonetheless, throughout his time with Drake, he proved invaluable. His local knowledge, his aptitude for building, his language skills, and perhaps his talent for subterfuge, made a formidable combination. Having proved his worth during the adventures of 1572–3, he was an obvious choice when Drake set sail once more in 1577.

---

* Africans had already come to North America with the Spanish, such as Juan Garrido and Esteban Dorantes, who travelled through Florida, Texas and Arizona in the 1520s and 1530s.
† Today, the island of Sulawesi.

Diego was treated well because he was useful to Drake. When Drake or other Englishmen encountered Africans they wished to trade with, or ally with against the Spanish, they approached them with respect. Those with less to offer they were all too happy to exploit or even enslave. Drake's treatment of Maria was so callous that even his contemporaries remarked on his shameful conduct. William Camden recounted in 1625 that Drake sailed round the world 'to the admiration and laudable applause of all people, and without purchasing blame for any other things' except executing Doughty, abandoning de Silva at Guatulco and 'for having most inhumanely exposed in an island that *Negro* or Black-more-Maide, who had been gotten with Child in his Ship.'[94]

On 12 December 1579, the by then heavily pregnant Maria was 'set on a small island to take her adventure', along with two African men.[95] This was 'Crab Island' in the Banggai Archipelago, Indonesia, a small, heavily wooded island, with a large population of crabs.[96] The manuscript of the anonymous account that describes this episode in the most detail has some perplexing amendments:

> at their departure Drake left behind him upon this Island the two negroes which he took at Guatulco and likewise the negro wench ~~Francesca~~ Maria she being gotten with child in the ship, and now being very great was left here on this Island which Drake named the Ile Francisca after ~~the woman~~ of one of the ii negroes name.[97]

The original text, in which the island is named 'Francisca', after a woman named 'Francesca', makes more sense than an island named 'Francisca' (a feminine form) after an unspecified man. Neither of the men is named at any other point in the narrative and there is some confusion over their identities: John Drake's testimony contradicts this account, reporting that one African came from Paita, the other from Guatulco. On the other hand, the woman is named Maria earlier in this narrative and also by John Drake in his recollections some years later.[98] If any of these individuals, or the island, were truly named Francis or Francesca, it might have been in tribute to Francis Drake. Could Maria have been baptised on the voyage and renamed after the Captain? Could bearing the feminine form of Drake's first name reflect a tie between the two? The altered text reduces the importance of the woman. Had the island been named after her, it might suggest Drake felt some level of affection for her.

Why was Maria abandoned on Crab Island? The cynical answer is that, being heavily pregnant, she was no longer of use to a ship full of lustful sailors. Perhaps these supposedly pious Christians finally began to think of the consequences of arriving in Plymouth with such evident proof of sinful behaviour on the voyage. A kinder interpretation would be that Maria was left on the island because Drake feared that she and her child would not survive the long journey home.[99] There is, however, no evidence for this. The episode is not mentioned in the account of the voyage published by Richard Hakluyt in the first edition of his *Principal Navigations* in 1589, or in the version of events published as *The World Encompassed* by Drake's nephew, also Sir Francis Drake, in 1628. The only other explanation of the events we have is that given by John Drake, when he was examined on 24 March 1584 by Alonso Vera y Aragon in Santa Fé in modern-day Argentina. He had fallen into Spanish hands after a calamitous series of events, which began with what became known as the 'troublesome voyage' of Edward Fenton. In 1582, John Drake was chosen to command the *Francis* (named for his cousin) as part of Fenton's voyage to the East Indies. The fleet broke up on the coast of Brazil, after its commanders could not agree on a route or strategy. John Drake took the *Francis* up the River Plate in search of provisions, but the ship hit a rock and was wrecked. He and his crew survived, only to be held captive by the local Charrúa people for the following thirteen months. John Drake and three others eventually escaped in a canoe and crossed the river to Buenos Aires, where the Spanish received them with some sympathy until John Drake's relationship to their hated enemy, Francis, was revealed. He was then handed over to the Inquisition for questioning.[100]

Was John Drake a reliable witness? He was recalling events that had taken place seven years earlier, when he was a boy of fourteen or fifteen. He might also have wanted to portray his cousin in the most positive possible light. According to him, 'they left the two negroes and the negress Maria, to found a settlement, leaving them rice, seeds, and means of making fire.'[101] The presence of the two African men makes the idea of forming a settlement slightly more plausible. Maria was not left alone on the island, and may therefore have stood a better chance of survival. That said, the three may have come from completely different parts of Africa and might not have had a common language, though they may have been able to communicate in Spanish or rough English.

Crab Island was a welcome refuge for the English; they rested there from mid-November until their departure on 12 December. It was well-supplied with delicious land lobsters or crayfish 'of such a size that one was sufficient to satisfy four hungry men at a dinner.'[102] Whether it was a suitable location for permanent settlement is more doubtful. It lacked its own water supply, which meant Drake and his men had to make regular trips to the neighbouring island. The English thought this larger island was inhabited, though John Drake said that they did 'not know by what people, because [they] never saw them nearby.'[103] Whether this was good or bad for the castaways depended entirely on the attitude of the native people. If they were friendly, they might provide much help, but if they were hostile, the Africans would be entirely at their mercy. They had been left with food, but not weapons. Ultimately, the idea that they would be able to survive and 'found a settlement' seems optimistic. William Camden's use of the word 'exposed' certainly suggests that back in England it was assumed Maria was left there to die.

A few decades later, a story seemingly mirroring Maria's plight could be seen on the London stage. It was that of the 'damned witch Sycorax', mother of Caliban, in Shakespeare's The Tempest. Sycorax, a native of Algiers, 'was hither [to the island] brought with child, /And here was left by th' sailors.' According to Prospero, Caliban was 'got by the devil himself/Upon thy wicked dam.'[104] Of course, it's far more credible that the sailors who abandoned her were responsible. Caliban survives, only to be enslaved by Prospero: a reminder of how vulnerable the four Africans would be should any other people, whether Europeans or local inhabitants, encounter them on the island.

Drake's biographers have often sought to minimise the damage of this episode to his reputation, or rather ignored it altogether.[105] In the late nineteenth century, a prominent naval historian tried to dismiss the anonymous narrative which details Maria's treatment as full of 'the kind of vulgar slanders a dissatisfied seaman would naturally invent'.[106] However, these 'slanders' were confirmed by Camden, and while the whole affair does not appear in the official accounts of the voyage, John Drake records, if not Maria's rape then at least her abandonment, heavily pregnant, which rather implies the former. Maria's story sounds a note of caution to any who try to use the tale of Diego and the Cimarrons to paint a picture of equality between English and Africans in either Drake's mind or his world. Equality may have existed to some extent among men, but invariably the lot of women at sea was to be exploited.

On future voyages Drake brought more Africans back to England, including Edward Swarthye, who returned with Drake after he raided the Spanish Caribbean in 1585–6. After his arrival in England, Swarthye found work as a porter in a gentleman's house in Gloucestershire. He later became the first African in English history to whip a white man.

4

Edward Swarthye,
the Porter

Sir Edward Wynter had a reputation for violence. In his youth he had killed a man in a duel, fought against the Spanish Armada, raided the Caribbean with Francis Drake and spent four years imprisoned in France after seeking to 'follow the wars' on the continent. Yet as he approached forty, in the winter of 1597, he was serving as a Justice of the Peace in Gloucestershire. Still, all was not peaceful at home. Wynter had summoned one of his servants, John Guye, to appear before him in the Great Hall of White Cross Manor, where a small crowd of local men had gathered. At first they exchanged only words; Wynter accused Guye of gross negligence. But when Guye did not appear to be the least bit contrite, Wynter called for his porter, Edward Swarthye. On his master's command, Swarthye took up a rod and brought it down hard and fast on Guye's back. Guye cried out in pain. The assembled company looked on in shock as a man of good standing was soundly whipped. Sir Edward struck a few blows himself before it was over. As Guye limped away, he 'bade him depart like a knave', dismissing him from his service for good. Edward Swarthye looked down at the rod in his hands, then back at the man he had dined with every day in that very hall. In the future he would have to turn him away from the gate. He gripped the rod very tightly, and the colour drained from his dark skin. For Edward Swarthye had another name. His alias was 'Negro': he was a Black Tudor.

I
N WILLIAM BLAKE's lurid 1796 engraving 'The Flagellation of a Female Samboe Girl', a near-naked woman hangs by her arms from a tree while two men lurk behind her, whips in hand. Horrific scars cover the entire back of Peter, a slave from Louisiana, in a photograph published in *Harper's Weekly* in April 1863; his master's cruelty writ large upon his flesh.[1] When asked about the relationship between Englishmen and Africans in the past, it is images such as these that come to mind. Our conception of their relationship is firmly rooted in the idea of the white master and his black slave. The fact that Edward Swarthye whipped John Guye in Gloucestershire in 1596 shows that it was not ever thus. His experience forces us to question whether the development of racial slavery in the English colonies was inevitable. In his story, we glimpse a time before racism became a dominant prejudice in British society. The whipping was considered shocking, even 'unchristian like', by those that witnessed it, but not for the same reasons that we might find it so today.[2] It was acceptable, even normal, for a Tudor gentleman to inflict corporal punishment on his servant, but the people of Lydney were stunned when such a well-educated, high-status servant was publicly humiliated. From a modern perspective, it is far more surprising that a black man was allowed to publicly whip a white man. How then did Edward Swarthye end up whipping John Guye at White Cross Manor in 1596? And how did an African man end up working as a porter in rural Gloucestershire?

The parish of Lydney lies some thirteen miles southwest of Gloucester, between the River Severn and the Royal Forest of Dean. Beyond the forest to the east are the southern parts of Wales, while a journey southwest along the river takes one past Chepstow to Avonmouth, the bustling trading port of Bristol, and out into the Bristol Channel and the Atlantic Ocean.[3]

White Cross Manor lay just beyond the south-west end of Lydney, off the Chepstow road.[4] The house had been built by Edward's father, Sir William Wynter, on land given to him by Queen Elizabeth I. He named it White Cross in honour of his promotion to Admiral of the White, the second-highest rank in the Navy, after the Battle of Gravelines against the Spanish Armada in 1588, in which father and son served together on the *Vanguard*.

Detail from John Speed's 1610 map of Gloucestershire –
Lydney is in the bottom left hand corner.

The Wynter family was originally from Wales, but by the sixteenth century they had been merchants of Bristol for several generations. Sir Edward's cousin John had captained the *Elizabeth* on Drake's circumnavigation voyage of 1577–80. Both Sir Edward's father, William, and his grandfather, John, were in royal service, as treasurers of the Navy. Queen Elizabeth knighted William for his services and William Cecil, Lord Burghley, considered him a man 'to be cherished.'[5] Despite their success at court, the Wynters risked their prosperity by deciding not to relinquish their Catholic faith when the Reformation came. This was a dangerous choice, as Catholics, or 'Papists', were increasingly unwelcome in England. In 1581, it was made high treason to convert to Catholicism, and over the following thirty years more and more anti-Catholic legislation was passed. By 1603, one hundred and ninety-one Catholics, both priests and laymen, had been executed.[6]

Catholics were politically suspect, especially between 1585 and 1604, when England was intermittently in conflict with Spain, and in the aftermath of the 1605 Gunpowder Plot, which resulted in further measures against 'Papists'. Despite this, the Wynters continued to practise their faith. When they were in London, it came to the notice of the authorities that they were not attending the required Church of England services: Sir Edward Wynter and his wife, Lady Anne Wynter, were listed amongst those not attending 'church, chapel or any usual place of Common Prayer' on 25 June 1615, 'nor at any time during the three months then next following'. Recusants (those who refused to attend Church of England services), were fined the huge sum of £20 a month. This was not enough to ruin a gentry family, but if they did not pay they ran the risk of their lands being confiscated by the Crown to service the debt. Although the Wynters were able to conduct their affairs more privately at home in Gloucestershire, their faith continued to mark them out as untrustworthy.[7]

In most other ways, the Wynters were a typical county gentry family. Edward Wynter had an education fit for a gentleman's son. In 1577, he matriculated at Brasenose College, Oxford, aged seventeen, and remained there for two years before moving on to the Middle Temple, one of London's Inns of Court. His time at Oxford coincided with the period in which Richard Hakluyt, of Christ Church, began giving public geography lectures, presenting 'instruments of this art' and showing how the 'old imperfectly composed' maps, globes and spheres had been 'lately reformed'. These demonstrations were, according to Hakluyt, made to 'the singular pleasure and general contentment of my auditory'. The pre-eminent English geographer of his age, Hakluyt went on to publish *The Principal Navigations, Voyages, Traffiques and Discoveries of the English Nation*, a compendium which included accounts of the first English voyages to Africa.

When Wynter moved to Middle Temple, he had the chance to meet Hakluyt's older cousin, also named Richard. At this time, Hakluyt the elder was working on his *Inducements to the Liking of the Voyage Intended towards Virginia*, in which he listed the purposes of the voyage as: '1. To plant Christian religion. 2. To trafficke. 3. To conquer. Or, to do all three.' When the younger Hakluyt visited in 1568, he was fascinated by the collection of maps and cosmographic books in his cousin's chamber. Years later he recalled the passage from the Bible his cousin had shown him: 'they which go down to the sea in ships, and occupy by the great waters, they see the works of the Lord, and his wonders in the deep'.[8] Given his later exploits, it seems that Edward Wynter was also inspired at a young age to travel and observe the world for himself. What is more, his later relationship with Edward Swarthye would be informed by the latest scholarship on the subject of Africa and Africans.

In Elizabethan England, knowledge of Africa was drawn from ancient writers, some newly rediscovered as a consequence of the Renaissance, and the emerging body of travel literature produced by European explorers. Richard Hakluyt the younger encouraged the translation of Portuguese, Spanish and Dutch texts, though the business of translation was not always easy. 'Within two hours' conference' with Duarte Lopez's *Report of the Kingdom of Congo*, Abraham Hartwell, a Member of Parliament and secretary to the Archbishop of Canterbury, who Hakluyt had persuaded to translate the work, found 'two most honourable Gentlemen of England' referred to as pirates. It was all he could do to stop himself tearing the book into as many pieces as 'his Cousin Lopez the Doctor was quartered'. Hartwell had mistakenly assumed that the author was related to Dr Roderigo Lopes, the *converso* physician who had been hung, drawn and quartered for plotting to poison his patient, Queen Elizabeth I, in the summer of 1594.[9]

While Pliny the Elder wrote in his *Natural History* that '*ex Afrique semper aliquid novi*' – out of Africa, something new always comes – Tudor writers were reproducing some very old stories about the continent. One traveller boasted to Sir Robert Cecil that he had 'seen above twenty men at one time together with heads like dogs'. Ancient and modern tomes, as well as still-popular medieval works such as *Mandeville's Travels*, bristled with tall tales of dog-headed men, cannibals, monopods, Amazons and other monstrous beings. Like Shakespeare's Desdemona, readers thrilled to hear stories 'of the Cannibals that each other eat . . . and men whose heads / Do grow beneath their shoulders'. Not all mythical African figures were negative. There were also the likes of Prester John, the fabulously wealthy and powerful Christian emperor; his ancestor, Balthazar, one of the Three Magi, who brought myrrh to the baby Jesus; and the Queen of Sheba, thought to rule over Ethiopia.[10]

This woodcut from Sebastian Munster's *Cosmographia* (1544) shows some of the monstrous beings Tudor voyagers thought they might encounter in faraway places like Africa. There is a Monopod, a Cyclops, conjoined twins, a headless man and a cynocephalus, or dog-headed man.

Those who perused the writings of contemporary voyagers would also find detailed descriptions of the language, customs and religion of the inhabitants encountered on trading and exploratory voyages. But no doubt it was the more monstrous tales that stuck in young minds such as Edward Wynter's, and fuelled their ambitions to go to sea and discover the world for themselves. It was this ambition of Wynter's that ultimately led to Swarthye's employment as his porter at White Cross Manor.

In September 1585, aged around twenty-five, Wynter took command of a ship named the *Aid* and set out with Sir Francis Drake's fleet, bound for the Spanish Caribbean.[11] Unlike the rest of Drake's captains, he had no previous military experience. His education had been 'at school and Court', and it was no doubt these court connections, fostered by his father, who had personally invested in the expedition, that secured his appointment. Wynter was not the only courtier keen to embark with the hero who had successfully circumnavigated the globe a few years before. Sir Philip Sidney and his friend Fulke Greville were also loitering with intent in Plymouth that summer, but were recalled to court by the Queen. Greville later wrote that it was 'no delight' for a young man to 'rest idly at home'. These young noblemen did not want to 'soften their manly virtue' by pursuing the arts of 'courtly flattery': they sought adventure, fame and fortune. Sidney was to find all three, and an early death, in the Netherlands the following year. They also appreciated the danger of allowing Spain's power to grow unchecked. Greville identified two ways to attack the enemy: 'to set fire to his own house' or 'to fetch away his golden fleece'. The latter had the advantage of enriching the aggressor. Both were to be a feature of this voyage. Theirs was a dangerous ambition, and many of the company, including Edward Wynter's younger brother Nicholas, would not return.[12]

Drake was on a mission to raid the Spanish colonies. Although the two countries were not technically at war in the summer of 1585, Philip II had placed all English ships in Spanish ports under arrest. The Queen ordered Drake to sail for Vigo, on the Galician coast, where most of the English ships were detained, to negotiate. This was clearly never going to be a diplomatic mission. The

Spaniards knew Drake as *El Draque*, the dragon, and considered him a dangerous pirate. In a later report, Captain Carleill described the English activity at Vigo as the 'usual pillage'. Nonetheless, Drake succeeded in getting the local governor, Pietro Bermudez, who said he had 'no orders to annoy or trouble any English', to release their ships.[13] Edward Wynter's letter to Sir Francis Walsingham from the port, dated 24 October, was the last anyone at home heard of the expedition for the next nine months.[14]

The pillaging and pilfering spree, with some holding to ransom thrown in, continued as Drake's fleet called at São Tiago in the Cape Verde Islands, Santo Domingo in the modern-day Dominican Republic, Cartagena in Columbia, and San Agustin in Florida. At every one of these ports, Africans, both men and women, ran away from their Spanish masters to join the English.[15] Although they cannot have known what would become of them aboard Drake's ships, this unknown future was clearly preferable to their lives in the Spanish colonies. It is possible that, like Diego, they had heard there were no slaves in England, and were willing to risk their lives to get there.

But first, they had to survive the rest of the voyage. In February, Drake gave a commandment 'for the general well-usage of Strangers, namely Frenchmen, Turks & Negros', suggesting that decent treatment of others did not come naturally to his men.[16] One episode shows how Drake reacted when Africans were not 'well-used'. While the English were at Santo Domingo, Drake sent an African boy to talk to the Spaniards, presumably because he was fluent in the language of his former masters. Although both sides carried white flags, at the end of their discussion a Spaniard ran the boy through with his pike. Fatally wounded, the boy was just able to report to Drake before expiring. Incensed, Drake ordered the execution of two captive Spanish friars and threatened to hang two more prisoners each day until the man responsible for the murder of the African boy was handed over. The Spaniards swiftly complied, and executed the man at the scene of his crime.[17]

By the time they reached Cartagena, in February 1586, Captain Wynter was keen to see some action. He swapped control of his ship, the *Aid*, for a land command and was in the vanguard when the English attacked.[18] A pair of African men fishing in the bay had revealed that Hicacos Point remained unguarded. The English disembarked there in the dead of night, and marched along the spit named La Caleta, dodging sharp poisoned stakes planted in the sand, to surprise the city. By mid-morning the fighting was over. Drake took up residence in the home of a Spanish Captain named Alonso Bravo and spent the next two months negotiating as large a ransom for the city as he could muster. In the end they came away with 110,000 ducats, much bolstered by payments extracted from private citizens, and plunder.[19] This was a sizeable sum, enough to purchase a small Italian dukedom.[20] They also left with a number of Africans. The Spanish reported that 'most of the slaves and many of the convicts from the galleys went off with the English as did some of the negroes belonging to private owners.'[21]

Most of the hundreds of Africans who joined Drake on the voyage did not make it to England. Like many of the English crew, scores died when a terrible storm hit the fleet in mid-June 1586 while they were anchored at Roanoke, in modern-day North Carolina, the nascent colony Walter Ralegh had founded two years earlier. One man aboard the *Primrose* reported that the tempest was so ferocious that all the ships either broke or lost their anchors, and so were forced out to sea. The hailstones that rained down upon them were 'as big as hen's eggs' and the seas appeared to rise up high enough to reach the heavens. The hurricane raged for three days and nights.[22]

Once the storm had abated, the survivors, including the Roanoke settlers, headed for home. There were at least three Africans amongst them, one of whom travelled on to France. Less than a month after the voyage returned to Portsmouth on 28 July 1586, Edward Stafford, ambassador to France, reported that an African man with a cut on his face was going about Paris saying he had sailed with Drake, and stole away from him after landing in England. The African appears to have been in cahoots with the Spanish Ambassador, Bernardino de Mendoza, who was using him to spread rumours that Drake had 'brought home little or nothing, and has done less, and that his taking of Cartagena, Nombre de

Dios and the rest is false'. Word of Drake's return had not yet reached France, so Stafford begged to be told the latest news, 'and as much as may be known of the particular successes of his journey' so that he could 'make them blown abroad to his honour', and better combat Mendoza's anti-English propaganda.[23]

The African had a good chance of freedom in France at this time. As Francois de Belleforest wrote in his *L'Histoire Universelle du Monde* (1570):

> The custom is such that not only the French, but foreigners arriving in French ports and crying '*France et liberté!*' are beyond the power of those that possess them; [their owners] lose the price of the sale and the service of the slave, if the slave refuses to serve them.

This was put into action in 1571, when a Norman merchant arrived in Bordeaux with a cargo of slaves. After he attempted to sell them, he was arrested, and the Parlement of Guyenne freed the men because 'France, the mother of liberty, does not permit any slaves'. The principle was followed by no less an authority than King Henri III, who freed between 2,000–3,000 Spanish galley slaves after they were shipwrecked at Calais.[24]

Two other Africans stayed in England. In October 1587, a Cornish mariner, John Lax of Fowey, brought an 'Ethiopian Negar' to London, where he sold him (illegally) to the Portuguese *converso* physician Hector Nunes for £4 10s. The African man had come from 'Santa Domingo in Nova Spayne beyond the seas', one of the ports Drake had raided a few months before. The following year, Nunes reported to the Court of Requests that the man 'utterly refuseth' to 'tarry and serve' him, but admitted that he had no legal means to compel him to do so.[25]

Another 'blackamore' was brought to Petworth House in Sussex, the home of Henry Percy, ninth Earl of Northumberland, during the winter of 1586–7. The young earl had only recently succeeded to the title, and vast estates in the north of England, after his father's suicide in the Tower of London, where he had been imprisoned on suspicion of treason. The African was brought to his Sussex home by 'Mr Crosse's man', an employee of Captain Robert Crosse, who had sailed with Drake as commander of the *Bond*. The African he sent to Petworth was still there in May 1588, when he was bought a new pair of shoes for the princely sum of 18d.[26]

The voyage of 1585–6 was by far the most feasible opportunity for Swarthye to have joined the Wynter household, as Edward Wynter was in no position to acquire an African servant during the next few years. After serving in the Armada battle of 1588, he 'resolved to follow the wars' on the continent the next year. This decision was made in the wake of his father's death, and his being granted a royal pardon for killing Henry Walsh, the son of the High Sheriff of Gloucestershire, in a duel in Marylebone. The wars overtook him pretty quickly. He sailed for the French coastal town of Dieppe, but a storm drove his ship north along the Normandy coast and he was captured by the wife of the governor of Eu and Tréport. Her husband then sold him to Mendoza, the Spanish ambassador. For the next four years he was a pawn in the diplomatic game between the warring powers, imprisoned at Antwerp Castle in the Spanish Netherlands, in the custody of Christobal Mondragon, forced to spend 'the sweetest time of my youth in all melancholy'. In the end he was forced to pay his own ransom: the eye-watering sum of £4,500. It was all he could do to breathe 'some words only of choler, which otherwise might have burst out more violently'. His wanderlust well and truly sated, he retired to life at White Cross Manor in Lydney. In 1595 he married Lady Anne Somerset, daughter of the Earl of Worcester, and was knighted. They went on to have ten children.[27]

Their home also became Edward Swarthye's home. Swarthye's first name suggests that Wynter had recalled Hakluyt the elder's dictum that the first priority of the voyager must be 'to plant the Christian religion'.[28] When King Nzinga a Nkuwu of Kongo and his queen were baptised by Portuguese missionaries in May 1491, they took the names of the King and Queen of Portugal: João and Eleanor. Their son Nzinga Mbemba became Afonso, after the prince of Portugal, and their courtiers followed suit, taking the names of prominent Portuguese nobles. Dederi Jaquoah, who we will meet in Chapter Seven, was given the baptismal name John in 1611, after John Davies, the merchant who brought him to London. Edward Swarthye almost certainly got his name from Edward Wynter in the same way. His surname seems more like a nickname inspired by his dark skin, though lacking the 'wit' of John Blanke's.

As porter, Swarthye's job was to answer the door and turn away undesirable visitors. While the word now conjures up images of someone carrying luggage in a train station, airport or hotel, the duties of a Tudor gentleman's porter were closer to those of an Oxbridge college porter or an apartment block concierge. He was the first person visitors met at the gate or lodge of the manor, and so their first impression of the household. As Erasmus remarked to the Earl of Surrey in the Elizabethan play *Sir Thomas More*:

> You saw, my lord, his porter
> Give entertainment to us at the gate
> In Latin good phrase; what's the master, then,
> When such good parts shine in his meanest men?[29]

One wonders what impression visitors to White Cross got when Edward Swarthye answered the door. Wynter was certainly displaying that he was a well-travelled man.

Swarthye was not the 'meanest' or lowliest member of the Wynter household, which would have numbered around twenty servants. A contemporary book of household regulations stipulated that the porter should eat his meals seated next to the yeoman of the chamber. Seating at meals reflected the hierarchy of the household: the lord of the manor dined at the top table with his family and the senior household officers, while the lowliest servants sat nearest the kitchen, at the far end of the hall. The yeoman of the chamber was allowed access to the bedchamber, and so was obviously a trusted servant.[30] A seat beside him indicates that the porter was of a similar status.

Swarthye's position in the Wynter household was not unique. He was one of about two dozen Africans serving in Tudor and early Stuart gentry and aristocratic households. The most famous of these employers included Robert Dudley (Earl of Leicester), Henry Percy (ninth Earl of Northumberland), William Cecil (Lord Burghley), Sir Robert Cecil, Sir Walter Ralegh, Ralegh's brother-in-law Sir Arthur Throckmorton, Endymion Porter and Alethea Howard (Countess of Arundel).[31] In 1560, Sir John Young of Bristol had an African gardener, as did Sir Henry Bromley of Holt, Worcestershire, in 1607. An anonymous, posthumous portrait of Peregrine Bertie (Lord Willoughby de Eresby, who died 1601), which now hangs at Grimsthorpe Hall in Lincolnshire, depicts him on horseback, attended by a black page. 'Grace Robinson, a blackamoor', worked as a laundress alongside 'John Morockoe, a blackamoor', in the kitchen and scullery for Richard Sackville, the third Earl of Dorset, at Knole in Kent between 1613 and 1624. Henry Bourchier, the fifth Earl of Bath, employed 'James the Blackamoor' as a cook in Tawstock, Devon, from 1640 to 1646. Edward Wynter's father, Sir William Wynter, had an African servant, Domingo, who worked in the Wynter's London home, The Abbey Place, in East Smithfield. When he died of consumption in August 1587, the parish clerk noted that the forty-year-old was originally from Guinea.[32] Domestic service may sound little better than slavery today, but there was no shame in being a Tudor servant. It was an extremely common occupation. Even the sons of aristocrats spent some time in a great household as part of their education.

The roles of these African servants were practical, not decorative. Seventeenth- and eighteenth-century portraits of aristocrats attended by 'blackamoor' servants dressed in rich clothes and pearls, such as that of Charles II's mistress, Louise de Kéroualle, by Pierre Mignard (1682), give the impression that Africans existed in these households purely as exotic pets, accessories or props.[33] The records that survive of the clothes bought for Africans working as household servants tell a different tale. The African ladies at the Scottish court wore plain fabrics such as kersey and russet; practical clothing that reflected the work they did. The laundress Grace Robinson was more likely to be found elbow-deep in urine and blisteringly hot water than bedecked with jewels, since protecting a new garment against stains involved placing it, complete with ruffles and silk embroidery, in warm urine for half an hour then boiling it.[34]

* * *

Sir Edward Wynter's behaviour since returning to live at White Cross had not ingratiated him with his neighbours. James Bucke, whose father had gone to court against Sir William Wynter, owned two smaller estates in nearby Aylburton, and held the position of Verderer of the Royal Forest of Dean, meaning he was charged by the crown to protect the deer and the trees.[35] These trees were increasingly at risk from the acquisitive Sir Edward, who had begun to enclose the common land, threatening 'that he would bury in the ditches there whomsoever should dare to' try to open the forest up again. The community depended on this woodland for firewood, but Wynter was hell-bent on keeping it all to himself. His actions were in keeping with the wider trend of landowners flouting anti-enclosure legislation by appropriating land for their private use that was previously open to all.[36] White Cross Manor did not suddenly require large amounts of fuel to heat it; rather, Wynter had embarked on a project that required prodigious amounts of firewood. He had begun to produce iron.

The Lydney estate was unusually rich in mineral deposits, a site of iron-working since the twelfth century.[37] It was a potentially lucrative business. The Earls of Rutland enjoyed a considerable income of over £500 a year from their works at Rievaulx Abbey in Yorkshire, while Robert Dudley, Earl of Leicester, received £400 a year from his in Cleobury, Shropshire.

On his return to White Cross, Wynter built an iron furnace and a forge on the Newerne stream, which he dammed to create large ponds. The problem was that iron-works required a constant supply of fuel, in the form of charcoal. The Earl of Rutland arranged for a rotational supply system from more than twenty parts of his estate, to avoid permanent destruction of the forest, but the Wynters' much more modest holdings did not provide enough wood to keep up with demand.[38] This was why Sir Edward had resorted to making 'great wastes and spoiles' of the Royal Forest of Dean.

Voracious attacks on the royal woodland were never going to go unnoticed. In February 1596, Henry Herbert, second Earl of Pembroke and President of the Council of the Marches of Wales, accused Wynter of abusing his position. Herbert demanded that

Wynter promise to pay up to £100 compensation to the Crown if he was found to be breaking the laws of the forest in future.[39] Closer to home, James Bucke found his neighbour's bullying tactics increasingly aggravating, especially when Wynter set about enclosing Aylburton Wood, which was right on Bucke's doorstep.

However, just as antagonism mounted between the heads of the Wynter and Bucke households, an unlikely romance blossomed between two of their respective members when John Guye, the manager of Wynter's iron works, fell in love with James Bucke's daughter, Anne. John Guye had been taken into the Wynter household as a child. His father, Thomas Guye, a Bristol shoemaker, would have arranged this with Sir Edward's father, Sir William Wynter, who had frequent business in that city.[40] A noble or gentry household was a good place to get an education, and Guye was a bright boy. The Wynters noticed his 'wit and towardness' and had him educated in Latin, Greek, French 'and in other good sciences'. Given the modest size of the household, he almost certainly shared the Wynter children's tutor. Guye became a man 'of honest account, credit, and estimation' and Wynter appointed him to 'the chief rule and ordering of the estate', for which he was paid £60 a year, a vast sum in comparison to the average servant's wage of £4 a year. The twenty-seven-year-old's high wages and gentle education combined to make him quite the eligible bachelor. Anne Bucke certainly thought so. Unfortunately, when Sir Edward discovered their attachment, he made Guye promise to forget about her. It was a promise Guye would not be able to keep.

In the summer of 1596, Sir Edward travelled to London on business. The cat away, John Guye and two of Wynter's most experienced iron workers, Henry Hyley and Francis Watkins, absconded to Bristol in hope of securing a passage to Ireland. With his heart set on marrying Anne Bucke, Guye could not continue in Wynter's service. Wynter would not countenance an alliance between one of his most trusted servants and the daughter of his 'mortal enemy'. A new life in Ireland might provide a way out.

It was not the most auspicious moment to visit the Emerald Isle. The Nine Years' War had broken out two years earlier, when the

Gaelic Lords rose against English attempts to extend their rule and impose the Protestant religion. Their leaders, Hugh O'Neill (Earl of Tyrone), and Red Hugh O'Donnell, appealed to their fellow Catholic, Philip II of Spain, for help, even offering the crown of Ireland to his nephew, Archduke Albert of Austria, as an incentive. Philip sent his 'Invincible' Armada to join the struggle, but thanks to a storm off Cape Finisterre in October 1596 the fleet never arrived. Although the war continued until 1603, and fear of a Spanish invasion lingered, when John Guye left Lydney the real fighting was in the northern province of Ulster. In the south, the English continued with the 'planting' of Munster, where, after putting an end to the revolt of Gerald Fitzgerald, the fifteenth Earl of Desmond, in 1583, Queen Elizabeth granted more than 574,000 acres of forfeited land in the province to English 'undertakers' or 'planters', who imported tenants from England to work their new lands.[41]

Guye's experience of managing the iron works at Lydney, plus the fact that he had persuaded two ironworkers to come with him, suggests he planned to find similar work across the Irish Sea, where the Munster planter and promoter Robert Payne had identified an area rich in iron stone and lead ore, and with enough wood to maintain 'divers Iron and lead works (with good husbandry) forever'.[42]

All did not go according to plan. One of the two iron workers Guye had persuaded to go with him fell ill while they were waiting to embark from Bristol. Guye pressed on to Ireland with the other man, but returned before Wynter got back from London. Perhaps he didn't like what he found, or maybe this first trip was a reconnaissance mission that he had hoped to carry out without his master's knowledge.

Back in Lydney, John Guye married Anne Bucke in secret. Their marriage could not be celebrated publicly, as the relationship between Wynter and Bucke was deteriorating rapidly. Bucke had formally complained to the Council of the Marches of Wales that Wynter had unlawfully dispossessed him of the bailiwick of Awre, part of the Royal Forest of Dean. The regional body had a reputation for cheap and swift justice, and its Lord President, the Earl of Pembroke, had cautioned Wynter about his behaviour earlier that year. Towards the end of September, Bucke appeared at the gate of White Cross Manor, brandishing a summons from the Council. Wynter was incensed, exclaiming that he was tempted to stab Bucke there and then with his dagger. He swore that thenceforth he would do more and say less.

A few weeks later, James Bucke was walking close to the boundary of the White Cross estate when he was set upon, assaulted and badly wounded. John Guye ran into the manor house brandishing a rapier, albeit undrawn, crying: 'My father-in-law is murdered!' He appealed to Lady Wynter for help; she sent her maid, Elizabeth Dixton, to fetch white wine to wash Bucke's wounds. On returning from this errand, Elizabeth observed that her mistress was troubled and asked what ailed her. Lady Anne – as well she might – replied that she was somewhat afraid.

While Bucke recovered at home, his new son-in-law busied himself trying to track down those responsible. Bucke was either too badly hurt, or retained too hazy a recollection of the attack to identify the culprits, but as the assault had taken place some twenty paces from the boundary of White Cross park, and given Bucke had no enemies in the county other than Wynter, he and his retainers were the main suspects. Circumstantial evidence mounted: the door of the White Cross cider house, an ideal base from which to launch the attack and shelter from the hue and cry afterwards, had been ajar on the morning of the crime. The movements of Wynter's servants in the days following the attack were scrutinised. Why had one left for London the following day? Why had another been taken to Wales? When two of Wynter's retainers, Samuel Parker and John Bromfield, were arrested by the constable William Hammond, Sir Edward demanded to know how Hammond dared to 'be so bold as to arrest any man in my house', even if he were suspected of felony or murder. Wynter put up bail for his men, which only heightened his guilt in the eyes of the victim and his friends. And there was a rumour that one Thomas Bridgman had crossed Wynter and been threatened with a fate similar to Bucke's as a result.

By early December, when Wynter was due to hold a session at White Cross in his role as Justice of the Peace, it was clear he could no longer trust John Guye. It was bad enough that Guye had absconded to Ireland over the summer, leaving Wynter's iron works unsupervised and short of two key workers, but to have married Anne Bucke and virtually accused Wynter of attempting to murder her father was something else entirely. Guye had turned from the family to whom he owed his education and livelihood. His loyalties now lay with the Buckes.

Wynter bided his time, saying nothing when Guye delivered his accounts as usual at the end of November. He wanted a public reckoning with the man, and on 3 December he had it. More than twenty people bore witness to what happened that day at White Cross Manor. Wynter asked Guye if he was behind in paying his wages. 'No,' came the reply. 'Do I owe you anything else?' asked Sir Edward. 'No, sir,' answered Guye. 'What would you desire of me otherwise?' demanded Wynter, before launching into a speech of vitriolic condemnation:

> Now John Guye, I have performed with you in all I have promised you and have been a good master unto you: I have given you threescore pounds by your wages to do my business, but you notwithstanding have dealt very badly with me in neglecting my business and going into Ireland at your pleasure, persuading two other of my servants to go with you, leaving your charge of two or three thousand pounds very carelessly and lewdly which may be to my great loss! And therefore you have deserved correction at my hands, being so good a master unto you and always willing to prefer you. And therefore you shall have punishment for your great abuse!

With these words, he commanded Edward Swarthye to strike Guye, who had remained silent throughout. Swarthye administered the 'odious' punishment. He whipped Guye, landing at least four or five strokes upon his back, his legs and 'sundry parts of his body'. There, in the hall of White Cross Manor, a minor Elizabethan gentry house in rural Gloucestershire, a black man whipped a white man, and no one tried to stop him.

Wynter himself joined in, and hit his servant on the head, dismissing him from his service for good. The warring neighbours' accounts differ as to how viciously Wynter had struck. Wynter claimed that he had not hit Guye hard, but only struck him once on the head with a little riding wand, a blow that could not have drawn blood, or even caused much pain. Bucke asserted that Wynter had used a 'cudgel' to beat Guye violently about the head and shoulders. Given the scale of Guye's betrayal and Wynter's propensity for violence, Bucke's version of events rings more true.

Bucke was sufficiently recovered from his injuries to be able to sue Wynter in the Court of Star Chamber the following year. An offshoot of the King's Council, named for the star-spangled ceiling of the room in the Palace of Westminster where it sat, the Court derived its authority from the King's ancient right to give legal judgments. It dealt with 'a better class of accused' from the beginning of the Tudor era in 1485 until 1641, when it was abolished by the Long Parliament, whose members saw it as one of many means by which Charles I abused his powers.[43] Bucke's Bill of Complaint detailed Wynter's illegal enclosure of land and use of wood from the Royal Forest of Dean. He blamed Wynter for the assault he had suffered and held the whipping of John Guye to be a malicious act that was far more violent than the admonishment of a wayward servant warranted.

Thanks to his starring role in this final scene, Edward Swarthye was called as a witness. He and the other witnesses travelled to Gloucester to give their evidence in the presence of two Justices of the Peace. Swarthye swore an oath on the Bible to tell the truth and answered the questions prepared for him by the lawyers in London. He admitted that Wynter had commanded him to whip John Guye, but testified that he was 'not prepared of his rods' beforehand, rather the command had come 'on the Sudden', and so the alleged crime was not premeditated. He may have only been saying this to protect his master, as he also made light of his involvement, supporting Wynter's claim that he had only hit Guye on the shoulder with a 'little riding wand.'

Swarthye's answers, together with the original Bill of Complaint and the other papers relating to the case, would have been read aloud before the members of the Privy Council, who, alongside two common law judges, made up the judicial bench in Star Chamber cases. In 1597, the council had eleven members, including Lord Burghley, his son Sir Robert Cecil, the Earl of Essex, the Archbishop of Canterbury, the Chancellor of the Exchequer and the Lord High Admiral.[44] Swarthye's testimony was therefore heard by some of the most prominent politicians and noblemen in Elizabethan England. As with Jacques Francis, the fact that he was accepted as a witness in an English court of law confirms that he had been baptised and shows that he was not considered a slave. The lawyers who interrogated Swarthye treated him just like the other servants in the Wynter household.

Unfortunately, the decree and order books of the Star Chamber, which gave the final judgments, do not survive, so the outcome of the case is unknown.[45] However, the ultimate victory in the war between the two families was Wynter's. He purchased James Bucke's estates at Aylburton in 1599, and went on to serve as an MP in 1601, and also as a member of the Council of the Marches of Wales.[46]

The summer before the Privy Council heard Swarthye's testimony, it issued a licence to a certain Caspar Van Senden to 'take up . . . Blackamoores here in this Realm and to transport them into Spain and Portugal', in a document often misinterpreted as an edict expelling Africans from England. Van Senden was a merchant of Lubeck, and the protégé of the bankrupt former Treasurer-at-war, Sir Thomas Sherley. Van Senden had brought back eighty-nine English prisoners of war from Spain and Portugal, and had hatched a plan with Sherley to make money from selling the Africans on his return. But the Council added the key proviso that the Africans could only be taken 'with the consent of their masters'. This would prove disastrous to Van Senden's scheme. He later complained that:

> together with a Pursuivant [he] did travel at his great Charges into divers parts of your highness Realm for the said Blackamoores. But the masters of them, perceiving by the said warrant that your orator could not take the Blackamoores without the Master's good will, would not suffer your Orator to have any one of them.[47]

Had Edward Wynter been approached in this manner, he would probably have given Van Senden short shrift. Wynter had once been sold himself, to the Spanish ambassador as a prisoner in France, and highly valued Swarthye's services. Swarthye's continued presence in his household, and treatment by the court in 1597, contradicts the notion that Africans were expelled from England by this Privy Council letter.[48]

In 1619, Sir Edward Wynter died. He was succeeded by his son John. If Edward Swarthye had come to England in 1586, he must have then been at least twenty, which would make him thirty at the time of the whipping and in his fifties when Wynter passed away. He may have lived on to serve Sir Edward's son, who was thought by Samuel Pepys to be a worthy man. John Wynter was knighted in 1624 and became secretary to Queen Henrietta Maria in 1638. If Swarthye were still alive he would have been an old man of over seventy. We cannot know whether he lived to see his master choose the losing side in the Civil War, or resort to burning White Cross Manor to the ground in April 1645.[49] Or, indeed, if he remained in service all his life. Not all Africans working in gentry households remained in them forever. Henry Jetto, for one, left his position as Sir Henry Bromley's gardener at Holt Castle in Worcestershire in around 1608 and made a home for himself in the village of Holt with his wife and family. When he died in 1627 he was the first known African wealthy enough to leave a will bequeathing legacies to his children and grandchildren.[50]

John Guye distanced himself so successfully from the ignominious events at White Cross that they are not recorded in later accounts of his life. After being dismissed from Edward Wynter's service he returned to Bristol, where he had been born. On 20 February 1597, he was admitted into the liberties, or given the freedom of the city, entitling him to trade and hold property. His career progressed rapidly: he became Sheriff of Bristol in September 1605, and a member of the Spanish Company (merchants trading to Spain) the same year. In 1608 he set sail on a reconnaissance mission to Newfoundland. James I granted the Newfoundland Company its patent on 2 May 1610 and John Guye led the first group of English colonists to Canada that summer.[51]

It is no surprise that iron working was on Guye's Newfoundland agenda. On 6 October 1610 he wrote from Cupers Cove to Sir Percival Willoughby about iron ore samples from Belle Island, the 'island of iron'. Willoughby was an investor in the Newfoundland Company, and the two men hoped to profit from iron working together. This great hope was never realised. As Francis Bacon remarked, 'the hope of mines is very uncertain' and serves only 'to make the planters lazy in other things'.[52]

Guye's meeting with a group of Beothuk in Newfoundland.

On his third trip to Newfoundland in 1612 Guye encountered the native people, the Beothuk, for the first time. One wonders what effect, if any, his years living and working alongside Edward Swarthye had on his impression of them. In his journal he wrote that they greeted the English party with a dance, 'laughing and making signes of joy, and gladness, sometimes striking the breasts of our company and sometimes their own'. The Beothuk and the

Englishmen proceeded to eat and drink together; the Beothuk preferred the English *aqua vitae* to their beer.[53] This was the first – and last – friendly encounter between the English and the native people of Newfoundland.

Guye returned to Bristol in April 1613, where he became mayor in 1618 and an alderman the year after. The biographer John Aubrey described him very briefly in his *Brief Lives* (1669–1696) as 'the wisest man of his time in that city. He was as their oracle and they chose him for one of their representatives to sit in Parliament'. Guye sat in the Parliaments of 1621 and 1624, where he brought in a bill for lowering of interest rates from 10 to 8. He died in 1629 and was buried at the church of St Stephen's in Bristol. He left half of his considerable estate, which included his Bristol house, estates at Doynton and Gaunt's Earthcott, near Almondsbury in Gloucestershire and Kingston Seymour in Somerset, and his share in the prisage (customs duties) on wines imported into Bristol to his son John, the eldest of ten children, and half to his 'loving wife' Anne; the same Anne he had first met in Lydney.[54]

Had Anne Guye not been quite so loving, John Guye not so ambitious or Sir Edward Wynter so violent, we might never have known of the existence of Edward Swarthye, alias Negro. Instead, the knowledge that Swarthye whipped Guye forces us to reassess our preconceptions about the status of Africans in Tudor society. That said, Edward Swarthye was still a servant, which in the modern mind is easily elided into something little better than slavery, even though many English people were in service then. But not all Africans who came to England followed this path. Some, like Reasonable Blackman, a silk weaver in Southwark, were able to use their skills to make an independent living.

5

Reasonable Blackman,
the Silk Weaver

Death had taken little Jane first. His son Edmund died three days later. That left Reasonable, his wife, and five-year-old Edward shut up in their house as the plague continued to ravage the city. The red cross on their door was beginning to fade, but they were still locked away, in grave danger of infection. Those who could afford to, the sort who liked to wear the fine silk Blackman wove, had left for their country estates long ago. The silk weaver and his family, like so many others, had no such luxury. Blackman thought of Jane and Edmund, and thanked God he'd been able to bury them in coffins. There was a churchyard across the river that had run out of space and forbidden coffins altogether.[1] But they had been so tiny, those boxes of wood. He shuddered to think of their small bodies, cold, stiff and lifeless, inside.

REASONABLE BLACKMAN MADE a living as a silk weaver in Elizabethan Southwark. Given his profession was not long established in the English capital, where did he learn it? And what of his name; was it a reference to his 'reasonable' prices? Whatever his rates, they allowed him to support a family. He had at least three children, though two of them died young in the plague of 1592. His wife was probably an Englishwoman, considering the relatively small numbers of Africans in Elizabethan London. How accepted would this family have been in the

Southwark community? He was a skilled craftsman, which shows us that not all Black Tudors worked for a master. It also causes us to wonder how many of the other Africans in Tudor England whose occupations are unrecorded were financially independent.

A surname alone cannot confirm a person's ethnicity.[2] Although Reasonable's surname would seem to indicate the colour of his skin, it is in fact an old English surname, derived from the Old English *Blaec mann*, as are 'Black', 'Blackmore', 'Moor/More' and 'Morris'. It could also be spelt Blakeman, Blakman, Blackmon or Blackmun. A John Blakman was living in England in 1206 and the name was fairly common until the thirteenth century. By the Tudor period, the name was found in Eynsham, Oxfordshire, Fowey, Cornwall, and Berkhampstead, Hertfordshire.[3] Henry VI had a chaplain named John Blacman, a fellow of Merton College, Oxford. A different John Blackeman was buried at Grey Friars Church, London, in July 1511. A third man of the same name was a benefactor of St John's Hospital, Coventry.[4] None of these men was African.

'Blackman' may have originated in reference to a dark complexion, but by the sixteenth century it cannot be assumed to signify African ethnicity. As William Camden noted in 1586, 'surnames began to be taken up . . . in England about the time of the Conquest, or else a very little before'.[5] Theoretically, a man called More in 1566 could have had a Moorish ancestor from five hundred years before, but it is a rather remote possibility. We cannot even assume that 'Blackman', or names like 'Moor' or 'Niger', were originally assigned to men of African origin. Wilfred Niger was nicknamed Niger or 'the Black' in around 1080, after he painted his face with charcoal to go unrecognised amongst his enemies at night.[6] The names could also refer to dark hair (Black), or to someone who came from a place called Moore (in Cheshire), More (in Shropshire), Blackmore (Essex), Blackmoor (Hampshire, Somerset) or Blakemere (Herefordshire), or even to someone who lived on or near a moor.[7] In Scotland, the surnames 'Muir, Mure, Moor, Moore, More' referred to ancient 'residence beside a moor or heath'.[8]

It is only because Reasonable Blackman was also described as 'blackmor' and 'a blackmore' that we know he was African.[9]

'Blackamoor' or its variants was the most popular term Englishmen used to describe Africans, appearing in some 40% of references to individuals in the archives, and in literature from at least 1525.[10]

To the modern ear, his first name, Reasonable, sounds as if it could have been a trading name, advertising the reasonable prices of his silk weaving business. Might Blackman have invented this name for himself, much as people with foreign names that are difficult for the English to pronounce still do today? It may have been a Christian name received at baptism, along the lines of 'Praisegod' or 'Charity', or a nickname bestowed on him by his neighbours and friends. Nicknames were widely used in Tudor England: Queen Elizabeth liked to invent them for courtiers (Robert Dudley was her 'eyes', Burghley her 'spirit') and even foreign princes; her suitor the Duc de Anjou was her 'frog'.[11] Notably, both Sir Thomas More and Sir Francis Walsingham were known by nicknames meaning African. More was referred to by Erasmus in punning mode as 'Niger', while Walsingham was 'the Moor' to his Queen because of his constant nature.[12] But any distinctive characteristic could give rise to a nickname, or byname, which could be pejorative, humorous, or both. Sometimes nicknames were used to distinguish people with similar names. A merchant named Thomas Palmer became known as 'Whiskers' Palmer, after the beard he had adopted in Turkey, where he lived for many years before returning to London. Robert Taylor (alias Rutt) called John Ledge, the apparently unctuous constable of his Essex village, 'Smooth Boots'.[13]

In 1579, Reasonable Blackman was living south of the River Thames on the 'West Side' of St Saviour's parish in Southwark. 'Resonablackmore' purchased two tokens to reserve his place to take communion at St Saviour's on Easter Sunday 1579.[14] St Saviour's parish began at London Bridge and stretched west, through the site of today's Borough Market, to what is now the Tate Modern. The 'West Side' where Blackman lived was actually at the eastern end of the parish, near the church (now Southwark Cathedral). The area lay between 'The Close' (now Montague Close) and 'Chain Gate' (one of the gates to the churchyard).

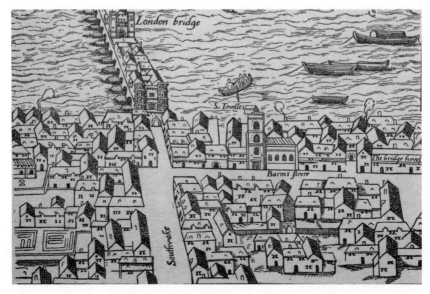

Tooley Street (then *Barms Street*) in the 1560s.

By 1587, Blackman lived in the neighbouring parish of St Olave's, Tooley Street. St Olave's ran east from London Bridge along both sides of Tooley Street to Tower Bridge, incorporating the sites of today's Shard and City Hall. The church of St Olave's, situated on the main thoroughfare of Tooley Street, was dedicated to Olaf II Haraldsson (995–1030), a Norwegian king, celebrated in England for helping Ethelred expel the heathen Danes from several English cities, towns and fortresses.[15]

Southwark, south of the river, and so outside the jurisdiction of the City of London, was a notoriously dissolute area. It was crowded, with almost 20,000 inhabitants in 1600, making up 10% of London's population. Many were immigrants; by 1603, there were 2,004 'alien' households in St Olave's alone.[16] It was also known for being home to the poor, unemployed, criminals and vagrants. In 1596, the Court of Aldermen, with the encouragement of the Privy Council, ordered that 'all manner of rogues, beggars, idle and vagrant persons' in the area be apprehended. Southwark had a notably high concentration of alehouses, brothels, theatres and bear-baiting gardens. The playwright and pamphleteer, Thomas Dekker, commented in 1608 that 'every fourth house is an alehouse'.

And, as Christopher Hudson complained in 1631, 'Alehouses are nests of Satan where the owls of impiety lurk and where all evil is hatched, and the bellows of intemperance and incontinence blow up'. The sleeping inhabitants of Southwark might well have thought Satan's owls of impiety were on the loose one night in October 1582, when 'certain lewd persons . . . did very disorderly disguise themselves and went up & down the street . . . almost stark naked, with their swords drawn in their hands, making great noises, shoutings and cryings'.

Although various monarchs, most recently Henry VIII, had attempted to shut down Southwark's brothels, they continued to flourish illicitly. Theatres such as The Rose, built on Bankside in 1587, were said to be frequented by 'light and lewd disposed persons, as harlots, cutpurses, cozeners, pilferers &c., who under colour of hearing plays, devised divers evil and ungodly conspiracies'. The area boasted five prisons: the Clink (which inspired the slang term for a gaol, possibly from the sound the gates made when they shut on a prisoner), the Compter, the King's Bench, the Marshalsea and the White Lion.[17] Yet, cheek-by-jowl with all this was an established community of craftsmen and artisans. Some worked south of the river because they could not afford City rents, others because their alien status (which in Tudor London included anyone born outside England) made them ineligible to work there. Foreigners were officially barred from completing apprenticeships and so rendered ineligible to obtain the freedom of the City.[18]

It was a good time to be a silk weaver. As wealthy aristocrats, ladies, gentlemen and merchants spent more time in the capital, attending court, Parliament or the law courts, there was a growing demand for silk clothing and accessories, and other luxury goods. Clothing was used to proclaim status, with Queen Elizabeth leading the way. In 1561, she received her first pair of silk stockings from Mrs Alice Montague, one of a dying breed of gentlewomen, known as 'silk women', who made various silk accessories or 'narrow wares', but did not manufacture cloth on an industrial scale. The Queen asked for more: 'I like silk stockings well; they are pleasant, fine and delicate. Henceforth I will wear no more cloth stockings.'[19] Elizabeth's courtiers aped her expensive tastes. They decked themselves out in all sorts of silk: velvet, satin, damask and taffeta.[20] Sir Walter Ralegh for one was keen on silk stockings.[21] By the 1590s many courtiers were spending up to £1,000 a year on clothes.[22] Their efforts were satirised by Thomas Dekker who wrote of: 'those changeable Silk gallants, who . . . read no books but a looking glass'.[23] The desire for silk was echoed on stage. In *The Taming of the Shrew*, Petruchio promises Kate 'silken coats and caps, and golden rings'. The fatal handkerchief Othello gives Desdemona is made of silk, spun by 'hallow'd worms'.[24]

It was not just the elite who wore silk. Although there were strict laws in place dictating who could wear what, as befitted their social station, they were largely ignored. 'It is very hard to know,' Philip Stubbs complained in 1583, 'who is noble, who is worshipful, who is a gentleman, who is not: for you shall have those, which are neither of the nobility, gentility, not yeomanry, go daily in silks, velvets, satins, damasks, taffetas and such like, notwithstanding that they be both base by birth, mean by estate and servile by calling'.[25] The specifics of the often-flouted sumptuary laws reflect just how fashionable it was to wear silk. Even those who could not afford to deck themselves in silk from head to toe still sought to flaunt a flash of silk somewhere about their person. The 1533 edict forbade the wearing of taffeta, satin, damask, outer garments containing silk and velvet garments (except jackets and doublets) unless you had an income of £100 a year. The 1554 law prohibited the wearing of silk accessories unless you were the eldest son of a knight or had an income of £20 a year. Those who continued to illegally wear silk 'hats, bonnets, nightcaps, girdles, hose, shoes, scabbards or spur leather' would face three months' imprisonment, and a fine of £10 for every day they had worn the offending item.[26]

Silk was also used in theatrical costumes. The diary that Philip Henslowe, owner of the Rose Theatre, kept between 1591 and 1609 lists two hundred and seventy-four silk and lace items (the production of lace involved the use of silk).[27] The actors' dress was in stark contrast to the rags of London's poor. One observer wrote to Walsingham in 1580 that it was 'a woeful sight to see two hundred proud players jet in their silks where five hundred poor people starve in the streets'.[28]

Silk weaving was a relatively new industry in London and under-went a dramatic expansion during Blackman's time; imports of raw silk increased five-fold between 1560 and 1593.[29] Silk had been produced in China for thousands of years and latterly made its way into Europe along the trading route known as the Silk Road. As demand increased in the West, the skills required to produce it slowly made their way there. By the fourth century, there were silk-weaving workshops in Constantinople, Syria and Egypt. Production spread across North Africa, to centres such as Tunis and Fez; Othello's silk handkerchief was made in Africa.[30] The Moors introduced the craft to Spain in 712, where the profession took root in Andalusia. It reached Italy in the thirteenth century and three centuries later their silks dominated the European market. The art then made its way into France and the Netherlands, reaching Antwerp, a key centre for cloth production, in the 1530s.[31] By 1584, the Antwerp silk industry employed some 4,000 people, producing satins, damasks, thin bourats, coarse grogram taffeta, velvets and the heavy, usually black, armoisin.[32]

Antwerp's days as a centre of trade and industry were numbered, for the Netherlands were shortly to be wracked by eighty years of war that began when the people of the Low Countries revolted against Spanish rule in 1568. The Netherlands had been ruled by the Spanish since 1506 when Charles V inherited his father's Dukedom of Burgundy and became Lord of the Netherlands. In 1516, he inherited the Spanish crown from his mother and three years later was elected Holy Roman Emperor, a title previously held by his paternal grandfather, Maximilian I. Charles was born in Ghent and as monarch he returned to the land of his birth regularly, maintaining a fairly harmonious relationship with his Dutch subjects. Things changed when his son Philip II succeeded him in 1555. Unlike his father, Philip was not born in the Netherlands, and after 1559 he never visited it; not that this prevented him from continuing to impose taxes on its people. This, combined with his insistence that he would not rule over heretics, led to a series of uprisings known as the Revolt of the Netherlands, which in 1618 segued into the Thirty Years' War.[33]

Some 50,000 refugees arrived in England from the southern

Netherlands between 1550 and 1585, bringing the art of weaving silk with them.[34] As John Stow recounted in his *Survey of London*, 'Among the trading strangers that came over into England from Flanders and those parts for their religion, in the said Queen Elizabeth's Reign, there were divers of this Sort that dealt in dressing and preparing Silk for the other trades.'[35] The number of immigrant heads of households and their servants recorded as working in silk manufacture in London more than doubled, from two hundred and thirty-seven in 1571 to five hundred and twenty-two in 1593. The best silks were still imported from Italy, but the refugees focused on making cheaper alternatives, mixing raw silk with linen or wool. These cheaper fabrics, amongst other purposes, were used for lining expensive garments and fine bed curtains, and making silk handkerchiefs. Spitalfields would later become London's silk-weaving centre, but at this early stage the trade was widely dispersed throughout the city, with silk weavers to be found in Bishopsgate, Cripplegate and Blackman's Southwark. In 1571, of the fifteen foreign silk weavers living in St Olave's parish, twelve were from Flanders, Brabant or Holland.[36]

That Blackman was a silk weaver living in Southwark suggests he came to London from the Netherlands, which, as well as being a centre for his craft, was home to a number of Africans, due to its connections with Spain and Portugal. In the sixteenth century, Antwerp is thought to have had the second-largest black population in Europe, after Lisbon, so Blackman may well have arrived from there. While the Netherlands were governed from Spain, the status of Africans there followed the Spanish example. Most were enslaved, but some, for example Antoine Rodrigues, became free: this 'African from Cape Verde' was manumitted in Antwerp in 1566.[37]

Africans are recorded in the city's artwork as well as its archives. When the German painter Albrecht Dürer visited Antwerp in 1521 he drew a portrait of a twenty-year-old African woman named Katherina. She was the servant of João Brandão, the Portuguese royal factor who oversaw the trade at the Indiahouse, the hub for selling Portuguese colonial goods. A few years later, Jan Mostaert, an artist working at the court of Margaret of Austria in Mechelen, just to the south of Antwerp, painted a high-status African Christian courtier.[38] Over the next century, portraits of Africans appear in

Dürer's portraits of Katherina and an unidentified African man.
Although the latter is dated 1508, this is considered unreliable
and, like Katherina, this man may also have been a member
of João Brandão's household.

works by a range of Dutch artists including Pieter Breughel the
Elder, Wenceslaus Hollar, Rubens and Rembrandt, who lived in
the same area as a group of several free African men and women
in 1630s Amsterdam.[39]

Blackman was not the only independent African businessman
working in the cloth industry in Tudor London. Some thirty years
earlier, in the reign of Queen Mary, Elizabeth's older, Catholic half-
sister, 'there was a Negro made fine Spanish needles in Cheapside,
but would never teach his Art to any'. Like silk weaving, 'Spanish
needles', fine sewing needles made of steel, were new to England.
Before this, needles were made of wood, bone or ivory, or were
crude iron needles produced by blacksmiths. This man, who like
his needles was probably from Spain, clearly made the most of his
monopoly. He taught no one else his craft so that he could continue
to charge a premium for his unrivalled wares. After his death, the

art was lost to England until it was reintroduced by a German, Elias Crowse, in 1566.[40] Technologies ranging from silk weaving to weapon manufacture were closely guarded national secrets in a time of intense rivalries between European powers; not unlike the way the blueprint for making atomic bombs was treated during the Cold War.

The needlemaker's place of business, Cheapside, was known for its metal work. Goldsmith's Row, in the heart of Cheapside, was a centre for gold and silver work. In 1500, an Italian traveller wrote:

> the most remarkable thing in London, is the wonderful quantity of wrought silver . . . In one single street, named [Cheapside], leading to St Paul's, there are fifty-two goldsmiths' shops, so rich and full of silver vessels, great and small, that in all the shops in Milan, Rome, Venice, and Florence put together, I do not think there would be found so many of the magnificence that are to be seen in London.

He goes on to say that 'artificers . . . have congregated there from all parts of the island, and from Flanders, and from every other place'.[41] No African appears in the clerk's lists of the occupants of Goldsmith's Row for 1558, the last year of Mary's reign, yet the diarist Henry Machyn, who died in 1563, recorded that Number 29 had the sign of 'The Black Boy'.[42] This sign was still in place in 1577, when 'the black boy in chepeside' was referred to in a Bridewell court case.[43] Could this establishment have been named after the black craftsman? Another reference to the African needlemaker can be found in the crest that the Worshipful Company of Needlemakers had adopted by 1780, which remained in use until at least 1915. In the strange yet poetic language of heraldry, the crest was described as 'A Moor's Head couped at the shoulders in profile proper wreathed about the temples Argent and Gules vested round the shoulders Argent in his ear a Pearl'. In other words, the bust of a Moor in profile, who wore a red and silver wreath around his temples, silver about his shoulders, and a pearl earring. It is believed to be an allusion to the man who first brought the art of steel needle making to England.[44]

The engagement of these craftsmen, silk weavers and needle-maker, in the larger project of England's cloth industry was no accident. The enterprise was central to the Tudor economy and a number of other Africans in London were involved. The subject of the next chapter, Mary Fillis, was a servant to Millicent Porter, an East Smithfield seamstress. Simon Valencia, 'a black moore', who died in the parish of St Botolph's Aldgate in 1593, worked for Stephen Drifield, a needlemaker.[45] If he was from Spain, as his surname might suggest, he may have been able to teach his master how to make fine Spanish needles. Around the same time, two African women worked for hat or hat-band makers in the capital.[46] Having learnt the skills of their master's trade while in service, these individuals might have taken the opportunity to set out on their own. In all likelihood, Blackman did just that.

By 1587 Blackman was married.[47] This was a sign of his growing prosperity, as marriage was a serious financial undertaking that required a large initial outlay to acquire all the furniture, uten-sils and other accoutrements necessary to establish a household.[48] His business was successful enough to enable him to support a family of at least five. In turn, the whole family presumably helped their father in his work.[49] His son Edward was baptised in February 1587 at St Olave, Tooley Street. We know he was also the father of Edmund and Jane, who both died in 1592. 'John Blakemore son of Reasonable Blakemore,' who was baptised at St Saviour's on 26 October 1579, might be a fourth child.[50] Although the surname was different, 'Reasonable' was such an uncommon first name that John was almost certainly his son. Tudor spelling and naming is not known for its consistency; no two of the six surviving versions of Shakespeare's signature are spelt the same way.

The name of Blackman's wife is not recorded and we have no other information about her. Parish registers did not consistently name the mothers of children unless they were born out of wedlock. It has recently been suggested that Mrs Blackman was the African woman alluded to in the exchange between Lorenzo and Launcelot Gobbo in Shakespeare's *Merchant of Venice* (1597):

LORENZO: I shall answer that better to the commonwealth than you can the getting up of the Negro's belly; the Moor is with child by you, Launcelot.

LAUNCELOT: It is much that the Moor should be more than reason; but if she be less than an honest woman she is indeed more than I took her for.

LORENZO: How every fool can play upon the word![51]

For Shakespeare, the main attraction of making Gobbo's mistress a 'Negro' could be the opportunity it provides to make a pun on 'Moor' and 'more'. However, her identity is of no consequence to the plot, so it could well be a reference to something happening in London at the time.[52] Shakespeare's use of the words 'more than reason' has led some scholars to imagine an affair between Will Kemp, the actor who played Launcelot Gobbo, and the widow of Reasonable Blackman.[53] The only connection is that both Kemp and the Blackman family lived in Southwark, which is circumstantial evidence at best.

Furthermore, Blackman's wife was probably English. There are only a handful of known records of marriages between Africans in this period. Three took place in Stepney, early in the seventeenth century: 'Peter & Mary both nigers' were married at the church of St Dunstan's and All Saints in July 1608; the following February saw the nuptials of 'John Mens of Ratcliffe a niger & Luce Pluatt a niger'; and in September 1610, 'Salomon Cowrder of Poplar a niger sailor' was united with 'Katheren Castilliano a niger also'.[54] Outside Stepney, we know of only one other marriage between two Africans before the Civil War, that of the trumpeter named Antony Vause and his wife Anne, who was buried in 1618 at St Botolph's Aldgate.[55]

Both Blackman and his wife would have been baptised. Blackman bought a token for Holy Communion at St Saviour's in 1579 and only Christians could be married. The Book of Common Prayer stipulated that 'The new married persons (the same day of their marriage) must receive the holy Communion'. We can see how this played out in the case of Samuel Munsur of Greenwich, who seems to have been baptised with marriage in mind. He was christened on 28 November 1613, a month before his wedding to Jane Johnson on 26 December 1613. This would allow just enough time for the banns giving notice of the marriage to be read out in church on three Sundays before the ceremony. James Curres's status as a baptised Christian was explicitly confirmed when he was described as 'a Moore Christian' in the record of his marriage to Margaret Person in 1617.[56]

'An old black ram is tupping your white ewe.' The villainous Iago's words to Desdemona's father Brabantio drip with disgust yet no archival evidence has been found that interracial relationships met this kind of hostility off stage. Tudor England was a far cry from the American colonies, which began passing anti-miscegenation laws, forbidding marriage between different races, in the 1660s. In 1578, George Best, who lived in the maritime hamlet of Ratcliffe, reported 'I myself have seen an Ethiopian as black as coal brought to England who taking a faire English woman to wife, begat a son in all respects as black as the father'. His tone of is one of curiosity rather than repulsion or condemnation.[57] As we shall see in Chapter Nine, skin colour was no obstacle to sexual relationships between black and white Tudors, whether they took place within the sanctity of marriage or not.

If not *the* first, Blackman was definitely one of the first financially independent family men of African origin to live in Tudor England. Others followed in Cornwall, Kent, Worcestershire and Hertford.[58]

In Truro, Cornwall, we find the family of 'Emmanuel the Moor', whose daughter, Maria, was buried at St Mary's Truro in August 1611. There is no baptismal record for her, which suggests the family had only recently moved to the area. Her brother Richard was baptised in October 1612. As with the Blackman family, there is no record of the mother, but the children were not labelled bastards so it follows that their parents were married. Emmanuel died in August 1623.[59] There is no reference to his being in service, so in all likelihood he was making his own living to support his family. We can assume the same was true for 'George a blackamoore' who married Marie Smith at All Saints' church in Staplehurst, Kent, in 1616. Their son, George, was baptised in February 1620 and their daughter, Elizabeth, in May 1622.[60]

There are two known examples of men previously in service who left to establish independent households. We learnt in Chapter Four of Henry Jetto, who left his post as Sir Henry Bromley's gardener at Holt Castle. His contemporary, John Accomy, was a servant to the Cappell family of Hadham Hall, Little Hadham, until 1614, when he left to live in Hertford with his second wife Temperance Swain. Like the Jettos, they went on to have five children, who were all baptised.[61]

The baptisms of John and Edward Blackman, Richard and Maria Moor of Truro, George and Elizabeth in Staplehurst, the Jetto children in Worcestershire and the Accomy children in Hertford are significant. As we shall see in the next chapter, in the highly religious world of the Tudors, the ritual signalled acceptance into both the parish community and Tudor society more broadly. With their offspring, these families were, as the priests intoned as they made the sign of the cross upon the child's forehead, received 'into the congregacion of Christes flocke.'[62]

In the summer of 1592 the plague swept through London, reaching St Olave's parish in July. The parish register departs from its usual brief listings of names, and notes in large writing that 'the 14th day of this month the plague did begin, Margaret the wife of Hugh Jones, the first buried of the same.'[63] By the end of the month twenty-six people had died. In August the figure was one hundred and eighty, in September 248, in October 158, and in November ninety-six.* The burials column of the register, usually contained in one column on a single page, becomes half-a-dozen columns over several pages. On 10 September, the Privy Council wrote to the Lord Mayor and Aldermen of London that 'by the weekly certificates, it doth appear that the present infection within the city of London doth greatly increase, growing as well by the carelessness of the people as by the want of good order to see the sound severed from the sick.'[64]

As the contagion spread, measures were put in place to combat it. Bonfires were lit in the streets 'to purge and cleanse the air.'[65]

---

* The plague died down over the winter and spring but came back to the parish with a vengeance the following summer: 146 died in July 1593, 269 in August, 300 in September, 163 in October.

Dogs, thought to be carriers of infection, were culled by parish authorities.[66] Clothes belonging to the dead were also suspect. In Kent, in 1610, a man sold a coat belonging to his lodger, who had recently died of the plague. Unfortunately, the man who bought it died soon afterwards, as the coat was 'not well aired or purified'.[67] Great efforts were made to stop crowds from gathering. Theatres, many of which were located in Southwark, were closed on 23 June, and did not open again until August 1594.[68] The Westminster law courts were prevented from beginning their new term in October, and by the end of the month it was decided to hold them in Hertford instead. The High Court of Admiralty, which usually met in Southwark, was relocated to Woolwich. On 11 October, the usual ceremonies held to inaugurate the new Lord Mayor of London were cancelled, and the Queen suggested the money was spent on relieving 'those persons whose houses are infected' instead.[69]

Southwark, crowded and poverty-stricken, was one of the capital's most vulnerable areas. The Blackman household was amongst the contaminated. The silk weaver's daughter Jane, and his son Edmund, fell ill. James Balmford, the curate of St Olave's, Tooley Street, observed that some sufferers lost their minds, leaping out of windows or running into the Thames. He put much of the blame for the spread of disease on the 'bloody error' that many people made, in thinking that the 'Pestilence' was not contagious. He dedicated his *A Short Dialogue concerning the Plagues Infection* of 1603 to his parishioners: a publication in which he 'set down all that I have publicly taught' and tried to disabuse them of this fatal misconception that led 'men, women and children with running sores' to 'go commonly abroad and thrust themselves into company'.[70]

Once their children's illness was discovered by the parish searchers, the Blackman's house was shut up and marked with a red cross to warn others away. Shakespeare describes the way plague victims were quarantined in *Romeo and Juliet*:

> the searchers of the town,
> Suspecting that we both were in a house
> Where the infectious pestilence did reign,
> Seal'd up the doors, and would not let us forth.'[71]

This added to their misery. As Balmford put it, those who were isolated in this way 'think it an hell to be so long shut up from company and their business: the neglecting whereof is the decay of their state'. The loss of business was a very real concern for those of modest means, such as the silk weaver. Balmford callously dismissed such concerns, remarking that those infected should be 'content to forbear a while, since in the Plague they usually mend or end in short time'.[72]

The plague could attack the lymphatic system, or spread into the lungs or blood. The first type, bubonic plague, manifested itself in red, grossly inflamed and swollen lymph nodes, called buboes (hence the name), high fever, delirium and convulsions. If it got into the lungs (pneumonic plague), the victim would begin coughing up blood, and if it got into the bloodstream (septicemic plague), there would be bleeding under the skin, from the mouth, nose and rectum, and gangrene would cause the fingers, toes and nose to turn black.[73] Thomas Dekker likened the advent of plague to Death pitching his tents in the 'sinfully polluted suburbs', from where he commanded his army of 'Burning Fevers, Boils, Blaines, and Carbuncles'. These generals led his rank and file: 'a mingle-mangle' of 'dumpish Mourners, merry Sextons, hungry Coffin-sellers, scrubbing Bearers, and nastie Grave-makers'.[74]

Reasonable Blackman and his wife could have done little to save their children from death's onslaught. Various remedies against the plague were prescribed in the twenty-three books published on the subject between 1486 and 1604.[75] Some came with royal authorisation, others most definitely did not. It was popularly thought that beer and ale had medicinal qualities, and alehouses were notably busier at times of plague.[76] The official government advice, first issued in 1578, suggested a host of preventative measures and cures, such as potions and lotions made up of ingredients like vinegar or various herbs and spices, or what to burn to purge the air. If you could not afford the ingredients, this was no obstacle: 'The poor which can not get vinegar nor buy Cinnamon, may eat bread and Butter alone, for Butter is not only a preservative against the plague, but against all manner of poisons'.[77] Simon Kellwaye's

1593 tract, *A defensative against the plague*, suggested applying live plucked chickens to the plague sores to draw out the disease. A later pamphlet gave more detailed advice as to how this would work:

> Take a cock chicken & pull all the feathers of his tail very bare, then hold the bared part of the pullet close upon the sore & the chicken will gape and labour for life & will die; then do so with another pullet till it die, & so with another: till you find the last chicken will not die cannot be killed by the infection being altogether extracted, for when all the venom is drawn out the last chicken will not be hurt by it & the patient will mend speedily: one Mr Whatts hath tried this on a child of his, & 8 chickens one after another died & the ninth lived, & the sore being hard & hot was made soft by the first chicken as papp, the 2nd drew it clean away.[78]

This method was used in St Olave's parish, but Balmford referred to the use of pigeons instead. The poor had to make to do with what they had.[79]

The Blackman children finally succumbed to Death's advances in mid-October 1592, in a week when the plague took one hundred and ninety-eight lives in London.[80] Other silk weavers' children were buried at St Olave's as the epidemic raged on, and Africans also died in other parts of the city. At St Botolph's Aldgate, three 'blackamoors' in their twenties: Simon Valencia (the needlemaker's servant), Cassango, and Robert, were buried in the late summer and autumn of 1593, their entries in the register marked with the word 'plague'.[81] The historian John Stow recorded that this outbreak claimed 10,675 Londoners between December 1592 and December 1593.[82] When it was over, the capital had lost 8.5% of its population. So many had died that rumour-mongers whispered England would no longer be able successfully to resist a Spanish invasion. Some thought the plague was the result of divine judgement, 'the will of God rightfully punishing wicked men'. To their way of thinking, taking action to prevent the plague was to rebel against God, and no human efforts could stop people from dying at their appointed time. The Privy Council threatened to imprison anyone who shared 'such dangerous opinions'.[83]

Others blamed immigrants for bringing the plague to London. The 'filthy keeping' of foreigners' houses was identified by the city authorities as 'one of the greatest occasions of the plague'.[84] This might have helped to trigger the anti-immigrant feeling expressed by London apprentices in the spring of 1593. The trouble began in April when they set up 'a lewd and vile ticket or placard' on a post in London threatening violence against 'the strangers'. A series of 'divers lewd and malicious libels . . . published by some disordered and factious persons' appeared in the following weeks. One castigated the 'beastly brutes, the Belgians, or rather drunken drones, and fainthearted Flemings: and you, fraudulent father, Frenchmen' and threatened that if they did not 'depart out of the realm' by 9 July, more than 2,000 apprentices would rise up against them. The verse set upon the wall of the Dutch church at Austin Friars in the City of London in early May did 'exceed the rest in lewdness': 'Strangers that inhabit in this land! . . . Egypt's plagues, vexed not the Egyptians more / Than you do us; then death shall be your lot'.[85] The threatened violence never actually erupted. Some of the culprits were rounded up and 'put into the stocks, carted and whipped, for a terror to other apprentices and servants'. The Privy Council encouraged the Lord Mayor to use torture if necessary to prevent these 'lewd persons' from their 'wicked purpose to attempt anything against strangers'. For 'out of such lewd beginnings, further mischief doth ensue'.[86] These rumblings of discontent were directed at a wide array of foreigners, prompted by a broad-brush xenophobia. Those named by nationality were European strangers. The Blackman family were not beastly Belgians or fraudulent Frenchmen. Their dark skin would of course make them immediately identifiable as strangers in the street, but Africans were not the primary target of the apprentices' vitriol.

The plague that struck the Blackman family so tragically in 1592 may have arrived in a Devon port from Portugal, which had suffered an epidemic in 1589. This outbreak was merely a skirmish in the long campaign Death waged on the capital under the command of this most devastating of his Generals, ever poised to snatch lives away in an instant. Between 1540 and 1666, there were nine serious outbreaks of plague in London. The most famous of these, the so-called 'Great Plague' of 1665, killed 12% of the population yet, in percentage terms, the plagues of 1563 and 1603 were almost twice as devastating.[87] The Black Death of 1348 had been another matter entirely. It wiped out almost a third of the European population, which had a seismic impact on every aspect of society from the feudal system to religious faith.

Plague burials took place at dusk, when there were fewer people about, to minimise the chance of the disease spreading. Not all took heed, however, and Balmford grieved to see how 'the poorer sort, yea women with young children, will flocke to burials, and (which is worse) stand (of purpose) over open graves, where sundry are buried together, that (forsooth) all the world may see that they feare not the Plague.'[88]

At the peaks of these plague epidemics, the usual burial rituals had to be set aside as parishes struggled to cope with the numbers of corpses. Two centuries earlier, a Florentine chronicler recorded that his city's plague pits were:

> as wide and deep as the parish was populous; and therein, whosoever was not very rich, having died during the night, would be shouldered by those whose duty it was, and would either be thrown into this pit, or they would pay big money for somebody else to do it for them. The next morning there would be very many in the pit. Earth would be taken and thrown down on them; and then others would come on top of them, and then earth on top again, in layers, with very little earth, like garnishing lasagne with cheese.[89]

However, such pits were only resorted to in extremity. At St Bride's, Fleet Street, the parish officials dug a plague pit in August 1665 when they often had more than thirty bodies to bury each day.[90] The week Jane and Edmund died, St Olave's parish had about forty bodies to dispose of but mass graves would not have been needed.

Six other people were buried alongside Jane on 13 October and four others beside Edmund, who died on 16 October.

The Blackman children received proper burials, with due ritual. Although there are no baptism records for Jane and Edmund, the fact that they were buried in the parish churchyard indicates that the church authorities knew them to be Christians. Some Africans were baptised shortly before their burial, suggesting they were already ill and preparing for the worst. 'John the Blackamoor' was baptised thirteen days before his burial at St Mary the Virgin, Aldermanbury, London in 1565.[91] When Mark Antony was buried in January 1617 at St Olave, Hart Street, the record stated he was 'a negro Christian': he had been baptised just two days earlier.[92] Those not known to be Christian were buried elsewhere: an anonymous 'neger' was laid to rest 'on Catt downe' an area to the east of Plymouth, close to the sea and the Plym estuary, in 1593–4.[93]

The unusually detailed accounts of St Botolph's Aldgate reveal more about the funerals of the Africans buried there. When Domingo, Sir William Wynter's servant, died of consumption in August 1587, the parish provided 'the best cloth' to cover his coffin. In 1552, St Botolph's had a hearse cloth of tawny velvet, the borders 'embroidered with Jesus', but this was confiscated as a piece of Popish frippery by Edward VI's government in 1553, and so by the 1580s, the 'best' cloth was probably rather less grand.[94] In October 1593, one of the black men who died of the plague in the parish, Cassango, had one bearer and was given the best cloth – for which his employer, Mr Barber, was charged 9d – though it wasn't used because he already had a black cloth. That November, another African plague victim, 'Robert a negar being servant to William Mathew a Gentleman' had the second cloth and four bearers. Three years later, 'a negar, supposed to be named Francis', servant to a beer brewer, Peter Miller, had four bearers and the finest cloth when he died of scurvy aged twenty-six.[95] Some of these funerals were grander than those recorded for non-African parishioners.

Nothing more is known of Blackman's life after the death of his children, but there is a tantalising record that suggests his son Edward carried on his father's trade. On 6 March 1614, when Edward Blackman would have been twenty-seven, a certain

'Edward Blackmore of Mile End, silk weaver' married 'Jeane Colle of Stepney' at St Dunstan's and All Saints Church, Stepney.[96] A mere three miles from Southwark, Mile End was on the eastern edge of Spitalfields, which became the centre of London's silk-weaving industry later in the seventeenth century. It is possible that Edward and Jeane knew each other as children, for a Jane Colle, daughter of the porter William Colle, was baptised at St Olave's, Tooley Street, in August 1590, three years after Edward.[97] The couple had three children – Jane, Mary, and William – born in 1614, 1617 and 1619. Only Mary achieved adulthood; William died at the age of two and Jane when she was three.[98]

The majority of documents recording the lives of black people at this time do not state their occupations and where one is recorded, it is usually domestic service. But if Reasonable Blackman was a Black Tudor who made his own way, with his son Edward possibly taking up his father's trade, then it is plausible that some of the many Africans whose occupations are not recorded could also have been financially independent. Just as Blackman doubtless learnt his trade in a master silk weaver's household, other Africans began as servants, and later set out on their own.

On the other side of the Thames, another African worked in the cloth trade. Mary Fillis was a servant to Millicent Porter, a seamstress, and thanks to the unusual enthusiasm of the parish clerk of St Botolph's Aldgate we know more about her than most.

6

Mary Fillis,
the Moroccan Convert

'Our Father, which art in heaven . . .' The strange words echoed
around the church. 'Hallowed be thy name . . .' Mistress Porter
had helped her learn this verse, and what it meant, in prepa-
ration for the day. When she'd reached the end of the Lord's
Prayer, Reverend Threlkeld asked her to rehearse the articles
of her belief and she did so, carefully and fluently. Then he
asked, did she desire to be baptised? 'Aye,' she replied. And so
they went to the font. The whole congregation called on God
the Father through the Lord Jesus Christ to receive her into
Christ's Holy Church. She had been in London thirteen or
fourteen years now, since she was six or seven. She had seen
the church spires every day, towering over the city streets. She
had heard these people speak of their God, of his great
Providence, of his Heaven. And of his wrath. Finally, Reverend
Threlkeld said 'I baptise thee in the name of the Father, and
of the Son, and of the holy Ghost. Amen.' And it was over. She
was a Christian, and she could go forth and 'daily proceed in
all virtue and godliness of living'.

MARY FILLIS WAS one of many Africans baptised in
Tudor England. Like her, most were either adults or
teenagers at their christening, and as there was no
specific ritual outlined in the Book of Common Prayer for such
cases before 1662, they are really better classed as conversions.[1]

Did these ceremonies signal true integration and acceptance into the Tudors' theocratic society? Mary Fillis had lived in London for thirteen or fourteen years before becoming a Christian; why did she wait so long to convert? The exceptionally detailed account of her baptism given by Thomas Harridance, the parish clerk of St Botolph's, Aldgate, gives us some clues.[2] He not only names Fillis's current mistress, the seamstress Millicent Porter, but also a widow, Mrs Barker of Mark Lane, her previous employer. Who was Mrs Barker? What brought the young Mary Fillis into her household and why did she leave? Mary Fillis lived through a period in which England's trading and diplomatic relationship with her country of birth, Morocco, was rapidly evolving. How did this affect her life and the way she was treated?

Mary Fillis was born in Morocco in 1577. She was the daughter of Fillis of Morisco, a basket-weaver and shovel-maker. In contrast to the way 'morisco' was used as an adjective to describe Jacques Francis the diver, Harridance employed the word 'Morisco' as a noun, meaning Morocco. The name Fillis might be linked to the profession of basket-weaving, as 'fillis' is 'a kind of loosely twisted string, made of hemp (*hemp fillis*) or jute (*jute fillis*), used by horticulturists as a tying material', which could have also been used to weave baskets.[3] There may be a connection between her father's profession and the area of London Fillis found herself in, as in Edward IV's time, 'Basket-makers, wire-drawers, and other foreigners' were only allowed to have shops in the manor of Blanch Appleton, which lay at the north end of Mark Lane, where Mary Fillis worked for Mrs Barker.[4] There is, however, no indication that Mary's father ever came to London.

When Mary Fillis was born, her country was about to enter a twenty-five-year period of peace and prosperity under the rule of Sultan Ahmad Al-Mansur. But before this could begin, three kings had to die. In the earlier part of the sixteenth century, Morocco was divided between a northern kingdom, ruled from Fez by the Wattasid dynasty, and a southern kingdom, ruled from Marrakesh by the Sa'adian family. Fez was founded by Idris I, Morocco's first Muslim ruler, in 789. Known as the 'Mecca of the West', the city was home to some 100,000 people and the world's oldest university or madrasa, *Al Karaouine*, which boasted international alumni including Leo Africanus, the Dutch scholar Nicholas Cleynaerts and the tenth-century Pope Sylvester II.[5] Marrakesh was the second-largest city in Morocco, with a population of 20,000. Leo Africanus described it as 'one of the greatest cities in the whole world'; its buildings were 'cunningly and artificially contrived' with 'most stately and wonderful workmanship'. A thriving trading centre, it was well placed to benefit from the trans-Saharan caravan trade which brought gold, ivory, spices and slaves from the south.[6]

The two kingdoms were united under the rule of the Sa'adian Mohammed ash-Sheikh in 1549. To succeed, he had not only to eliminate the Wattasids but also to resist the Spanish and Portuguese who had established various trading posts along the Moroccan coast over the preceding century.[7] Mohammed ash-Sheikh took many of these key cities, most significantly Safi and Agadir, back under Moroccan control in 1541.[8] Soon only Ceuta, Tangier and Magazan remained in Portuguese hands.[9]

The Ottoman Turks watched ash-Sheikh's mounting successes with growing displeasure. For the past hundred years, they had enjoyed a period of prodigious military expansion. Pushing west, they took Constantinople in 1453, much of Hungary in 1526 and threatened Vienna more than once. Their naval presence in the Mediterranean caused serious vexation to the European powers throughout the century, despite the much-celebrated 1571 victory at Lepanto, when a coalition of Catholic powers known as the Holy League defeated the Turks in an epic battle. They also expanded east, encroaching into Persia and taking Baghdad in 1534. To the south, they invaded Syria and from there made their way into Egypt, Tripoli, Tunisia and Algiers. By the mid-sixteenth century the Ottoman Sultan, Suleiman the Magnificent, ruled over some 15 million people on three continents.[10]

And still the Ottomans were not satisfied. Looking to expand further into North Africa, they assassinated ash-Sheikh in 1557. His head was mounted on a spike above the walls of Constantinople.[11] The crown passed to his son, Abdallah Al-Ghalib, but when he died of natural causes in 1574, civil war broke out. His son, Abu Abdallah Mohamed, attempted to secure the throne by executing one of his brothers and imprisoning the other. This did not deter his uncle, Abd al Malik, who had been living in exile in Algiers, from claiming the crown himself. He invaded Morocco and captured Fez in 1576, driving his nephew to seek refuge in the Spanish-held fortress of Penon de Velez.[12]

In 1578, King Sebastian of Portugal made a suicidal intervention in this dynastic dispute. He aligned himself with the ousted Abu Abdallah Mohamed and invaded Morocco. Juan da Silva, Philip II's ambassador in Lisbon, despaired to watch the King depart 'without a single man knowing what we are undertaking, and whereas victory seems impossible, defeat seems certain because we are depending totally on a miracle; may God grant it.' On landing at Tangier, Sebastian insisted on marching inland, separating his troops, who had 'no knowledge of the military arts', from their naval support. Juan da Silva reported that 'all are sure he leads them to a certain death.'[13]

On 4 August 1578, all three rulers died in the Battle of Alcazar, also known as the Battle of the Three Kings, or The Battle of Makhazen River. Abd al Malik was fatally ill before the fighting started, and died in his tent as the battle raged around him. The contemporary rumour was that he had been poisoned, but a modern medical assessment of his symptoms suggests he suffered a perforation of the oesophagus that led to sepsis and multi-organ failure. His councillors made every effort to conceal his death from his troops, propping the corpse up with cushions and continuing to issue commands in his name for some hours, until the news could no longer affect the battle's outcome. His nephew, Abu Abdallah Mohamed, who could not swim, was thrown from his horse and drowned in the River Makhazen while trying to flee from the onslaught. The young Portuguese King was so intent on slaughter that he battled on even as three horses were shot from under him. He became isolated from his guard and was cut down on the field. The bodies of the three kings were displayed in a tent that evening by Ahmad Al-Mansur, Abd Al-Malik's brother. Al-Malik's body was buried with due ceremony in Fez, but his nephew's corpse was flayed, stuffed with straw, and mounted on an ass to be paraded through the streets of Fez and other cities and towns. He was henceforth known as Mohammed Al-Mutawakkil (the Flayed). Sebastian's body was handed over to the governor of Ceuta in December, before being transported to Faro. He was eventually buried at the Jerónimos Monastery of Belém in Lisbon.[14]

Mary Fillis was born the year before this decisive battle. In the aftermath, Ahmad Al-Mansur took the crown and much of the credit for the outcome: 'Al-Mansur' means 'the Victorious'. He succeeded in uniting Morocco after years of civil war, and ensured it remained independent, despite the machinations of the Turks. In 1591 he invaded present-day Mali, conquering the extensive Songhai Empire, his victory assured by the fact that his soldiers bore English-imported muskets, while their victims had only lances and javelins. This conquest brought great riches to Marrakesh: Al-Mansur received an annual tribute of 1,000 slaves and 100,000 gold pieces from his new fiefdom.[15] He reigned in peace for twenty-five years, finally dying of the plague in 1603, five months after Elizabeth I. Like the English Queen, he did not manage the succession well. She had no children and refused to name an heir; he failed to make it clear which of his three sons should succeed him. Their rivalry dragged the country into civil war once more, and the kingdom their father had made strong was destroyed.[16]

The battle had repercussions across the globe. King Sebastian of Portugal had died aged only twenty-four, unmarried and without an heir. As a teenager he had shown little interest in women, preferring the company of 'dissolute' young men, with whom he frequented beaches and woods in the middle of the night. Some historians have taken this behaviour, alongside indications that Sebastian contracted gonorrhoea and/or chlamydia at the age of ten, to mean that the prince was sexually abused by his Jesuit tutor Luís Gonçalves da Câmara. They claim that as a result he was so spiritually tormented that his fervour for military glory in Africa was in fact a barely concealed death wish.[17] Whatever its ultimate cause, his death was excellent news for Spain. As Philip II commented before the battle, 'If he succeeds, we shall have a fine nephew, if he fails, a fine kingdom'. The Portuguese were well aware of this. An agent for the Fuggers – a powerful German banking family – in Lisbon reported: 'It is a woeful matter to lose in one day their King, their husbands and their sons . . . but what is even more terrible is that this kingdom must now fall under Spanish rule, which they can brook least of all'.[18]

After Sebastian's death, the Portuguese throne passed to his great-uncle, Cardinal Henry. The Pope refused to grant this churchman a dispensation to marry, and so he became the last of the Aviz family to rule Portugal. On his death in 1580, Philip II of Spain claimed the Portuguese throne. His title was through his mother, Isabella of Portugal, Cardinal Henry's younger sister. The only other candidate was Don Antonio, Prior of Crato, the illegitimate son of Luis of Portugal, Duke of Beja, the older brother of Cardinal Henry and Isabella. Don Antonio had previously served as governor of Tangier. He managed to survive the Battle of Alcazar, escape his Moroccan captors, and find his way home. However, his illegitimacy seriously compromised his position, and his forces were unable to resist when Philip II invaded in the summer of 1580. The Spanish King took the crown, and with it acquired a trading empire that encompassed the coast of Africa, part of India, the Spice Islands and Brazil. Don Antonio fled to France, and then England, in search of military aid to regain the throne.

A few years later, the six- or seven-year-old Mary Fillis arrived in England and became a servant to the Barker family: John Barker, a merchant, originally from Ipswich, his second wife, Anne, and their new-born daughter, Abigail. The Barkers made their home in Mark Lane, in the parish of St Olave's, Hart Street. Originally 'Mart' or 'Market' Lane, the street runs between Great Tower Street and Fenchurch Street. Its proximity to Leadenhall Market, the customs house, weigh house and the quays made it an ideal address for a merchant, especially one who traded in cloth with the Spanish as John Barker did; Clothworkers' Hall is situated in Dunster Court, just off the street where he lived.[19] As well as trading, Barker was a Member of Parliament, representing Ipswich in the parliaments of 1584, 1586 and 1589. He had lived in London since at least 1582, when records show he was assessed for tax on £300 worth of goods in Tower Ward, which included the parish of St Olave's. If he was not actually resident in the parish then, he was by 1584, as his daughter Abigail was baptised there in March of that year.[20] A wealthy man, at his death in June 1589 he bequeathed £100 a year to his two sons from his first marriage, and provided a marriage portion of £1,000 for his daughter.

Anne Barker came from a wealthy background. Her father Henry Herdson was an Alderman of London, while her stepfather, Sir Richard Champion, had served as Lord Mayor. She had been married before, to George Stoddard, a member of the Grocers' Company. An unscrupulous businessman and loan shark, Stoddard no doubt left her a merry widow when he died in October 1580.[21] She wore a gold chain every day, and owned two pearl bracelets and two diamond rings. Her London home boasted quite an array of expensive linen, gilt and silver plate, upholstery and embroidered silk cushions. Tapestries hung in the Great Chamber and another bedchamber. As well as dozens of silver spoons, gilt goblets, pots, trenchers and candlesticks, she possessed silver bowls marked with her stepfather's coat of arms, and a ewer and basin marked with the arms of both her first husband and the Grocers' Company. Her bed was bedecked with a new red cloth bedspread embroidered with black, yellow and white, and there were matching bed curtains and cushions. Six of her 'best' chairs, those covered with crimson-figured satin, were specifically 'for gentlewomen to sit on'. Such was the opulence that Mary Fillis would have seen all around her as she was growing up. Images spring to mind of her laundering the contents of Mrs Barker's seemingly bottomless linen cupboard and polishing her extensive collection of plate.[22]

Fillis was not the only African in the Barker household. In 1593, Leying Mouea, a 'blackamoor of 20 years' was recorded 'at Mistress Barker's'.[23] Two years later, 'George, a blackamore out of Mrs Barker's' was buried at St Olave's, Hart Street.[24] How might Mary Fillis, Leying Mouea and George have come to be living there? John Barker was a factor in the Spanish trade for Robert Dudley, Earl of Leicester, in the 1570s.[25] We know that Leicester had an African in his household; an inventory from Leicester House, the earl's townhouse on the Strand, records that a mattress was given to 'the blackamore' in March 1583, and another account book records that he received a reward of five shillings at Wanstead in

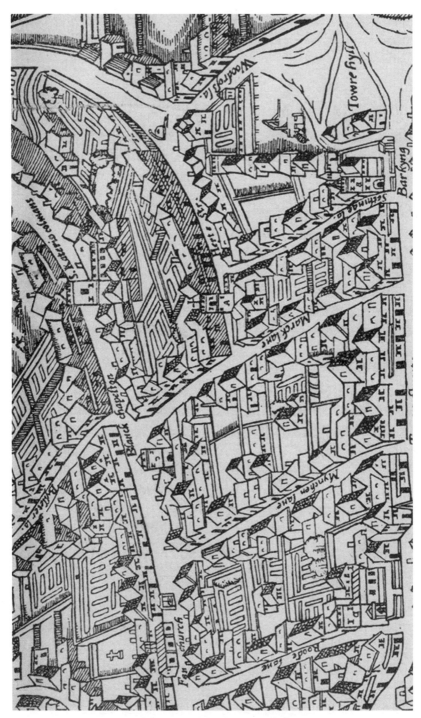

St Olave's, Hart St. (marked 'A'), in the 1560s.

April 1584.[26] Shortly after Mary Fillis arrived in England, Leicester's interest in the burgeoning trade to Morocco was formalised when the Queen issued Letters Patent to a group of merchants trading to Barbary. The charter of July 1585 gave great power to Leicester, who was named as governor, and to his brother, Ambrose Dudley, the Earl of Warwick.[27] All in all, forty merchants of London traded with Barbary at this time; it was very much a going concern. The following month, Leicester signalled a more personal interest by sending Sultan Al-Mansur a gift of horses, care of Henry Roberts, the English ambassador to Morocco.[28]

Regular English trade with Morocco began in the summer of 1551, when a group of prominent London merchants* clubbed together to sponsor Captain Thomas Wyndham's voyage in the *Lion of London*.[29] He returned to Morocco the following May accompanied by two more ships, the *Buttolfe* and a vessel that had been purchased from some Portuguese men in the Welsh town of Newport. It took two weeks to reach the port of Safi, whence some of their merchandise was transported overland to Marrakesh. They went on to Agadir, where, after a bit of bother with a French ship whose captain did not know whether or not his country was currently at war with the English, they sold 'linen, woollen cloth, coral, amber, jet and divers other things well accepted by the Moors', including hardware, guns, and copies of the Old Testament, which were sold to the significant Jewish population. They spent three months in the port, leaving with their ships full of the sweet cargo they had sought: 'sugar, dates, almonds, and molasses or sugar syrup'. On the way home they passed Tenerife, where they got into a fight with the Spaniards and took the ageing governor of the island prisoner. Having made peace, they narrowly avoided being attacked by the Portuguese before finally arriving home with their valuable cargo towards the end of October.[30]

The hostility Wyndham and his men encountered in the Canaries was symptomatic of a bigger problem; the Iberian powers did not welcome interlopers to the trade they had monopolised. Portuguese

---

* Three of whom would go on to invest in John Hawkins's slaving voyages in the 1560: William Chester, William Garrard and Thomas Lodge.

merchants in England threatened that if they found English merchants trading in Morocco they would treat them as 'mortal enemies, with great threats and menaces'. Almost thirty years later, one of Francis Walsingham's advisers warned that 'if the Spaniards take you trading with them [the Moroccans] you die for it'.[31] Before 1550, African goods had mostly come to England via Spain, Portugal or the Spanish-controlled Netherlands. However, the wars of the 1540s disrupted English trade with Spain and the Antwerp cloth market collapsed following the Revolt of the Netherlands, leaving English merchants to seek new markets for cloth and to develop the means to obtain exotic imports such as gold, sugar and meleguetta pepper directly from African sources rather than via Spanish and Portuguese middlemen.[32] By 1558, the Moroccan trade had developed into a more permanent enterprise, based on trade factors resident in the country, most of whom were in the ports of Larache, Safi and Agadir.[33] By 1576, English trade with Morocco was worth £17,775, equivalent to £3.3 million today. This was twice the value of their trade with Portugal.[34] As a cloth merchant, John Barker would have taken a keen interest in this new and developing market for his wares.

What particularly disturbed the Iberian powers, and what attracted the Earl of Leicester's attention, was the fact that the new Anglo-Moroccan trade was also a trade in arms. The English obtained saltpetre, a key ingredient for making gunpowder, from Morocco. In return, they exported weapons and ammunition. Jehan Scheyfve, the Imperial ambassador to the court of Edward VI, reported to Charles V in 1551 that Thomas Wyndham's cargo contained pikes and armour.[35] In 1574, an intelligencer wrote to Don Luis De Requesens y Zuñiga, the Governor of the Netherlands, that the English took 'great quantities of arms and ammunition to Morocco'.[36] Such reports were explosive at a time when Iberian trading posts in the region were threatened by an increasingly united and powerful Moroccan kingdom. The Papal nuncio in Madrid blamed Queen Elizabeth for the Moroccan victory at the Battle of Alcazar: 'There is no evil that is not devised by that woman, who, it is perfectly plain, succoured Mulocco [Abd Al-Malik] with arms, especially artillery'.[37] England's enemies were equally disturbed that she was receiving a steady supply of saltpetre from Morocco, where it was 'more plenty and better than in any country'.[38] When the merchant Edmund Hogan led an embassy to Morocco in 1577, negotiating a supply of saltpetre was one of his principal concerns. The Earl of Leicester, who had advocated military intervention in the Netherlands and subsequently led an English expedition there, took a keen interest in the supply of Moroccan saltpetre, samples of which he had viewed as early as 1575. In 1581, his agent John Symcot was granted a licence to 'bring into this our realm so much saltpetre as he shall have in exchange in Barbary'.[39] As John Barker acted as a factor for Leicester in the 1570s, it is quite plausible that he played a similar role when the Earl later took an interest in the Barbary trade. Certainly, this connection would go some way towards explaining the arrival of a young Moroccan girl in his household in 1583 or 1584.

In the late 1580s, Barker also became involved in privateering. Although too late to account for Fillis's arrival, this may be how the other Africans came to be in his household. Privateering was essentially piracy by royal approval. When a captain had been robbed at sea, he could be given letters of marque or reprisal by a monarch that authorised him to seize enemy goods equal in value to that which he had lost. In 1586, Barker and some other Ipswich merchants were granted such letters of reprisal, authorising them to recover losses up to £19,000.[40] Privateering was hugely popular amongst Tudor merchants; between 1575 and 1630, far more capital was invested in privateering ventures than in any trading company. An estimated £4.4 million was invested in privateering during this period, £2.9 million in the East India Company, and just £7,100 in the Guinea and Binney Company.[41] Unsurprisingly, privateering tended to peak during periods of war. More than two hundred vessels made reprisal voyages between 1589 and 1591, in the years immediately following the attack of the Spanish Armada.[42]

In 1601, one observer noted that 'great numbers of Negroes and blackamoors . . . are carried into this realm of England since the troubles between her highness and the King of Spain'.[43] Spanish ships almost always had at least a few Africans on board, even if they were not slaving ships. There was an African aboard the *San Pedro Mayor*, wrecked near Salcombe in South Devon in November 1588 after the Armada battle, who died shortly afterwards.[44] In February 1589, the English intercepted the *Francis* of Lisbon on its way home from the Portuguese trading fort at Elmina in modern-day Ghana. As well as a plentiful cargo of meleguetta pepper and gold, they found eight Africans on board.[45] We don't know what became of them, but other such encounters led to Africans being brought back to England; 'two Negroes formerly belonging to Don Luis Vasconcelos' arrived on the Isle of Wight aboard the *Castle of Comfort*, a privateering ship belonging to Sir Henry Compton in November 1571. Their Portuguese master, Vasconcelos, was *en route* to take up the governorship of Brazil but bad weather drove him to the Canaries where he 'and all his people' were 'captured and murdered' by the crew of the *Castle of Comfort* in concert with a crew of French Huguenot corsairs.[46] The two Africans were the only survivors.

The largest group of Africans known to have come to England as a result of privateering in this period arrived in Bristol in October 1590, on a prize (a ship captured legally in war) brought in by her Majesty's ship, the *Charles*.[47] The prize bore 734 chests of sugar and 13 hogsheads of molasses. There were 32 Spaniards and Portuguese and 135 Africans on board. The Bristol authorities put them up in a barn for a week before shipping them back to Spain, asking Lord Burghley for £302 13s 3d to cover their expenses.[48]

Not all Africans who arrived in England in this way were shipped back to their enslavers' lands.[49] A prisoner of war in Spain, John Hill of Stonehouse, Plymouth, was released in 1597 on the condition that he return to England to procure two Africans taken by Captain Clements of Weymouth the year before. He was to return to La Coruña with the Africans or a 'true certificate why they could not be obtained', at which point his fellow prisoners would be released.[50] But Clements had seen no reason to return the Africans, one of whom, according to Hill, was now in the service of Lady Ralegh. Hill asked the Privy Council to allow him to take this man back to Spain with him. Their response to his request is not recorded but presumably, as had been the case with Caspar Van Senden the year before, they told him the African could only be taken with his master's or mistress's consent, a consent the Raleghs were unlikely to have given.

Many merchants engaged in privateering had Africans in their households.[51] In the case of John Barker's neighbour, Paul Bayning, the connection is clear. Bayning was also a parishioner of St Olave Hart Street, in fact his name comes directly after John Barker's in the 1582 tax assessment. The two men must have known each other, especially as John's son, Robert Barker, was a business partner of Bayning's by the mid-1580s. Bayning was one of the leading privateering magnates of his generation, contributing a ship to Drake's attack on Cadiz in 1587, and investing heavily in Sir James Lancaster's 1595 venture to Pernambuco in Brazil and the Earl of Cumberland's Puerto Rico expedition of 1598. In June 1599, his ship the *Golden Phoenix* took a prize ship near Havana and sent it home. The following February she took another near Barbados, which had 125–130 African slaves on board; the English sold them for 60 ounces of pearls at La Margarita.[52]

Bayning had at least five Africans in his household. In 1593 'three maids, blackamores', are recorded as lodging there. In March 1602 'Julyane a blackamore servant with Mr Alderman Bayning' was christened at St Mary Bothaw, half a mile west of St Olave's, close to today's Cannon Street station. In 1609, 'Abell a Blackamor' appeared before the Governors of the Bridewell and was punished for being stubborn and incorrigible. Finally, Bayning's 1616 will mentioned an African servant named Anthony.[53] It is most likely that these Africans ended up in Bayning's household as a direct result of his involvement in privateering. In this, he would have been part a larger trend that included John Barker, and others in London, Southampton and Barnstaple.

The parish of St Olave, Hart Street, where the Barkers and the Baynings lived, saw three baptisms and twelve burials of Africans between 1588 and 1638. The neighbouring church of St Botolph's Aldgate had one baptism (Fillis's) and seventeen burials between 1583 and 1631. Some Africans worked in gentry households, such as Sir William Wynter's servant Domingo, and a man named

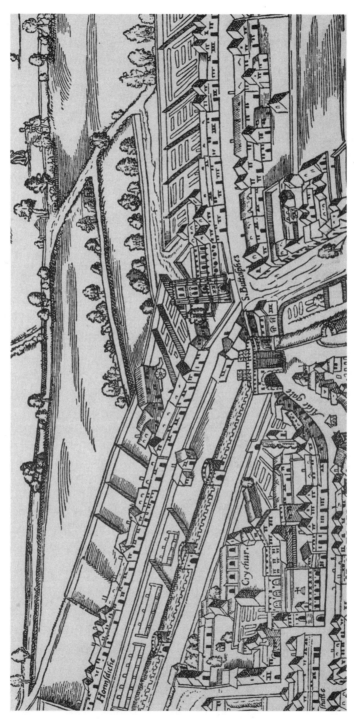

St Botolph's Aldgate in the 1560s.

Robert, who worked for William Matthew, 'a Gentleman dwelling in a garden being behind Mr Quarles his house and near unto Hogg Lane in the liberty of Eastsmithfield'. Others lived with merchants, such as Thomas Barber or the Portuguese *converso* Francis Pinto. And some were in more lowly households, such as those of Peter Miller, a beer-brewer, and Stephen Drifield, the needlemaker mentioned in the last chapter. Still others were not recorded as being part of a household, and could have been financially independent.[54]

Another prominent household in the neighbourhood with African servants was that of Dr Hector Nunes and his wife Leonor. Jewish *conversos*, refugees from the Portuguese Inquisition, they had been resident in Mark Lane since 1549.[55] Nunes was a physician to the court. His patients included William Cecil (Lord Burghley) and his wife. He was also a merchant, importing Spanish wool and Brazilian sugar, and a marine insurance broker. With his trading network and court connections, Nunes was in a good position to provide intelligence to men like Burghley and Walsingham. In September 1578, he sent Burghley a description of the Battle of Alcazar, quoting letters he'd received from Lisbon.[56] He later kept Walsingham informed of the preparations of the Spanish Armada in 1588. Like a handful of the eighty or ninety other *conversos* in London, Nunes and his brother-in-law Ferdinando Alvarez employed black servants. Besides the unnamed 'Ethiopian Negar' Nunes acquired illegally from John Lax of Fowey in 1587, there were three women, Elizabeth, Grace and Mary, working for them between 1576 and 1590.[57] These Africans presumably either came to London with the family from Portugal or arrived later through their Iberian trade connections. When some of Nunes's creditors brought a Chancery lawsuit against him between 1588 and 1596, they tried to discredit him by claiming he and his family still observed Jewish rituals. Thomas Wilson, a former servant of Ferdinando Alvarez, although he had not actually seen anything untoward himself, testified that he was told by 'their blackmores which they kept' that a week before Easter, 'they did commonly . . . light a great wax candle and set the same in a basin with four white loaves about the candle in the midst of a great room in the said Ferdinando's house.' This rather confused description contains elements of Shabbat, Passover and Yom Kippur.[58] Did the Jews consider it sensible to hide their practices from their English servants, while trusting the Africans to keep their secrets?

Of all the Africans living in this area of the City of London at this time, Mary Fillis is the only one known to be from Morocco. Very few were described as being from anywhere in particular; although Sir William Wynter's servant Domingo was said to be from Guinea, this is quite a vague term. The majority probably came from West Africa, arriving in London either via southern Europe or with English privateers. If Mary was the only Moroccan in her neighbourhood, did the locals see her differently to the West African residents? All we know is that the parish clerk, Thomas Harridance, recorded her and her father as dark-skinned 'black mores', the same words used to describe many of the other Africans recorded in the parish, despite the fact that he knew her to be from Morocco. What did Mary and her African neighbours make of each other? They were few enough that we can imagine they knew each other, or had at least a nodding acquaintance on the street or at church.

Morocco would not have seemed quite as foreign to the Londoners of the time as we might imagine. Before the 1620s there were more Britons resident in North Africa than in North America and merchants had brought back accounts of the place since the 1550s.[59] The markets of Safi, Agadir and Marrakesh were known as the source of the delicious sugar, dates and almonds that merchants supplied to the sweet-toothed, and wealthier, people of the capital. News of the Battle of Alcazar not only made it back to Dr Hector Nunes, Fillis's neighbour on Mark Lane, but into London's playhouses. The battle became the inspiration for George Peele's play *The Battle of Alcazar*, as well as *The Famous History of Captain Thomas Stukeley*, whose author remains anonymous.

Thomas Stucley, an English soldier who'd fought and died in the battle, was a playwright's dream. A spendthrift mercenary Catholic and a veteran of the 1571 Battle of Lepanto, he was rumoured to be an illegitimate son of Henry VIII. Burghley accused him of 'the highest degree of vain-glory, prodigality, falsehood and vile and filthy conversation of life . . . altogether without faith, conscience, or religion'.[60] John Barker crossed paths with him *en route* to Lisbon in the spring of 1578, in the course of his work for the Earl of Leicester. He wrote to the earl that 'the King of Portugal doth go for Barbary, and Stucley with him'. Embarking on his doomed expedition was part of Stucley's wider Catholic mission; King Sebastian had promised him that after victory in Morocco, he would join him in an invasion of Ireland. Barker reported that Stucley had 'threatened the English nation'. The plan, backed by Pope Gregory XIII, was to invade Ireland, muster Catholic support there and then launch an attack on England. Stucley was also, according to Barker, giving rosaries to people who came aboard his ship, recommending they used them to pray for 'the reducing of the English nation to the Catholic faith.'[61] Mary Fillis's first employer was well versed in recent Moroccan politics and how they fitted into the wider religious struggle.

By the time Mary Fillis was eleven years old, the people of London no longer needed to look to the stage to see her countrymen. The first Moroccan embassy arrived in London in 1589.[62] Ahmad Bilqasim, known in England as 'Mushac Reyz', landed at St Ives in Cornwall on 1 January 1589 with Henry Roberts, the Queen's ambassador to Morocco. Bilqasim was a Morisco, or Moorish convert to Catholicism, who was born in Spain and spoke fluent Spanish.[63] As Richard Hakluyt later reported, 'the chiefest merchants of the Barbary Company well mounted all on horseback, to the number of 40 or 50 horse' escorted him into the City of London by torchlight on 12 January.[64]

The visit heralded the beginning of a new era in Anglo-Moroccan relations. Where before the main impetus for friendship had been a desire for trade, the deterioration of England's relationship with Spain now gave way to a new and urgent agenda. In September 1579 there was a treatise on 'the intentions of Spain and how the plans of the King of Spain and France may be frustrated by forming a league with the King of Barbary'.[65] A year after the Battle of Alcazar, the threat of Philip II taking the Portuguese crown and its empire was very real, but it was only after the English defeat of the Spanish Armada in 1588 that Al-Mansur began to see Elizabeth I as a credible ally. When news of the Spanish defeat reached Marrakesh, the jubilant English merchants lit bonfires and paraded the streets with a banner they had painted showing Queen Elizabeth triumphant over Philip II. Al-Mansur decided to send an ambassador to the English court at the end of that year. The Spanish ambassador to France, Bernardino de Mendoza, described the visit in a letter to Philip II:

> A man had arrived from Fez to see the Queen and Don Antonio [the pretender to the Portuguese throne], and in order to beguile the people they had christened him ambassador of the Sherriff [Sultan] and asserted that he had brought a great sum of money for Don Antonio. They caused the merchants of London to go out and meet him with 200 horsemen, and the Queen received him with the ceremonial of an ambassador, Don Antonio doing the same, sending him a coach in which to visit him.[66]

Bilqasim's arrival was wonderful news for Don Antonio. His initial hopes for a speedy return to Portugal at the head of an English invading force had been stifled for eight years by a spiral of debt, ill-health, and political and commercial intrigue but the Moroccan envoy's arrival breathed new life into his ambitions.[67] Bilqasim conveyed to the Queen and Don Antonio that his master, Al-Mansur, would provide 'men, money, victuals, and the use of his ports, and his own person' in return for English ships and mariners, and help with strengthening the Moroccan navy. He offered to pay 150,000 ducats towards the expedition, but only once English troops had arrived in Morocco ready to join him in a joint attack on Spain, starting with Spanish-occupied Tangier.[68]

In April, Bilqasim left England 'dressed as a Portuguese' on the expedition led by Francis Drake and John Norris to Portugal. They aimed to exact revenge on the Spaniards for the Armada attack and put Don Antonio back on the throne. Bilqasim's objective, according to a Spanish spy known as 'David', was 'to carry the news of the landing to the Sheriff [Al-Mansur] who will then send a force of Moors, or perhaps try to land them in Andalusia'.[69] From the start, the expedition was a fiasco; an over-ambitious amalgamation of conflicting objectives. The Queen's priority was to destroy the remaining Armada ships sheltered in the ports of Santander and San Sebastian; Don Antonio wanted to seize the throne in Lisbon; Walsingham and Drake had their eyes on the Spanish silver fleet in the Azores. In the end, no one got what they wanted.

Drake and Norris wasted two weeks in a fruitless siege of La Coruña. The invading force decided to march on Lisbon from Peniche, forty-five miles to the north, costing them both the element of surprise and the lives of several men who died on the road due to heat, hunger and sickness. On top of that, the people of Portugal showed little interest in having 'King Antonio' restored to them. The English abandoned the idea of the Azores and returned home in disarray in July, having lost dozens of ships and thousands of men.[70] The promised help from the Moroccans had not materialised. Edward Perrin, who'd been sent to collect money from Barbary, reported 'the Moor would never give a real'.[71] The English and the Moroccans might have shared a common enemy, but they did not share a common plan of attack. England simply did not have the resources or the inclination to aid Al-Mansur in the joint land invasion of Tangier and Andalusia that he had envisaged.

Mary Fillis had more immediate concerns that summer. Early in June, John Barker died. He left neither her, nor any of his other servants, anything in his will.[72] After his death, Mary worked for his widow for several years.

By the time Mary Fillis was nineteen, Morocco was once again a potential ally in the ongoing struggle against Spain. But on this occasion Al-Mansur made a more substantial effort to aid the English. He was better placed to do so, following his successful subjugation of the rich Songhai Empire. In the summer of 1596, he sent three galleys with supplies to support the English attack on the port of Cadiz, which was being led by Lord Thomas Howard and Sir Walter Ralegh, and dispatched ships to carry out a simultaneous attack on the Spanish in the Canaries. This joint offensive may have been negotiated by an ambassador to London in 1595, but this embassy is only referred to in a letter from an English merchant in Morocco; there is no record of a Moroccan delegation arriving in England. Al-Fishtali, a court scribe in Marrakesh, wrote that Al-Mansur 'may God be with him, prepared for jihad against the enemy of religion [Philip II] to punish him for what he had done to Islam'.[73] Besides sending ships, Al-Mansur 'showed her [Elizabeth I] his willingness to help confront him [Philip II] by supplying her with copper to cast cannons, and saltpetre for ammunition, which he permitted her to buy from his noble kingdoms. He also supplied her with metals that were not found in her lands'.[74]

The attack on Cadiz was a success. The English sacked the city, the Spanish fleet was burnt and many Spaniards were taken hostage. English accounts didn't give Al-Mansur as much credit for the victory as Al-Fishtali, but nonetheless, Morocco had finally proved herself as a military ally. Later that year, Shakespeare included a 'Prince of Morocco' as one of Portia's three suitors in *The Merchant of Venice*. The prince makes the wildly exaggerated boast that with his scimitar he not only killed the Shah of Persia, but bested the Ottoman Sultan, Suleiman the Magnificent, in the field three times.[75]

By 1597 Mary Fillis had left the service of Widow Barker, and was the servant of Millicent Porter, a seamstress dwelling in East Smithfield. East Smithfield, in Middlesex, was a village surrounded by fields. It lay just outside the city walls and was beyond the jurisdiction of the City authorities. The village had a community of foreigners, mostly Dutch and French, who used St Katherine's Docks to unload their cargoes, as they were not allowed to do so inside the City. The nearby Cistercian monastery, which Edward III had established to commemorate the victims of the Black Death buried in the plague pits there, had been surrendered in 'the late general suppression' of the monasteries under Henry VIII. In 1560, the Navy Victuallers Yard, 'a large storehouse for victuals, and convenient ovens, for baking of biscuits to serve her majesty's ships' was built in its place.[76]

Millicent Porter lived in 'Mr Crew's rents', accommodation rented from one of the family of bakers of that name, who probably baked biscuits for the Navy.[77] Her immediate neighbours included Edward Harwin, an embroiderer and 'drawer of linen cloth', William Pearce, a gentleman and sea captain, and John Pavy, a clerk of the Ordnance in the Tower. In 1597, she was fifty-eight years old and a widow. Her daughter had the uncommon name of Lucrezia, presumably not out of an admiration for the infamous Lucrezia Borgia, nor in homage to the ninth-century Spanish martyr Lucrezius.[78] Lucrezia Porter had married a local beer brewer's clerk, Robert Whitaker, in 1594, and provided Millicent with three granddaughters, the third of whom was also named Millicent. The newlyweds initially moved in with Widow Porter, but by 1596 they had moved to rented accommodation in Nightingale Lane. Widow Porter had recently lost two young servant girls to consumption: Frances Warkeup, aged ten, in June 1595, and seven months later the twelve-year-old Margaret Nynnie. Their deaths left a vacancy, which was filled by Mary Fillis.

Why did Fillis move from a wealthy merchant household to the lowlier establishment of a seamstress? Mrs Barker lived until 1610, so it was not a result of her death. The move suggests that Mary was able to choose her employer. Maybe she met Millicent Porter when the seamstress made some dresses for Mrs Barker, the wealthy widow. Working for Widow Porter gave her the opportunity to learn a trade. As the seamstress did not have a large household, she would be heavily reliant on Mary Fillis for help with everything from household chores to the more skilled aspects of her profession. Fillis would doubtless have learnt to sew, to make and mend clothes, and develop an appreciation for the intricacies of Tudor dress. Her work for Mrs Porter puts paid to the popular assumption that African servants of this time were mere playthings for the aristocracy. The domestic servants we know of were doing practical work in a range of households, from the likes of White Cross Manor, where Edward Swarthye was one of many servants, to much more lowly establishments such as Millicent Porter's, where Mary Fillis was probably her only employee.

* * *

When Fillis started working for Millicent Porter, she, 'now taking some hold of faith in Jesus Christ, was desirous to become a Christian.' It would seem that the Barker family had not thought it necessary to provide their young maid with a Christian education during her first thirteen years in England but Millicent Porter encouraged Fillis in her faith. She went to the curate of St Botolph's Aldgate to arrange for Fillis to talk to him. Later, she became Fillis's godmother. In 1584, the then forty-five-year-old Millicent Porter had been charged with being 'one that liveth very suspiciously', and had done public penance at St Paul's, despite denying she was 'guilty of fornication or adultery'. Could this experience have made her one of those reformed characters that make the most zealous evangelicals?[79] However, it is the Barkers' lack of interest that is more surprising, given the intense religiosity of the times. Did they really not care or were they merely waiting until Fillis was old enough to fully understand the significance of baptism?

Millicent Porter had good reason to consider it her duty to give Mary Fillis a Christian education. The Book of Common Prayer exhorted that not only 'fathers and mothers', but also 'masters, and dames' should ensure that 'their children, servants, and apprentices (which have not learned their Catechism)*' went to 'Church at the time appointed, and obediently to hear, and be ordered by the Curate, until such time as they have learned all that is here appointed for them to learn'.[80] Christopher Threlkeld, the curate of St Botolph's Aldgate, also had a special interest. A few years before the Bishop had specifically admonished him to catechise children, apprentices and servants.[81]

Mary Fillis had many opportunities to hear the word of God. In the year leading up to her baptism on 3 June 1597 there were on average seven sermons a month at St Botolph's Aldgate. They were often preached at funerals, and sometimes twice on Sundays. Threlkeld was a regular preacher, but the parish also received sermons from a range of visiting lecturers, some boasting an Oxford

---

* A summary of the Christian faith in the form of questions and answers, used for instruction.

or Cambridge education, some from neighbouring parishes and some at the invitation of members of the congregation.

As well as Millicent Porter, Fillis's other godparents were William Benton and Margery Barrick. This was a serious responsibility. The Book of Common Prayer stated that godparents should ensure the child understood 'what a solemn vow, promise, and profession he hath made', and encourage him or her to hear sermons. They were to see to it that the child learnt the creed, the Lord's Prayer and the Ten Commandments 'and all other things which a Christian man ought to know, and believe to his soul's health'. It was their duty to see 'that this child may be virtuously brought up, to lead a godly, and a Christian life'.[82] Although Mary was no longer a child, this duty of care would have remained, and wouldn't have been taken lightly by god-fearing people.

Millicent Porter's support of Mary Fillis's conversion is placed in sharp relief by an episode that occurred in eighteenth-century Westminster. In November 1760, *Lloyd's Evening Post* reported:

> Last week a Negro girl about nine years old, having eloped from her mistress on account of ill-usage, was brought to a Church in Westminster by two housekeepers, to be baptized. But the mistress of the girl, getting intelligence of it, while the Minister was reading the churching service, seized upon her in the face of the congregation and violently forced her out of the Church, regardless of her cries and tears; telling the people about her that she was her slave, and would use her as she pleased.[83]

Despite the woman's assertion, no positive statute law was ever passed to legalise slavery in England. By the final quarter of the seventeenth century the legal status of Africans who had been enslaved in the colonies, but were then brought to England, was a vexed question that was not to be truly resolved until slavery was abolished throughout the British Empire in 1834. When the question came before English judges, however, a key element of the deliberation was often the religious status of the African or Africans involved. Therefore, this woman's aversion to the girl being baptised sprang from the fear that, in seeking to become a Christian, the girl was trying to confirm her freedom.

It had long been held invidious to enslave Christians. In his Bull *Sicut dudum* of 1435, Pope Eugenius IV sentenced to excommunication 'all who attempt to capture, sell, or subject to slavery, baptised residents of the Canary Islands, or those who are freely seeking Baptism'. The scholar and diplomat Thomas Smith explained in his *De Republica Anglorum* of 1583 that when the English became Christian 'men began to have conscience to hold in captivity and such extreme bondage him whom he must acknowledge to be his brother . . . that is who looketh in Christ and by Christ to have equal portion with me in the Gospel and salvation'. He was discussing the manumission of villeins, the feudal serfs of medieval England, but the idea that fellow Christians should not be enslaved was also applied to Africans. In 1624, the General Court of Virginia ruled that 'John Phillip a negro' was qualified, as a free man and a Christian, to give testimony because he had been 'Christened in England 12 years since'.[84] But as slavery developed in the colonies, such principles became impossible to uphold. In 1667, the Virginia Assembly declared that conversion to Christianity would not give an African freedom, implying that it previously had.[85]

The Protestant ideal of a personal faith, based on an understanding of the scriptures, meant that Mary Fillis and others like her could not just convert on the spot. They had to be educated to a level where they could understand the basic tenets of the religion and convince clergymen and the congregation of their faith.[86] Other employers also took the responsibility to educate their servants in their faith seriously. When Paul Bayning died on 30 September 1616, he bequeathed £10 to John Simpson, the minister of St Olave, Hart Street, of which half was to be used for 'instructing Anthony my Negro in the principles of the Christian faith and religion when he shall be fit to be baptised'.[87]

How the process of conversion worked in practice can be seen in the case of an Indian boy brought to Kent in 1633 from Armagon on the Coromandel Coast by an East India merchant named Nicholas Bix. Over the next two years, the boy was 'instructed in the English tongue', and 'catechised in the rudiments of Christian religion'. He regularly attended church, where he was 'a diligent hearer of the word preached' and 'joined with the congregation in prayers'. In July 1635, when he was thirteen, a petition was submitted on his behalf to the Canterbury Archdeaconry Court, asking for a baptism licence. Reginald Ansell, the parson of Fordwich, certified that the boy 'doth now desire to be baptised & to be made a member of the Church'. The licence was granted, and the very next day, an 'Indian Manchild of 14 years old, of Armagon', was baptised 'Thomas' at St Mary, Fordwich.[88]

Thomas Harridance said Mary Fillis was 'desirous to become a Christian'. On the occasion of her baptism, the curate, Christopher Threlkeld, specifically 'demanded of her if she were desirous to be baptized in the said faith', it being necessary to confirm the will-ingness to become a Christian. This inclination is often emphasised in contemporary accounts of conversions.[89] When Pocahontas was baptised in Virginia in 1614, the colony's Governor, Sir Thomas Dale, not only records her education in the religion, but also her wish to convert:

> Powhatan's daughter I caused to be carefully instructed in Christian Religion . . . who after she had made some good progress therein, renounced publicly her country Idolatry, openly confessed her Christian faith, [and] was, as she desired, baptised.[90]

Edward Terrill, a member of the Baptist church led by Nathaniel Ingelo in Bristol, also emphasised this desire in his account of an African woman named Frances, who joined the congregation in the 1640s. She was, he said, 'truly convinced of Sin' and 'truly converted to ye Lord Jesus Christ':

> which by her profession or declaration at ye time of her reception together with her sincere conversation she gave great ground for charity to believe she was truly brought to Christ; for this poor Aethiopian's soule savoured much of God, and she walked very humble and blameless in her Conversation to her end.[91]

Of course, it is not always easy to unpick the true motivations of the convert from the zeal of the author in these accounts.

What were Mary Fillis's motivations? She was a foreigner, which might well have caused those she met to question her religious identity. Public baptism would go some way towards dispelling such suspicion, at least amongst her fellow parishioners. In Morocco, Mary would have been born into a Muslim family, yet she was so young when she came to England that she is unlikely to have retained much of that faith, which she couldn't have practised openly in London. She grew up amidst a zealously Protestant population, who marked out their lives by the Church. She may truly have believed in a Christian God; her new mistress may have asked her about her faith for the first time and given her the opportunity to make it official. Protestant Christianity was not only a private conviction, but a very public indicator of full participation in post-Reformation Tudor society.[92] Anyone who had not been baptised would never be fully accepted as a member of the community. On a more personal level, the ritual of baptism, with the acquisition of godparents and the approbation of the congregation, signalled an acceptance into the parish, and would have strengthened Fillis's relationships with her neighbours.

One good reason for Fillis to become a Christian would be so that she could get married, or at least be able to marry if she met someone. Although most of the known examples of inter-racial marriage at this time are between African men and English women, it also happened the other way round. In August 1600, the parish register of St Philip and St Jacob, Bristol, recorded the baptism of 'Richard a Bastard, the son of Joane Maria a Black Moore & now the wife of Thomas Smythe'.[93] Smythe was a skilled craftsman who made a living making 'bills', polearm weapons similar to the halberd but with a hooked blade.[94] In marrying him, Joane would have gained a certain level of social status. Whether Thomas Smythe was Richard's father or not isn't clear, but the child's existence had not prevented Joane Maria from marrying. There was a Biblical precedent; according to the popular Geneva translation, Moses had married 'a woman of Ethiopia'.[95]

It was not at all uncommon for Africans in England to be baptised as adults. When Christopher Adam was christened in Chislehurst, Kent, in April 1593, he was noted to be 'a man grown'. Some parish register entries record exact ages. Gylman Ivie was thirty at his baptism in Dyrham, Gloucestershire, in 1575. Julyane, one of Paul Bayning's maids, was baptised at the 'age of 22 years' in 1602. In other cases, we can deduce that individuals were adults because they are recorded as getting married or giving birth shortly afterwards. 'Grace (a blackmore)' was baptised in Hatherleigh in May 1604, and had a child two years later in August 1606.[96]

When a person is baptised as an adult they are conscious, in a way that a baby cannot be, of what they are doing. When Fillis was asked to say the Lord's Prayer at her baptism, she demonstrated her knowledge of the faith. The ritual was actually more like that usually required at a confirmation, which was to be performed as 'soon as the children can say in their mother tongue, the articles of the faith, the Lordes prayer, the ten commandments, and also can answer to such questions of this short Catechism'.[97] The confession of the faith was a specific requirement laid out by the French theologian John Calvin in *The institution of the Christian religion*, first translated into English in 1561. He insisted that the ritual had to signal a personal spiritual acceptance of God, and be as far from the 'stage-like pomps, which dazzle the eyes of the simple and dull their minds' that he associated with Catholic practice.[98]

The conversion of an African was a deeply significant occasion for the Church of England and its ministers, as was reflected in the sermon preached by Meredith Hanmer, the vicar of St Leonard's Shoreditch, on the occasion of the baptism of Chinano in October 1586. Chinano was one of the hundred Turks recently released from Spanish enslavement in Cartagena by Francis Drake. Originally from Chalcis, the capital of the Greek island of Euboea, which had been under Turkish rule since 1470, he spent twenty-five years enslaved and was forty years old by the time he was once again free. At the Hospital of St Katherine by the Tower, Meredith Hanmer contrasted Chinano's conversion to Protestant Christianity with the fact that he had refused to convert to Spanish Catholicism during his captivity. After his arrival in England, Hanmer reports that Chinano saw:

courtesy, gentleness, friendly salutations of the people, succour for him and his countrymen, pity and compassion of the Englishmen, and withal he learned that the poor, the aged, the impotent, the sick and diseased Christians were provided for, whereas in his country and where he had been in captivity the poor, sick and diseased were scorned, despised and accounted of as dogs.

He was said to have concluded that 'if there was not a God in England, there was none nowhere'. The experience of coming to England should, preached Hanmer, result in conversions like this. The English people should do their best to inspire such thoughts. England should set an example, as Jesus said in the Sermon on the Mount: be 'the light of the world', 'a city that is set on a hill' and so 'cannot be hid'. 'And whereas now one silly [insignificant] Turk is won', Hanmer declared, 'ten thousands no doubt would receive the faith'.[99]

Edward Terrill was similarly enthused in his account of Frances's baptism in Bristol. For him, her conversion was an eloquent confirmation of his faith, and the universality of God's word. He concluded his account with the remark that Frances's Christianity showed 'Experimentally, that scripture made good . . . that is, God is no respecter of faces: But among all nations, &c. Acts X 34: 35'.[100] The biblical passage he cited reads:

> Then Peter opened his mouth, and said, Of a truth I perceive that God is no respecter of persons: But in every nation he that feareth him, and worketh righteousness, is accepted with him.[101]

Terrill emphasised that Christianity is for everyone, and was more than happy to recognise Africans as members of his church. His approach was part of a wider evangelical mission to expand Christianity's reach across the world, which can also be seen by Spanish, Portuguese and, latterly, English efforts to baptise the 'noble savages' they found in the Americas.

To some, these baptisms, and the giving of Christian names, seem an effacement of African identity, an arrogant assertion of

English cultural superiority.[102] These arguments are rooted in a modern political perspective that would have made no sense to the Tudors. This was a time when people died for their faith. They believed there was only one way to heaven, and that by bringing Africans into their church they were saving their lives. Not only religious men believed this. In 1621, William Bragge, a merchant and privateer, who had encountered a group of thirteen 'heathens . . . negroes or Indian people' in Bermuda a few years before, wrote that they were: 'Created after the Image, Similitude, and Likeness of God, our most heavenly, most sweet Comforter, whom in Troubles is ready always to be found'. He explained that:

> the Lord Jesus hath suffered Death as well for them as for all you, for in time the Lord may call them to be true Christians, the which I most humbly beseech thy Great and Glorious Majesty in Thy good appointed Time, that thou wilt, Good Father, out of Thy most great, sweet and careful Love call them all home in Thy most good appointed Time, most merciful and most loving sweet Father, which must Good Lord be done, if it pleaseth Thy great and glorious Majesty, before that most heavenly kingdom of thine is finished . . .

This heartfelt prayer, which continues for another two paragraphs, shows that the ideal of conversion had spread beyond the pulpit.[103] It was so universal a precept that it was even followed by William Longcastle who, as we saw in Chapter Two, was so impious as to be hanged as a pirate in 1609. He had baptised the African boy who later testified against him, an act pronounced as 'the most virtuous & blessedst deed that he did show in his whole life'.[104]

Baptism was a public event, witnessed by the whole parish community. According to John Calvin, the person to be baptised should be 'presented to the whole assembly of the faithful, and be offered to God, the whole Church looking on as a witness: and praying over him'.[105] The Book of Common Prayer stipulated that christenings should take place on Sundays and other holy days, 'when the most number of people may come together' so that the 'congregation there present may testify the receiving of them that be newly Baptized into the number of Christ's Church'.[106] Although Mary Fillis was baptised on a Friday, many people attended. As well as her godparents, others present at the ceremony were the curate's wife, Mrs Magdalene Threlkeld, Matthew Pearson, Mrs Young, Thomas Ponder, the sexton and his wife Gertrude, Thomas Harridance and 'divers others'. Similarly, in 1621, Maria, a five-year-old black girl who had come from Spain with the courtier Endymion Porter, was baptised '*in presentia multos*' (in the presence of many) at St Martin in the Fields, Westminster.[107]

The large congregations who bore witness to these events testify to the curiosity of parishioners keen to witness a relatively unusual event, but they also represent a ritualised welcoming of the new convert into the wider community. The words of the ceremony ordained that the convert was now 'regenerate' and would be 'grafted into the body of Christ's congregation'.[108] Frances's experience of the Baptist church in Bristol in the late 1640s illustrates how an African could become an accepted member of a community in this way. Having become a full member of the church, she was not forgotten by her friends as she lay on her deathbed:

> one of the Sisters of the Congregation, coming to visit her in her Sickness, she solemnly took her leave of her, as to this world, and prayed the Sister to remember her to the whole Congregation.[109]

After baptism, an African convert would take part in parish life, attending church regularly and interacting with other members of the congregation, as Thomas, the Indian boy brought to Kent by Nicholas Bix, had begun to do before his baptism.[110] Mary Fillis's baptism, and those of more than sixty other Africans recorded in this period, directly contradict the impression historians have previously gleaned from a draft proclamation of 1601 that asserted that 'most of them are infidels, having no understanding of Christ or his Gospel'.[111] This document, presumably penned by Caspar Van Senden and Sir Thomas Sherley, was a draft designed to be of 'some stronger purpose' than the 1596 Privy Council letter that granted

Van Senden a limited licence to transport individuals out of England with their masters' consent. The proposed draft of 1601 insisted that:

> if there be any person or persons which be possessed of any such blackamoores that refused to deliver them in sort aforesaid, then we require you to call them before you to advise and persuade them by all good means . . . if they shall eftsoons wilfully and obstinately refuse, we pray you to certify their names to us to the end her majesty may take such further course therein as it shall seem best in her princely wisdom.

This proclamation was never published. Robert Cecil, the Queen's Secretary of State, who himself had an African servant named Fortunatus, 'thought it not meet to have those kind taken from their masters compulsorily'.* Van Senden and Sherley tried to depict Africans as irreligious outsiders, but the parish registers across England tell a different tale.[112]

Two years after Mary Fillis was baptised, Millicent Porter died. She was buried at St Botolph's Aldgate on 28 June 1599. Thomas Harridance noted in his memorandum book that she had been 'long sick'; Fillis may well have taken on the burden of nursing her through her long illness. Porter was buried in the middle of the south churchyard and bells were rung. Four bearers, Thomas Harridance and the sexton, Thomas Ponder, were paid for their attendance. Presumably Mary Fillis was there too. A sermon was preached at the funeral by John Fulthorpe, a minister recently returned from a journey to 'the North Country some twenty miles beyond Newcastle'. His text was Acts 9:36, which tells the story of how St Peter resurrected a woman named Dorcas or Tabitha of Joppa (now Jaffa, part of modern-day Tel Aviv), who was a seamstress. If Fulthorpe drew a parallel with Dorcas's 'good works and

---

* 'Fortunatus, a blackmoore of the age of 17 or 18 years' was baptised at Cheshunt, near the Cecil house, Theobalds, in April 1570 and buried at St Clement Danes, London, in January 1602.

alms deeds', then it would seem that Widow Porter's reputation had recovered significantly in the parish since she was accused of fornication in 1584.

The year after Millicent Porter died, a new embassy from Morocco visited London. This ambassador is better known than his predecessors since he had his portrait painted during his visit. Abd-al-Wahid bin Masoud bin Muhammad al-Annuri, and fourteen others, arrived 'very strangely attired and behavioured' in August 1600. They stayed at Alderman Anthony Radcliffe's house near the Royal Exchange for six months, their food and 'all other provisions' paid for by the Queen. Radcliffe was Master of the Guild of Merchant Taylors; his daughter Ann later became an early benefactor of Harvard University, giving the family name to Radcliffe College. The Moroccans kept Halal, as John Stow observed that they killed all their own meat 'and turn their faces eastwards when they kill anything'. He criticised them for selling, rather than giving away, their leftover food to the poor. As their stay wore on, London merchants began to worry they were collecting information about the price of goods, which could prove injurious to English profits in future.[113]

Ultimately, the embassy was sabotaged by the Queen, who tried to enlist the ambassadors as mercenary soldiers without the involvement of their Moroccan lord. Al-Annuri refused, but other members of the party were tempted. The foremost were Hajj Mesa, an elder statesman, and Abdullah Dudar, an interpreter. Dudar had served as a mercenary in Italy, and now employed the Italian language to plot with the Queen. Rumours later circulated that al-Annuri and his advisers had poisoned both Mesa and Dudar. The newsletter-writer John Chamberlain reported unsympathetically on Mesa's death: 'the eldest of them, which was a kind of priest or prophet, hath taken his leave of the world and is gone to prophecy apud infernos [in Hell] and to seek out Mahomet their mediator'.[114] This same hostility meant the embassy had some trouble returning home. Chamberlain wrote that the English merchants and mariners refused to take them 'because they think it is a matter odious and scandalous to the world to be friendly or familiar with Infidels'.

The English Queen was not the only Christian ruler to overlook doctrinal differences when choosing allies. The French King Francis I had showed no scruples in joining forces with the Ottoman Sultan, Suleiman the Magnificent, against Charles V.[115] Chamberlain was obviously in two minds about the Moroccan alliance, as he went on to say that it was an honour 'that nations so far removed and every way different should meet here to admire the glory and magnificence of our Queen of Saba [Sheba]'.[116] The prejudice here was not racial, but religious, albeit the two are not always easily disentangled.

English readers had the opportunity to learn more about Morocco in 1600, when a Cambridge scholar, John Pory, published his translation of Leo Africanus's *Description of Africa* at the behest of Richard Hakluyt. Africanus had grown up and studied in Fez, before being captured by Spanish pirates and presented to Pope Leo X in Rome in 1520. He was freed and baptised by the Pope, who became his godfather, and stayed in Rome for some years, writing his book in Italian in 1526.[117] Pory dedicated his translation to Robert Cecil, noting that 'at this time especially I thought [it] would prove to be acceptable: in that the Moroccan ambassador (whose King's dominions are here most amply and particularly described) hath so lately treated with your Honour concerning matters of that estate'.[118] Africanus's account was especially detailed in its description of Morocco and the parts of North Africa he knew well. It bristled with information that would be useful to merchants, such as local produce and languages, and to statesmen, such as recent political history and military capability. Of course, by 1600 much of this information was out of date, so Pory did his best to update and expand on the original text. He also indicated that some of his readers may already be 'as well . . . informed as myself', suggesting that the English, or at least a small literate elite, were not entirely ignorant of Morocco and other parts of Africa by the close of the century.

When Al-Mansur heard the disastrous outcome of the embassy, he wrote angrily to the Queen that his ambassadors had told him all about her plans to circumvent him and enlist them as mercenaries: 'We listened with attentive ears until we understood them all, and became alert to all you had plotted'. England's relationship with Morocco deteriorated further after the deaths of both their rulers. In April 1603, Henry Roberts, English ambassador in Morocco between 1585 and 1589, wrote to James I urging him to conquer Barbary for King and Christ.[119]

After Millicent Porter's death, we lose sight of Mary Fillis. By this time she had no doubt learnt enough about making clothes to either be a useful addition to another seamstress's establishment, or be able to survive on her own account.

There are two burial records for African women named Mary in the parish registers of St Botolph's Aldgate: in 1623, when Fillis would have been forty-six, and in 1631, when she would have been fifty-four.[120] Mary was a fairly common name, so there is no way to definitively identify either woman as Mary Fillis. However, there are no other known records of African women named Mary in the City of London at this time. Both women were described as poor. The first, buried on 4 November 1623, was described as a 'poor woman being a Blacke Moore, Named Marie, who died in the street in Rosemary Lane'.[121] The second Mary, Mary Peters, interred on 16 February 1631, was described as 'a poor blackamore woman at Tower Hill'.[122] Could Mary Fillis have married a Mr Peters? A 'Christian Peters' appears in a list of people that received communion at St Botolph's Aldgate on Easter Sunday 1596, but no other record of him, or a wife, remains.

Whatever her fate, during her lifetime, which might have lasted into the 1620s or 30s, Mary Fillis witnessed the relationship between her native and adopted countries develop and change. She was born at a time of civil war, and probably lived to hear that Morocco had descended into that state once more after the death of Al-Mansur. She witnessed the evolution of a trading partner into a military ally, and the accompanying diplomacy. The excitement of the arrival of the Moroccan embassies in London in 1589 and 1600 might well have prompted curious questions from her neighbours and acquaintances.

As trade and contact with Morocco grew, English merchants had begun to travel further down the west coast of Africa, to

Guinea, Benin and, by the early seventeenth century, as far as South Africa, as they passed around the continent on their early voyages to the East Indies. These expeditions created opportunities for Africans to visit England directly from their own continent. The English intended to train them as interpreters and trade factors, but these men had their own agendas. Often of high birth, some were members of African royal families, such as Dederi Jaquoah, Prince of River Cestos, who was christened in London in 1611.

7

Dederi Jaquoah,
the Prince of River Cestos

*'Father, the English have arrived.' King Caddi-biah smiled at
his son. 'Yes, I know. Go to them, entertain them well, and
perhaps we will get what we want.' Prince Dederi Jaquoah
put on his cap and set off down river in his canoe with a
handful of his men to greet the visitors. The English, sweating
in their linen and hose, took them aboard their ship and
received their gifts of fruits, rice, ivory tusks and grains of
paradise. 'A-quio!' began one of the merchants, before
resorting to English, spoken in the slow and deliberate tone
of a man not sure if he would be understood. 'My name is
Edward Blitheman. I am a merchant of the East India
Company. We have stopped here to refresh ourselves on our
long journey to the Spice Islands of the East.' The Prince
smiled and held out his hand. 'Hello Mr Blitheman. I am
John Davies.' The Englishman gaped on hearing his mother
tongue fluently spoken and seeing the hand proffered in
greeting as it was at home. The Prince smiled again, in a
welcoming fashion, but privately enjoying the man's discom-
fiture and amazement. 'I spent two years in London, sir. With
Mr Davies at the Stocks.' 'Davies? The Haberdasher? The
Guinea merchant? Well, that explains why your English is so
good.' 'He taught me well', replied the Prince. 'Now, my good
sir, your General must come ashore and meet my father. The
King looks forward to welcoming you after your long journey.'*

ALONGSIDE THE REGULAR trade to Morocco the English developed in the second half of the sixteenth century, they began making forays further south, to the parts of West Africa they called 'Guinea'. As a result of this trade, some West Africans were brought to England, later to return home. Were men such as Dederi Jaquoah taken by force or did they come willingly? The idea of English merchants taking Africans away from their homes immediately conjures images of shackled men and women crammed into the confines of a ship's hold, of the backbreaking monotonous work, physical exploitation and mental persecution if they survived the crossing. The Swahili word *maafa*, meaning 'great disaster' or 'terrible occurrence', comes closer to describing the horrific enterprise that killed millions of Africans over three centuries than sanitised terms such as 'the slave trade'.[1]

Dederi Jaquoah's was a different experience. With the notable exception of John Hawkins's voyages in the 1560s, the Tudor and early Stuart trade with Africa was not about buying and selling people. What then was the nature of the early Anglo-African trade? If those Africans who travelled to England on merchants' ships were not taken by force, why did they embark on such a long and dangerous journey?

Prince Dederi Jaquoah was born around the year 1591. He was the son of Caddi-biah, King of River Cestos.[2] This river meets the Atlantic at the modern-day town of River Cess, south-east of Monrovia in Liberia, in between the states now known as Sierra Leone and Ivory Coast. Caddi-biah's kingdom stretched along the coast from the St John River to 'Croe', close to the present-day town of Settra Kru.[3] The coastline was flat and heavily wooded, as were the river's banks: 'on both sides it is set very pleasantly with Trees, very large and very tall'.[4] The narrow entrance to the river was marked by a ledge of rocks to the south-east, and another large rock in the 'havens mouth right as you enter'.[5] The King and his subjects were the most southern of the Kru people, known as 'Zeguebos'. They spoke a variant of a language called Kra, in which the people ('*bo*') addressed their leader as '*dabo*'.[6] The small village where Caddi-biah and his family lived was surrounded by palm and banana trees, and situated just a few miles up the River Cestos on the north-west bank. Dederi's mother would have been one of his father's many wives. As he was growing up, Jaquoah wore a cap to signify his princely status.[7] He ate the typical children's porridge made of boiled yams, and learnt how to navigate a canoe and catch the plentiful mullet, loach, pike, sardines, sole and other fish that frequented the river. One fish had a dart on its tail that was used to make arrowheads.

This late-seventeenth century map of River Cestos, drawn by French trader Jean Barbot, shows 'The King's Town', home to King Caddi-biah and his son Dederi Jacquoah.

King Caddi-biah, and his fathers before him, were well accustomed to trading with Europeans. It was the Portuguese who gave the river the name we now know it by in 1461. According to the Portuguese explorer Duarte Pacheco Pereira, writing in the early sixteenth century: 'the name is due to the fact that the negroes of this country come to the ships to sell pepper (which is very good and very plentiful here) in baskets, which they do not do elsewhere on the coast where this pepper is sold'.[8] *Cestos* is the Portuguese for 'basket'. These baskets were also used as a unit of measuring quantities of pepper. This was meleguetta pepper (*aframomum melegueta*) or 'grains of paradise'. Quite different to the black pepper (*piper nigrum*) native to South-East Asia, this spice, a member of the ginger family, was widely used in Europe. In England it was thought to revive stale wine and ale, and to have medicinal qualities. In *The Canterbury Tales*, the 'jolly lover' Absalom chews it with liquorice to freshen his breath before visiting Alison, the carpenter's young wife.[9] The plentiful meleguetta pepper gave its name to the whole coast. The Portuguese called it the *Meleguetta* Coast, the French *Meleguette*, and it was later anglicised as the 'Grain Coast'.[10] As one English merchant explained in an account of 1553, at 'the great river of Sesto', he found for sale:

> the grains of that country, which is a very hot fruit, and much like unto a fig as it groweth on the tree. For as the figs are full of small seeds, so is the said fruit full of grains, which are loose within the cod, having in the midst thereof a hole on every side. This kind of spice is much used in cold countries, & may there be sold for great advantage, for exchange of other wares.[11]

A century later, the French merchant Jean Barbot commented that the meleguetta pepper pods that grew on the River Cestos were 'the largest of all this part of the pepper coast'.[12]

It must have been quite a shock the first time Jaquoah's countrymen saw the pale Europeans. When Alvise Cadamosto, a Venetian merchant in Portuguese employ, went ashore on the Senegal River in 1455 'some touched my hands and limbs, and rubbed me with their spittle to discover whether my whiteness was dye or flesh'. In many African cultures, for example the Kongolese, white was the colour of the underworld. In their cosmology, the world of the living and the world of the dead were separated by water, and so the fact that the Europeans arrived from across the sea, together with their white skin and their powerful weapons, gave an impression of ghosts, evil spirits or wizards. To some, the threat they posed seemed more visceral. The Gambians believed that 'Christians ate human flesh, and . . . only bought blacks to eat them'.[13] These fears were coupled with fascination and the desire to acquire European goods and technologies. Over time, it became clear that the Europeans were more or less human, and could be useful trading partners.

The people of River Cestos began a regular trade with the Portuguese in meleguetta pepper, ivory and slaves. It did not take long for the Cestos merchants to realise the value of their goods to the strangers, and they quickly raised their prices. Pacheco complained in 1505 that one *alquier* of meleguetta pepper now cost five or six *manillas*, where previously it had been one. The price of one slave also rose, from two metal shaving basins to four or five.[14]

For almost a century, the Portuguese enjoyed a monopoly on the African trade. By 1530, however, French and English traders were beginning to frequent the coast. In the time of Louis XIV, the French claimed that merchants from Dieppe and Rouen had in fact discovered this area, naming River Cestos '*Petite Dieppe*' in 1364: a fabrication intended to justify that King's desire for territory in West Africa. For the kings of Cestos, new customers meant more bargaining power. The French merchants did their best to ingratiate themselves by offering better gifts than the Portuguese. Although the Portuguese had no trading forts in the River Cestos area, they fiercely defended their monopoly, resulting in regular confrontations with the newcomers. In 1557, the people of River Cestos witnessed three French ships attack and burn a Portuguese caravel, killing the entire crew, apart from one African, who they set ashore. He was found there by the English a year later. In 1568, the *Mary Fortune*, a ship owned by Sir William Wynter, was sunk by the Portuguese near the river.[15]

The people of River Cestos met their first Englishman when John Hawkins's father William made a series of voyages to Brazil, via Guinea, in the 1530s. Hakluyt relates that *en route* to Brazil 'he touched at the River of Sestos, upon the coast of Guinea, where he trafficked with the Negroes, and took of them Oliphant's teeth [ivory], and other commodities which that place yieldeth'.[16] In 1553, Thomas Wyndham called at River Cestos but did not trade there, preferring to press on to the Gold Coast and, eventually, as far as Benin in modern-day Nigeria. This decision was made against the wishes of the Portuguese pilot Antonio Anes Pinteado, who was guiding the English ships along the coast. Pinteado feared that it was too late in the season to continue, and that they should make for home, but Wyndham cursed him as a 'whoreson Jew' and threatened to 'cut off his ears and nail them to the mast' if he did not take them to Benin. Wyndham's insult may have had some basis in truth; if Pinteado was a Jewish *converso*, it would explain why he had been forced to flee Portugal and offer his services to the English. Once they arrived at Benin, the men began to die of fever at the rate of four or five a day. Before long, both Captain Wyndham and his Portuguese pilot lay among the dead. Of the one hundred and forty men who set out, only forty survived the voyage and yet they returned with enough gold (150 lbs) and meleguetta pepper to encourage further voyages.[17]

The following year, the *Trinity*, *Bartholomew* and *John Evangelist*, under the command of John Lok (an ancestor of the philosopher John Locke), spent a week at River Cestos towards the end of December. Lok bought a ton of meleguetta pepper to take back to England, ivory tusks 'as big as a man's thigh above the knee' and the head of an elephant, which was displayed to the public in the house of Sir Andrew Judde, a wealthy merchant and former Lord Mayor of London. The head was 'of such huge bigness' that it provoked much wonder, and even religious contemplation. One observer 'beheld it, not only with my bodily eyes, but much more with the eyes of my mind and my spirit, considering by the work, the cunning and wisdom of the workmaster'.[18]

Such strange new treasures clearly inspired London's merchants and investors. Three further voyages set out to West Africa in 1555, 1556 and 1558, under the command of William Towerson.[19] Over the following decades, the English made several other journeys to the area, resulting in the establishment of the first Guinea Company in 1588, when Elizabeth I granted a group of merchants from London and Devon the exclusive right to trade with West Africa for the next ten years. Don Antonio, the claimant to the Portuguese throne, was in London and the English took full advantage of his presence; as 'King of Portugal', Antonio could authorise trade to Africa. The patent specified that Don Antonio was to receive 5% of the merchants' profits, one-third of goods seized from any interlopers and a quarter of their prize goods.[20] A separate right to trade to Sierra Leone, the region immediately to the north-west of River Cestos, was granted to Thomas Gregory of Taunton and his associates in 1592.[21] Six years later the Lord High Admiral Charles Howard, Earl of Nottingham, who had commanded the fleet that defeated the Armada, and the courtier Sir John Stanhope, negotiated an extension of the right to trade to Guinea. In the same year Hakluyt dedicated the second edition of the *Principal Navigations*, which included accounts of voyages to Guinea, to Nottingham.[22] It has been estimated that the English made fewer than fifty voyages to Guinea before 1600, rising to one hundred and fifty by 1650.[23] By then, they were being overtaken by the Dutch, who only began trading to Africa early in the seventeenth century, but sent some two hundred ships there between 1599 and 1608 alone.[24] 'Guinea' being such a vague term, it is not always clear where exactly the English called, but at least some of these voyages included a stop at River Cestos.[25]

With the exception of the four Hawkins-sponsored voyages of the 1560s, the English Guinea trade in this period was not a slave trade. In 1620, Captain Richard Jobson was offered the chance to buy some young female slaves on the Gambia River, but refused. He told the African merchant, Buckor Sano, that the English were 'a people who did not deal in any such commodities, neither did we buy or sell one another, or any that had our own shapes'.[26] This was largely true for the Tudor period, and remained so for the first four decades of the seventeenth century.[27] The enslaved Africans Hawkins procured to sell in the Spanish Caribbean during the 1560s came from Sierra Leone. Dederi Jaquoah and his father would not have known the English as slave traders.[28]

At around the time Jaquoah was born, a merchant named John Davies began trading to Africa from London. A haberdasher, specialising in hats, buttons, ribbons and other paraphernalia, he became a member, or freeman, of the Haberdasher's Company on 21 February 1584. Just three days later, his master John Best died and ten days after that Davies married Best's daughter Marie at St Mary Woolchurch Haw. The marriage lasted only two years, as Marie died in June 1586. Davies remarried the following year, taking as his wife Margaret Fynn, the daughter of a fishmonger.[29] By the early 1590s, he had moved on from being a 'retailing haberdasher' and begun investing in overseas trade and sponsoring privateering voyages. Despite the fact that his ships were often attacked, meaning he was continually in debt, he managed to continue to live 'in the world with good credit and reputation'.[30] In 1600 he was authorised, alongside a gun founder named Thomas Browne, to export the Queen's old and unserviceable cast iron ordnance.[31] The people of River Cestos 'were very eager for old or new iron' and so their river may have been among the 'places remote and unknown' where Davies sold the ordnance.[32] By 1607 Davies was the leading figure in the Guinea trade, with a particular interest in importing redwood (used for the dyeing of cloth) from Sierra Leone.[33] Two years later, the Earl of Nottingham granted him permission to send the ship *Resistance* to 'the parts beyond the seas, namely Guinea, Binney [Benin] and Brazil'.[34]

Late in the summer of 1610, Dederi Jaquoah and his father King Caddi-biah received one of John Davies's ships at River Cestos. The *Abigail* of Southampton, captained by Roger Newse, arrived laden with silks, satins, taffetas, velvet, thread, ribbon, broadcloth, cottons, linen, hats, brass basins (used in the process of hat-making), brass axes, kettles, rings, bugles, iron, wines and aquavitae; the stock-in-trade of John Davies and his partner, the mercer Isaac Kilburne.[35] The merchants of Cestos were keen to buy these goods, exchanging them for rice, meleguetta pepper and ivory. However, this voyage was unlike the others in one important respect: when the *Abigail* departed for England, Prince Dederi Jaquoah was amongst its passengers.

Prince Jaquoah may not have had a particularly pleasant voyage to England. When the *Abigail* returned home, Davies complained to the authorities of the Trinity House at Deptford about the conduct of Captain Roger Newse, his pilot Thomas Addison, the master's mate John Addison and various other crew members, including the boatswain and the gunner. They had not done their best 'towards the performance of the voyage, as they ought to have done' and had 'been very turbulent, factious and mutinous'. Mutiny was not uncommon, and the 'turbulence' natural to sea voyages, where men were confined in a small space under often difficult conditions, was exacerbated as long journeys into uncharted territory became increasingly common. The year after the *Abigail*'s voyage, Captain Henry Hudson learnt this to his cost after his crew mutinied and set him adrift in the icy waters of the Canadian bay which thereafter bore his name.[36] By 1631, the Admiralty court was receiving complaints daily regarding 'disobedient and mutinous mariners' who conspired 'to depose a master who does not conform to their wishes and put another of their choosing in his place'. The ringleaders sheltered their identities by use of the 'pernicious phrase one and all' or by a 'Round Robin', where all the mutineers' names were written in a circle so that the ringleader could not be detected.[37]

The *Abigail*'s crew seem to have stopped short of full mutiny, or at least there cannot have been an uprising against the captain, since he was named amongst the offenders. Davies instead accused them of breaking the terms of the charter-party, the original agreement made before they put out to sea, which usually included the safe delivery of the cargo amongst its requirements. Was Davies unhappy with how Newse and the others had conducted their trade at River Cestos? Did he object to the fact that they'd returned with Jaquoah aboard? Whatever they had done, or failed to do, the Trinity House decided that the accused would not be paid their wages and stated that they deserved a greater punishment than it was in the House's power to inflict. Was there tension during the voyage between these 'mutinous' mariners and the rest of the company, who had 'carried themselves well'?[38] These disagreements, both during and after the voyage, gave Jaquoah a rude introduction to English culture, or the lack of it.

On the same day that Trinity House passed this judgment, New Year's Day 1611, Dederi Jaquoah was christened at St Mildred Poultry. The parish register records the baptism of 'John Jaquoah, a king's sonne in Guinnye':

Dederi Jaquoah about the age of 20 years, the son of Caddi-biah king of the river of Cetras or Cestus in the country of Guinea, who was sent out of his country by his father, in an

English ship called the *Abigail* of London, belonging to Mr John Davies of this parish, to be baptised. At the request of the said Mr Davies and at the desire of the said Dedery, and by allowance of authority, [he] was by the Parson of this church the first of January, baptised and named John. His sureties were John Davies haberdasher, Isaac Kilburne mercer, Robert Singleton churchwarden, Edmund Towers, Paul Gurgeny and Rebecca Hutchens. He showed his opinion concerning Jesus Christ and his faith in him; he repeated the Lord's prayer in English at the font, and so was baptised and signed with the sign of the Crosse.[39]

Dederi Jaquoah was christened John, after John Davies, just like Edward Swarthye had taken Edward Wynter's name. Like Mary Fillis, he had learnt the Lord's Prayer, and the parish clerk emphasised his desire to be baptised. His 'sureties', or godparents, included some of Davies's associates in the Guinea trade, Isaac Kilburne and Edmund Towers. Kilburne had done business with John Davies since about 1600 and the two were friends. Unfortunately, their 'old familiarity and acquaintance' did not survive the strains of their professional dealings. Kilburne was later to wish he had never known Davies, 'a man of most subtle cunning disposition intending only to defraud', full of 'subtle devices and malice and plots'.[40] Edmund Towers had been John Davies's resident factor in Guinea, sending him advice as to which goods were 'best vendible' there.[41] We do not know where exactly in Guinea Towers lived. Could it have been River Cestos? He may have spent the year there on a 'factory ship', a vessel from which merchants' factors traded, or hired from the King a warehouse or lodge fashioned from mud and straw, or banana trees leant up against one another.[42]

Davies's long career of trading to West Africa meant Dederi Jaquoah was not the first African to be associated with him in London. In 1597, the register of Davies's parish church, St Mary Woolchurch Haw, recorded that 'a blakmore belonging to Mr John Davies, died in White Chapel parish, was laid in the ground in this church yard *sine frequentia populi et sine ceremoniis quia utrum christianus esset necne nesciebamus* (without any company of people

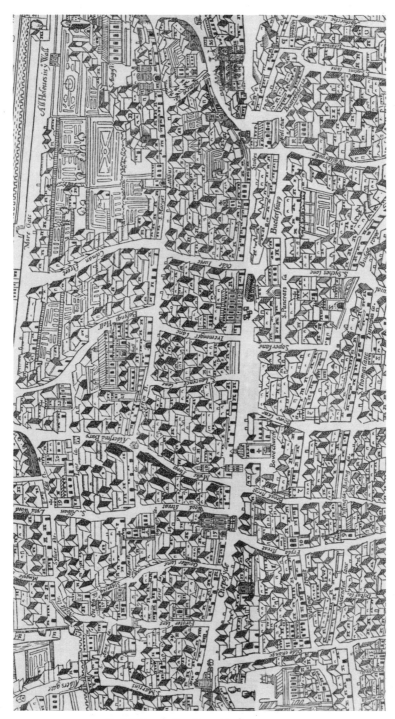

St Mildred, Poultry, in the 1560s.

and without ceremony, because we did not know whether he was a Christian or not)'.[43] When the clerk records this African as 'belonging' to Davies, this does not mean that he owned him. At the time, the word 'belong' could merely signify membership of a household. In 1568, the Returns of Aliens, a poll tax on foreigners, recorded that Peter Martin, a Spaniard, 'belongith to the Spanish Ambassador'. In Shakespeare's *Twelfth Night*, Duke Orsino asks Lady Olivia's servants, 'Belong you to the Lady Olivia, friends?' and the Clown answers: 'Ay, sir; we are some of her trappings'.[44] Nonetheless, it is perplexing that although this man was part of Davies's household, the parish authorities did not appear to know him well enough to judge whether he was a Christian. Nor do we know what he was doing in Whitechapel, about a mile east of Davies's home, and there is no record of his death in the register of the parish church, St Mary Matfellon.[45]

Jaquoah was neither the first nor the last black man to arrive in London from Africa on an English merchant ship during this period. In 1555, a group of five Africans from Shama in modern-day Ghana had arrived with Robert Gainsh and John Lok. Of the five, sometimes erroneously cited as the first Africans to come to England, we know the names of three: Anthony, 'Binne' (or 'Binny') and George.[46] Two unnamed African men were brought to London by Anthony Dassell in 1592. A few years after Dederi arrived in England, a South African named Coree stepped off an East India Company ship, the *Hector*, on her return from Bantam in western Java in 1613. She had been part of the Company's eighth voyage to the East Indies since its incorporation by Elizabeth I in 1600. Following in the wake of the Portuguese and the Dutch, the East India Company was making a killing importing black pepper, spices such as cloves, nutmeg and cinnamon, medicinal drugs, aromatic woods such as sandalwood, perfumes and silks. The profit made by subscribers to the eighth voyage was an eye-watering 221%. Investment grew and by 1620 the Company had established more than twelve factories in the East Indies, employing more than two hundred factors. It had also built seventy-six of its own ships in its two purpose-built shipyards on the Thames at Deptford and Blackwall.[47] As we will see in the next chapter, Company ships were soon bringing both Africans and East Asians back to England from the East Indies.

Like Dederi Jaquoah, the other Africans who were brought to England by merchants at this time were high status. One of the five who came to London in 1555 was the son of 'the Captain' of the town, and the fact that the others had gold with them suggests they were also from wealthy families.[48] The men who arrived with Anthony Dassell in 1592 were described as: 'two chief young negroes . . . sons to the chief justice of that country'.[49] Coree was later observed wearing a 'perfum'd Cap', which may also have indicated high status. This was part of a wider trend of African nobility visiting Europe. As early as 1487, Bumi Jeleen, the ruler of Senegal, sent his nephew as his ambassador to Portugal. In 1508, King Afonso of Kongo sent his son Henry to study with the order of St John the Evangelist in Lisbon.[50] He went on to become the first sub-Saharan Catholic bishop (and the last for more than two hundred and fifty years). In 1600, the ruler of the Itsekiri kingdom of Warri, in modern-day Nigeria, sent his eldest son to Lisbon, where he received a Christian education and was christened, and returned eight years later with a Portuguese wife, and a priest to help him establish a Catholic state.[51] So when the St Mildred's Poultry baptism register asserted that Jaquoah was 'sent out of his country by his father . . . to be baptised', it was not without precedent.

What was the motivation behind these baptisms? African rulers were impressed by Europeans' ability to navigate oceans when out of sight of land, and by the deadly power of their firearms. On a practical level, they may have converted in order to obtain weapons; the Portuguese refused to sell firearms to non-Christians. But the Africans might also have believed that Christianity imbued the weapons with a special spiritual force. In 1515, three Portuguese missionaries journeyed to Benin in the hope of converting Oba Ozolua and his people. Ozolua, who was at war, told his visitors that he needed time to contemplate the 'deep mystery' of their faith. He took them with him on his campaign, subjecting their Christian faith to trial by combat. Successful in battle, the Oba finally agreed that the missionaries could baptise his son and some of his highest-ranking noblemen.[52] The situation at River Cestos a century later was a little different, as the English did not bring missionaries with them. This, together with the Protestant insistence on a Christian education before baptism, explains why the prince would have to travel to England to convert.

Clearly, there were other advantages to visiting their trading partner's homeland. Jaquoah would be able to learn more about the market for meleguetta pepper and ivory, and bring back useful commercial knowledge. It was just this sort of industrial espionage that English merchants had suspected the Moroccans of in 1600, and such fears were raised again after Coree the Saldanian returned to South Africa in 1614. He informed his countrymen that the brass they so admired was 'but a base and cheap commodity in England' and after that the English no longer had 'such a free exchange of our brass and iron for their cattle'. The merchant John Milward subsequently complained that 'They demanded ably for their Cattle, which we thought proceeded from Coree, who had been in England, and (as we suppose) acquainted them with our little esteem of Iron and Copper'. Coree also explained about guns to his countrymen. Where once just one gun 'would cause a multitude of them to fly', by 1617 John Jourdain, a captain in the East India Company, lamented that Coree, 'understanding our manner, hath made them so bold' that they 'did not greatly care' when they saw one.[53] Such a change of attitude disrupted the English objectives. Edward Terry, a ship's chaplain, commented that it would have been better if Coree had never seen England, and Edward Blitheman, the Company man who met Jaquoah at River Cestos on the same trip, wrote of the Saldanian that 'it had been good in my opinion either he had been hanged in England or drowned homeward'.[54]

Travelling to London also gave Africans the opportunity to learn English. At this time, much of the trade between English and Africans relied heavily on the use of signs. In 1555, William Towerson reported that two of the King's servants at River St Vincent, south-east of River Cestos, 'made us signs that if when we had slept we would come again into their river, we should have store of Grains'. Towerson and other merchants made some effort to learn a few key words and phrases, such as 'Have you enough?', 'give me bread', 'hold your peace' and 'you lie!', but it cannot have been easy for the English and Africans to understand each other.[55] The East India merchants at the Cape of Good Hope were particularly flummoxed by the Khoi Khoi language. Sir James Lancaster reported in 1601 that:

> their speech is wholly uttered through the throat, and they cluck with their tongues in such sort, that in the seven weeks which we remained here in this place, the sharpest wit among us could not learn one word of their language; and yet the people would soon understand any sign we made to them.

They resorted to using sounds: a 'Language, which was never changed at the confusion of Babel . . . *Moath* [Moo] for Oxen . . . and *Baa* for Sheepe: which Language the people understood very well without any Interpreter'.[56] Gabriel Towerson, William Towerson's son and the Captain of the *Hector*, wanted to take Coree to England because once he had learned some English, he would be able to tell them more about his country, revealing things 'which we could not know before'.[57] The advantage cut both ways.

Although Africans might choose to visit England for various reasons, sometimes the choice was taken out of their hands. William Towerson admitted in 1556 that the Africans brought from Shama by Robert Gainsh and John Lok had been taken by force. When he called at the town, 'none of them would come near us; being as we judged afraid of us: because that four [actually five] men were taken perforce the last year from this place'. Towerson made further efforts to negotiate, but was attacked by the Africans, in concert with the Portuguese, 'whom before they hated'. He decided to 'go from this place, seeing the Negroes bent against us'. On his second voyage, Towerson attempted to repair the damage he had done by returning three of the men, one of whom was named as George. Though the people were very glad to see the trio, who then facilitated trade, they still demanded to know where the other two were. Towerson did his best to reassure them that 'Anthonie and Binne' would be brought home on the next voyage.[58]

The best thing for English merchants to do was to leave some of their own men behind when they took Africans away. In 1582, when Edward Fenton set out on his abortive voyage to the East Indies, which was to call at the West African coast, he was given instructions to 'settle . . . a beginning of a further trade', by bringing back 'some few men, and women if you may' from his travels, leaving Englishmen 'for pledges, and to learn the tongue and secrets of the Countries'.[59] But not all English trading expeditions needed to learn from Towerson's mistakes. When William Hawkins brought a Brazilian king to London in 1531, he left behind one of his crew, Martin Cockerham of Plymouth, to reassure the people of their King's return. The King met Henry VIII at Whitehall, and stayed in England for almost a year before setting off for home with Hawkins.[60] Unfortunately he died on the return voyage, but Hawkins managed to persuade the Brazilians to allow Martin Cockerham to re-join his countrymen. On a smaller scale, we saw in Chapter Three how John Drake exchanged men with the Cimarrons the first time they met.

The Portuguese, Spanish and French had made such exchanges for years.[61] In 1483, the Portuguese explorer Diogo Cão left four missionaries at the mouth of the Congo River and took four Kongolese hostages back to Lisbon in exchange. He had these men taught Portuguese so that they could act as interpreters, before returning them two years later. They were welcomed home 'as though they had seen them resuscitated from under the earth'.[62] Columbus brought native Americans back to Spain with him in 1493, 'to learn the Spanish tongue, to the intent to use them afterwards for interpreters'.[63] A century later, the merchant Anthony Dassell declared there was 'no nation better welcome to ye negroes nor so well beloved' than the French. This 'proceedeth chiefly by bringing negroes with them into France & returning them again to the increasing of further love and Amity'.[64] Certainly, an exchange of hostages was more conducive to friendship than the seizure of Africans and something both sides could use to their advantage. In January 1577, Walter Wren reported that the people of Cape Verde refused to release the Englishmen who were living with them until the English returned three of their people who had been taken in an English ship three weeks before.[65]

John Blanke and the other trumpeters herald the beginning of the Westminster Tournament, held in February 1511 to celebrate the birth of a short-lived son to Henry VIII and Katherine of Aragon.

The trumpeters signal the end of the day's jousting and the assembled company proceed to the banquet. In the *Westminster Tournament Roll*, Blanke has large eyes and he wears a turban – could these be clues to his ethnic and cultural identity?

African musicians were present at courts across Europe: this group appears in a Lisbon altarpiece, *The Engagement of St. Ursula and Prince Etherius*, commissioned in 1522 by Eleanor, Queen of Portugal.

A black trumpeter performs in this French tapestry depicting a wrestling match during the meeting of Henry VIII and Francis I at the Field of the Cloth of Gold in 1520.

The German artist Christoph Weiditz observed this African drummer playing at the ceremonial entrance of Katherine of Aragon's nephew, Emperor Charles V, into a city during his Spanish progress of 1529.

This portrait of an anonymous member of the Habsburg court of Margaret of Austria, the ruler of the Spanish Netherlands, not only reflects the extent of the black presence there, but shows not all Africans in Renaissance Europe were enslaved.

An African groom holds the Queen's horse in this 1617 portrait of James I's wife, Anne of Denmark, who had performed in Ben Jonson's *The Masque of Blackness* a dozen years before. Could he be the African servant recorded in her Edinburgh household in the 1590s?

By the time Charles I and Henrietta Maria are depicted embarking on a hunting expedition in the early 1630s, the African groom figure has become so exoticised that one wonders if this was a real person at the Stuart court.

The masts of the *Mary Rose* sink beneath the waves as Henry VIII watches from Southsea Castle in the foreground. Unlike the sailors we see drowning here, Jacques Francis, the African diver later sent to salvage the wreck, could swim. (Courtesy of Kester Keighley and the Mary Rose Trust)

Africans diving for pearls by the Caribbean island of Margarita, off the north coast of Venezuela, in 1586.

Does this jewel given to Sir Francis Drake by Queen Elizabeth I in the wake of the Armada victory of 1588 symbolise the desire for an English–African alliance against Spain?

Sir Francis proudly wears the Drake Jewel around his waist in this 1591 portrait, which also features a globe in reference to his successful circumnavigation voyage of 1577–80.

Maroon communities of Africans who had escaped Spanish captivity, like the ones Drake found in Panama, were in existence across the Spanish Empire. Here, a Maroon leader from Esmeraldas in Ecuador visits Quito with his father and brother to sign a peace treaty in 1599.

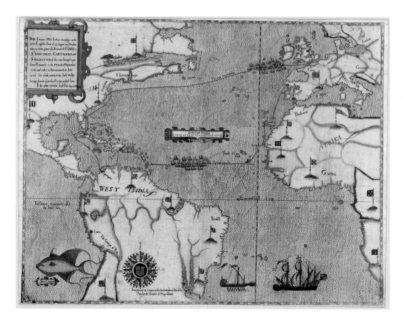

Africans joined the English at each of the ports Drake raided on his West Indian voyage of 1585–6.

Drake's attack on Cartagena in February 1586. The English soldiers can be seen marching along the beach towards a weak point in the city's defences as recommended by a pair of African men they found fishing in the bay.

Edward Swarthye was one of several Africans serving in Tudor gentry households, like this page portrayed c. 1601 with his master Peregrine Bertie, Lord Willoughby de Eresby.

An African child appears in the centre foreground of this c. 1575 image of a village festival by Marcus Gheeraerts the Elder, a visual echo of the various African children who appear in contemporary baptism records.

Painted in 1580s Bologna, Carracci's portrait of an unidentified woman later belonged to Philip V of Spain and was given to the Duke of Wellington during the Peninsular War. The needles in her bodice suggest that she, like Mary Fillis, was a seamstress.

Mary Fillis's countryman Abd-al-Wahid bin Masoud bin Muhammad al-Annuri led an embassy from Morocco to the court of Elizabeth I in 1600. Two of his entourage were later rumoured to have been poisoned.

The question of whether Africans came to England willingly or by force was raised again in a case before the High Court of Admiralty in 1592. Don Antonio of Portugal accused the London merchant Anthony Dassell of bringing 'two Negroes out of the said Country [Guinea] against their wills and contrary to the proclamation and commandment of the king of the said coast of Guinea'.*
In his defence, Dassell claimed that the young men had 'of themselves made suit to come, and voluntarily came to see England'. The trip could well have seemed like a great adventure to the chief justice's sons; curiosity causing them to flout their King's commandment. Julius Caesar, the Judge of the Admiralty Court, examined the men himself and found 'by them' that they came to England 'by consent of their friends to see the country'. Dassell insisted that he fully intended to take the two men home, to foster greater trust in his African trading partners. Certainly, antagonising the people he wished to do business with would jeopardise his future trading prospects. His agent, Richard Kelly, said as much: 'by such indiscreet dealing it is greatly to be feared that the trade into those parts will be very much hindered'. Kelly himself refused to return to Guinea unless 'some order be taken for the safe bringing back of the said two Negroes into the said country'.[66]

Despite what William Towerson and others had learned about the negative effects kidnapping Africans had on trade, Coree the Saldanian was brought by force from the Cape of Good Hope, South Africa, to England by the East India Company in 1613. The Europeans called Coree's home 'Saldania' at this time, after the Portuguese Antonio de Saldahna who landed there in 1503. Edward Terry, who was not on the voyage but met Coree when he travelled to South Africa a few years later, recounted that Captain Gabriel Towerson's decision was made 'very much against both their [the Africans'] minds'. The other man who was taken aboard the *Hector* alongside Coree was apparently so upset that he died shortly after

---

* With creditors harassing him daily for payment of the £8,000 or more he had spent since arriving in London, Antonio was actually more concerned with the fact that Dassell hadn't been paying him a share of his profits as the Guinea Company charter of 1588 prescribed.

they put to sea, 'merely out of extreme sullenness though he was very well used'. In May 1614, Captain John Saris visited Saldania and found that 'the Naturalls of this place are very treacherous at the present, making signs unto us of the forcible carrying away of two of their people'.[67] The East India Company merchants would have to learn William Towerson's lesson all over again; relations improved only after Coree was returned to the Cape.

Jaquoah spent 'two years in England with Mr Davis at the stocks', from the autumn of 1610 until the summer of 1612.[68] This was not a reference to their daily activities, but an address; the Stokes (or Stocks) market specialised in selling fish and meat. The market was situated at the junction of Lombard Street and Cornhill, on the site of the present-day Mansion House, the official residence of the Lord Mayor of London, immediately adjacent to Davies's parish church of St Mary Woolchurch Haw and across the road from St Mildred's Poultry, the church where Jaquoah was baptised. John Davies and his second wife Margaret had been married since May 1587. They had no children.[69] By the time Dederi Jaquoah came to live with them in 1610, Davies was about fifty years old, and his wife was probably not much younger; she died at the end of June 1612, around the same time that Jaquoah returned home.[70]

What would it have been like to be the guest of a London merchant for those accustomed to life on the Guinea coast? The five men who arrived in 1555 presumably stayed at the houses of either Robert Gainsh or John Lok, where they were, according to William Towerson, 'well used'. They were 'tall and strong men, and could well agree with our meats and drinks' although 'the cold and moist air doth somewhat offend them'.[71] In 1592, Anthony Dassell, who was living in the parish of Holy Trinity the Less, Little Trinity Lane, kept the two Africans he had brought from Guinea at his 'own house at . . . great charges', where they were 'courteously used and well entertained for the honour & credit of our Prince and Country'.[72]

One wonders whether Jaquoah was as homesick as Coree, who, having learnt a little English, 'would daily lie upon the ground, and cry very often thus in broken English, "Coree home go, Saldania go, home go".[73] Coree spent six months at the London house of the Governor of the East India Company, Sir Thomas Smith, in Philpott Lane 'where he had good diet, good clothes, good lodging with all other fitting accommodations'. He even had a suit of armour made for him in brass, 'his beloved Metal', which was much admired in Saldania.[74] Edward Terry noted that Coree and his countrymen were so taken with it that 'if a man lay down before them a piece of gold worth two pounds sterling, and a piece of brass worth two pence, they will leave the Gold, and take the brass'.

Coree may have met some Native Americans whilst he was in London. Smith was also Governor of the Virginia Company, and two Virginians, 'out of Sir Thomas Smith's house' were buried at the local church of St Dionis Backchurch in late October and early November 1613.[75] This was not the first multi-racial household in England. Africans lived alongside Native Americans in the Ralegh home during Manteo of Croatan and Wanchese of Roanoke's stay in 1584, and that of Prince Cayowaroco of Guyana and a handful of other men from the New World in 1594–6.[76]

The visitors would have been provided with English clothes to keep them warm, as well as to satisfy the English sense of propriety. The Native Americans living with Ralegh were 'clad in brown taffeta'.[77] When an African arrived at Saltram Hall, Devon, in 1628, Sir James Bagg insisted he should be 'handsomely clad'.[78] Clothes could make a big difference to the way foreign visitors were perceived. In 1501, two men from Newfoundland appeared before Henry VII 'clothed in beasts' skins and ate Raw flesh and spoke such speech that no man could understand them . . . in their demeanour like to brute beasts'. But within two years they were seen at Westminster Palace 'apparelled after English men' so that the anonymous observer had to admit that he 'could not discern [them] from English men till I was learned what men they were'.[79]

Appearances could be swiftly altered, but communication was another matter. The English were hardly proficient in non-European languages. For Africans such as Dederi Jaquoah, it could take several months to learn English well enough to act as a useful interpreter and trade factor. The five Africans who arrived in London in the summer of 1555 'were there kept till they could speak the language', the idea being that 'then they should be brought again to be a help to Englishmen' in Guinea.[80] The first three left London in September 1556, so it had taken them about a year, or more if we count their months on board ship, to become fluent. When Lupold Von Wedel, a German visitor to London, met Manteo and Wanchese at Hampton Court on 18 October 1584, 'nobody could understand their language'.[81] But just two months later they were able to convey information to potential investors about the 'singular great commodities' of their homeland.[82] Jaquoah was in London for two years. When he was baptised in January 1611 he had been in the country for a few months and was able to 'repeat the Lord's Prayer in English at the font'. The fact that the record specifically states that he recited the prayer *in English* suggests he did not speak in that tongue throughout the ceremony. According to the parish register he '*showed* his opinion concerning Jesus Christ and his faith in him', so it seems he was not completely fluent in English, and we can only guess what signs he used to communicate his faith.

How did Dederi Jaquoah and the other African 'students' in London learn English? In 1584, when Thomas Hariot taught Manteo and Wanchese for eight months at Durham House, he developed a phonetic system to facilitate the mastery of any language. It was entitled *An universal Alphabet containing six and thirty letters whereby may be expressed the lively image of man's voice in what language soever: first devised upon occasion to seek for fit letters to express the Virginian speech, 1585*. This was the first attempt to devise a non-alphabetic system to represent the sounds of a language. A fellow scholar who saw it said the sinuous characters looked 'like Devils'.[83] Was this system used by Dederi's teachers? It was designed more for recording foreign languages than teaching English; Dederi probably had to pick up the language piecemeal during his two-year stay in the Davies' household. The tuition available in London was not always first-rate and without regular practice it may have been difficult to retain much of what he learned after he returned home. When the French captain Augustin de Beaulieu encountered Coree at the Cape in 1620, he found that 'his English was good only when he asked for bread'.[84]

No doubt Jaquoah attended church regularly while he was in London, either at St Mildred, Poultry, where he was baptised, or at the Davies parish church of St Mary Woolchurch Haw, across the road. He might well have seen one of the first copies of the King James Bible, which was printed in London in May 1611. *The Tempest* was first performed in this year, and some critics have suggested that Dederi's father's name, 'Caddi-biah', inspired Shakespeare to name his character 'Caliban'.[85]

After two years in London, Dederi Jaquoah returned home in the summer of 1612. Other Africans had been delighted to return home and were met with a warm welcome. When George and two of the other Africans returned to Guinea with William Towerson in 1556, the people of Hanta, a town close to Shama, wept with joy to see their people returned, and:

> were very glad of our Negros, specially one of their brother's wives, and one of their aunts which received them with much joy, and so did all the rest of the people, as if they had been their natural brethren.[86]

When Coree returned to Africa in June 1614, aboard the *New Year's Gift*, captained by Nicholas Downton, 'he had no sooner set footing on his own shore, but presently he threw away his *Clothes*, his *Linen*, with all other *Covering*', and eagerly 'got his sheep's skins upon his back, guts about his neck', and 'a perfum'd Cap . . . upon his head.'[87] Initially, it appeared he was open to further dealings with the English; he gave Captain Downton a young steer (a castrated bull, good for beef), but on 18 June he went away 'with his rich armour and all his wealth in the company of his friends' and did not return.[88]

On 10 July 1614, a fleet of three East India Company ships, the *Samaritan*, the *Thomas* and the *Thomasine*, under the command of Captain David Middleton, stopped at River Cestos, *en route* to Bantam.[89] Edward Blitheman, assistant to Mr Bailey, the principal merchant on the *Thomasine*, wrote to Sir Thomas Smith that they had met 'an Indian' (an indigenous person) who 'spoke very good

English and had formerly been two years in England with Mr Davis at the stocks and is known by the name John Davis, being as we perceived the king's son of that place'.[90] Why was Prince Dederi now referring to himself not merely by his baptismal name, John, but actually as 'John Davis'? Perhaps it was an attempt to foster better relations with potential trading partners. Jaquoah appears to have started a tradition. Some seventy years later Jean Barbot noted that the King of Cestos, whom he called 'Barsaw', also used the name Peter, for "tis customary with the Blacks of note on this coast to take a European name'. King Barsaw/Peter was described by Barbot as 'an old man of 65 or 66' in 1681, so he could have been Dederi Jaquoah's son and heir, born a few years after his return from London.[91]

After his time in London, Jaquoah was well equipped to engage in trade with visiting English merchants. He invited Captain Middleton to his father's court and showed him their stores of ivory. 'A great quantity more' could be procured, Jaquoah told him, if the Englishman so desired. King Caddi-biah gave Middleton 'very kind entertainment'. We can get some idea of what this visit might have been like from the account of French merchant Jean Barbot, who visited the King of Cestos in 1681, and sketched a picture of their meeting. He and his party were received in the Meeting Hut in the King's village, where Barbot was 'melting all the time as if I were in an oven'. The King, flanked by some twenty men, was 'sitting on his heels, as they do in that land', smoking a pipe and wearing a flowing white robe and a ceremonial headdress made of straw 'decorated with goats' horns, small porcupine tails and other trifles'. Barbot presented the King with two iron bars, a bundle of glass beads, two flasks of brandy and a few knives. In return he received a large basket of rice and two hens, which the French immediately killed and cooked on the spot 'so that the alliance . . . could be sealed'.[92]

King Caddi-biah and his son made 'great proffers and promises of trade' if Middleton 'would stay there with his ships', but Middleton decided not to trade on this occasion and the fleet set sail again the next morning. Middleton was on a tight schedule for the East Indies, and was keen to make progress southwards while the weather was fair. 'Had not the time of the year been so

Barbot's sketch of his meeting with King Barsaw or Peter
of River Cestos, c. 1681. The hens on the right were shortly
afterwards killed and cooked to seal the trading agreement.

precious,' Blitheman reported, Middleton might well have tried to
trade some of the 'petty commodities,' such as 'knives, coarse felts
of all colours, looking-glasses, scissors, iron etc.' he had on board
for the ivory and meleguetta pepper available at River Cestos.
However, as well as the time of year, Middleton also took into
consideration how expensive it was to service the fleet, concluding
that 'the charge of the fleet would have eaten away all the profit'
he could have made by trading there.[93]

Although Jaquoah was unsuccessful in persuading the English to
trade in 1614, his language skills and familiarity with the English
and their commercial needs would stand him in good stead over
the years. Other Africans who had learnt English in London used
it to communicate and trade with English merchants once they
returned home. Those who had come to London in 1555 were
instrumental in facilitating trade on William Towerson's voyages.
In January 1557 at Cape de Tres Puntas, the most southerly tip of

modern-day western Ghana, the locals were wary of the English and kept their distance until 'we sent George our Negro a shore, and after he had talked with them, they came aboard our boats without fear' to trade. George seems to have been so keen to help the English that after they returned him home he followed them for at least ninety miles in a small boat, and 'when he came, the Negroes and we soon concluded a price'.[94] The cooperation continued: when Towerson called at their coast again in June 1558, George and 'Binny' (who had, as promised, been returned) came to see him with two pounds of gold to trade.[95]

Despite his disappearance after returning to South Africa in 1614, Coree acted as a mediator for English merchants in later years. He welcomed Walter Peyton of the *Expedition* to the Cape in June 1615, taking some of the Englishmen to see his house, wife and children. There, they saw his suit of armour, which he kept in pride of place. Peyton credited Coree for a change in the locals' manner towards the English, remarking that they were 'nothing so fearful of us nor so thievish as in former times'. Coree also appeared to have taught his countrymen a little English, as they chanted the phrase 'Sir Thomas Smith English Ships' repeatedly and 'with great glory'. Some of the people 'desired to go for England with us, because they esteemed Coree to have sped so well, returning rich with his suit of copper'. Indeed, Coree himself spoke of returning to England with one of his sons when the East India Company ships called at the Cape 'homeward bound'. But by the time the fleet returned, in January 1617, the atmosphere had changed and Coree had moved his family further away 'for more security from strange Ships'. Peyton believed the Dutch had scared him away, as they were wont to eschew trade altogether and send raiding parties of one hundred men to capture cattle. Nonetheless, Coree continued to play a key role in trading negotiations whenever the English called at the Cape until he met his death at the hands of the Dutch in 1627, when he refused to provide them with 'fresh victuals' out of loyalty to, or at least familiarity with, the English.[96]

Englishmen continued to visit River Cestos after Blitheman's visit of 1614. At some point in the mid-seventeenth century they established a factory, or trading post, there but this was abandoned by 1667. A French visitor observed 'about three leagues [nine miles] up the River the English had formerly a house, but there is nothing of it left but the Walls'.[97] If Barbot is to be believed, the English had abandoned this lodge 'when they failed to find enough trade to support the agents'.[98]

John Davies continued to trade to West Africa after Dederi Jaquoah's return home, but he did not send his ships to River Cestos. He became the leading figure in the Guinea trade, establishing the first English factory on the African coast, at Sherbro, in Sierra Leone, in 1618, the same year that he formed the Gynney and Bynney Company, which promoted three unsuccessful voyages to the Gambia over the next three years. In 1620, Davies was granted a monopoly of the redwood trade with Sierra Leone.[99]

River Cestos was not particularly popular with the East India Company either. Blitheman had praised it as 'a convenient place for trade' because it 'lies very little out of the ordinary course'. 'Elephants' teeth and grain' were 'to be had in great abundance and for small trifles', and 'there is very good refreshing for men that shall stop there, for they may water there in a great river'. However, his arguments did not hold sway with his employers. Instead, the Cape of Good Hope, South Africa, became the preferred 'refreshing point', hosting twenty-five English fleets in the first twenty years of the seventeenth century. Thereafter, Madagascar became the main pit stop.[100]

As English traders became more established on the African coast, and more permanent trading forts or settlements were set up, the need to bring Africans to England to learn the language diminished. In 1633, the Guinea Company established a factory on the Gold Coast at Wiampa, and the local kings granted them the use of the port of Warracoo. The King of Aguema sent them one of his sons 'for a pledge' and the Prince travelled to England twice with the Guinea merchants, eventually returning to become a factor at their base, the Castle of Cormantine, established two years earlier. The most prominent merchants involved in the Guinea Company at this time were Humphrey Slany and William Cloberry, so presumably the prince stayed with one of them, but as yet no record has been found of him in London. Not long afterwards, the King of

Aguema sent the English another of his sons, named Asheney. However, rather than travel to England, Asheney lived at Cormantine for three or four years and learnt to speak English there.[101] As more permanent trading forts or settlements were set up abroad, this became the standard practice.

These permanent bases would alter the balance of power on the African coast and the nature of the African trade was to change dramatically. The first known English voyage to transport enslaved Africans across the Atlantic, after Hawkins's last slaving voyage in 1568, was that of the *Star*, which arrived in Barbados with 'a cargo of Negroes' in 1641. By this time, a new market for enslaved African labour was developing in England's nascent colonies in America and the Caribbean. In the first half of the seventeenth century, the English established colonies in Virginia (1607), Bermuda (1612), New England (1620), St Kitts (1622), St Croix (1625), Barbados (1625), Providence Island (1630), and Nevis, Antigua and Monserrat (1628–1632).[102] These early settlements were small, and in constant danger of being wiped out either by disease or attacks from native peoples, such as the Virginia Massacre of 1622, or the Spanish, such as on Providence Island in 1641. However, between 1630 and 1642 there was a huge wave of migration, inspired by religious dissent and widespread promotion of the colonial ideal.[103] As the new territories developed it became clear that they would be reliant on crops that could only be harvested by intensive labour. At first, small numbers of enslaved Africans were supplied to the colonies by privateers who captured them from Spanish or Portuguese ships, but as demand increased, English merchants started importing enslaved Africans themselves.

The trade developed rapidly after 1641: more than one hundred voyages were undertaken in the following two decades.[104] For the first time the purchase and sale of enslaved Africans was an explicitly stated objective in the charter of the Company of Royal Adventurers Trading to Africa in January 1663; an objective they met.[105] By 1667, the Company stated it was delivering more than six thousand enslaved Africans each year to the English plantations.[106] Few of these men and women were likely to have been obtained at River Cestos. When the Royal Africa Company was incorporated by Charles II in 1672, River Cestos was listed amongst the territories that their members had the right to trade with, but while other regions were mentioned as good places to acquire 'negroes', River Cestos was listed only as a source of ivory.[107]

While men like Dederi Jaquoah only spent a few months aboard English ships, travelling as passengers, other Africans found permanent employment at sea. Diego had become part of Francis Drake's crew as a result of the Englishman's vendetta against the Spanish, and many other Africans arrived in England as a result of less high-profile privateering activity while the two countries were at war. But what brought Africans to England after James I made peace with Philip III in 1604? The story of John Anthony, an African mariner of the port of Dover in 1619, shows that while some things had changed, much of what happened at sea and on shore remained the same.

8

John Anthony,
Mariner of Dover

John Anthony was desperate to set sail for Virginia. The Silver
Falcon *lay at anchor in Dover harbour, ready, like he was, to
depart as soon as they received word from Lord Zouche. They
should have been at sea by now, on their way to buy tobacco
from the colonists and to trade with the native peoples. They
were to venture as far north as Canada. But terrible rumours
had halted their departure. Word had reached England that the
governor of Virginia and thirty of his men had met their deaths
on the same route. It was said they had been poisoned by
Spaniards when the* Neptune *stopped in the Azores. John
Anthony had met plenty of Spaniards in his time as a pirate
with Captain Mainwaring. He wondered that any Englishman
had been so foolhardy as to accept their hospitality. When the
news reached Dover, investors had withdrawn their funds and
men previously keen to join the ship suddenly lost their appetite
for the adventure. John Anthony viewed their cowardice with
contempt. He ached to be back at sea, working, instead of this
endless hanging around the port with nothing to do but spend
money he didn't have. Still the* Silver Falcon *did not fly.*

THE YEAR THE *Silver Falcon* left Dover for Virginia, 1619,
is significant in Black Atlantic History, for it was in August
that year that the first enslaved Africans arrived in an
English colony on the North American mainland. Yet that same

year John Anthony was in paid employment aboard an English ship, recorded not only as a 'Blackmore' and a 'Negar' but also as a 'mariner of the town and port of Dover'.[1] What, or who, brought him to Kent?

Africans worked as sailors on English ships from Drake's time to John Anthony's and beyond. In 1625 a 'negro called by the name of Brase' helped a certain Captain Jones work his ship from the West Indies to Virginia.[2] Africans were employed by sea captains in both Dover and London; the burial of an unnamed 'blackamore of Captain Ward's'* at St Mary's, Dover, in November 1618 shows that John Anthony was not the only African present in the port.[3] 'John Come Quicke, a blacke-moore so named', buried in November 1623 at St Botolph's, Aldgate, had been a servant to Sir Thomas Love, a naval officer close to the Duke of Buckingham. His unusual name reflects the demanding nature of work on board ship.[4] There were black sailors living in Stepney, like 'Salomon Cowrder of Poplar a niger sailor', who was married there in 1610, and Thomas Jeronimo, who died *en route* to the Philippines on the East India Company ship the *Peppercorn* in 1621 or 1622, having previously lived in Ratcliffe from about 1616 to 1618 with his wife Helen, who was also a 'moor'.[5]

Cowdrer and Jeronimo may have been some of the first Lascars (sailors from the East Indies) in London; certainly there were Indians and South East Asians in the city by this time. John Saris took fifteen Japanese sailors to England and back on the *Clove's* voyage of 1613–14.[6] In December 1616, 'an East Indian was christened by the name of Peter' at St Dionis Backchurch, and in August 1623, St Katharine by the Tower saw the baptism of 'Phillip, an Indian blackmore, borne in the East Indies at Zarat [Surat]'.[7] Jeronimo was described as a 'moor', but his East India Company employ may indicate an Asian rather than African origin, while Cowdrer 'came out of the East Indies'. This in itself is not definitive, as Africans were taken to the East Indies by the Portuguese, and later the Dutch, but also could have joined East India ships in London.[8]

---

* This may actually have been William Warde, the Mayor of Dover, who appears later in the chapter.

In 1612, Captain John Saris described some of his men as 'swarts' [blacks] brought out of England'.[9] The East India Company's voyages provided a new route for African sailors to make their way to England. In an echo of Drake's experiences in the Spanish Caribbean some forty years earlier, when the Company fleet arrived in the Philippines in 1621, 'divers blacks and slaves had run away from the Spaniards and were keeping themselves in the woods, in hope of getting to the English ships'.[10]

After 1604 England was nominally at peace with Spain, and so the Crown stopped issuing letters of reprisal, but this did not deter some Englishmen from continuing to attack Spanish ships. As one sea captain observed, 'those that were rich rested with what they had; those that were poor and had nothing but from hand to mouth, turned Pirates'.[11] The early years of the seventeenth century saw a piracy boom, with bases appearing everywhere from Ireland to Morocco. By 1608, the 'ocean waters' were 'swarming with pirates'; King James I 'declared that they may possibly number five hundred ships'.[12] This was the heyday of the 'Barbary pirates'. Some were Moroccan, or *moriscos,* originally from Spain, but others were Englishmen based in Morocco.[13] Prominent amongst them was Henry Mainwaring.

It is highly likely that John Anthony arrived in England thanks to Mainwaring, a man he referred to as his 'worshippful master' in 1619. Mainwaring was the scion of an ancient Shropshire family, educated at Brasenose College, Oxford, and the Inner Temple, who in the summer of 1613 took to the high seas in high dudgeon. He later claimed that he became a pirate 'not purposely but by mischance', but the English ambassador to Venice, Edward Wotton, told a different story. Wotton told the Doge of Venice that Mainwaring 'went off in disgust' after the Spanish ambassador, Don Pedro de Zuniga, prevented him from accompanying Sir Robert Shirley on an expedition to Persia. De Zuniga suspected the voyage was secretly bound for the West Indies, to attack Spanish shipping. Setting off with the *Resistance* and the *Nightingale* of Chichester, Mainwaring exceeded the ambassador's worst fears. He 'very soon found himself master of thirty or forty ships which he had taken, mostly at the expense of the Spaniards,' with six or seven hundred men under his command.[14] They made their base at Mamora [Mehedia], twenty miles north of Salé on the west coast of Morocco, at the mouth of the River Sebu. A popular pirate haunt, Mamora reportedly harboured forty pirate ships and 2,000 Pirates.[15] Such was the extent of Mainwaring's plunder of Spanish shipping that in January 1618 the Spanish ambassador, Diego Sarmiento de Acuña, Count of Gondomar, tried to recover 80,000 ducats from him.[16] Two years later, when Gondomar visited him in Dover, Mainwaring 'went to meet him on the beach, for which courtesy he said in jest, that he would excuse him [Mainwaring] twelve crowns out of the million he owed the Spaniards, if he would pay the rest'.[17]

John Anthony may have been captured aboard one of the Spanish ships Mainwaring took. During Mainwaring's three years of piracy, more than 16,000 Africans embarked on slaving ships headed for the Spanish New World. Alternatively, they may have met in Mamora, or in Tunis, which Mainwaring haunted for some five months.[18] At least one other African sailed aboard Mainwaring's ships. In 1624, 'John Phillip a negro' testified that he had been with Mainwaring when they took a Spanish ship near Cape St Mary, south of Faro, Portugal, and carried her to Mamora.[19] Pirate crews were, by their very nature, made up of men from a range of ethnic and national groups. One Plymouth ship raiding the Adriatic in 1604 and 1605 was 'a ramass of rogues, some of Genoa, some of Savoy, some of Barbary, and the master of her is English'. In 1718, sixty of Blackbeard's hundred-man crew were black. It has been estimated that by the eighteenth century up to 30% of pirate crews were of African descent, though this was partly because by this time the Caribbean was becoming the pirates' preferred pillaging ground.[20]

For Mainwaring, Mamora was not long a safe haven. The Spanish sent a fleet of ninety-nine ships there in the summer of 1614 to clear out the pirates' nest.[21] When they arrived, Mainwaring was in Newfoundland, acquiring new recruits and supplies from the fishing fleet. On his return, with four hundred new crew members, 'many volunteers, many compelled', he simply relocated to Villafranca (now Villefranche-sur-mer), near Nice, in the south of

France.[22] The Duke of Savoy had declared Villafranca a 'free port' in 1613 and according to the Venetian ambassador to Savoy, it had since become 'an asylum and refuge for all scoundrels, offering safety to everyone of whatsoever sect, religion, creed, outlawed for whatsoever crime'.[23]

Mainwaring achieved the greatest feat of his Mediterranean sojourn on Midsummer's Day 1615. '5 sail of the King of Spain's men of war' came upon two of Mainwaring's ships, intent on his capture. Against the odds, the pirates inflicted a bruising defeat on the Spanish, killing many of their men and causing 'great hurt' to their ships. The battle was won by Mainwaring's exceptional seamanship and the superior range of his guns. The pirates were able to inflict serious damage on the Spanish ships while remaining beyond the reach of their broadsides. The Spanish were so 'roughly handled' that 'they were glad to withdraw from the contest' and retreat to Lisbon.[24]

Pirate ships were thought to be an excellent training ground for developing nautical skills, and John Anthony would have gained considerable experience by sailing with Mainwaring. Life aboard Mainwaring's ships was strict (or so he later told James I). His men were 'the most uncivil and barbarous seamen' and yet 'by constant severity' he 'kept them all in a short time in so good obedience, and conformity', that he 'never had any outrageous offence, but had them all aboard my ships in as good civility and order'.[25] According to the Venetian ambassador Pietro Contarini, who was considering recruiting Mainwaring, he was unsurpassed in 'nautical skill, for fighting his ship, for his mode of boarding and resisting the enemy'.[26] Contarini later added that 'for nautical experience and for sea-fights, and for a multitude of daring feats performed afloat, he is in high repute, being considered resolute and courageous, and perfectly suited to that profession, understanding the management of first-rates [the largest ships] better, perhaps, than anyone'.[27]

The pirate later distilled his knowledge into a 'Seaman's Dictionary' of nautical terms that would form the basis of many a maritime manual.[28] His exploits soon became the stuff of legend. Jean Chevalier, a neighbour of Mainwaring's on the Isle of Jersey in the 1640s, dined out on the story that once, 'being attacked by a superior force, and his shot expended, he beat off the enemy by loading his guns with pieces of eight'.[29]

John Anthony's adventures with Mainwaring came to an end when, under heavy diplomatic pressure from France and Spain, James I issued an ultimatum: if Mainwaring did not immediately desist and return to England, the King would send an English fleet against him.[30] Given Mainwaring's legendary prowess and the comparatively lacklustre performance of the English navy in the period, it is a little surprising that the pirate chose to call it a day.[31] The rulers of Spain, Savoy, Florence and Tunis all extended offers of pardon. In Tunis, Mainwaring could have followed in the footsteps of another notorious pirate, John Ward, who retired to live like a king in 'a faire palace beautified with rich marble and alabaster stones'.[32] Mainwaring did dine with the Dey of Tunis, 'a very just man of his word', who 'swore by his head (which is the greatest asseveration they use) that if I would stay with him he would divide his estate equally with me, and never urge me to turn Turk'.[33] Yet in the end Mainwaring chose to return home, weary, perhaps, of the exigencies of life at sea, his desire for both adventure and riches well sated.

John Anthony probably arrived in England in the winter of 1615, either in November via Ireland, where Mainwaring waited while the negotiations over his pardon took place, or by sailing direct to Dover aboard one of the pirate's ships in December.[34] And as far as we know, John Anthony lived in the town from his arrival in the winter of 1615 until the spring of 1619. His master, and all who sailed with him, were formally pardoned in June 1616. Mainwaring's 'principled' avoidance of attacking English vessels, and efforts to free various Englishmen from captivity may have helped his cause. He himself claimed this 'patriotic' approach rendered his piracy a '*Pulchrum Scelus*' (an honourable crime). James I may also have been in a forgiving mood, perhaps hoping that Mainwaring, who allegedly had enough silver to use it as ammunition, might be persuaded to pour some into the royal coffers.

In the early seventeenth century, Dover was a thriving port with a population of some 3,000 people. The town was the leading member of the Cinque Ports, a confederation formed by Sandwich, Romney, Dover, Hythe and Hastings, plus the two 'ancient towns' of Rye and Winchelsea, which retained certain privileges in return for providing men and ships to the Crown. Dover had once had six parish churches, but after the Reformation it had only two: St Mary's and St James's. The famous white cliffs towered over the town, atop them the imposing Dover Castle, the Key to England. Situated at the easternmost extremity of Kent, Dover was then, as now, the 'most easy, speedy and convenient [place for] passing into France and other foreign ports beyond the seas'. As Walter Ralegh wrote to Elizabeth I, 'no promontory, town or haven, in Christendom, is so placed by nature and situation, both to gratify friends, and annoy enemies, as this town of Dover'. Its harbour, well-fortified against those enemies, was always busy with travellers and merchants. Both Henry VIII and Elizabeth I had spent considerable sums to improve the harbour, which had a natural tendency to fill with silt, as well as being vulnerable to 'the raging of the sea' and 'frequent and furious storms'. In 1606, James I transferred responsibility for the port's maintenance and improvement to a forerunner of the Dover Harbour Board, saving the Crown from further expenditure.[35]

Other Africans arrived in England as a result of piracy around this time. As we saw in Chapter Two and Chapter Six, in the summer of 1608 an African boy joined the crew of William Longcastle, Captain of the *Ulysses*, who had him christened. To be more precise, the pamphlet account of Longcastle's trial states that he had 'bought' the African 'to be his boy' less than a month before he attacked the *Susan* of Bristol off the coast of Safi, Morocco, on 12 July, so the boy, whose name is unrecorded, must have joined Longcastle's ship in the second half of June. In the normal course of events, the boy might have returned to England with Longcastle, but the Englishman accidentally left him behind in the *Ulysses* when he made off with the *Susan* to the West Indies.[36] The master of the *Susan*, Anthony Wye, was also left on the ship and it was he who took the boy to England. The boy provided damning testimony against Longcastle in the winter of 1609, but after that he disappears from the record.

Another African who came to England in this way was a man named Diogo. In 1607, the twelve-year-old Diogo was captured near the Canary Islands while on his way from Lisbon to Bahia, Brazil, with a Portuguese man called Luis Vaz Paiva. Diogo was sold in Algiers to a pirate named Camarit, who converted him to Islam and gave him the name 'Tombos'. For the next seven years, Diogo served Camarit as he attacked European vessels in the Atlantic and Mediterranean. He was then taken by an English pirate captain, with whom he sailed for four months until the Englishman decided to return to home and throw himself on the mercy of the Crown. He was pardoned by the King in 1614, and his crew was allowed to disembark. But after only four months in London, Diogo headed for Lisbon once more to seek his original Portuguese master, Francisco de Paiva Mercado.[37] His arrival in England seems to have closely mirrored John Anthony's, but while Diogo chose to leave, John Anthony decided to stay.

By 1619, John Anthony was working as a sailor aboard the *Silver Falcon* of Dover, a small, light pinnace of 40 tons. Henry Mainwaring had commissioned Phineas Pett to build the *Silver Falcon* in the summer of 1616. Pett was a well-known shipwright, who had made ships for Drake, Ralegh and King James I at his yard in Chatham. He had even produced a miniature boat for King James's son, Prince Henry, who died aged eighteen in 1612.[38] Mainwaring had asked Pett to build the *Silver Falcon* on behalf of Edward, Lord Zouche, warden of the Cinque Ports and a senior member of James I's Privy Council. A veteran of Elizabeth I's reign, Zouche was one of the signatories of Mary Queen of Scots' death warrant in 1587.[39] On 6 August 1616, Pett sailed the finished ship from Woolwich to Dover with Sir Walter Ralegh and his sons, Henry Mainwaring, and others aboard. Quite possibly John Anthony was also present, and was part of the *Silver Falcon*'s crew from the beginning.

Mainwaring had not entirely left off his piratical ways. Pett recorded in his diary that:

Towards the whole of the hull of the pinnace and all her rigging and furniture I received only £100 from the Lord Zouche, the rest Sir Henry Mainwaring cunningly received in my behalf without my knowledge, which I could never get from him but by piece-meal, so that by the bargain I was loser £100 at least.[40]

This said, Pett himself was a notorious thief, one of a handful of men who treated the Royal Navy as their private slush fund. Samuel Pepys, the diarist and Navy official, had amongst his papers a list of items Pett was said to have stolen. Pocketing things along the course of one's duties was accepted practice, a perk of the job, only penalised when it got out of hand.[41]

John Anthony had a useful patron in Mainwaring. The former pirate found favour with James I, who made him a gentleman of the bedchamber, and knighted him in 1618. Mainwaring dedicated his discourse *The Beginnings, Practices and Suppression of Pirates* to the King, advising his majesty that the only way to stop this criminality, which he estimated had grown tenfold since the end of Elizabeth's reign, was to 'put on a constant immutable resolution never to grant any Pardon, and for those that are or may be taken, to put them all to death, or make slaves of them'.[42] Evidently Mainwaring was confident that his rehabilitation in the eyes of the King was complete. The suggestion also shows that slavery was by no means conceptualised in racial terms at this time, but was a perfectly plausible fate for errant Englishmen. Mainwaring saw plenty of Englishmen reduced to slavery during his time in North Africa; in the mid-seventeenth century there were 35,000 Christian slaves in Algiers alone.[43]

Lord Zouche had ambitious plans for his new pinnace. An exciting new business opportunity presented itself: the tobacco trade. There had long been a market for tobacco in England, but the Spanish had monopolised the trade; the only supply came from their colonies in the West Indies. This might go some way to explaining King James I's hatred of smoking, which in his *Counterblast to Tobacco* (1604) he described as 'a custom loathsome to the eye, hateful to the nose, harmful to the brain, dangerous to the lungs, and in the black stinking fume thereof nearest resembling the horrible Stygian smoke of the pit that is bottomless'.[44] But in 1612,

John Rolfe pioneered the cultivation of Spanish tobacco, or *Nicotiana tabacum*, in the new Virginia colony. The native *Nicotiana rustica* was judged 'poor and weak, and of a biting taste', but Rolfe managed to acquire some seeds of the Spanish variety from Trinidad or Venezuela. The first shipment was brought to England by Captain Robert Adams aboard the *Elizabeth* in July 1613, and was a great success. In 1617, 20,000 pounds of tobacco were shipped to England, and double that the following year.[45] Such was the profit that the colony concentrated on the crop to the exclusion of all else. When Rolfe visited England on a promotional trip with his wife Pocahontas in 1617 he heralded tobacco as 'the principal commodity the colony for the present yieldeth'.[46]

In the autumn of 1618, the *Silver Falcon* was being prepared for its voyage to Virginia. William Warde, the Mayor of Dover, oversaw the day-to-day business on Lord Zouche's behalf and sent regular progress reports to him at his home in Philip Lane, Hackney.[47] The projected itinerary was ambitious. They intended to leave certain people in the country to plant tobacco and corn and to exchange commodities with the English colony, to 'discover and trade with the savages for furs' and other merchandise and to 'fish upon the coast of Canada, and carry the said fish being salted into Virginia'.[48]

It was a risky business. Just that summer, the Governor of Virginia, Lord De La Warr, and thirty of his men had perished *en route* to the colony.[49] According to William Camden they had died at sea shortly after being 'splendidly entertained' at a feast hosted by the Spanish governor of the island of St Michael's in the Azores, 'not without suspicion of poison'. The news of De La Warr's death had 'discouraged some that promised to adventure money' in the *Silver Falcon* and 'deterred others that offered to go in person'.[50] Zouche, a member of the Virginia Company since 1609, was out of pocket himself, having invested £100 in De La Warr's voyage.[51] Although being poisoned by Spaniards in the Azores was not a common fate – if indeed it happened at all – there were many other hazards to deter would-be adventurers. As well as storms, pirates and shipwreck, a host of diseases threatened seafarers. Chief among them was scurvy, which Sir Richard Hawkins (son of John) called 'the plague of the sea and the spoil of mariners'; he had seen 10,000 men 'consumed of this disease' during his twenty years at sea. After just six weeks at sea, a lack of vitamin C could result in lethargy, aching joints, swelling and bruises, which would soon progress to bleeding and rotting gums, teeth falling out, old wounds reopening and eventually fatal internal haemorrhaging.[52]

John Anthony, with his long experience at sea, was not deterred. Nor was the principal investor in the voyage and part-owner of the ship, Jacob Braems, who was taking quite a gamble on the venture, claiming that he had had to invest more than he 'intended or could well spare' to make up for others dropping out.[53] Braems was a merchant from Sandwich, where he held the position of Customer, and he also operated in Dover. His family was of Flemish origin. His great-grandfather Jasper had come to England from Cassileberg near Dunkirk during Queen Mary's reign. One of his ancestors was said to have been secretary to the Holy Roman Emperor for the province of Flanders.[54] As well as setting out the ship, Braems also undertook to pay all the men's wages on their return. The other investors ranged from Lord Zouche, who apart from providing the ship itself invested £200 in the enterprise, to more minor players, such as the ship's steward, Francis Augur, who ventured 'victuals, goods and commodities', including twenty hogs, men's and women's clothes, embroidered gloves and soap. Braems estimated the entire cargo to be worth between £900 and £1,100.

As well as the 'sufferings and danger incident to actions of this Nature' there was also the threat of the 'cruelty' of the 'Virginian Monopolists'. Braems feared that they might put an embargo on the voyage, or not allow them to trade in tobacco or sassafras, 'a kind of wood of most pleasant and sweet smell, and of most rare virtues in physic for the cure of many diseases', which were the main commodities they hoped to obtain.[55] Outlining his project to Lord Zouche, Braems attempted to circumvent the Virginia Company's strictures by promising that if the voyage resulted in 'any extraordinary benefit which may seem any way hurtful to the Company or Colony', he and the other adventurers would make a compensatory payment. In

closing with the hope that 'this intended voyage may be so pros-
perous as our desires and purposes therein are honest and lawful',
the merchant protested too much.[56]

The voyage was further delayed when the ship's Captain, Thomas
Andrews, died during the winter of 1618–9. His brother-in-law,
Walter Upton, was mooted as a possible replacement, but Lord
Zouche impressed on Warde that a 'man of experience and suffi-
ciency' was needed. As it happened, Upton was more than happy
to remain at home. Eventually, a gentleman of London, John Fenner,
was appointed, and encouraged to invest in the voyage himself.[57]
The ship's master was to be Henry Bacon, who had just returned
from Guiana with Sir Walter Ralegh. Lord Zouche granted the
Silver Falcon a warrant to travel to Virginia on 15 February and
the ship duly set sail from Dover on 2 March 1619.[58] There were
twenty-five men on board; John Anthony was one of them.

What might John Anthony have expected to find on the other side
of the Atlantic? The Virginia colony had been established twelve
years previously when Jamestown was founded in 1607. Life there
was precarious. Many of the early settlers were gentlemen or skilled
craftsmen, not accustomed to, or willing to perform, the hard
labour required to plant and harvest corn. During the 'starving
time' of 1609–10, the colonists resorted to eating snakes, rats and
dogs. Some even turned to cannibalism, feeding 'on the corpses of
dead men, and one who had gotten insatiable, out of custom to
that food, could not be restrained until such time as he was executed
for it'. Another man 'murdered his wife, ripped the Child out of
her womb and threw it into the river, and after chopped the mother
in pieces and salted her for his food'. There were two hundred
people in Jamestown in October 1609; in May 1610, there were
only sixty and by 1615, 900 men and women had died in the colony.
As well as hunger, there was disease; many succumbed to dysentery
and malaria. Others were the victims of Native American arrows,
or worse. In December 1607, a labourer named George Cassen
was captured, stripped naked and tied to a tree. His fingers were
cut off one by one, the skin was scraped from his head and face,
and finally he was disembowelled and burnt.[59] Despite such horrors,

the Virginia Company continued to promote their enterprise and encourage new settlers and investors.

When the *Silver Falcon* sailed there were no Africans living in Virginia. The first arrived in August 1619, when John Rolfe bought twenty at Point Comfort, near Jamestown, from the Cornish privateer Captain John Colyn Jope of the *White Lion*. Jope had, in concert with Daniel Elfrith of the *Treasurer*, captured the Africans off the coast of Mexico from a Portuguese ship called the *São João Bautista*, which was coming from Angola.[60] Although the first Africans to arrive in Virginia had been enslaved by the Portuguese, and purchased by Rolfe, once in the colony their status, and that of those who arrived soon after, remained undefined. Jack, an African who arrived in Charles City County, Virginia in about 1636, possessed a contract proving his status to be an indentured servant, not a slave.[61] Anthony Johnson, a black man living with his wife Mary on Virginia's Eastern shore in the 1650s, was a free man and owned his own slaves.[62] Legislation clearly identifying Africans as slaves was not passed in the colonies until the 1660s. Some of these measures forbade inter-racial marriage and asserted that baptism did not confer freedom, which suggests that, before these laws were passed, marriages had taken place between English and Africans, and that converting to Christianity might have set some Africans free.[63]

In the early days of the colony, some of the Africans in Virginia had travelled there from England. John Phillip, the other African who sailed with Mainwaring, told the Virginia court in 1624 that he had been christened in England twelve years previously.[64] In 1667, a man named Fernando asserted that he had lived in England for many years before coming to Virginia.[65] The Africans listed in the early 'musters' of the inhabitants of Virginia in February 1625, such as 'Antonio, a negro' who arrived on the *James* in 1621, 'Mary, negro woman' on the *Margaret & John*, in 1622 and 'John Pedro, negro' on the *Swan* in 1623, may have also come directly from England.[66]

On average it took eleven-and-a-half weeks to sail from England to Virginia, so the *Silver Falcon* should have arrived there in June 1619.[67] Had the voyage been completed as intended, John Anthony, a free man employed as a sailor, would have been the first African to arrive in an English colony in mainland North America.*

But the *Silver Falcon* never reached Virginia. 'Near the Bermudas they met with a frigate of the West Indies and had trucke with her', exchanging their goods for 'upwards of 20,000lb weight' of tobacco.[68] Bermuda, some seven hundred miles south-east of Virginia, had been settled by the English since 1609, when the *Sea Venture* was shipwrecked there *en route* to the new colony, an episode that inspired Shakespeare's *The Tempest*.[69] By 1619 it had a total population of just under a thousand, including at least forty Africans, most of whom had been brought to the island by privateers sponsored by the Earl of Warwick, one of Bermuda's major landholders.[70] The *Silver Falcon* does not seem to have called at the island itself. Given it was provisioned for a much longer voyage, perhaps there was no need.

While Braems claimed the tobacco was acquired in a fair trade, one Francisco de Conynge, of Seville, alleged it had been stolen from a Spanish ship. This was not a far-fetched accusation, despite Braems's assertion that they had a 'contract of the merchants and others of the company of the said frigate' with details of the legal exchange of goods. Bermuda was becoming a popular base for attacking Spanish ships passing the island on their way back to Europe. In 1613, the Duke of Medina Sidonia (who had commanded the Spanish Armada in 1588) wrote to Philip III that the Spanish should uproot the English from the island because it was an ideal place 'from which to overrun everything on the route of the fleets and armadas, because . . . everything that comes from the Indies must pass to the south or the north of it'. By 1620, the island was 'much frequented with men of war and pirates, with whom the inhabitants there are grown in great liking, by reason of the commodities they bring unto them'. One Bermudan minister even commended the 'robbing of Spaniards' because they were 'limbs of the Antichrist'.[71] At only 40 tons the

---

* As we saw in Chapter Three, Diego, Maria and the two other unnamed African men aboard the *Golden Hinde* had set foot in California with Drake in June 1579.

Silver Falcon was much smaller than the usual transatlantic trading vessels, which typically weighed 100 tons or more. Braems's choice of a small ship suggests piratical activity may have secretly been on the agenda from the start.[72]

While Braems insisted that tobacco was the only commodity the *Silver Falcon* had brought back from Bermuda, some of his investors claimed she returned 'richly laden with tobacco, plate, pearls and other rich goods worth some £40,000'. They were sure they had been cheated of a huge profit from these glamorous goods, which must have been sequestered in some remote port in the west of England.[73] Plate, or silver, and pearls were typical West Indian cargoes found on Spanish shipping. Considering the commodities the *Silver Falcon* had aboard when she left Dover, it is scarcely believable that such a valuable haul could have been obtained in a fair trade.

Even more suspiciously, instead of returning to her home port of Dover, the *Silver Falcon* now docked at Flushing in the Netherlands in mid-June 1619. Flushing, or Vlissingen, was one of the principal ports of the Dutch state of Zeeland. Situated on the island of Walcheren, at the mouth of the River Scheldt, it controlled the approach to Antwerp. The town had been held by the English from 1585 to 1616 as part of their alliance with the Dutch against Spain, so English mariners were familiar with the port, and many English people lived there. Braems denied that he had planned to have the ship dock in Flushing. He was backed up by his younger brother, Arnold, who was adamant the decision had been made 'by the advice, consent and direction of the Master and company then in her' and not Braems, for he was 'not at Dover when the said ship passed by to Flushing, but was at London or in his way to Dover, not then knowing any thing of the said ship's return'.[74] Their cousin, Daniel Braems, kept to the family script, confirming that Jacob had indeed been at his house in London at the time. If this were so, had Captain Fenner and the ship's master, Henry Bacon, turned to piracy and absconded to Flushing to avoid the difficult questions that would surely await them on their return to Dover? Or had Braems agreed this itinerary with Captain Fenner, in an effort to sidestep the 'Virginia Monopolists' whose interference he feared at the voyage's outset?

Whatever the truth of the matter, once Braems learnt that the *Silver Falcon* was in Flushing, he hurried across the Channel to meet her.

Flushing, where the *Silver Falcon* mysteriously docked in 1619.

Braems's factor in Flushing, John Vandhurst, paid the customs required for the ship to be unloaded. Thomas Lawley, an English merchant based in Holland, agreed to buy half the tobacco on board for seven shillings a pound, but would not pay for it until he had sold it on.[75] Lawley, Vandhurst and Braems then made a bargain with some merchants of Amsterdam, who agreed to purchase the tobacco at eight shillings and sixpence a pound. They looked set to make a fine profit, and Braems boasted that his investors would have a tenfold return on their investment.

Unfortunately for Braems, Lord Zouche was incensed when he heard that his pinnace had gone to Flushing 'contrary to my order and the command I gave'. He immediately dispatched the Mayor of Dover, William Warde, to find the ship and 'see what goods she hath and to get into your hands and bring on with you to Dover so much thereof as ye shall think fitting in your discretion'. Accompanied by Thomas Fulnetby, the lieutenant of Deal Castle, who had also invested in the voyage, Warde tracked down the wayward vessel and confiscated one hundred and fifty rolls of the best tobacco on Zouche's behalf. When the Amsterdam merchants found out, they backed out of their deal with Braems. Even though he offered them 'the value of the said 150 rolls of tobacco and one thousand pounds Flemish more to hold their said bargain', they 'utterly refused so to do'.[76]

To make matters worse, before Braems was able to sell any of the *Silver Falcon*'s cargo to anyone else, it was arrested, on a procuration sent from Spain, as 'stolen goods', after Jacob Dragoboard claimed ownership on behalf of Francisco de Conynge of Seville. Braems suffered a further blow in 1621 when, 'after the peace expired between the Hollanders and the Spaniards', the 'officer of the States of the Netherlands did attach and arrest . . . the ships lading as Spanish goods'. The tobacco, much of it 'rotten, spoiled and nothing worth', lay under embargo in a Flushing cellar, while the English, the Spanish and the Dutch disputed its ownership. As Daniel Braems put it, Lord Zouche's 'taking and carrying away of the said tobacco' was a 'great hindrance and loss' and ultimately led 'to the overthrow of the gain of the said voyage'.

Jacob Braems was not only taken to court in The Hague. In England, his investors were far from happy, despite his attempts to pay them off. Over the next few years, he became embroiled in legal proceedings in the Chancery Court at Dover – where the case was presided over by none other than Sir Henry Mainwaring – as well as the High Court of Admiralty and the Exchequer Court in London.[77]

By mid-September 1619, John Anthony had returned to Dover aboard the *Silver Falcon*. The dispute between Lord Zouche and Jacob Braems, which would have a significant bearing on his future, grew increasingly bitter, and was not to be resolved overnight. Zouche ordered William Warde 'to seize and make stay of all such wines, pepper, currants, tobacco and other merchandises' found in Jacob Braems's cellar 'bought or exchanged for the goods or merchandise which were brought into Flushing which were in the pinnace called the Silver Falcon' and 'to seize and make stay of the said pinnace itself called the Silver Falcon which lieth in your harbour'.

While Braems was still in Flushing, Warde went to his house. Arnold Braems, who had been entrusted with his brother's goods, refused to hand over the key to the warehouse, so Warde 'threatened to break open the said storehouse door'. Ultimately, Warde 'took possession of the storehouse and sold and carried away all the said goods and merchandise', which consisted of 'Spanish wines, ten bales of pepper, Tobacco, and currants being all worth about five hundred pounds'. Zouche was seriously displeased. 'I hold him not worthy of any favour for he hath so ill managed the trusts I reposed in him', Zouche said in a letter to Warde, furious at 'how ill he hath dealt with me'. He demanded Braems appear before him at Dover Castle on 23 September, but Braems and his wife remained in Flushing, leaving Zouche to order Warde to 'make stay of him on his arrival and commit him to Dover Castle'.[78] When Braems finally returned to England in mid-December, Warde, having gone to his home to detain him, found him 'sick in his bed of a fever', and so 'commanded him to keep his house and not to stir abroad'. Braems asked Zouche to name a time for them to meet, promising to give 'good satisfaction concerning his business and accounts'. Zouche approved of Warde's forbearance, writing that he did not desire to use 'extremities', and allowed Braems 'liberty to take the benefit of the air' at a friend's house, on the proviso that he swore 'to yield himself prisoner at Dover Castle on eight days warning'.[79]

A sketch of Dover Castle by Wenceslas Hollar.

While their employers fought over the profits of the voyage, John Anthony and the rest of the crew were left waiting in Dover for their pay. It was not forthcoming. Over the next few months, Anthony became 'indebted for his diet, lodging and washing'. He owed at least £3, and had to mortgage his 'best apparel' to pay the debt. As the 'winter's season' drew on, he feared that 'he shall endure great extremity if he may not have his money'. He desperately needed to pay his debts and to buy some 'necessary apparel', presumably warmer clothes for the winter and new ones for sea.

During the winter of 1619, Anthony twice petitioned Zouche, and the rest of the Privy Council, for payment of his wages. In his first petition, he explained that he had been informed the sum of £30 due to him 'for his wages and service' in the *Silver Falcon* was 'deposited in the hands of' the Mayor of Dover, but he had not yet received any part of it because Zouche had ordered Warde 'not to pay the said money or any part thereof'. Anthony asked that 'your honour to be pleased to give order to Mr Mayor to pay him'. In his second petition, he was desperate. He 'in all humble and dutiful manner beseecheth' Zouche 'to give order to Mr Mayor of Dover that he may pay unto him such moneys as remaineth in his hands', even suggesting that if the money cannot be released directly to him, it might be 'delivered into the hands of Sir Henry Mainwaring, knight . . . his worshipful master'. By now, Anthony was willing to settle for less than he was owed, 'at the least so much thereof as may pay his debts and defray the charges on necessary apparel fit and meet for sea'.

Sailors needed specialised clothing and equipment. Their clothes had to allow for plenty of movement and so were amply cut, though not so loose as to tangle in the rigging. A rare example of a sailor's outfit from this period, held at the Museum of London, exhibits these qualities. It comprises a loose-fitting pullover top and full breeches, known as 'slops' or 'galligaskins'. Although they were made of very strong linen, needed to endure the hard, rough work, they have been heavily mended and patched with a variety of materials, and the breeches are stained with tar across the front from hauling ropes. An illustration in Cesare Vecellio's costume book of 1598 shows an English sailor dressed in these kind of loose garments and wearing a Monmouth cap (a shaggy, brimless woollen hat, its long pile designed to shed water). Their clothes were as warm and waterproof as the natural materials available at the time allowed. Sir Richard Hawkins's crew wore 'rugge gowns', made of coarse woollen cloth, to protect them against the 'fresh and cold' nights they endured, even in hot countries. To stay dry, sailors made a sort of waterproof tarpaulin petticoat by coating canvas or sailcloth with tar. They had thigh-high boots with double soles, and many sailors wore mittens when the temperature called for it.[80] All in all, the 'charges on necessary apparel fit and meet for sea' could be quite high.

The £30 John Anthony claimed was a relatively high amount, especially considering the voyage had lasted only a few months. Most sailors earned in the region of £1 to £2 a month, although the more skilled might get £3 or £4, and ship-masters £5 to £6. Anthony's earnings suggest he was a skilled worker, perhaps a quartermaster, carpenter or gunner. The normal practice was to pay sailors half wages while in port, so some of the £30 could have been owed from the months Anthony waited in Dover for the *Silver Falcon* to set sail. Of course, Anthony might have petitioned for more than he was owed.[81]

'An English Sailor' in Vecillo's 1598 costume book.

Anthony's fortunes were caught up in the larger struggle between Lord Zouche and Jacob Braems. Zouche was delaying making payments relating to the voyage until he himself had received satisfaction. This was not uncommon, as ship-owners were not legally obliged to pay the crew until they themselves had been paid by the merchants who had hired the ship. Although Braems had undertaken to pay the men's wages, by this time that responsibility had passed to Zouche. In January, Zouche asked Warde for an account of the goods seized from Braems and in February requested 'all the money which you have received for any such goods'. Zouche wrote to Mainwaring on 24 February 1620: 'As soon as I receive the money which the Mayor is to send me for such goods of Braems I will give order for the payment of the purse man that looks to the pinnace'.

Soon, Zouche began to suspect that Braems was not the only one who had 'deceived his trust'. On 1 March he wrote to William Warde that his account of the profits made from selling the goods seized from Braems and moneys spent in relation to the *Silver Falcon* did not add up: 'I much doubt whether the things mentioned in your note of receipt be all the goods of Braems that went to your hands'. He accused Warde of juggling the books, of meddling, of 'foul play' and said he would not be 'satisfied with such shuffling'. Zouche ordered him to provide 'a more honest account than you have yet given me, which if you will not perform, I will trouble you if you live, and yours when you are gone, for I will not be cozened by all your running'. He signed this letter, the last he was to write to Warde: 'yours as you shall deserve'!

On 20 March, Mainwaring, whom Lord Zouche had appointed lieutenant of Dover Castle the month before, wrote to Zouche from the Castle that 'the blacke boy is come her[e] for his money & the Mayor hath very honestly payed him 17s 6d for half a year's interest'. For payments to be delayed was hardly unusual; the state papers and High Court of Admiralty records are littered with similar cases.[82] What is significant is that Anthony was being paid just like everybody else, and that his petitions were taken seriously by senior members of the administration. He was even paid interest, in acknowledgement of his long wait. Zouche replied to Mainwaring's letter the same day, commenting 'I mislike not that you gave Ward order to pay the poor man for his pains about the pinnace'.

John Anthony's paid employment indicates that he was not enslaved. To the modern eye it might be suspicious that in one of his petitions he suggested his wages be paid to Sir Henry Mainwaring, but other sailors' wages were paid to their masters in the same way.[83] Sailors often empowered third parties to receive their wages, usually a wife or relative; Anthony might well simply have invoked Mainwaring's influential name in an attempt to expedite matters. John Anthony called Sir Henry Mainwaring his 'worshipful master', but as he was in debt for his 'diet, lodging and washing', he clearly did not live in his household.[84] Anthony might not formally have been Mainwaring's servant, but rather seen him as his patron.

John Anthony is one of several Africans, including John Blanke and 'James the Blackamoor', cook to Henry Bourchier the fifth Earl of Bath in Tawstock, Devon, who were paid wages in this period. But wages were not the only way in which servants of all ethnicities were compensated for their labour. Harry Domingo, a 'moir' employed by the Burgh of Aberdeen in the early seventeenth century, was paid for specific tasks, such as 'sounding the trumpet at the proclaiming' of letters 'from the council', rather than receiving a regular wage.[85] Some worked only for board and lodging, often being provided with clothing at the household's expense. 'Nageir the Moor', who worked for Lord Regent James Stewart, Earl of Moray, had various outfits made for him in the late 1560s, including a cloak lined with velvet at the neck. Others received the occasional cash reward, such as the six shillings given to 'the blackemor' by a member of the Cecil family in 1622.[86]

Having received his wages, John Anthony was on the lookout for new employment. As he wrote in his petition to Zouche, he was keen to return to sea and sought to obtain 'clothes and other necessaries fit to be used at sea, where he intendeth speedily to employ himself'. He also planned to invest some of his wages, writing that 'some of the said £30 may be put out to some profit'. Did he want to put money into a voyage? A more common course for mariners was to purchase a 'venture', goods that they could trade on their own behalf while at sea.[87]

The *Silver Falcon* did not sail again for some time. In March 1620 Zouche asked Mainwaring to look for a 'cheupman', or purchaser, for the vessel, as he was concerned 'she will decay if she be not much used'. Robert Barrett, a Jurat (municipal officer), of Dover bought her for £160, about half of the £300 Braems thought her to be worth. The legal wrangles over her 1619 voyage outlasted the lives of many of those involved; by 1625, Zouche, Warde, Fenner and Bacon were all dead. A 'John Anthony of the town and port of Dover in the county of Kent, shipwright', who had a wife called Elizabeth and a son called Richard, made his will in Lisbon in 1650, having sailed on voyages to Bahia, Brazil, and Luna, northern Italy. But as the will makes no mention of the testator's ethnicity, we cannot be sure that this was the John Anthony who went to sea aboard the *Silver Falcon*.[88]

The story of John Anthony, the sailor aboard the *Silver Falcon*, who was eventually paid his wages with interest, ends on a positive note. His connection with Mainwaring suggests that once the golden age of Elizabethan privateering came to an end, Africans still came to England as a result of similar activity, which, without the veneer of legality provided by letters of reprisal, was plain piracy. His role as a waged sailor aboard the *Silver Falcon* in 1619, and the agency he demonstrated in pursuing payment of his wages, provides a stark contrast to the experience of the Africans who arrived in Jamestown that same year. And while the English were happy to employ African men as sailors, there were fewer viable careers for African women in England. Some were left with no choice but to join the world's oldest profession.

9

Anne Cobbie,
the Tawny Moor with Soft Skin

Anne slathered the unguent over her arms, her shoulders, her breasts, her belly, her legs and her back. It was her daily ritual. Her soft skin was what the punters remembered, what they were willing to pay above the odds for. They would give a gold coin for the chance to touch her. Not that she got to keep it all. Mrs Bankes took her share, but it was from her house that Anne did her most profitable business. Westminster offered richer pickings than Clerkenwell or Southwark. Crowded with courtiers, politicians, merchants, men in town to pursue a case at the law courts, as well as the apprentices and servants who found the money from God-knows-where. She had bedded them all. There, she was ready. What did the French character in that old play call the black maid? A 'black swan, silk'ner then Signet's plush'.

HISTORIANS AND LITERARY critics have asserted that many African women worked as prostitutes in Tudor and early Stuart England. One has written that Africans were 'used . . . in three capacities: as household servants (the majority); as prostitutes or sexual conveniences for well-to-do Englishmen and Dutchmen; and as court entertainers'. Another claims that there were 'several' black courtesans in Clerkenwell during this period.[1] The most-often cited example is a woman known as Lucy Negro, 'tentatively identified' as the Dark Lady of Shakespeare's sonnets in 1933.[2] Yet there are almost as many theories about who 'Lucy Negro' was as there are about the Dark Lady. Is there any truth in the idea that Shakespeare was enamoured of an African prostitute, and was her name Lucy Negro? How representative was the experience of Anne Cobbie, who worked in a brothel in 1620s Westminster, of the experiences of other African women in England at this time?[3]

In 1626, Anne Cobbie was in her prime, so she was probably born in the early years of the century.[4] A fellow prostitute described her as a 'tawny Moor'.[5] The word 'Moor' is derived from the Latin '*maurus*', which specifically referred to the predominantly light-skinned inhabitants of the ancient province of Mauretania in North Africa. However, by the sixteenth century the term indicated dark skin. As early as 1489, William Caxton wrote: 'He was so angry for it, that he became as black as a Moor'.[6] In 1550 William Thomas, in his *Principal rules of the Italian grammar*, defined 'Moro' as 'a Moore or blacke man', as if the two were synonymous.[7] Shakespeare described Othello, and Aaron in *Titus Andronicus*, as 'Moors', but references to Othello's 'sooty bosom' and Aaron's 'coal-black' visage make it clear that both were conceived as being dark-skinned.[8] A brief glance at Henry Peacham's drawing of a staging of *Titus Andronicus* confirms that Aaron was played as a black man.[9] Standing alone, it seems 'moor' had come to signify black skin.[10]

Peacham's sketch of a scene from *Titus Andronicus* is the only contemporary illustration of a Shakespeare play known to exist.

With the addition of 'tawny', meaning brown, 'tawny-moor' referred to lighter-skinned North Africans. In *The Merchant of Venice*, Shakespeare described the Prince of Morocco as a 'tawnie Moore', and his Cleopatra as having a 'tawny front'.[11] John Pory, the scholar who translated Leo Africanus' *Description of Africa* in 1600, spoke of the 'tawnie Moores' who inhabited North Africa.[12] One Welsh squire wrote that the sunburnt peasants of Pembrokeshire 'are forced to endure the heat of the sun in its greatest extremity, to parch and burn their faces, hands, legs, feet and breasts in such sort as they seem more like tawny Moors than people of this land'.[13] But other than in these literary sources, 'tawny' was rarely applied to a person's complexion; to date, Anne Cobbie is the *only* person found in the archives of the period to be described this way. 'Tawny moor' suggests a North African origin; that she was either from Morocco, like Mary Fillis, or from one of the other 'Barbary States' (Algeria, Tunisia and Tripoli) which, unlike Morocco, were part of the Ottoman Empire. Or, perhaps, given her English surname, she was the mixed-race child of a Black Tudor and an Englishman or woman.[14]

By 1626, Anne Cobbie was a well-known and sought-after prostitute who was often found at the St Clement Danes's bawdy house of John and Jane Bankes.[15] The most eastern parish of Westminster, St Clement Danes ran from Somerset House along the Strand to Temple Bar, and the gate to the City of London. To the north lay Lincoln's Inn Fields and the Inns of Court. To the south, 'to the Thames-ward', as one 'silver-tongued' poet put it in 1590, 'all along the Strand, The stately houses of the nobles stand'.[16] Butcher's Row – so named for the butchers' stalls ranged on its southern side – ran north of and almost parallel to the Strand from Temple Bar to Wych Street. Brewers and market gardeners were also to be found here, outside the City of London's walls.[17] A mile or so upriver was the heart of Westminster: the site of Parliament, the Law Courts and the royal court at Whitehall Palace. Beyond these monumental establishments and the main thoroughfares lay a complex of narrow alleys and squalid streets running off the Strand and Fleet Street, known as 'the Straits' or 'the Bermudas' because they were infested with 'land pirates' and other miscreants.[18] John and Jane Bankes's bawdy house was doubtless situated on such a street.

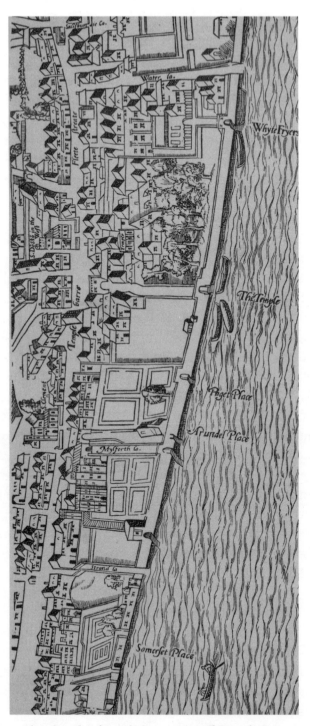

The church of St Clement, just off Temple Bar.

As it lay outside the City of London, the 'Liberty' of Westminster benefited from certain traditional immunities. A draft Act of Parliament in 1585 described Westminster as the site of 'sundry great murders, Riots, Routs, frays, robberies . . . Adulteries and other incontinent life . . . and many other the like shameful sins'. By 1620, there were said to be almost a hundred taverns along the Strand between Charing Cross and Temple Bar.[19] The number of bawdy houses in Westminster grew substantially in the Tudor period. One street on the south side of Petty France even earned itself the name 'Codpiece Row'.[20] When Henry VIII officially shut down the sanctioned brothels of Southwark in 1546, their prostitutes scattered across the capital. This 'privatisation' of prostitution was recounted in verse by the poet John Taylor in 1630:

> The Stews in England bore a beastly sway,
> Till the eight Henry banish'd them away:
> And since these common whores were quite put down,
> A damned crew of private whores are grown,
> So that the devil will be doing still,
> Either with public or with private ill.

As Bishop Latimer put it in a sermon preached before Edward VI in 1549: 'Ye have but changed the place, and not taken the whoredom away . . . there is now more whoredom in London than ever there was on the [South] Bank'.[21] By the late 1570s there were at least one hundred 'houses of salary sensuality' in the city, where men could 'have harlots as readily and commonly as men have vittles honestly in vitteling houses for their money'.[22]

Africans had lived in Westminster since at least 1571, when 'Margrueta, a Moore' was buried at St Martin in the Fields.[23] Between 1586 and 1624, eleven other Africans were buried in Westminster's four parishes, three of them in Cobbie's parish of St Clement Danes. Five Africans were baptised in Westminster between 1620 and 1634. While many were not recorded as belonging to a particular household, some worked for courtiers, including Fortunatus, servant to Sir Robert Cecil. Mary was a maid to William Stallenge, the former MP for Plymouth and the Keeper of the King's silkworms. She was buried in 1609, the same year Stallenge published his treatise *Instructions for the Increasing of Mulberie Trees*, and the King employed him to set up a mulberry garden in Westminster.[24] The Crown sought to establish a native production of the silk that, as Reasonable Blackman could attest, was so fashionable and profitable at this time.

Some of the Africans in Westminster were brought there from southern Europe by members of the nobility or gentry. In 1621 a five-year-old child named Maria was baptised at St Martin in the Fields. She was '*valde nigra*', (very black). Born in Barbary, she'd been taken to London from Spain by the courtier Endymion Porter.[25] With a Spanish grandmother and an uncle in the Spanish diplomatic service, it was only natural for the young Endymion to spend time in Spain. He served as a member of the Duke of Olivares's household from 1605 to 1607, and returned to the country at least twice in the following two decades.[26] Another African girl was brought to Westminster in July 1623 by Aletheia Howard, Countess of Arundel. The letter-writer John Chamberlain reported the event to Dudley Carleton, the English ambassador to the Netherlands:

> The Countesse of Arundel is now upon her return for she hath sent some forerunners before, three Italian massaras [female servants] (whereof one is a blackamore) and a Gondola, which I doubt will not so well brook our river, where there is commonly so much wind.[27]

To Chamberlain, the idea of a gondola being blown about the Thames was far more incongruous and noteworthy than the arrival of an African servant at Arundel House, one of the stately mansions that lined the Strand. Like the gondola, she hailed from Venice, where the Countess had lived since 1620, spending most of her time collecting art.[28] As we saw in Chapter Two, there had been Africans in Venice for more than a century by this time. For visiting English aristocrats, they were literally part of the picture: Anthony Van Dyck included African attendants both in his portrait of the diplomat George Gage, a friend of the Arundels, and in *The*

Continence of Scipio, featuring the Duke of Buckingham.[29] He painted both these works during Lady Arundel's sojourn in Italy, where he was part of her circle.

Few women voluntarily chose prostitution as a career. Many recounted that they had been tricked into it by 'fair words and great promises'. Some had received guarantees of marriage that proved as worthless as the men who gave them once the deed was done, leaving them with little choice but to turn to prostitution.[30] Others were preyed upon by 'women-brokers' who were said to visit households, 'demanding of . . . Maid-servants if they do like of their services: if not, then they will tell them they will help them to a better service, and so allure them' to abandon their employment. The maids who left boarded with one of these brokers and while awaiting their new, better job, 'they be oftentimes made Harlots' by 'lewd young men that resort to those houses . . . to their undoing, and the great hurt of the Common-wealth'.[31]

Unscrupulous masters and mistress sometimes forced their servants into the trade. In April 1605, Eme Finch said 'her mistress would often times force her to go up into a room to be naughty with divers men who resorted to the house'.[32] Being 'naughty' had a far stronger sexual connotation then, as 'naught' or 'nothing' was slang for the female genitals, which lacked a 'thing'.[33] Hence, when Ophelia says 'I think nothing my lord', Hamlet's response is 'That's a fair thought to lie between maids' legs'.[34]

Some women were the victims of their own parents. Judith Hill, a widow, pimped out her own daughter in 1603, and James Baron, a tailor of St Margaret's Westminster, was accused in June 1627 of 'procuring his daughter and a gentleman to meet together whereby she was got with child'.[35] The Bankes themselves may have abused their daughter Frances in this way. Although one lodger described her as 'a modest civil maid', another asked 'hath your mother sold your maidenhead?' Frances was supposedly so upset at this suggestion that she died of grief.

In the grip of extreme poverty, some women thought it better to prostitute their bodies than to steal. Young women who arrived in London from the countryside could not always find the respectable work they sought. Bawds haunted the typical drop-off points and preyed on new arrivals, enticing them to work in their brothels: in 1612, the Clerkenwell madam Katherine Fuller took 'country wenches from the carriers' and 'put them into gentlemen's apparel' to 'play the whore'.[36]

Anne Cobbie 'often' frequented the Bankes's house, but she didn't live there. She may have been one of the women who worked at various bawdy houses, such as Anne Smith, who had 'layen at Wattwood's, Marshall's, Jane Fuller's, Martyn's, Shaw's, and other naughty houses'.[37] At least eight other women worked from the Bankes's house at this time, but most of them resided elsewhere. Only two actually lived there: Anne Edwards, a minister's wife, and a young woman named Mary Hall. This fits with the average number of women lodged in a bawdy house, which was two or three.[38] Some lived nearby on the Strand: Margaret Hammond lived near the White Hart and Mary Etherington at the Windmill. Elizabeth Ratcliffe was also close at hand, lodging at a broker's house near Scroope's Court in Holborn. Further afield were Elizabeth Hales, in Cloth Fair by Smithfield, and Sara Waters, near the Three Tunnes at Ratcliffe. Both Elizabeth and Sara lived with their mothers. Sara's sister Jane had previously boarded with the Bankes, but by February 1626 she had died. Another woman named Mary, of unknown address, 'resorted daily' to the Bankes's house.

John Bankes was a tailor by trade, but by the 1620s he and his wife were making quite a substantial amount on the side by keeping a bawdy house. It may have been Mrs Bankes who masterminded the business, as the majority of bawds were women, though some houses were kept by husband and wife teams.[39] The Bankes would have had connections with several pimps who supplied them with women, such as the 'broker' who lived near Scroope's Court in Holborn, where Elizabeth Ratcliffe lodged. They needed a regular supply of fresh recruits. One of their workforce, Jane Waters, had died recently and another, Thomasine Greene, was very ill from 'the pox'. And if their late daughter Frances had worked for them, then she too needed to be replaced.

Mary Hall had heard Anne Cobbie herself, and various men, say that 'they had rather give her a piece to lie with her than another five shillings because of her soft skin'. A piece was a gold coin worth 22 shillings. In the eyes of these men, Cobbie was worth almost five times more than other women. The 'set price of a strumpet's soul' varied enormously. In the 1590s Thomas Nashe spoke of 'sixpenny whoredom' in the same breath as he declared the normal fee to be half-a-crown (two shillings and sixpence).[40] In Dekker's 1630s comedy, *The Honest Whore, Part II*, a bawd is asked 'how many twelve-penny Fees, nay two shillings Fees, nay, when any Ambassadors have been here, how many half-crown Fees hast thou taken?'[41] High-class courtesans commanded the steepest prices, while streetwalkers could be considerably cheaper. Elizabeth Compe, 'a very lewd quean and a notorious whore', was said to be 'naughty with anyone' for two pence in 1609.[42]

Anne Cobbie and the other women of the Bankes's house would have been dressed in 'gorgeous attire'. The Bridewell court books are full of descriptions of sumptuous costumes of silk, satin, velvet, tufted taffeta and fur, decorated with gold embroidery or pearls. Mistress Hibbens kept a wardrobe full of 'silk gowns of several colours, as also silk rash gowns and other stuffe gowns, petticoats of durance with two or three yards velvet as also smocks of Holland' for use in her bawdy house. The heroine of Thomas Cranley's 1635 poem, *Amanda: or the Reformed Whore*, has gowns, jewels, ruffs, muffs, fans and perfume in abundance:

> Now in the richest colours maybe had,
> The next day, all in mourning blacke, and sad . . .
> The next time, rushing in thy Silken weeds,
> Embroyder'd, lac't, perfum'd, in glittering shew,
> Rich like a Lady, and attended so.

Mistress Frances, of Thomas Nashe's *Choice of Valentines* (c. 1593), appears 'in her velvet gowns / And ruffs, and periwigs as fresh as May', and confounds the 'hero' Tomalin with her 'rattling silks'.[43] Such dress was par for the course, especially for women like Anne Cobbie who aimed to attract a higher class of clientele.

Cobbie's occupation was less salubrious than Reasonable Black-man's but, like his, it made her financially independent. There is no suggestion that she was directly employed by the Bankes, nor that she was any more dependent on them than the other women who worked from their house, all of whom would have given Mrs Bankes half their takings. Katherine Jones 'had to do carnally with many men' in Jane Fuller's house on St John Street in Clerkenwell, 'and she had her half always of the money for her whoredome'. Lodging and food cost another four to six shillings per week, but as Cobbie didn't live at the Bankes's, she may have paid less to use of one of their rooms.[44] Her popularity allowed her to demand higher rates, which could have proved quite lucrative over time. If, like the Clerkenwell prostitute Elizabeth Kirkham, she entertained up to four clients a day she could have made hundreds of pounds a year, and even after losing half to Mrs Bankes, she would still have made a tidy profit.

Working in St Clements Danes put Anne Cobbie in a good position to attract well-to-do clients. A constant flow of gentlemen came to Westminster to attend Parliament, to attend the royal court at Whitehall in search of preferment, to pursue legal suits, or even simply to shop, especially after James I opened the New Exchange shopping centre that he called 'Britain's Burse' in 1609. Well-to-do visitors often rented accommodation from men such as John Cleeves of St Clements Danes, who kept a large and 'fair' house 'by the sign of the Black Boy' to lodge gentlemen during term-time for thirty years from 1605. In the 1620s, large houses with gardens intended for 'the use of some great person' were built in Drury Lane. In the following decade, the Earl of Bedford continued this trend, with his development of Covent Garden. St Clements Danes was also one of the two main churches attended by the gentry.[45] Despite what they might hear from the pulpit, gentlemen in town for business, and away from home, might be tempted to visit women like Anne Cobbie, who just happened to be very close by.

The Bankes's house was also well placed for the Inns of Court and Chancery, especially St Clements Inn, which was, as the name suggests, close by the church of St Clements Danes. In Thomas Dekker and John Webster's *Westward Ho!* (c. 1604) Luce boasts of Inns of Court men amongst her long list of clients. She has so many that she can 'suffer one to keep me in diet, another in apparel; another in Physic; another to pay my house rent'.[46]

Not only gentlemen and lawyers called. One sample of 219 Elizabethan clients whose status can be identified from the Bridewell records shows that 39% were apprentices and servants, 12% craftsmen and tradesmen, 11% gentlemen, 11% foreign merchants, 7.8% ambassador's retinues, 5% servants of bishops and aristocrats, 3% young men of the Inns and 2% aristocrats.[47] There were 20,000–30,000 thousand unmarried apprentices in seventeenth-century London. Such was their propensity for visiting prostitutes that every Shrove Tuesday they rioted and pulled down bawdy houses, to remove temptation during Lent.[48] In the 1612 ballad, *Whipping Cheer*, the prostitutes sing: 'If the London Prentices, / And other good men of fashion / Would but refrain our companies, / Then woe to our occupation'.[49] Thomas Nashe said that servants and apprentices stole money from their masters in order to purchase sex, though of course he blamed the women: 'Prentices and poor servants they encourage to rob their masters'.[50]

Cobbie's customers were not necessarily all Englishmen; there is more evidence of African men visiting prostitutes in this period than of African women working as prostitutes. In May 1577, 'Peter Peringoe, a blackamore' confessed before the Bridewell Court that he'd had 'the use of the body of one Margery Williams here present . . . in one Sawyers house in Clerk Alley in Bishopsgate on Mondaye last'. Although she denied it, Richard Dobson, Beadle of the Ward, testified that 'they were taken a bed together'. In December of the same year, 'Jane Thompson a harlot' was whipped because 'she consented to commit whoredom with one Anthony a blackamore'. They were also caught in bed together, with 'the door locked to them'. In her evidence to the Bridewell court in January 1578, Elizabeth Kirkham testified that Rose Brown, a 'common bawd' and a 'whore of evil fame', had 'divers serving men blackamores and other persons resort to her house whilst this Elizabeth dwelt there'.[51] Elizabeth and Rose were both prostitutes; they worked for Gilbert East, who ran a brothel in Turnbull Street, and Lucy Baynham, who ran another brothel in Clerkenwell. So, some of Anne Cobbie's encounters may also have been with African men who did not lack the wherewithal to pay for sex.

* * *

Contemporary evidence of what went on behind locked doors is hard to come by, especially from a woman's point of view. Nashe's *Choice of Valentines* provides a man's account. Despite the romantic title, it is so explicit that it went unpublished until 1899, and even then was only available to private subscribers. Nashe describes a young man named Tomalin's visit to a 'house of venerie'. He is met by 'a foggie three-chinned dame / That used to take young wenches for to tame'. She insists he pays in advance, only unlocking the door after Tomalin has handed over the money. 'Dame Bawd' leads him 'by blind meanders and by crankled ways' until they come to a 'shady loft / where Venus' bouncing vestals skirmish oft'. There he is seated in a leather chair and introduced to a pair of women, 'To choose of them which might content mine eye'. He rejects both, insisting he must 'have fresher ware'. Eventually the bawd produces Frances, the young woman he came to see, all the while warning him that her charms will come at a higher price. What follows seems more the product of Nashe's feverish imagination, designed for what Pepys called 'one-handed reading', than an accurate report.[52] The poet's 'hero' suffers premature ejaculation at the sight of Frances's 'lofty buttock bared with azure veins', and although she is able to raise his 'silly worm' from its 'swoon', he is unable to keep it up for long, and all too soon 'life forsakes his fleshly residence' once more.[53] At this point she whips out a dildo, which 'stands as stiff, as he were made of steel' and 'plays at peacock twixt [her] legs right blithe, /And doeth [her] tickling swage with many a sigh'. Nashe's harlot is a woman who enjoys sex:

> With Oh, and Oh, she itching moves her hips,
> And to and fro, full lightly starts and skips.
> She jerks her legs, and sprawleth with her heels,
> No tongue may tell the solace that she feels.[54]

We cannot know exactly what Anne Cobbie did with her clients or how she felt about it. However, Peter Lowe, a Scottish surgeon who worked for Henry IV of France, commented that 'common women take not so great pleasure, because they are accustomed night and day to exercise venerie'.[55] His words sound much closer to the truth than Nashe's fantastical verse.

Anne Cobbie said herself that men were prepared to pay above the odds for her soft skin; they don't appear to have been put off by its colour. Indeed, in one play of 1658, a 'wencher' boasts that he has 'tasted . . . of all complexions / From the white flaxen to the tawny-moor'.[56] Not everyone shared this character's attitude. In *A Midsummer Night's Dream* (c.1595), Lysander rejects Hermia with the line: 'Away you Ethiop!'[57] In Ben Jonson's *Masque of Blackness* and its sequel, the *Masque of Beauty*, performed by Queen Anne of Denmark and her ladies at court in 1605 and 1606, the black daughters of Niger seek beauty and become white, thanks to the rays of the British sun, which represented King James.[58] To render herself unattractive to other men, Pamphilia of Mary Wroth's 1621 sonnet cycle, 'Pamphilia to Amphilanthus', wishes to be a 'Black-moore or any thing more dreadful'.[59] However, these very same texts also include references to black beauty. Jonson's Niger praises his daughter's looks, 'their beauties conquer in great beauty's war', which 'no age can change'; a seventeenth-century precursor to the modern phrase 'black don't crack'.[60] In the end, Wroth's Pamphilia marries the noble and heroic Rodomandro, King of Tartaria, whose skin is dark.[61]

Ambiguous attitudes to skin colour also appear in poetry. In one of his Dark Lady sonnets Shakespeare proclaims 'now is black beauty's successive heir' while in another he speaks of a 'woman colour'd ill'. Some critics have argued these verses should be renamed the 'black woman sonnets'. Not only are the Lady's breasts 'dun', but 'black wires grow on her head' and her eyes are 'raven black'.[62] New evidence of African women living in Shakespeare's London only strengthens this proposal. Other seventeenth-century poets certainly contemplated the beauty of black women, in verses such as *On an Ethiopian Beauty*, *One Enamour'd on a Black-moor* and *Sonnet of Black Beauty*.[63]

On the stage, Cleopatra, who has a 'tawny front' like Cobbie and is 'with Phoebus's amorous pinches black', is so desirable that Antony is tempted to leave Rome, and ultimately to die for her. As his friend Enobarbus comments: 'Age cannot wither her, nor custom stale / her infinite variety. Other women cloy / the appetites they feed, but she makes hungry / where most she satisfies'. There are even literary echoes of the emphasis on Cobbie's soft skin. In *Lust's Dominion* (1600), the Queen of Spain talks of her lover as the 'soft-skinned Negro'. The Frenchman Montferrat of Beaumont and Fletcher's *The Knight of Malta* (1616–18) tells the black maid Zanthia or Abdella: 'thou art more *soft* / And full of dalliance than the fairest flesh, And farre more loving'. He calls her his 'black swan, silk'ner then Signet's plush'. Anne Cobbie's skin may have attracted similar compliments. And, like Zanthia, she might well have replied 'I . . . know . . . I am as full of pleasure in the touch / As ere a white-fac'd puppet of 'em all'.[64]

After Henry VIII closed down the last legal brothels in 1546, prostitutes lived with the constant threat of arrest and punishment. One of Dekker's 'whores' was 'burnt [deflowered] at fourteen, seven times whipt, sixe times carted, nine times duck'd, search'd by some hundred and fifty Constables'.[65] Much of the blame for the existence of the sex trade was laid at the door of the women involved: they were lustful creatures who lured poor innocent men into their clutches. In July 1614, Sir Thomas Myddelton, the Lord Mayor of London, wrote to the Lord Chamberlain, that he 'had informed himself, by means of spies, of many lewd houses, and had gone himself disguised to divers of them, and finding these nurseries of villainy, had punished them according to their deserts, some by carting and whipping, and many by banishment'.[66] One wonders why exactly he felt the need to go in person, and indeed how he disguised himself on these visits. When it came to the punishments, however, he was absolutely sincere. Many prostitutes were sent to the London Bridewell, which had been established as a 'house of correction' in 1553. For women who worked in Westminster, 'lewd and disorderly behaviour' was also dealt with at the Westminster Quarter Sessions, which met in Westminster Hall from 1618.[67] As the Lord Mayor said, punishments included being taken through the streets of London in the back of a cart, flogging, a fine, banishment from the city, or imprisonment in Bridewell prison, where inmates were forced to beat hemp and spin flax. In the 1612 ballad *Whipping Cheer, Or the woeful lamentations of three Sisters in the Spittle when they were in new Bridewell* the women sing:

Gold and silver hath forsaken,
Our acquaintance clearly:
Twinned whipcord takes the place.
And strikes t'our shoulders nearly.

'If the wheel leave turning', they are whipped. If they stop thumping the hemp, they are whipped. Their hands are blistered and the eldest sister 'cannot endure the labour / which is thrust upon her'.[68]

By the early 1630s, some prostitutes were being banished to Virginia. In Massinger's *The City Madam* (1632) 'Strumpets and Bawds' are 'shipp'd thither', 'For the abomination of their life, / Spew'd out of their own Country'.[69] Some thought this wasn't enough. In 1583, the Puritan pamphleteer Philip Stubbes had proposed a return to the medieval practice of facially branding women found guilty of prostitution. The clergyman Donald Lupton called for nothing less than the death penalty.[70]

Bawds such as the Bankes took precautions to avoid detection. Their houses had 'back-doors to come in and out by undiscovered; sliding windows also, and trap-boards in floors, to hide whores behind and under, with false counterfeit panes in walls, to be opened and shut like a wicket'[71] But no one could evade suspicion forever. In March 1624 the Provost Marshal, Daniel Powell, accused Mrs Bankes of 'supposed misdemeanours' before the Westminster Sessions.[72] Although the marshals were meant to police the 'houses of persons notoriously suspected . . . for lewd and incontinent life', they were not always particularly effective. In 1602, one commentator complained that 'there be more notorious strumpets and their mates about the city and the suburbs than ever were before the [Provost] Marshall was appointed'.[73] So it proved for Jane Bankes; Powell failed to 'manifest' his accusations, and she escaped punishment.

Only when a private citizen pursued the Bankes, with the collusion of one of their own lodgers, were they were brought to justice. Towards the end of June 1625, Clement Edwards, a Cambridge graduate and former rector of Witherley in Leicestershire, came to London in search of his wife, Anne.[74] He found her lodging in the Bankes's bawdy house, where she was 'suspected to live incontinently', and on 24 June, he lodged an indictment before the Westminster Sessions.[75] The formal Latin of the document is punctuated with the English phrase 'keeping a common brothel house'. The Latin word used to mean brothel was *lupanum*, derived from the word *lupo* for wolf. The Italians used the related word *Lupanerie* to describe 'those secret chambers of harlots wherein they filthily prostituted their bodies to sale . . . because they after the manner of ravening *she-wolves* catch hold of silly wretched men and pluck them into their holes'.[76] Edwards's indictment complained that the Bankes's house contained:

> divers persons of evil behaviour and manners committed adultery and fornication by day as by night, to the great displeasure of Almighty God, the corruption and destruction of youth, the great disquietude of the neighbours dwelling near the aforesaid house and to the evil and perilous example of others in the like delinquent.[77]

It seems the court was very busy that year, as the case was not mentioned again until the February 1625 Epiphany Session, presided over by Dr Roger Bates, chaplain to Charles I.[78] By this time, Clement Edwards had found an ally in Mary Hall, the other woman who, like his wife, permanently lodged at the Bankes's house. No doubt Hall blamed Mrs Bankes for luring her into the business. According to the written information she supplied to the court, Mrs Bankes had sold her maidenhead twice, first to 'one Master Freake' and 'the second time to one Master Waferer'. She may have been particularly put out by how much of the money found its way into Mrs Bankes's pockets and how little of it into hers. Mr Freake had paid Mrs Bankes ten 'pieces' (£11) and Hall £2 2s. Her cut from Mr Waferer's visit had been £1 7s, while Mrs Bankes had received £7 14s. Both instances were a long way from the usual 50/50 split between bawd and prostitute.

Mary Hall's testimony was taken before Roger Bates on 23 February 1626. As well as recounting the two instances where Mrs Bankes had sold her virginity, and describing Anne Cobbie, she provided the names and addresses of nine 'whores' who 'resort . . . daily to the said Bankes his house'. In the same session, recognisances (bonds) were taken for the key individuals – Mr and Mrs Bankes, Anne Edwards and Mary Hall – to appear at the next sessions, to be held in the Trinity Term. Their neighbours promised to ensure their appearance, on pain of a financial penalty if they did not. In the mean time, all were enjoined to be 'of good behaviour'.

The Trinity session was presided over by Dr Peter Heywood. Heywood was one of those who had discovered the Gunpowder Plot in 1605. He was supposedly the man who seized Fawkes's lantern in the cellars of the Houses of Parliament. He met his end on 21 November 1640, when a Catholic assassin stabbed him in Westminster Hall as he showed a friend a list of local 'suspected and notorious Papists'.[79] Clement Edwards himself appeared before the court on 4 June 1626, after which the Grand Jury committed the case for trial at the next Quarter Session.[80] John and Jane Bankes were placed on remand. Their names appear on the list of 'prisoners remaining in the custody of the Keeper of the Gatehouse since the last sessions', dated 23 June 1626. It was of the Gatehouse Prison, close to Westminster Abbey, that the poet Richard Lovelace wrote: 'Stone walls do not a prison make, / Nor iron bars a cage'.[81] It was a real enough prison for the Bankes. In July they were summoned by the court to formally deny the charges made against them, but even though they were to 'appear at the next sessions' there is no mention of them in Michaelmas 1626, nor thereafter, and they do not appear on the next list of prisoners in October.[82] As for Anne Cobbie, it seems that the Westminster authorities took no interest in pursuing her, in spite of Mary Hall naming her as a prostitute.

Venereal disease was as much of a danger to prostitutes as the law. Another regular at the Bankes's house had succumbed; Mary Hall reported that Thomasine Greene 'now lies sick of the pox in Turnbull Street and is almost consumed with them'. The 'pox' was a general term for sexually transmitted diseases, but most likely referred to gonorrhoea or syphilis.

The blame for the pox was always placed elsewhere. The English called it 'the French pox', in France it was 'the Spanish pox' or 'the evil of Naples', while others thought it originated in the New World. Wherever it came from, syphilis was widespread in England by this time. The surgeon William Clowes called it 'the pestilent infection of filthy lust . . . a sickness very loathsome, odious, troublesome and dangerous, which spreadeth itself throughout all England and overfloweth as I think the whole world'. It was all the result of 'the filthy life of many lewd and idle persons, both men and women, about the city of London'.[83] Young men were warned to avoid brothels for fear of infection:

> Breathe, breathe awhile, my over-heated Muse,
> Before you enter their accursed Stews;
> Where Aches, Buboes, Shankers, Nodes and Poxes,
> Are hid in Females Damn'd Pandora's Boxes.[84]

Prostitutes were blamed for incubating the disease, and one part of their body in particular was described as the site of infection: 'the mixture of so many Seeds does occasion such a Corruption in the Passage of the Matrix, that it degenerates into a proper virulent Ferment'.[85] The disease could result in unsightly ulcers, paralysis, blindness, madness and 'saddle nose', where the bridge of the nose collapses entirely. Sir William Davenant – poet, playwright and godson (and, as he would have it, actual son) of William Shakespeare – 'got a terrible clap of a Black* handsome wench that lay in Axe-yard, Westminster . . . which cost him his Nose'.[86]

There was no effective cure, but plenty of suggested remedies. These ranged from mercury treatment – hence 'A night with Venus, a lifetime with Mercury' – to stewed prunes, which were often served in brothels.[87] In 1615 Gervase Markham's *The English Huswife* included a recipe for an ointment made with grains of paradise, which could have come from River Cestos.[88] It was also thought that 'hard pissing' immediately after coitus would flush out the disease and to this end, two chamber pots were kept under each bed.[89] Most thought on prevention and cure focused on the male victims, with little concern spared for the women, who were thought of as disease carriers. The prevailing wisdom was that

* When used like this, 'Black' is more likely to refer to the colour of the woman's hair than her skin.

women couldn't easily contract syphilis, because the uterus was supposedly cold, dry and dense.[90] In reality, many women died of venereal disease, and prostitutes were at high risk. If Anne Cobbie did contract such a disease, even if did not kill her, it would eventually have left her unable to work.

Sex work was hard work, and it took its toll, as many contemporary commentators noted. John Taylor ended his poem on 'A Whore' with the lines: 'And so I leave her . . . To mend or end, when age or / Pox will make her / Detested, and Whore-masters all forsake her'.[91] 'Ere they come to forty, you shall see them worn to the bare bone', Thomas Nashe wrote, 'At twenty their lively colour is lost, their faces are sodden & parboiled with French surfeits [syphilitic sores]'.[92] The playwright Henry Chettle estimated that most women were broken after seven years of such work. Barnabe Rich wrote in *My Lady's Looking Glasse* (1616) that 'the harlot that is once past thirty-five years is fitter to furnish a Hospital then to garnish a bed chamber'.[93] Had Anne Cobbie required medical treatment for venereal disease, she could have sought help at St Thomas's or St Bartholomew's hospitals, which both treated such cases. From 1622 'foul women' were sent to Kingsland Hospital in Hackney, but there were only twenty beds and the care was expensive, not to mention mostly ineffective.[94]

Another consequence of having regular sex was that Anne Cobbie might have become pregnant. On 3 July 1626, shortly after the Bankes were imprisoned in the Gatehouse, an abandoned child was found in Somerset yard, a large stable to the west of Somerset House. This palace, situated at the western end of St Clements Danes, had been built by Edward Seymour, Duke of Somerset, during Edward VI's reign, but by 1626 it was in royal hands; the architect Inigo Jones was in the process of remodelling it for Queen Henrietta Maria. The child was baptised 'Elizabeth' at St Mary Le Strand, Westminster. It was noted 'the father [was] supposed to bee a blackmore' as contemporary medical theory credited the male seed with determining a child's physical characteristics.[95] The ancient Greek doctor Galen, who still held currency in sixteenth-century England, had written that 'the female semen is exceedingly weak and unable to advance to that state of motion in which it could impress an artistic form upon the foetus'.[96] African women giving birth to dark-skinned children fathered by Englishmen would have confused Tudor doctors. It's impossible to know if this child was Anne Cobbie's, but she could have been.

Cobbie wouldn't have been the only African woman in England with an illegitimate child. There were at least twenty-six such children, born to black mothers, recorded between 1578 and 1640. Sixteen of these were baptised or buried in Devon, six in London, two in Bristol, the rest in Cornwall, Dorset and Kent. Edith, the daughter of Katalina 'a blacamore', was a typical case. On her baptism at Sherborne Abbey, Dorset, in January 1631, the parish clerk summarised the circumstances of her birth with the Latin word 'spuria' (from which we derive the word 'spurious').[97] Illegitimacy was common enough, regardless of ethnicity; 4% of children were born illegitimate in the late sixteenth and early seventeenth century. While Tudor and Stuart society disapproved of sex outside marriage, communities were used to dealing with it.[98] The parish authorities were always keen to establish the identity of the father because if they didn't they became responsible for the child's maintenance. To this end, they put pressure on midwives to do their best to extract this information during the throes of labour. If the supposed father failed to support his child, the courts could pursue him, even if the child hadn't yet been born. We know the names of about half of the fathers of illegitimate children born to African mothers in this period. Some are known to us because they were held to account for their misdemeanours, just as other men were in cases involving Englishwomen. For example, in Poole in 1609–10, the town authorities received £1 15s from Francis Kent:

> for releasing him of his punishment, inflicted on him at the quarter sessions, the which he was adjudged unto for begetting a bastard on the Blackmore Elizabeth Ferdinando which was given towards the reparacon of the Church.[99]

Anne Cobbie's liaisons with the men of Westminster were one extreme of a spectrum of inter-racial relationships that existed in this period: from prostitution, via fornication, where no money changed hands, to long-term relationships and the occasional marriage. The church courts policed the moral crime of fornication alongside offences such as drinking during divine service, slander and failing to pay church tithes. The worst sentence that could be passed by the English church courts was excommunication. From 1563, adulterers in Scotland could be given the death penalty, in line with the thinking of Protestant reformers including John Knox, Luther, Calvin and Zwingli. In reality, the sentence was rarely carried out.[100]

Both African men and women were punished by the church courts for having sex outside marriage. In February 1593, Joanna Bennett of Grays Thurrock, Essex, was brought before the Church court at West Ham and charged with 'having carnal knowledge and abusing her body with a certain blackmore now dwelling in the town'. The following January one Agnes Musby did penance for 'fornication with Paul, a blakemore' in Aldingbourne, West Sussex. Paul himself didn't respond to the court's summons and in so doing he risked being banned from entering church.[101] These relationships show a very physical acceptance of Africans into Tudor and early Stuart society.

As the popularity of family history and genealogy soars, and the accuracy of DNA tests increases, more and more people are discovering they have African ancestry. A man named Peter Bluck, living in Wales, recently traced his family tree back to Henry Jetto, who as we learnt in earlier chapters was the gardener to Sir Henry Bromley in Worcestershire, before he left to establish his own household some time before he died in 1627. Other Jetto descendants are currently living in Birmingham, Bristol, Cheshire, Durham, Manchester and Surrey, as well as in Australia and in the USA.[102] The North Carolina descendants of Adam Ivey (1640–1710) of Virginia have been found through DNA testing to have Mandinka genes, from Western Gambia, and are investigating whether this could have come via Gylman Ivie, an African who lived in Gloucestershire in the 1570s.[103] When West African DNA was found in seven Yorkshiremen with the surname 'Revis' in 2007, it was assumed they had a shared ancestor who had come to England as a slave in the eighteenth century. Our new-found knowledge of the Black Tudors means that their shared genes could be traced back to Anne Cobbie's time or earlier.[104] Generations of intermarriage later, modern descendants of the Black Tudors and Stuarts bear no visual markers of African identity. There may be hundreds of residents of Britain and her former colonies walking around oblivious of this genetic inheritance, but modern science has the power to render these connections visible once more.

If Anne Cobbie survived the perils of punishment, pox, and pregnancy, she might have gone on to become a bawd with her own establishment. In Shakespeare's *Measure for Measure*, Mistress Overdone, now a 'powdered bawd', was once a 'fresh whore'. In Thomas Cranley's *Amanda: or the Reformed Whore*, 'The Mistress of the house where thou dost lie / Hath formerly been of the self-same trade: / One that long since hath sold her honesty, / And now is turn'd from Whore unto a Bawd'.[105] Or Cobbie might even have left the bawdy world behind and married. Just as some women fell into prostitution having received false promises of marriage, some wed and left it behind them.[106] There is a record at St Clements Danes for the marriage of an Anne Cobbie and Richard Sherwood on 11 June 1626. He may have been the haberdasher of that name who took on an apprentice in 1629.[107] We can't be sure this was the same woman, but the timing of the wedding fits well with the dates of the Westminster Sessions case. The Bankes were called to appear before the court in the first few days of that month, and were imprisoned by 23 June. It certainly would have been an opportune moment for Cobbie to move on with her life.

Modern writers have exaggerated the number of African prostitutes in Tudor and Stuart London, reading later trends back into the earlier period, imagining the African prostitutes in the works of Hogarth and Rowlandson were also commonplace in Shakespeare's London.[108] If they were, their names would appear in the copious records of London prostitution produced by the Bridewell court, yet they do not. A heavy evidential burden has been placed on the quasi-mythical character of 'Lucy Negro' even though there is no concrete archival proof that she ever existed.[109] The only references to her come from literary texts. A 'Lucy Negro' appears in the surviving script for the entertainment performed at the Gray's Inn Revels of 1594.[110] The character is a Clerkenwell bawd, who may well have been a topical reference to one of two women who had the nickname 'Black Luce' in the period, Latinised in the play as 'Lucy Negro'. One was Lucy Baynham, 'the infamous Black Luce of Clerkenwell', who ran a brothel there in the late 1570s. The other was Lucy Morgan, committed to the Bridewell for keeping a bawdy house in 1600.[111] There is no evidence that either of these women was African. Nonetheless, the idea of an African prostitute named Lucy Negro has been embraced by people who like the idea that Shakespeare's Dark Lady sonnets were written to an African woman.

There is one African woman, who did exist, that scholars have sought to identify as a prostitute working in London at this time. However, the evidence to support this proposition is ambiguous at best. She is referred to, but not by name, in a letter written in May 1599 by Denis Edwards of Southampton to Thomas Lankford, the Earl of Hertford's secretary:

> I wrote to you as concerning my negroe where or in what place she was or whether you have taken pains to succour her, or no. If you have not I pray make enquiries for her for she is certainly dwelling in Turnbull Street at the sign of the Swan at one Danes house who selleth beer it is hard by Clerkenwell.[112]

Her address in a Dane's (or Mr Danes) beer shop in the notorious Turnbull Street has been enough for most historians to assume she was a prostitute. Turnbull Street, now Turnmill Street, where Thomasine Greene lay dying of the pox in 1626, was 'the most disreputable street in London, a haunt of thieves and loose women'.[113] In Shakespeare's *Henry IV, Part II*, Falstaff says of Justice Shallow that he 'hath done nothing but prate to me of the wildness of his youth, and the feats he hath done about Turnbull Street'.[114] The street was so notorious that its name was used as a synonym for licentiousness. In 1625, Ellen Tilbury accused her neighbour of being a whore simply by saying 'Turnbull Street is a more fit place for thee'.[115] However, one wonders at the wording of Edwards's letter. He seems concerned with her wellbeing, and asks his friend to succour her. When he asks 'what place' she was in, could he mean to enquire whether she had found a 'place', that is, domestic employment? He can't be asking where she is, because he already knows that she's dwelling in Turnbull Street. When he asks Lankford to 'make enquiries for her', could he not be asking if a job as a domestic servant might be found for her?

Anne Cobbie is exceptional. She was the only African prostitute active during this period of whose existence we are certain. Her presence in 1626, a decade after Shakespeare's death, will do little to help those still seeking to identify his 'Dark Lady'. Nonetheless, her soft skin might have inspired poetry, had the right client appeared at the Bankes's house at the right time. As it is, we have only the stark words of Mary Hall to record her beauty. If African prostitutes were rare, how did African women who were not married or employed as domestic servants support themselves? Our final story takes us back to the rural Gloucestershire that Edward Swarthye called home, to a village not far from Bristol, where a single woman named Cattelena made a life for herself.

Cattelena of Almondsbury, Independent Singlewoman

The cow lazily chewed the grass on the village green, her udders heavy with milk. The tower of St Mary's Church soared above her, dwarfed in turn by the steep, wooded slope of Almondsbury Hill. Villagers passed by the common, as did the few travellers who used the Aust Ferry to cross the Severn, on their way to Bristol or Wales. No one gave the cow a second glance. The sun grew lower in the sky, and the cow's mistress came to collect her. She called her fondly by name. The animal was her livelihood and provided her with enough milk, butter and cheese to sustain herself and to sell to others. It was the hour for evening milking. She quietly sat beside the cow and gently began the familiar process of tugging at her teats. It was a meditative, repetitive action. As she sat there, she daydreamed a little. She thought of the twists and turns her life had taken, of the strange series of events that had brought her to Almondsbury. There she was, a single woman with her cow on a village common. A wholly unremarkable sight in rural England. And yet, in this case, it was remarkable. For she was not of Gloucestershire stock like her cow. She was African.

THE MAJORITY OF the Africans in Tudor and early Stuart England were not recorded as having a master or mistress. Without a job in someone's household or aboard a ship, were they abandoned or destitute?[1] Anne Cobbie, Reasonable

Blackman and the anonymous needlemaker of Cheapside made a living in the city, but what of the Africans who lived in the countryside, in particular the women? The only record that survives of Cattelena of Almondsbury is an inventory of her goods made after her death.[2] Like large swathes of the English population, her life was committed only to the 'short and simple Annals of the Poor'.[3] About one million probate inventories survive for the period from around 1580–1720.[4] These lists of objects, from livestock to armour, chamber-pots to musical instruments, provide an intimate insight into the daily lives and material culture of ordinary people. The more detailed ones allow us to imagine the rooms the objects furnished, the daily rituals of their owner, and estimate their social standing. What can Cattelena's possessions tell us about her daily life and how she supported herself? And how did she come to be living in a small village in Gloucestershire?

In the inventory of her goods, Cattelena was described as 'a negra deceased of Almondsbury in the county of Gloucester single woman'.[5] Her status as an unmarried woman was not very unusual. An estimated 30% of the English adult female population were single women, and very few of the African women we know about were married in this period.[6] Use of the word 'negra' was quite rare, especially in the Bristol area. It is simply the female form of the Latin (also Spanish, Portuguese and Italian) 'negro', meaning black. The word 'negro' was new to England in the sixteenth century. Its first recorded use in an English text was in 1555, in Richard Eden's translation of Peter Martyr's *Decades of the New World*, where he used it to describe the inhabitants of 'the coast of Guinea and the mid parts of Africa'.[7] I have only found the female form 'negra' employed to describe seven other individual Africans between 1598 and 1640. The word 'negro' was also used to describe women: there are eighteen known examples between 1586 and 1627. In one case in Bristol in 1612, a woman was described as a 'blacke negra', which seems to demonstrate some uneasiness with the foreign word 'negra'. None of the other Africans in Bristol were described as 'negroes' or 'negras', so the term was still unfamiliar there.[8] We don't know where Cattelena was from, but her Hispanic-sounding name suggests that she, like many others, had arrived in England via the Spanish or Portuguese-speaking worlds.

This late-eighteenth century view of Almondsbury Church
by Samuel Lysons shows the broach spire and cows,
like the one owned by Cattelena, grazing on the common.

Cattelena's village, Almondsbury, lies seven miles north of Bristol. It was originally a 'bury' or camp, and possibly the burial-place, of the Saxon prince Alomund, or Ealhmund (active around 784), father of King Egbert, the first sole monarch of England. Almondsbury was listed in the Domesday Book of 1086, when it had two hundred and sixty-two inhabitants and covered two hides, or 240 acres.[9] Set on a steep, wooded hill, the village looks down across the Severn estuary to the hills of South Wales, and over the Royal Forest of Dean. At the foot of the hill is St Mary's Church, with its tall lead-clad broach, or octagonal, spire, the village green before it. Adjoining the churchyard is the Bowl Inn, named after the shape of the surrounding land. The lead for the church spire was locally mined. In 1639, the Berkeley estate steward and local historian John Smyth wrote that it had 'in good plenty been digged' in the hilly part of the parish, and that the roof of nearby Berkeley Castle (the site of Edward II's murder in 1327) was covered with lead from the same source.[10]

Moments of drama occasionally interrupted this pastoral scene. In 1621 the vicar, Hieronimus Brown, noted a matter:

which should never be forgotten as long as the Sun & moon endureth; that is, a very fearful example of God's just judgement against that detestable sin of drunkenness, manifested upon William Crosseman, son of John Crosseman, who, amidst his excessive drinking in ye Church house, on 10 April, in the year of our Lord 1621, was suddenly killed by Timothy Wright, a lewd serving-man, sometimes dwelling with Mr Thomas Chester.[11]

The village was also the scene of the Princess Caraboo hoax in 1817, in which the impostor Mary Willcocks persuaded the locals that she was a royal personage, kidnapped by pirates from her home on the island of Javasu in the Indian Ocean.[12]

Many of the lives in this book have been lived in the bustling streets of London or ports such as Southampton, Plymouth and Dover, where you'd expect to find foreigners. By contrast, Cattelena is one of several Africans who were living in the Tudor and early Stuart English countryside. Parish registers record the baptisms and burials of Africans, or the children of Africans, in villages in Cornwall, Cambridgeshire, Devon, Dorset, Gloucestershire, Kent, Northamptonshire, Somerset, Suffolk and Wiltshire. The earliest is the burial of 'Thomas Bull, niger' in Eydon, Northamptonshire, in December 1545.[13] The entries from southern coastal counties are explained in part by their proximity to the ports, where ships returning from Africa and Atlantic privateering voyages might arrive. But it is nonetheless startling to find more Africans in the small village of Hatherleigh, Devon, than in the county town of Exeter. Some of the more obscure locations where Africans were living include Bluntisham-cum-Earith in Cambridgeshire, where 'Dido And a more' was buried in 1594, Stowell in Somerset, where 'Galatia the black negra' was buried in 1605 and Sibton in Suffolk, where 'Christianna Niger Anglice a blackamore' was baptised on Christmas Day 1634.[14]

There may have been more Africans living in rural locations: not all the parish registers have been systematically searched for such entries and some do not survive. In such cases, these individuals were probably the only dark-skinned person in their village. Indeed, some are referred to as 'the' rather than 'a' blackamoor. Beyond the fact that they were accepted into the parish community through baptism and Christian burial, there is little evidence to tell us how these Africans were regarded and treated. Some clearly had relationships with local people, as their children were also baptised. Gylman Ivie, a 'negro' or 'Ethiop', had two children with Anna Spencer of Dyrham, Gloucestershire; their daughter Elizabeth was baptised in October 1578, and their son Richard in February 1581, only to be buried two years later in June 1583.[15] In St Keverne, Cornwall, 'Constance the base child of a blackmore ye reputed father John the servant of John Langford' was baptised in January 1605.[16]

What brought Cattelena to Almondsbury? The village lies close to Bristol, home to at least sixteen Africans between 1560 and 1640. As far as we know, the first African to live in the city was a man Sir John Young 'did appoint to keep possession of his garden' in around 1560.[17] Four Africans were baptised in the city's churches in the period 1600–1636, and nine were buried from 1595–1632.[18] Almost half were women. Joan Maria married the weapons-maker Thomas Smyth and died of the plague in 1603, three years after her son Richard was baptised. Katherine, a 'blacke negra, servant at the horshead' – that is, the Horsehead Tavern on Christmas Street – was buried at Christ Church in January 1612. In September 1632, Grace Claun and Mary, servant to William Edmonds, were both buried at St Augustine the Less. And in August 1636, an unnamed woman gave birth to a daughter called 'Maudlinge'* in Bristol's Bridewell prison.[19] As we saw in

---

* This was an alternative spelling of Magdalene, as in Mary Magdalene, whence we get the word 'maudlin' and so might refer either to her penitence or tearfulness, or both.

Chapter Six, in the 1640s a woman named Frances, who worked for 'a man who lived on the Back of Bristol' was part of the Baptist congregation led by Nathaniel Ingelo. Was Cattelena another African woman of Bristol?

Like the Ethiopian 'negar' who 'refused to tarry and serve' Hector Nunes, Cattelena might have run away from her employer. Servants who abandoned their work broke the terms of their service and were regarded as idle or vagrant in the eyes of the law.[20] Augustina Patra, a 'blackamoor servant', was punished by the London Bridewell in January 1601 'for running away diverse times'.[21] Her mistress was Lady Elizabeth Berkeley (1576–1635), the daughter of George Carey, Baron Hunsdon. Elizabeth, who married Sir Thomas Berkeley in 1596, was a godchild and a cousin of Elizabeth I; her grandfather was the son of Mary Boleyn, Anne's sister. The family seat of Berkeley Castle was not far from Almondsbury, only about fourteen miles to the north-east. Another African woman, Mary, absconded from the Weymouth household of the French privateer Captain Peter Sallenueve in 1633 and got as far as Dorchester before the authorities caught up with her. The Dorchester Offenders' Book records that:

> Mary a Black moore servant to Captain Sallanova of Weymouth and Melcombe Regis . . . is taken within this Borough this day being Run away from her master & she confesseth having no leave of either her master or mistress & is ordered to be sent home again this day in the Afternoon.[22]

Alternatively, Cattelena may have first arrived in the area as part of one of the local gentry households. The nearest was the Chester household at Knole Park, which lay half a mile to the south of the village. Another local manor house was Over Court, built around 1580 for the Bristolian John Dowell, son of a wealthy merchant.[23] In the eighteenth century, Sir James Laroche employed two African servants there: James Long (died 1773) and Charles Morson (died 1776).[24] The third manor in the vicinity was Gaunt's Earthcott, which had been purchased by the Bristol Corporation from the Crown after the Dissolution of the Monasteries. By the early seventeenth century, the bulk of this estate was leased to none other than John Guye, who we met in Chapter Four, and his brother-in-law Matthew Bucke. All three houses had connections to Bristol merchants, but the strongest case can be made for Knole Park, which also had a link to Southampton.

At the time of Cattelena's death Knole Park was occupied by Thomas Chester (1587–1653) and his wife Elizabeth. His grandfather, Thomas Chester (c.1518–1583), a wealthy MP, merchant, and mayor of Bristol, had purchased the manor of Almondsbury in 1569. The elder Thomas Chester had various business interests that might explain the arrival of a young Cattelena into his household. In 1556, he and Giles White were summoned to appear before the Privy Council concerning the 'sending forth of two ships into the coasts of Guinea', an association that connects him to the earliest known African in Bristol.[25] For it was Giles White's widow Anne who testified in 1560 that Sir John Young 'did . . . appoint a blacke moore to keep the possession of his garden'.[26] Chester later sold Young the site of today's Colston Hall concert hall, where Young built his 'Great House'.[27] In 1577, at the age of fifty-nine, Chester became a founding member of the Spanish Company. So it is possible that Cattelena came to Knole Park from Bristol.

Her other possible route to Knole Park was through the elder Thomas Chester's daughter Anne. She married John Caplin, MP for Winchester, merchant and comptroller of the custom house of Southampton, in 1574. As we saw in Chapter Two, there were as many as ten Africans resident in the households of wealthy Southampton merchants between 1594 and 1611. John Caplin paid the poll tax for an African in his household in the parish of Holy Rood in 1598 and 1599, and a relative, Francis Caplin, paid the same tax in 1611. Anne Caplin died some time before 1623.[28] The tax returns don't record the gender, or any other details, of the Africans in the Caplin household so we don't know if these records all refer to the same individual or not. Could Cattelena have served in the Caplin household before coming to Almondsbury?

The inventory of May 1625 listed Cattelena's possessions as:

One cow

One bed, one bolster, one pillow, one pair of blankets, one sheet, one quilt

Four little pots, one pewter candlestick, one tin bottle, one dozen of spoons

Three earthen dishes, two dozen of trenchers

One table cloth

All her wearing apparel

One coffer & two little boxes

Noticeable by its absence is any sort of furniture. There are no tables or chairs; even the 'bed' may actually refer to a mattress rather than a wooden frame.[29] The fact that she didn't own any other furniture suggests that she shared a house, or lived in someone else's house. It was rare for single women to live in their own home. Only about 5% of single women below the age of 45 headed their own households. About half lived with at least one parent, a third lived as servants, 5–11% lived as lodgers and 3–7% lived with some other relative.[30] Some African women in London are described as lodgers, 'borders' or tenants: Suzanna Pearis 'a blackamoore tenant' to John de Spinosa near the sign of the Fleur de Lys in East Smithfield in 1593, 'Mary a negro' who said she 'dwelte with Mr Conradus' in 1606 and 'Isabell Peeters a Black-more lodging in Blew Anchor Alley' in 1616.[31]

If Cattelena were a servant, this would surely have been recorded in the inventory. The fact that she named the widow Helen Ford her administrator, rather than a family member, suggests she was not living with relatives. Did Cattelena rent a room from Mrs Ford? It was common for single women and widows to live together in this period.[32] Unfortunately the parish registers for Almondsbury before 1653 do not survive, so it is difficult to discover more about Helen Ford. A Richard Ford of Almondsbury made a will in 1639, in which he left his son Robert a loom, which suggests he might have been a weaver.[33] It is possible that Helen was Richard's mother.

The term 'singlewoman', used to designate Cattelena's status in the inventory, was sometimes used to refer to prostitutes. In 1530, the scholar John Palsgrave translated the French '*putain*', as 'Syngle woman, a harlot'. John Stow, in his *Survey of London* (1598), wrote that: 'single women were forbidden the rites of the church, so long as they continued that sinful life, and were excluded from Christian burial, if they were not reconciled before their death'. London legal records mention two women being dunked in the Thames for being 'singlewomen', but these same records use the term for unmarried women whose probity was not in doubt.[34] There is no reason to believe Cattelena was a prostitute. In this patriarchal society, the authorities worried that all single women were little better than prostitutes, especially if they lived alone.[35] Living with someone else, perhaps Helen Ford, would make Cattelena less suspicious in this respect.

Cattelena owned a bed or mattress, and bedding: a bolster cushion, a pillow, a pair of blankets, a sheet and a quilt. Mattresses were commonly made of ticking, a canvas or heavy linen material, usually striped. The most basic were no more than a sack: hence the expressions 'hit the sack' and 'in the sack'. The most luxurious were stuffed with feathers and were held in beautifully carved wooden bedsteads. Some people, like Shakespeare, who bequeathed his 'second best bed' to his wife Anne Hathaway, had more than one. After the featherbed, the second-best sort was a flock-bed, stuffed with coarse tufts and refuse of wool or cotton. A less valuable mattress was stuffed with straw or chaff from oat or wheat. Whichever sort Cattelena had, she had plenty of other accoutrements to make herself comfortable at night. Her bolster cushion was 'a long stuffed pillow used to support the sleeper's head in a bed'.[36] In owning a soft cushion like this, Cattelena was benefiting from a general rise in living standards during the latter half of the sixteenth century. In 1577, William Harrison reported that the old men of his village could recall sleeping with 'a good round log under their heads instead of a pillow'. In their time, if a man 'had within seven years after his marriage purchased a mattress or flock-bed, and thereto a sack of chaff to rest his head on, he thought himself as well lodged as the lord of the town'. Pillows had also only recently become commonplace. Previously, they were thought only suitable 'for women in childbed'. Cattelena had only one sheet; it would have been better to have a pair. Given the choice, it may have been preferable for her to sleep above, rather than below the sheet. As William Harrison explained, a sheet under the body would protect 'from the pricking straws that ran oft through the canvas of the pallet' and 'razed' the hardened hides of the occupant.[37] Sleepers often also lay on their quilts rather than under them. Quilts were made of a thin layer of wool, flock, feathers or down, held between two large pieces of material by lines of stitching, often decorative; the 'Tree of Life' was a popular pattern.[38] So we can imagine Cattelena's bed as a mattress covered with a single sheet and a quilt, with a bolster cushion and a pillow to support her head, and a pair of blankets to keep her warm.

She would have kept her kitchen goods in the coffer. She had four little pots, one pewter candlestick, one tin bottle and a dozen spoons. The pots would have been deep, round, metal cooking vessels, usually with three feet, made to stand over a fire.[39] Pewter, an alloy of 80% tin with 20% lead, was more valuable than wood as a material for a candlestick, but pretty common nonetheless. Spoons were the principal utensil used for cooking and eating, as forks were not yet commonly employed. When Thomas Coryate saw forks used in Italy in 1611, he thought them so remarkable that he took to using them on his return home, earning himself the nickname 'Furcifer' or fork-bearer. In Jonson's *The Devil is an Ass* (1616), one of the characters hatches a business plan to introduce forks into the English market, bringing them 'into custom here as they are in Italy to the sparing of napkins'.[40] It would have been hard to manage without a knife, however. Presumably there was one she could share.

When Beatrice comments on Benedick's hearty appetite in *Much Ado About Nothing*, she calls him a 'valiant trencherman'. Trenchers were flat plates of wood, on which meat or other food was cut up and served. They were either square or circular; some of the former had a small depression in one corner for salt.[41] Cattelena had twenty-four trenchers, which seems rather a large number for a single woman, unless she was using them to present butter and cheese. She also had a tablecloth, which – not being essential – suggests a certain level of wealth, as well as some finesse in her daily dining habits.

All Cattelena's 'wearing apparel', or clothing, came to a value of £2. We can get some idea of what might constitute a typical woman's wardrobe from the clothes the Virginia Company purchased for a group of women they sent to Jamestown in 1621 to be wives for the settlers. Each woman received a petticoat, a waistcoat, two pairs of stockings, a pair of garters, two smocks, a pair of gloves, a hat and bands, one round band, an apron, two pairs of shoes, a towel, two coifs and one cross cloth (worn across the forehead), as well as worsted and yarn for stockings. One set cost £2.[42] These women were 'young, handsome and honestly educated maids', the daughters of artisans or gentry, and so their wardrobe rather more extensive than Cattelena's, but the basic constituents were probably the same.

The most valuable item that Cattelena owned was her cow, which was valued at £3 10s. A cow was an extremely useful possession. Alcon, a rustic character in a play from 1590 exclaims, 'My cow is a commonwealth to me!' Not only, he explains to a usurer who is threatening to take his cow away, does she allow him, his wife, and son, 'to banquet ourselves withal, butter, cheese, whey, curds, cream, sod milk, raw milk, sour milk, sweet milk and butter milk', she has also saved him 'every year a penny in almanacs'. The cow's 'very tail was a calendar'. If she 'set up her tail and have galloped about the mead[ow], my little boy was able to say "Oh Father, there will be a storm!"'[43] Three-quarters of labourers leaving inventories between 1560 and 1600 owned a cow, calf or heifer. Sir Kenelm Digby wrote in 1658: 'There's not the meanest cottager but hath a cow to furnish His family with milk: 'tis the principal sustenance of the poorest Sort of people . . . which makes them very careful of the good keeping and health of their cows'.[44]

Cows were given names. Some reflected their function, as well as the owner's sense of humour. Eleanor Cumpayne of Halesowen, Worcestershire, inherited a cow named Fillpayle from her father George in 1559. It is lost to history whether the name was spoken as an order 'Fill pail!' or as a compliment on satisfactory service.[45] Other recorded names reflect the affection with which these useful creatures were regarded: Gentle, Brown Snout, Lovely, Motherlike, Winsome and Welcome Home.[46] What Cattelena called her cow is not recorded, but this doesn't mean she didn't give it a name; it just wasn't commonplace to record cows' names in inventories or wills. Only seven of the four hundred and ninety-one cows (1.43%) bequeathed in 3,720 wills Essex dating from 1620 to 1635 had their names recorded.[47]

In 1615, Gervase Markham included a chapter on 'Dairies, Butter, cheese and the necessary things belonging to that office' in his guide for English housewives, which gave advice and recipes for every aspect of keeping a cow. The ideal cow should, he said, be 'of big bone, fair shape, right red, and deep of milk, gentle and kindly'. By 'kindly' he meant not of a sympathetic nature, but 'apt to conceive, and bring forth, fruitful to nourish, and loving to that which springs from her'. The best hours for milking were between 5 and 6am in the morning and 6 and 7pm in the evening.[48] From Whitsun to Michaelmas, a cow could produce a gallon of milk a day, which could be used to make a range of 'white meats', as Alcon called them.[49] Markham includes recipes for all sorts of cheese, from 'morning milk cheese' and 'a very dainty nettle cheese' to 'eddish, or winter cheese'. 'May butter' could even be used for medicinal purposes:

> if during the month of May before you salt your butter you save a lump thereof, and put it into a vessel, and so set it in the sun the space of that month, you shall find it exceeding sovereign and medicinable for wounds, strains, aches and such like grievances.

As we learnt in Chapter Five, butter was thought to be a preventative against the plague. None of Cattelena's kitchen utensils seem to be specifically for making butter or cheese – no churn is listed – but she may have shared these items. Her three earthen dishes were, as Markham notes, the best vessels for 'long-keeping' of milk.[50]

Milking cows and making cheese and butter was thought of as women's work. In one 1629 ballad, a man and his wife swap roles. She goes out into the fields and he stays at home. When the man tries to milk the cow things do not go well:

He went to Milk one evening tide,
A skittish Cow on the wrong side,
His pail was full of Milk, God wot,
She kickt and spilt it every jot,
Besides she hit him a blow o' the face,
Which was scant whole in six weeks space

He is no better when it comes to churning butter:

As he to Churn his Butter went,
One morning with a good intent,
The Cot-quean fool did surely dream,
For he had quite forgot the Cream,
He churn'd all day, with all his might.
And yet he could get no Butter at night.[51]

The poor man had forgotten to put the cream into the churn and so spent all day pumping an empty vessel in vain. Cattelena would have been far more proficient, and her neighbours would have attributed this in most part to her sex.

Single women like Cattelena pastured their cows on the common land and made a living by selling milk and butter to their non-farming neighbours. A cow was considered a starting point towards self-sufficiency. In the eighteenth century, parish authorities sometimes helped poor women to buy a cow so they could support themselves without further help from the parish.[52] There were various patches of common land in Almondsbury, and Cattelena was fortunate enough to live there when Sunday's Hill common was still open to all; it was enclosed in 1631.[53] The pace of enclosure set in the sixteenth century, by men such as Sir Edward Wynter, only accelerated in the seventeenth. This sparked agrarian riots, such as the Midland Revolt of 1607, which began in Northamptonshire, a county that had lost 27,000 acres to enclosure since 1578.[54]

Cattelena was not a wealthy woman, yet neither was she a pauper. Her goods were valuable enough in total to be listed and reckoned by the authorities. At a time when Africans elsewhere in the world were themselves property, it is significant that she was the legal owner of anything at all. Her relative independence as a woman is also significant. Not only was she *free*, as in not enslaved, but she seems to have been free from service or any family obligation. Thanks to her cow, she was able to support herself.

The only other African woman we know who possessed property in early seventeenth-century England was Helenor Myou. She was in London when Laurence Mereene stole 'certain bandes, a pillober and other goods' from her and made his escape across the River Thames with the help of Thomas Collingwood, a yeoman of the Strand by the Savoy, in 1612. She successfully pursued the culprits at the Middlesex Sessions, where another waterman, John Smith of Stepney, was exonerated after he was also accused of carrying away the 'felon who had robbed a blackamore woman'.[55] Myou owned 'bandes' (collars or ruffs), a 'pillober' (or pillowcase), and some 'other goods'. These mysterious items were also described as 'divers goods', suggesting they were numerous enough to have been for sale.[56] So Myou not only owned property in these goods, a fact accepted without comment by the court, but may have been in business. Her possessions suggest she might have been a seamstress, or that she worked for one, like Mary Fillis. Between 1571 and 1640, more than fifty African women were recorded without mention of masters or mistresses. One scholar has suggested they were all 'unattached (abandoned, destitute)', but there is no reason why many of them cannot have lived as Cattelena and Helena Myou did.[57]

One route to financial independence for Cattelena would be to have received a legacy of money or goods in the will of a dying employer that allowed her to leave the household and set up on her own. There are a few examples of Africans being left money in their employers' wills.[58] In August 1570, Nicholas Witchals of Barnstaple left five marks to 'Anthony my negarre'. This was a sizeable sum: £3 6s 8d. Mary Groce, widow of Lawrence Groce, a Southampton merchant, left 'three pounds in money' to her 'servant Joane the blackemore' in October 1612. In December 1600, the London merchant William Offley's will gave £10 to Frances, his

African maid. With such a legacy Cattelena could have bought her cow, some other necessaries, and still been able to afford rent while she established herself as a dairy provider.

Cattelena could also have inherited the cow, bedding, kitchen utensils and some of her clothes. It has been said that in this period 'the most important component of wealth was not wages, but inheritance, whether that inheritance consisted of a landed estate, or of a single cottage and garden, or even of a cow, a kettle, a brass pan and a bed'.[59] Other Africans were bequeathed such items, so why not Cattelena? As well as money, William Offley left Frances 'a gowne of twelve shillings the yard', while Mary Groce left Joane a flockbed, two blankets, a coverlet and two pairs of sheets.

These employers understood that their servants might not continue in their households, and provided them with enough money to leave. Nicholas Witchals specified in his will that Anthony be given five shillings 'so that he remain with my wife' or 'if she mind to not keep him' they should give him five marks 'and let him depart'. The fact that Anthony's baptism was recorded at St Peter's Barnstaple in 1565, but there is no record of his burial there, suggests that he left the town.[60] Five marks was equivalent to around half a year's wages for the average labourer, so quite a generous severance package.[61] While there are no records of Africans in service in the tax returns from Southampton after 1611, the parish registers do not survive, so Joane's fate remains uncertain. Nonetheless, with £3 to her name, she had the opportunity to become independent. William Offley's will specified 'to Frances my black a moore I give *for her relief* the sum of ten pounds', meaning she had the choice to remain in his household or to move on. In March 1625, 'a Christian negro servant unto . . . Lady Bromley', later described as 'a negro maid servant', left a legacy of £10 to the poor of St Mary's parish, Putney, 'to be employed as a stock for the relief and comfort of the said poor in bread, or otherwise at the discretion of . . . the vestry men'.[62] Lady Anne Bromley had been the wife of William Offley and by 1625 was also the widow of Sir Henry Bromley, the former employer of Henry Jetto at Holt Castle, who died in 1615.[63] She seems to have inherited Frances's service from her first husband. Yet in Offley's will Frances was given financial freedom; £10 was a huge sum of money, especially compared to the 50 shillings awarded to Offley's other maids. In the end, she seems to have kept the money for the next twenty-five years, allowing her to become a benefactor to the poor of Putney at her death.

After Cattelena died, she was presumably buried at St Mary's Church in Almondsbury. The parish registers only survive from 1653, so we cannot be sure. She died intestate, without making a will, which isn't particularly surprising. Most people did not make wills and very few single women did. The purpose of a will is to make sure your property is inherited by the people of your choice, particularly to provide for widows and younger children, whom the common law and local custom might overlook in favour of the heir. When an individual had many relatives, a will, as one Lincolnshire yeoman remarked in 1596, could prevent 'such troubles, unkindness and controversies as do most commonly grow where no such order is taken'. The single women who did make wills tended to leave their estate to a relative, though more often than not they made other women, such as sisters or nieces, their beneficiaries.[64] If, like Cattelena, you did not own a great estate or have any close family, the likelihood of controversy was much diminished and there was no great motivation to write a will.

Helen Ford would have had to apply to the Consistory Court of Bristol, the ecclesiastical court presided over by the Bishop of Bristol in Bristol Cathedral, for letters of administration. These gave her the authority to deal with Cattelena's estate. It was common for women's estates to be administered by other women. Administrators were normally close family members, such as wives, sons or brothers of the deceased. In the absence of a relative, the administrator was sometimes a creditor, someone the deceased owed money to, or a neighbour or other friend.[65]

The next step was for Cattelena's estate to be valued. On 24 May 1625 her goods were appraised by Thomas Cottwell, Maurice Perry and Thomas Haines. Thomas Haines was possibly a member of a local gentry family, the Haynes of Westbury-on-Trym, Wick and Abson.[66] At least two local men had to act as appraisers, and were given breakfast or supper for their services, although in the case of impoverished estates this might dwindle to just a drink, as the provisions had to be paid for from the deceased's estate.[67]

Cattelena's goods were worth a total of £6 9s 6d. Inventories were only required for estates worth more than £5, so this places the value of her possessions at the lower end of the scale. That said, she might have owned things not mentioned; probate inventories did not list land, only moveable goods. While cows, pigs and sheep were itemised, chickens, ducks and geese usually weren't. The inventory also often omitted debts owing.[68]

On 27 May, the inventory was exhibited: that is Helen Ford took it to show to the Consistory Court in Bristol Cathedral. All was deemed in order. After this, Cattelena's goods were almost certainly sold. Once the cost of her funeral, the appraisal, the court administration fees and any debts were paid, there may not have been much left. As she had left no will, the remainder of the property went to the Crown.

Cattelena's small-scale existence, using borrowed furniture in a shared house and working hard to get enough dairy produce from her cow to feed herself and sell to others, does not have the excitement of adventure on the high seas or in the bustling streets of London. Nor can we picture her at the royal court. Yet her very ordinary presence, with her cow, on an English village common, is extraordinary. Imagining her darker face in the pastoral scene forces us to reimagine rural life in this period. The twists and turns that brought an African woman to live in an English village may never be recovered, but a simple list of the goods she owned at her death shows that the authorities recognised that an African could own property and, in its quotidian detail, allows us to sketch the rhythms of her daily life. In the everyday motions of sleeping, preparing food, milking a cow and lighting a candle in the evening, it was a life no different to so many other inhabitants of the English countryside.

Conclusion

I N 1584, THE author of *Leicester's Commonwealth*, a scurrilous tract attacking the reputation of Elizabeth I's favourite, made a passing reference to 'the Black moors . . . that dwell in Guinea (whereof I suppose you have heard and seen also some in this land)'.[1] Africans were 'heard and seen' across England, from Hull to Truro, throughout the sixteenth century and thereafter. And yet their presence has been forgotten. In 1999, an eminent Liverpool professor, expert in the history of British and Portuguese West Africa, asserted that: 'Black Africans were hardly at all known in England itself, Anglo-African contacts being almost exclusively within Guinea'.[2] He was wrong. The presence of Africans in Tudor England was common knowledge at the time, and it needs to become common knowledge again.

The Black Tudors were not only present, but played an active part in some of the best-known stories of the age. John Blanke blew his trumpet at Henry VIII's coronation. Jacques Francis came face to face with the skeletons of sailors drowned on the *Mary Rose*. Diego and Maria joined Francis Drake on the first English voyage to circumnavigate the globe. African sailors like John Anthony crewed early Atlantic trading voyages, while African princes like Dederi Jaquoah visited London merchants' houses and returned home to facilitate trade. In England's capital city, people like Reasonable Blackman, Mary Fillis and Anne Cobbie made lives for themselves, while others like Edward Swarthye and

Cattelena of Almondsbury found work in the countryside. We have tantalising glimpses of their lives, granted to us only by the peculiar circumstances that brought them into contact with a law court, an unusually verbose parish clerk or a state official who mentioned them in a letter. Fleshing out these biographies from the meagre documentation that remains is not easy, but it is a mission that must be undertaken if we are to reclaim their stories. Those revealed in this book provide so much that challenges the preconceptions we have about the role of Africans in British history.

These ten men and women are but a small fraction of the hundreds of Africans who lived in Renaissance England. Many are recorded by no more than a one-line entry in a parish record or a tax return, their existences many times more enigmatic than the tales told here. Yet, more may still be revealed. No one has yet trawled the entire corpus of sixteenth- and seventeenth-century documents for these sorts of stories. But as increasing numbers of records become digitised, transcribed and electronically searchable, the task should become more manageable. And if what has already been found is anything to go by, it will prove worthwhile.

Why? Because anyone who assumes that all Africans in British History have been powerless, enslaved victims must be challenged. The Black Tudors actively pursued their own interests and were free to do so. We find them petitioning for the payment of wages or for a pay rise, guarding trade secrets to retain a monopoly, seeking baptism as a path to social acceptance. More often than not, their efforts were rewarded.

The presence and experience of the Black Tudors and Stuarts demonstrates that Elizabeth I's so-called 'expulsion of the black-amoors' is a myth born of modern assumptions, not reality. As debate about immigration becomes ever more vituperative and divisive, it is vital to understand that the British Isles have always been peopled with immigrants. The Black Tudors are just one of a series of different peoples who arrived on these shores in centuries past.[3]

Knowing about the Black Tudors brings a richer understanding of a fascinating period of history. Traditional narratives tell of the 'Age of Discovery', but the physical presence of Africans in England literally brings home the reality of the country's growing contact with the wider world. Tracing the journeys of individuals such as Diego, who came to Plymouth via Panama and ended his days in the Moluccas, makes the global story personal. Broadening our horizons to consider the political and military potential of Morocco, or the Cimarrons in the story of the English struggle against Spain, gives us a more accurate picture of international affairs at the time.

Few people know that the Tudors, or even the early Stuarts, traded with Africa at all. When they do think about it, they think of John Hawkins and imagine that any trade with that continent must have been a trade in human flesh. Through Dederi Jaquoah and the other Africans who went on to become interpreters and facilitators of trade after short stays in London, we discover most English merchants were far more interested in acquiring gold, ivory and grains of paradise from their sophisticated African counterparts.

Historians have often argued that the racialised chattel slavery that developed in Colonial America was based on a mind-set imported from England.[4] But the experiences of Africans in Tudor and early Stuart England described here show that slavery was not an inevitable result of the Anglo-African encounter. Coupled with evidence of free Africans in early Virginia, this book adds weight to the conclusion that American slavery was instead something that emerged in the very specific economic and social circumstances of the early colonies.

The intense physical requirements of harvesting lucrative colonial crops, especially sugar, created the demand for imported slave labour, following the decimation of the indigenous populations by Old World diseases; this led English merchants to begin transporting enslaved Africans across the Atlantic in earnest from the 1640s onwards. It is not that the Tudors were morally superior to those who came later. It is merely that, until the mid-seventeenth century, there was no market, and so no profit, to be made from slavery.

And yet, even once slavery was adopted by the English colonies, and the English overtook the Portuguese and the Spanish as the world's most successful slave traders, no statutes codifying slavery were ever passed in England. This caused confusion when

Englishmen brought home Africans they had legally purchased in the colonies. This was the very confusion that men like James Somerset were able to exploit when the question of their freedom came before English judges in the eighteenth century.

In the Tudor period, before the English colonies were established, there was a similar confusion when Africans came to England from southern European countries such as Spain, Portugal and Italy, where they might have been legally enslaved. As the Italian merchants in Southampton who contested Jacques Francis's reliability as a witness, and Hector Nunes, who found that the 'Ethiopian Negar' he'd illegally acquired refused to 'tarry and serve' him, discovered to their cost, Tudor England really had 'too pure an Air for Slaves to breathe in'.

The history of the Black Tudors is an aspect of British history that deserves a wider audience. It shows that when we ask new questions of the past we get new, and often surprising, answers. We thought we knew Tudor England, but this book reveals a different country, where an African could earn a living, marry and have a family, testify in a court of law, or even whip an Englishman with impunity.

Author's Note

When I began research for my Oxford D.Phil. thesis, 'Africans in Britain 1500–1640', in 2004, study of the subject was still in its infancy. Pioneering works of Black British History such as Edward Scobie's *Black Britannia* (1972), James Walvin's *Black and White: the Negro and English Society, 1555–1945* (1973) and Folarin Shyllon's *Black People in Britain, 1555–1833* (1977) only dedicated a few pages to the early modern period, citing a handful of examples. By the time Peter Fryer published *Staying Power: The History of Black People in Britain* in 1984 he was able to enumerate around 30 individuals living in England and Scotland, thanks in part to research carried out by Paul Edwards.

My own investigation owes a huge debt to Marika Sherwood, a founding member of the Black and Asian Studies Association (BASA), who was kind enough to provide me with a list of close to 100 references to Africans that she had recently published in a 2003 *History Today* article entitled 'Blacks in Tudor England', and the BASA newsletter. Kathy Chater, who was working on her book *Untold Histories: Black people in England and Wales during the period of the British slave trade, c. 1660–1807* (2009), also sent me references she had found from the earlier period. Using these as a starting point, I was able to compile a database of more than 400 references to more than 360 African individuals living in England and Scotland which became the Appendix to my thesis, 'Evidence of Africans in Britain, 1500–1640'. My criteria for inclusion were strict: although it would be tempting to assume that everyone with the surname 'Black' was of African origin, there are enough certain examples of people described as 'a' or 'the' 'blackamoor', 'negar' or 'Ethiop' that we can disregard more ambiguous possibilities.

Since I began my research, two other scholars have published their own findings: Imtiaz Habib included a detailed 'Chronological Index of Records of Black People 1500–1677' in his book *Black Lives in the English Archives* (Ashgate, 2008) while Onyeka's *Blackamoores: Africans in Tudor England, Their Presence, Status and Origins* (Narrative Eye, 2013) also listed and referenced many examples of Africans living in Tudor England.

This documentation means that statements such as that made as late as 1999 by Liverpool Professor Paul Hair, an expert on Portuguese and British West Africa, in his article 'Attitudes to Africans in English Primary Sources on Guinea up to 1650' that 'Black Africans were hardly at all known in England itself, Anglo-African contacts being almost exclusively within Guinea' are no longer tenable.

The evidence for the Black Tudor presence comes from a range of archival sources: parish registers of baptisms, marriages and burials; other church and municipal records; tax returns; household accounts; legal records; voyage accounts; wills and inventories; diaries and letters.

It is this archival record that must be consulted first when trying to understand the position of Africans in Tudor society. Until now, much of the discussion of this subject has relied upon literary texts such as Shakespeare's *Othello* and the various other contemporary plays that featured African characters and geographical texts, such as Leo Africanus's *Description of Africa* and the travel narratives gathered together by Richard Hakluyt and his friends. Few Tudors knew how to read, or regularly attended the theatre. Far fewer had ever travelled abroad. Printed texts only reflect the ideas of a small, literate or play-going elite. Such works are written to entertain or convey a polemical point, and cannot be quoted verbatim as evidence of attitudes without first analysing the context in which they were written, and why.

The archival material naturally comes with its own set of drawbacks and historical problems. The authors of England's parish registers, tax returns, household accounts, court records, and other administrative documents did not set out to entertain the reader. They simply recorded what actually happened to Africans in Tudor England; not what people thought of them in the abstract, but how they were treated on a day-to-day basis. These quotidian actions speak louder than words.

The Black Tudors are often only known to us from a line in a register recording their birth or death, or their presence in a household. The ten people featured in this book are better documented than most, often because they appeared in court, or in other cases, where petitions and the occasional more detailed baptism record give us the clues we need to piece together a biography. This approach was pioneered by Rosalyn Knutson in her inspired 1991 essay 'A Caliban in St Mildred, Poultry', which took the baptism of Dederi Jaquoah as its starting point, but went on to deploy a wide range of archival sources to place Jaquoah in a wider context, in particular examining the life of the merchant John Davies, who brought him to London. Gustav Ungerer also demonstrated what could be done with legal records when he used the High Court of Admiralty case of Erizzo v. Corsi to tell the story of Jacques Francis in his 2005 article 'Recovering a Black African's Voice in an English lawsuit: Jacques Francis and the Salvage Operations of the *Mary Rose* and the *Sancta Maria* and *Sanctus Edwardus*, 1545– c.1550'.

While my research into the African presence in Britain has been extensive, it has not been exhaustive. In particular, the legal sources that have proven so revealing warrant further investigation. The High Court of Admiralty papers for this period are not well catalogued and so are not easy to search systematically, but might well furnish further fascinating examples of Black Tudor lives. I hope this book will show what is possible, and inspire others to conduct further research into the subject, both in England and in other European countries. This in turn will hopefully feed into a wider debate about the status and experience of Africans in early modern European societies and why and how this was to change over the course of the seventeenth century.

Acknowledgements

There are so many people who have gone out of their way to help me with their time, enthusiasm and expertise since I made my first forays into this subject in 2004, that some of them are bound to remain unacknowledged. So my apologies and thanks to them in equal measure.

In the writing of *Black Tudors* I have been particularly fortunate that other scholars have been kind enough to answer odd questions, read chapters, or in some heroic cases, the whole manuscript, and provide me with invaluable feedback, discussion, suggestions and encouragement. A huge thank you to Richard Blakemore, James Davey, Kevin Dawson, Matthew Dimmock, Madge Dresser, Kelechie Ezie, Peter Fleming, Catherine Fletcher, Helen Hackett, Jonathan Healey, Simon Healy, Alex Hildred, Aaron Jaffer, Bernhard Klein, Rosalyn Knutson, Alisa Miller, Kate Morrison, Michael Ohajuru, David Olusoga, Onyeka, Peter Robison, Duncan Salkeld, Cassander L. Smith, Richard Stone and Christian Wilson.

I greatly appreciate the continued efforts and patience of my agent, Charlie Viney of the Viney Agency, and the editorial brilliance and moral support of his associate Val Hudson. Thanks also to Martin Sheppard, Tony Morris and Janet Gough, who each spurred me on in different ways to believe that my research could become a book.

As a first-time author I have been extremely fortunate to have Oneworld as my publisher. Sam Carter has made *Black Tudors* a better book in so many ways, with his genuine interest in the subject, wide-ranging knowledge and incisive editing. Jonathan Bentley-Smith has gently given me a more active, emphatic and less verbose voice, and dealt with my manifold queries both patiently and promptly. Ann Grand has been grand. James Jones and Kishan Rajani have produced the most wonderfully eye-catching and resonant jacket. Margot Weale has guided carefully my boundless enthusiasm for publicity.

Thanks to Philip Murphy, director of the Institute for Commonwealth Studies for giving Michael Ohajuru and me both an institutional base and the opportunity to establish the *What's Happening in Black British History?* workshop series, which has provided such an invaluable forum for wider debate and networking, allowing me to place my understanding of my subject in a wider context. Michael himself has been the most wonderful colleague, friend and sounding board; thanks also to his partner Ebun Culwin for her artistic presence and tolerating our never-ending shop-talk!

I am also indebted to Margaret McGregor, Annette Walton, Luca Zenobi and Eilish Gregory as well as the staff of the many record offices and archives I visited or contacted for their assistance with additional research, translation and transcription of sources. Thanks also to all the scholars, local historians and other enthusiasts including Kathy Chater, Sylvia Coldicott, Kelechie Ezie, Helen Good, Martin Ingram, Stuart Minson, Duncan Salkeld, Marika Sherwood, Gustav Ungerer and Annette Walton, who drew my attention to, and generously shared evidence of, Africans they had found in the archives.

Above all I am deeply grateful for the love and support of my family and friends, which has sustained me throughout. Zanna Bankes, Jessica Barrett, Ann Berry, Emily Boldy, Zahler Bryan, Rosie Collins, Philip Day, Kathryn De Jesus, Ruth Evans, Jesse Galdal-Gibbs, Ciorsdan Glass, Emily Hacker, Sparrow Harrison, Elizabeth Hunt, Sophie Knox, Sarah Legrand, Kate Maltby, Issy Millard, Alisa Miller, John Morgenstern, Fiona Pearce, Jacqui Unsworth, James Weekes, Josephine Wynne-Eaton and Emma Young have all provided both moral support and light relief. I look forward to fulfilling all the promises I've made to you that began with the phrase 'once I've finished with the book . . .' Aunt Loraine has always been a supportive source of wisdom. My parents, Johanna and Peter and my sisters, Augusta and Olivia, have continued to give me endless unconditional love, and been incredibly supportive, especially in helping me make time to work alongside the new responsibilities of parenthood. Finally, I would like to thank my husband Olivier Dechazal, though the words to do so adequately escape me (the dedication should do it) and my little angels, Sophie and Juliette, for daily cuddles, smiles, kisses and songs and for inspiring me to make them proud.

Bibliography

These are some of the key sources I consulted for this work. The full bibliography can be downloaded as a pdf from http://oneworld-publications.com/black-tudors-hb.html or http://www.mirandakaufmann.com/black-tudors-bibliography.html

Manuscript and archival sources

I found evidence of the African presence in Tudor and Stuart England in a wide range of the original documents that survive from that time: parish registers (which record baptisms, marriages and burials) and other church records, tax returns, household accounts, legal records, wills and inventories, diaries, letters, State papers and voyage accounts.

I visited record offices and archives across England, from Devon and Cornwall to Yorkshire, with a particular focus on ports such as Bristol, Plymouth and Southampton, to find my sources.

Many of the most fascinating documents I pored over are held in London. The British Library is home to Thomas More's letter describing Katherine of Aragon's arrival in London, the anonymous (and slanderous) account of Drake's 1577–80 circumnavigation voyage and Lord Zouche's correspondence with William Warde, Jacob Braems and Henry Mainwaring regarding the *Silver Falcon*. The Westminster Quarter Sessions records, held at the London Metropolitan Archives, contain the case against John and Jane Bankes for keeping a bawdy house detailed in Chapter Nine.

At The National Archives, Kew, I delved into a wealth of state papers, legal records and other miscellaneous documents. Amongst the Letters and Papers of Henry VII and Henry VIII was proof of John Blanke being paid his wages from December 1507 onwards, as well as his petition for a pay rise. The High Court of Admiralty provided the documents that allowed me to piece together the case brought against Peter Paulo Corsi, while the Bucke vs Wynter case before the Court of Star Chamber held the key to Edward Swarthye's story. Searching through the Elizabethan State Papers, I uncovered intriguing details about relations between the English state and Morocco, a proposal for a voyage to Guinea, an inquiry into Hawkins's attack on San Jan d'Ulloa and John Anthony's petition to Lord Zouche.

For further details, see the full bibliography available online, and the Appendix to my 2012 Oxford DPhil thesis 'Africans in Britain, 1500-1640', cited below, which contains more than four hundred archival references to Africans in Tudor and early Stuart England.

Printed primary sources

The Accounts of the Lord High Treasurer of Scotland, eds. Thomas Dickson, Sir James Balfour Paul, C.T. McInnes, and Athol L. Murray (Edinburgh: HM General Register House, 1877–1978), 13 vols.

Acts of the Privy Council of England, ed. John Roche Dasent (London: HM Stationery Office, 1890–1964), 46 vols.

Adams, Simon, ed. *The Household Accounts and Disbursement Books of Robert Dudley, Earl of Leicester, 1558–1561, 1584–1586* (Cambridge: Cambridge University Press, 1995).

Africanus, Leo, *The History and Description of Africa*, trans. John Pory, ed. Robert Brown, Hakluyt Society, 1st ser. (London: Hakluyt Society, 1896), 3 vols.

Alvarez, Francisco, *The Prester John of the Indies: A True Relation of the Lands of the Prester John, Being the Narrative of the Portuguese Embassy to Ethiopia in 1520*, trans. Lord Stanley of Alderley, eds. Charles Fraser Beckingham and George Wynn Brereton Huntingford,

Haklyut Society 2nd ser., 114 (Cambridge: Cambridge University Press, 1961).

Ames, Richard, *The Female Fire-Ships; A Satyr Against Whoring: In A Letter to a Friend, Just Come to Town* (London: Printed for E. Richardson, 1691).

Andrews, Kenneth R., ed. *The Last Voyage of Drake and Hawkins*, Hakluyt Society 2nd ser., 142 (Cambridge: Cambridge University Press, 1972).

Anglo, Sydney, ed., *The Great Tournament Roll of Westminster* (Oxford: Clarendon Press, 1968), 2 vols.

Annual Report of the Poor Law Commissioners for England and Wales, (London: HM Stationery Office, 1837), vol 3.

Anon., *Lust's Dominion*, prep. Mary Ellen Cacheado (Sheffield: Sheffield Hallam University, 2007), http://www.marlowe-society. org/docs/LustsDominionText.pdf.

Anon., *Sir Thomas More, A Play; Now First Printed*, ed. Alexander Dyce (London: Royal Shakespeare Society, 1844).

Aubrey, John, *Aubrey's Brief Lives* ed. R. Barber, (Woodridge, Suff.: The Boydell Press, 1982).

   Aubrey's Brief Lives, ed. L. O. Dick, (Ann Arbor: University of Michigan Press, 1957).

   '*Brief Lives*', *Chiefly of Contemporaries*, ed. Andrew Clark (Oxford: Clarendon Press, 1898), 2 vols..

Bacon, Francis, *The Essays, or Councils, Civil and Moral* (London: E. Holt for Timothy Childe, 1701).

Balmford, James, *A Short Dialogue Concerning the Plagues Infection Published to Preserue Bloud, through the Blessing of God.* (London: R. Rield for Richard Boyle, 1603).

Bannerman, William B., ed., *The Registers of St Olave, Hart Street, London, 1563–1700* Harleian Society Registers ser., 46 (London: Harleian Society, 1916).

Barbot, Jean, *A Description of the Coasts of North and South-Guinea* (London: Printed by assignment from Messrs Churchill for John Walthoe [etc.], 1732).

Beaumont, Francis and John Fletcher, *The Knight of Malta*, in ed. A.R. Waller, *The Works of Francis Beaumont and John Fletcher* (Cambridge: Cambridge University Press, 1909), vol. 7, pp. 78–163.

Bethune, C.R. Drinkwater, ed. *The Observations of Sir Richard Hawkins, Knt. In His Voyage into the South Sea in the Year 1593*, Hakluyt Society, 1st ser. (London: Hakluyt Society, 1847).

Blake, John W., trans. and ed., *Europeans in West Africa, 1450–1560*,

Hakluyt Society 2nd ser., 86–7 (London: Hakluyt Society, 1942), 2 vols.

Boorde, Andrew, *A Compendyous Regyment, or A Dyetary of Helth Made in Mountpellier*, ed. F.J. Furnivall (London: For the Early English Text Society by N. Trübner, 1870).
The Fyrst Boke of the Introduction of Knowledge, ed. F.J. Furnivall (London: For the Early English Text Society by N. Trübner, 1870).

Brome, Richard, *The English Moor, or The Mock-Marriage*, ed. Matthew Steggle (London: Richard Brome Online, 2010), https://www.hrion-line.ac.uk/brome/

Burke, Arthur Maredyth, ed., *Memorials of St. Margaret's Church, Westminster: The Parish Registers 1539–1660* (London: Eyre & Spottiswold, 1914).

Calendar of Letters and State Papers Relating to English Affairs Preserved in or Originally Belonging to the Archives of Simancas, ed. Martin A. S. Hume (London: Public Record Office, 1892–9), 4 vols.

Calendar of the Manuscripts of the Most Honourable the Marquess of Salisbury, K.G., &c: Preserved at Hatfield House, Hertfordshire, ed. Sir Robert Cecil, Richard Arthur Roberts, Edward Salisbury, *et. al* (London: HM Stationery Office, 1883–1976), 24 vols.

Calendar of Patent Rolls, 30 Elizabeth (1587–88), C66/1304–1321, ed. Simon R. Neal (Kew: List and Index Society, 2003).

Calendar of Patent Rolls, 34 Elizabeth, Part I to Part XV, C66/1379–1394, ed. Simon R. Neal (Kew: List and Index Society, 1999).

Calendar of the Plymouth Municipal Records, ed. Richard Nicholls Worth (Plymouth: Borough of Plymouth, 1893).

Calendar of State Papers, Colonial Series, 1574–1660, ed. W. Noël Sainsbury (London: Longman, Green, Longman, & Roberts, 1860), 10 vols.

Calendar of State Papers, Domestic Series, of the Reign of Charles I, ed. John Bruce (London: Longman, Green, Longmans, & Roberts, 1858–97), 23 vols.

Calendar of State Papers, Domestic Series, of the Reigns of Edward VI, Mary, Elizabeth and James I, 1547–1625, eds. Robert Lemon and Mary Anne Everett Green (London: Longman, Brown, Green, Longmans, & Roberts, 1856–72), 12 vols.

Calendar of State Papers, Domestic Series, of the Reign of James I, ed. Mary Anne Everett Green (London: Longman, Brown, Green, Longmans, & Roberts, 1857–1872), 5 vols.

Calendar of State Papers, Foreign Series, of the Reign of Elizabeth,

1558–1589, eds. Joseph Stevenson, Allan James Crosby, Arthur John Butler, *et. al* (London: Longman, Green, Longman, Roberts, & Green, 1863–1950), 23 vols.

Calendar of State Papers and Manuscripts, Relating to English Affairs, Existing in the Archives and Collections of Venice, and in Other Libraries of Northern Italy, ed. Rawdon Brown (London: Longman, Green, Longman, Roberts, & Green, 1864–1947), 38 vols.

Calendar of the State Papers Relating to Scotland and Mary Queen of Scots, ed. Joseph Bain, (Edinburgh: HM General Register House, 1898–1969), 11 vols.

Camden, William, 'Annals of King James I', in William Camden, *A Complete History of England: With the Lives of all the Kings and Queens Thereof* . . . (London: Printed for Brab. Aylmer [etc.], 1706), vol. 2.

Annales, the True and Royall History of the Famous Empresse Elizabeth Queene of England France and Ireland &c., trans. Abraham Darcie (London: Benjamin Fisher, 1625).

Remaines Concerning Britain (1605), ed. Robert D. Dunn (Toronto: University of Toronto Press, 1984).

Cameron, Annie I., ed., *The Scottish Correspondence of Mary of Lorraine*, 3rd ser. (Edinburgh: Scottish History Society, 1927), vol. 10.

de Castellanos, Don Juan, *Discurso del Capitan Francisco Draque*, prep. by Angel Gonzáles Palencia (Madrid: Instituto de Valencia de Don Juan, 1921).

Chamberlain, John, *The Letters of John Chamberlain*, ed. Norman Egbert McClure (Philadelphia: The American Philosophical Society, 1939), vol. 2.

Chapman, George, *The Comedies of George Chapman*, ed. T.M. Parrott (London: George Routledge and Sons, 1914).

Chaucer, Geoffrey, *The Canterbury Tales*, ed. David Wright (Oxford: Oxford University Press, 1986).

Clowes, William, *A Profitable and Necessarie Booke of Obseruations, For All Those That are Burned with the Flame of Gun Powder, &c* . . . (London: E. Bollifant for Thomas Dawson, 1596).

Colyer-Fergusson, Thomas Colyer, Sir, ed., *The Marriage Registers of St. Dunstan's, Stepney, in the county of Middlesex.* (Canterbury: Cross & Jackman, Printers, 1898), vol. 1.

The Copie of a Leter, Vvryten by a Master of Arte of Cambrige, to his Friend in London (Paris:, s.n., 1584).

Corrie, George Elwes, ed., *Sermons by Hugh Latimer, Sometime Bishop of Worcester, Martyr, 1555* (Cambridge: Cambridge University Press, 1844), vol. 1.

Coryat, Thomas, *Coryat's Crudities: Hastily Gobled up in Five Moneths Travels . . .* (Glasgow: James MacLehose and Sons, 1905), 2 vols.

Craig, J.T. Gibson, ed., *Papers Relative to the Marriage of King James the Sixth of Scotland with the Princess Anna of Denmark* (Edinburgh: Bannatyne Club, 1828).

Cranley, Thomas, *Amanda: or the Reformed Whore* (London: John Norton, 1635).

Cruwys, Margaret C.S., ed., *The Register of Baptisms, Marriages & Burials of the Parish of St. Andrew's Plymouth, Co. Devon* (Exeter: Devon & Cornwall Record Society, 1954).

Cummings, Brian, ed. *The Book of Common Prayer: The Texts of 1549, 1559, and 1662* (Oxford: Oxford University Press, 2011).

Danvers, Frederick Charles and William Foster, eds. *Letters Received by the East India Company* (London: Sampson, Low, Marston & Co., 1896–1902), 6 vols.

Davenant, William, *The History of Sir Francis Drake: Exprest by Instrumentan and Vocall Musick* (London: s.n.,1659).

Davis, Norman, ed. *Paston Letters and Papers of the 15th century*, Early English Text Society ser., (Oxford: Oxford University Press, 2004), 2 vols.

Dekker, Thomas, *The Dramatic Works of Thomas Dekker*, ed. Fredson Bowers, (Cambridge: Cambridge University Press, 1961), 4 vols.
The Wonderfull Yeare (London:Thomas Creede, 1603).

Devon, Frederick, ed. *Issues of the Exchequer: Being Payments Made Out of His Majesty's Revenue During the Reign of King James I* (London: John Rodwell, 1836).

The Diary of the Lady Anne Clifford, ed. Vita Sackville-West (London: William Heinemann, 1923).

Digby, Kenelm, *A Late Discourse Made in a Solemne Assembly ovf Nobles and Learned Men at Montpellier in France . . .*, trans. R. White (London: Printed for R. Lownes and T. Davies, 1658).

Drake, Francis, Sir, *Sir Francis Drake's West Indian Voyage, 1585–6*, ed. Mary Frear Keeler, Hakluyt Society 2nd ser., 148 (London: Hakluyt Society, 1981).

Dunbar, William, *The Poems of William Dunbar*, ed. Priscilla Bawcutt (Glasgow: Association for Scottish Studies, 1998).
The Poems of William Dunbar, ed. James Kinsley (London: Oxford University Press, 1979).
'The Flyting of Dunbar and Kennedy', trans. Michael Murphy (Clan

Strachan Scottish Heritage Society, n.d.) http://www.clanstrachan. org/history/Flyting_of_Dunbar_and_Kennedy.pdf.

Edelman, Charles, ed. *The Stukeley Plays: The Battle of Alcazar by George Peele, The Famous History of the Life and Death of Captain Thomas Stukeley* (Manchester and New York: Manchester University Press, 2005).

Elyot, Thomas, 'Extracts from the Accounts of the Burgh of Aberdeen', in *The Miscellany of the Spalding Club*, ed. John Stuart (Aberdeen: Spalding Club, 1841–52), 5 vols.

The Boke Named the Governour (s.n., 1531).

Florentine Chronicle of Marchionne di Coppo di Stefano Buonaiuti, trans. Jonathan Usher, Decameron Web, https://www.brown.edu/ Departments/Italian_Studies/dweb/plague/perspectives/ marchionne.php, Rubric 634a.

Freshfield, Edwin, ed., *The Register Book of the Parish of St. Christopher le Stocks, in the* (London: Rixon and Arnold, 1882).

Galen, Claudius, *Galen on the Usefulness of the Parts of the Body*, trans. Margaret Tallmadge May (Ithaca, NY: Cornell University Press, 1968), 2 vols.

Gesta Grayorum, or the History of the High and Mightie Henry, Prince of Purpool, Anno Domini 1594, ed. D. Bland (Liverpool: Liverpool University Press, 1968).

Gray, Thomas, *An Elegy Wrote in a Country Church Yard* (London: Printed for R. Dodsley, 1751).

Gray, Todd, ed., *Devon Household Accounts, 1627–59, Part II*, new ser., 39 (Exeter: Devon and Cornwall Record Society, 1996).

Greville, Fulke (Lord Brooke), *The Life of the Renowned Sir Philip Sidney*, (London: Henry Seile, 1651).

Hair, P.E.H., ed., *Hawkins in Guinea, 1567–1568* (Leipzig: University of Leipzig, 2000). Ed., *Travails in Guinea: Robert Baker's 'Briefe Dyscourse'* (Liverpool: University of Liverpool Press, 1990).

Hair, P.E.H., Adam Jones, and Robin Law, eds. *Barbot on Guinea: The Writings of Jean Barbot on West Africa, 1678–1712*, Haklyut Society 2nd ser., 175–6 (London: Hakluyt Society, 1992), 2 vols.

Hakluyt, Richard, *The Principall Navigations, Voiages, and Discoveries of the English Nation: Imprinted at London, 1589*, Hakluyt Society extra ser. (London: Hakluyt Society, 1965), 2 vols.

The Original Writings and Correspondence of the two Richard Hakluyts, ed. Eva G. R. Taylor, Haklyut Society 2nd ser., 76–7 (London: Hakluyt Society, 1935), 2 vols.

The Principall Navigations, Voyages, Traffiques and Discoveries of the English Nation: Made by Sea or Over-Land to the Remote and Farthest Distant Quarters of the Earth at Any Time Within the Compass of These 1600 Yeeres (Glasgow: James MacLehose and Sons, 1903–5), 12 vols.

Hanmer, Meredith, *The Baptizing of a Turke, a Sermon Preached at the Hospitall of Saint Katherin,* (London: Robert Waldegrave, 1586).

Hargrave, Francis, *An Argument in the Case of James Sommersett a Negro: Wherein it is Attempted to Demonstrate the Present Unlawfulness of Domestic Slavery in England: To Which is Prefixed a State of the Case* (London: Printed for the author by W. Otridge, 1772).

Hariot, Thomas, *A briefe and true report of the new found land of Virginia . . .* (London: s.n., 1588).

Harris, G.G., ed. *Trinity House of Deptford Transactions, 1609–35* (London: London Record Society, 1983), vol. 19.

Harrison, William, *The Description of England*, ed. Georges Edelen (London: Constable & Co., 1994).

Hayden, Roger, ed. *The Records of a Church of Christ 1640–1687* (Bristol: Bristol Record Society, 1974).

Haynes, Samuel, ed., *A Collection of State Papers, Relating to Affairs . . . From the Year 1542 to 1570* (London: William Bowyer, 1740).

Henry, David, comp., *An Historical Account of All the Voyages Round the World, Performed by English Navigators* (London: F. Newberry, 1773), vol. 1.

Hobbes, Thomas, *Leviathan, Or, the Matter, Forme and Power of a Commonwealth Ecclesiasticall and Civil*, ed. Michael Oakeshott (New York: Touchstone, 2008).

Hughes, Paul L. and James Francis Larkin, eds., 'The Information of Mary Hall, Westminster Sessions Roll (1626)', comm. Martin Ingram, in eds. Helen Ostovich and Elizabeth Sauer *Reading Early Modern Women: An Anthology of Texts in Manuscript and Print, 1550–1700* (New York and London: Routledge, 2004), pp. 40–2.

Tudor Royal Proclamations (New Haven: Yale University Press, 1964–9), 3 vols.

James I, King of England, *A Counterblaste to Tobacco* (London: R. B., 1604).

James, T.B., ed. *The Third Book of Remembrance of Southampton, 1514–1602* (Southampton: The University, 1952–1979), 4 vols.

Jobson, Richard, *The Discovery of River Gambra (1623)*, ed. David P. Gamble and P.E.H. Hair, Hakluyt Society 3rd ser., 2 (London: Hakluyt Society, 1999).

The Golden Trade: Or, A Discovery of the River Gambra, and the Golden Trade of the Aethiopians (London: Nicholas Okes, 1623).

Jonson, Ben, *Bartholomew Fair* (1631), in eds. Charles Harold Herford, Percy Simpson, and Evelyn Simpson *The Works of Ben Jonson* (Oxford: Oxford University Press, 1986), vol. 6.

The Devil is an Ass (1631) in eds. Charles Harold Herford, Percy Simpson, and Evelyn Simpson *The Works of Ben Jonson* (Oxford: Oxford University Press, 1986), vol. 6.

'An Epistle to Sir Edward Sackville, now Earl of Dorset' (1616), in *Ben Jonson: The Complete Poems* (London: Penguin Books, 1988), pp. 143–6.

The Characters of Two Royall Masques: The One of Blacknesse, the Other of Beautie (London: Thomas Thorp, 1608).

'Masque of Blackness' (1605), in David Lindley and Edward Gieskes, 'Court Masques: Jacobean and Caroline Entertainments 1605–1640', *Experimental Dermatology* 6:6 (1997), pp. 93–5.

Jovius, Paulus, *De Piscibus Romanis* (Basel: s.n., 1351).

Kingsford, Charles Lethrbridge, ed. *Chronicles of London* (Derby: A. Sutton, 1977).

Kipling, Gordon, ed. *The Receyt of the Lady Kataryne*, Early English Text Society ser., 296 (Oxford: Oxford University Press, 1990).

Kirk, R.E.G. and Earnest F. Kirk, eds., *Returns of Aliens Dwelling in the City and Suburbs of London: from the Reign of Henry VIII to James I*, Huguenot Society of London ser., 10 (Aberdeen: University Press Ltd, 1900–1908), 3 vols.

Laing, D., 'Notice Respecting the Monument of the Regent Earl of Murray, Now Restored, within the Church of St. Giles, Edinburgh', in *Proceedings of the Society of Antiquaries of Scotland*, 6, 1831, pp. 49–55.

Lang, R.G., Ed. *Two Tudor Subsidy Rolls for the City of London: 1541 and 1582* (London: London Record Society, 1993), vol. 29.

Lemaitre, Eduardo, *Historia General de Cartagena* (Bogotá: Banco de la República, 1983), vol. 2.

Letters and Papers, Foreign and Domestic, Henry VIII, eds. John S. Brewer, R.H. Brodie and James Gairdner (London: HM Stationery Office, 1810–1920), 21 vols.

Lindsay, Robert, *The Historie and Cronicles of Scotland: From the Slauchter of King James the First to the Ane Thousande Fyve Hundreith Thrie Scoir Fyftein Zeir*, ed. Æ.J.G. Mackay (Edinburgh and London: William Blackwood and Sons for the Scottish Text Society, 1899–1911), 3 vols.

The Liues, Apprehensions, Arraignments, and Executions, of the 19. Late Pyrates Namely: Capt. Harris. Iennings. Longcastle. Downes. Haulsey. and their Companies . . . (London: J. Bussy, 1609).

Lodge, Thomas and Robert Greene, *A Looking Glasse for London and England* (London: Barnard Alsop, 1617).

London Consistory Court Wills, 1492–1547, ed. Ida Darlington (London: London Record Society, 1967), vol. 3.

Lopez, Odoardo, *A Report of the Kingdome of Congo Drawen Out of the Writinges and Discourses of Odoardo Lopez a Portingall*, trans. A. Hartwell (London: John Wolfe, 1597).

Lovelace, Richard, 'To Althea, from Prison', in *The Poems of Richard Lovelace: Lucasta, Etc.*, Classic Reprint ser. (London: Forgotten Books, 2012).

Lowe, Peter, *An Easie, Certaine, and Perfect Method, to Cure and Prevent the Spanish Sickness* . . . (London: Iames Roberts, 1596).

Machyn, Henry, *The Diary of Henry Machyn: Citizen and Merchant-Taylor of London, 1550–1563* ed. John Gough Nicholls, 1st ser. (London: Camden Society, 1848).

Madox, Richard, *An Elizabethan in 1582: The Diary of Richard Madox, Fellow of All Souls*, ed. Elizabeth Story Donno, Hakluyt Society 2nd ser., 147 (London: Hakluyt Society, 1976).

Mainwairing, Henry, Sir, *The Life and Works of Sir Henry Mainwaring*, ed. George Ernest Mainwaring, Naval Records Society ser., 54, 56 (London: Navy Records Society, 1920–1922), 2 vols.

Mandeville, John, Sir, *Mandeville's Travels*, ed. M.C. Seymour (Oxford: Oxford University Press, 1967).

de Marees, Peter, *Description and Historical Account of the Gold Kingdom of Guinea (1602)*, ed. A. Van Dantzig and Adam Jones (Oxford: Published for the British Academy by Oxford University Press, 1987).

Markham, Clements R., ed. *The Hawkins' Voyages During the Reigns of Henry VIII, Queen Elizabeth, and James I*, Hakluyt Society 1st ser. (London: Hakluyt Society, 1878).

Markham, Gervase, *Countrey Contentments, Or, The English Huswife* (London: Printed for R. Jackson, 1623).

Martyr d'Anghiera, Peter, *The Decades of the Newe Worlde or West India* . . ., trans. Richard Eden (London: s.n., 1555).

Massinger, Philip, *The City Madam* (1658), ed. Cathy Shrank (London: Nick Hern, 2005).

McGowan, Alan Patrick, ed., *Jacobean Commissions of Enquiry, 1608 and 1618* (London: Navy Records Society, 1971), vol. 116.

Minutes of the Council and General Court of Colonial Virginia, 1622–1632, 1670–1676, ed. Henry Read McIlwane (Richmond, Vir.: Colonial Press, Everett Waddey Company, 1924).

More, Thomas, Sir, *The Correspondence of Sir Thomas More*, ed. Elizabeth F. Rogers (Princeton: Princeton University Press, 1947).

Myers, Alec Reginald, ed. *The Household of Edward IV: The Black Book and the Ordinance of 1478* (Manchester: Manchester University Press, 1959).

Nash(e), Thomas, *Christ's Tears Over Jerusalem* (London: Longman, Hurst, Rees, Orme, and Brown, printed by T. Davison, 1815).

The Choice of Valentines, online version, ed. W. Ingram (Ann Arbor: University of Michigan, n.d.), http://www-personal.umich.edu/~ingram/grinnell/Nashe%20Valentines.pdf

Nichols, John Gough, ed. *The Herald and Genealogist* (London: John Bowyer Nichols and Sons, 1863–74), 8 vols.

Nuttall, Zelia, trans. and ed. *New Light on Drake: a Collection of Documents Relating to His Voyage of Circumnavigation, 1577–1580*, Hakluyt Society 2nd ser., 34 (London: Hakluyt Society, 1914).

'Parishes: Richmond (anciently Sheen)', in *A History of the County of Surrey*, ed. H. E. Malden (London: Victoria County History, 1911), vol. 3, pp. 533–46.

'Parish Register of Stowell, Somerset', in *Somerset and Dorset Notes and Queries*, eds. Frederic William Weaver and Charles Herbert Mayo (Sherborne: J.C. and A.T. Sawwtell, 1893), vol. 3, pp. 4–8.

Orders, Thought Meete by her Maiestie, and her Priuie Councell, to be Executed Throughout the Counties of this Realme, in such Townes, Villages, and Other Places, as Are, or may be Hereafter Infected with the Plague, for the Stay of Further Increase of the Same (London: Christopher Barker, c.1578).

Parker, Martin, *The Woman to the PLOW; And the Man to the HEN-ROOST; OR, A Fine Way to Cure a Cot-quean* (London: Printed for F. Grove, 1629), held in University of Glasgow Library – Euing 397,, EBBA ID: 32024.

Payne, Robert, *A Briefe Description of Ireland: 1590*, ed. Aquilla Smith, Tracts Relating to Ireland ser. (Dublin: Irish Archeological Society, 1841), vol. 1.

Percy, Henry (Ninth Earl of Northumberland), *The Household Papers of Henry Percy, 9th Earl of Northumberland, 1564–1632*, ed. G. R. Batho, Camden 3rd ser. (London: Royal Historical Society, 1962), vol. 93.

Pett, Phineas, *The Autobiography of Phineas Pett*, ed. William Gordon Perrin (London: Navy Records Society, 1918), vol. 51.

Pepys, Samuel, *The Diary of Samuel Pepys*, eds. Robert Latham and William Matthews (London: Bell & Hyman, 1970), 11 vols.

Pepys, Samuel and Hyder Edward Rollins, eds., *A Pepysian Garland: Black-letter Broadside Ballads of the Years 1595–1639, Chiefly from the Collection of Samuel Pepys* (Cambridge: Cambridge University Press, 1922).

Philipot, John, *The Visitation of Kent: Taken in the Years 1619–1621*, ed. Robert Hovenden, Publications of the Harleian Society ser. (London: Harleian Society, 1898), vol. 42.

Pliny (the Elder), *Natural History*, trans. H. Rackham, Loeb Classical Library ser. (Cambridge, Mass: Harvard University Press, 1961), 10 vols.

Purchas, Samuel, *Hakluytus Posthumus, or Purchas his Pilgrims*, Hakluyt Society extra ser. (London: Hakluyt Society, 1905–7), 20 vols.

  Purchas his Pilgrimage. Or Relations of the World and the Religions Observed in All Ages and Places Discovered, from Creation unto this Present (London, William Stansby for Henrie Fetherstone, 1613).

Ralegh, Walter, Sir, *The Discouerie of the Large, Rich, and Bevvtiful Empire of Guiana . . .* (London: Robert Robinson, 1596).

Reddaway, Thomas Fiddian and Alwyn A. Ruddock, eds., 'The Accounts of John Balsall, Purser of the Trinity of Bristol, 1480–1', *Camden Fourth Series*, 7, (1969), pp. 1–28.

The Right Plesaunt and Goodly Historie of the Foure Sonnes of Aymon, trans. William Caxton, ed. O. Richardson (London: Early English Text Society, 1885).

Rogers, Woodes, Captain, *A Cruising Voyage Round the World: First to the South-Seas, Thence to the East-Indies, and Homewards by the Cape of Good Hope . . .* (London: A. Bell and B. Lintot, 1712).

Rolfe, John, *A True Relation of the State of Virginia Lefte by Sir Thomas Dale Knight in May Last 1616* (New Haven: Printed for Henry C. Taylor at Yale University Press, 1951).

Rowe, Margery M., ed., *Tudor Exeter: Tax Assessments 1489–1599*, New ser., 22 (Exeter: Devon and Cornwall Record Society, 1977).

Royal African Company, *An Answer of the Company of Royal Adventurers of England Trading into Africa to the Petition . . . Exhibited to the Honourable House of Commons by Sir Paul Painter, Ferdinando Gorges, Henry Batson, Benjamin Skutt, and Thomas*

Knights on the Behalf of Themselves and Others Concerned in His Majesties Plantations in America (London: s.n., 1667).

Rushworth, John, *Historical Collections of Private Passages of State* (London: J. D. for John Wright and Richard Chiswell, 1680), 2 vols.

de Santa Cruz, Melchor, *Floresta espanola*, ed. María Pilar Cuartero and Maxime Chevalier (Barcelona: Crítica, 1997).

Satow, Ernest M., Sir, ed. *The Voyage of Captain John Saris to Japan, 1613*, Hakluyt Society 2nd ser. (London: Hakluyt Society, 1900), vol. 5.

Scouloudi, Irene, ed., *Returns of Strangers in the Metropolis 1593, 1627, 1635, 1639*, Quarto ser. (London: Huguenot Society of London, 1985), vol. 57.

Shakespeare, William, *The Complete Works of William Shakespeare* eds. Stanley Wells, John Jowett, and William Montgomery, 2nd ed. (Oxford: Clarendon Press, 2005).
  The Merchant of Venice, eds. J. Russell Brown and Bernard Harris (New York: St. Martin's Press, 1964).

Smith, Thomas, Sir, *De Republica Anglorum*, ed. Mary Dewar (Cambridge: Cambridge University Press, 1982).

Smyth, John, 'A Description of the Hundred of Berkeley', in *The Berkeley Manuscripts: The Lives of the Berkeleys, Lords of the Honour, Castle and Manor of Berkeley, in the County of Gloucester, from 1066 to 1618*, ed. Sir John Maclean (Gloucester: John Bellows for the Bristol and Gloucestershire Archaeological Society, 1883–1885), 3 vols.

Sneyd, Charlotte Augusta, trans. and ed., *A Relation, or Rather a True Account, of the Island of England*, Camden Society old ser. (London: Camden Society, 1847), vol. 37.

Southampton Record Office and Southampton Maritime Museum, *Southampton in the 1620s and the 'Mayflower: an Exhibition of Documents by the Southampton City Record Office to Celebrate the 350th Anniversary of the Sailing of the 'Mayflower' from Southampton in 1620*, ed. S.D. Thompson (Southampton: City Record Office, 1970).

Squire, William, *Newes from Mamora, Or, A Summary Relation Sent to the King of Spaine . . .* (London: Printed by N. Oakes for Thomas Archer, 1614).

The Statutes at Large: Being a Collection of all the Laws of Virginia, ed. William Waller Henning (Richmond, Virg.: Franklin Press–W. W. Gray, 1809–1823), 18 vols.

Stow, John, *A Survey of the Cities of London and Westminster*, ed. John

Strype (London: Printed for A. Churchill [etc.], 1720).

Annales, or, a Generall Chronicle of England, ed. Edmund Howe (London: Richardi Meighen, 1631).

Survey of London: Containing the Original, Increase, Modern Estate and Government of that City, Methodically Set Down . . ., cont. Anthony Munday (London: Printed for Nicholas Bourn, 1633).

A Summarie of the Chronicles of England (London: Richard Bradocke, 1598).

Strype, John, *Annals of the Reformation and Establishment of Religion* . . . (Oxford: Clarendon Press, 1824), 2 vols.

Sydenham, *A New Method of Curing the French-Pox*, trans. William Salmon (London: John Taylor, 1690).

de Togores, Roca, Marquis de Molins, ed., *Crónica Del Rey Enrico Otavo De Ingalaterra* (Madrid: Alfonso Durán, 1874).

Tawney, R. H. and Eileen E. Power, eds., *Tudor Economic Documents* (London: Longman's Green, 1953), vol. 2.

Taylor, E.R.G., ed. *The Troublesome Voyage of Captain Edward Fenton, 1582–1583: Narratives and Documents*, Hakluyt Society 2nd ser., 113 (Cambridge: Cambridge University Press, 1959).

Taylor, John, 'A Whore', in *All the Works of John Taylor the Water Poet* . . . (London: Printed by I.B. [etc.] for Iames Boler, 1630), pp. 105–14.

Terry, Edward, *A Voyage to East-India. Wherein Some Things are Taken Notice of in Our Passage Thither, but Many More in Our Abode There, Within that Rich and Most Spacious Empire of the Great Mogol* . . . (London: T.W. for J. Martin, and J Allestrye, 1655).

Thomas, Arthur H., and Isobel D. Thornley, eds. *The Great Chronicle of London* (London: George W. Jones at The Sign of the Dolphin, 1938).

Thomas, William, *Principal Rvles of the Italian Grammer: With a Dictionarie for the Better Understandynge of Boccacce, Pethrarcha and Dante* (London: Thomas Berthelet, 1550).

Van Den Broeke, Pieter, *Pieter Van Den Broeke's Journal of Voyages to Cape Verde, Guinea and Angola*, ed. James D. La Fleur, Hakluyt Society 3rd ser., 5 (London: Hakluyt Society, 2000).

Vaux, W.S.W., ed. *The World Encompassed by Sir Francis Drake*, Hakluyt Society 1st ser. (London: Hakluyt Society, 1854).

Vick, Douglas F., ed., *Central Hampshire Lay Subsidy Assessments 1558–1603* (Farnham, Surrey: Douglas F. Vick, 1987).

Villaut, Nicolas, *A Relation of the Coast of Africa Called Guinee* (London: Starkey, 1670).

Virginia Company of London, *The Records of the Virginia Company of London*, ed. Susan Myra Kingsbury (Washington: US Government Printing Office, 1906), vol. 1.

Von Bulow, Gottfried, 'Journey Through England and Scotland Made by Lupold Von Wedel in the Years 1584 and 1585', *Transactions of the Royal Historical Society (New Series)*, 9, 1895, pp. 223–70.

Wernham, Richard Bruce, ed. *The Expedition of Sir John Norris and Sir Francis Drake to Spain and Portugal, 1589*, no. 96 (Aldershot, Hants.: Temple Smith for the Navy Records Society, 1988).

Wright, Irene Aloha, ed. *Documents Concerning English Voyages to the Spanish Main 1569–1580*, Hakluyt Society 2nd ser., 71 (London: Hakluyt Society, 1932).

Wright, Irene Aloha, ed. *Further English Voyages to Spanish America, 1583–1594*, Hakluyt Society 2nd ser., 99 (London: Hakluyt Society, 1951).

Wright, Louis B., ed. *A Voyage to Virginia in 1609: Two Narratives* (Charlottesville: University of Virginia Press, 2013).

Wright, Thomas, ed. *Queen Elizabeth and Her Times: A Series of Original Letters . . .* (London: Henry Colburn, 1838), vol. 2.

Secondary works

Adair, Richard, *Courtship, Illegitimacy, and Marriage in Early Modern England* (Manchester: Manchester University Press, 1996).

Adelman, Janet, *Blood Relations: Christian and Jew in the Merchant of Venice* (Chicago: University of Chicago Press, 2008).

Amussen, Susan Dwyer, *Caribbean Exchanges: Slavery and the Transformation of English Society, 1640–1700* (Chapel Hill: University of North Carolina, 2007).

Anglo, Sydney, 'The Court Festivals of Henry VII: A Study Based Upon the Account Books of John Heron, Treasurer of the Chamber', *Bulletin of the John Rylands Library*, 43, 1960, pp. 12–45.

Appleby, J.C., *Women and English Piracy, 1540–1720: Partners and Victims of Crime* (Woodridge, Suff.: Boydell & Brewer, 2015).

'Jacobean Piracy: English Maritime Depredation in Transition, 1603–1625', in *The Social History of English Seamen*, ed. Cheryl A. Fury (Woodridge, Suff.: Boydell Press, 2012), pp. 277–99.

'Thomas Mun's West Indies Venture, 1602–5', *Historical Research*, 67:162, 1994, pp. 101–10.

Ashbee, Andrew, ed., 'Groomed for Service: Musicians in the Privy

Chamber at the English Court, c.1495–1558', *Early Music*, 25:2, 1997, pp. 185–97.

Records of English Court Music (Snodland, Kent: Andrew Ashbee and Aldershot: Scholar Press, 1986–96), 9 vols.

Ashbee, Andrew and David Lasocki, eds., *A Biographical Dictionary of English Court Musicians, 1485–1714* (Aldershot: Ashgate, 1998), 2 vols.

Bardsley, Charles W., *English Surnames: Their Sources and Significations* (1884, reprint Newton Abbot: David & Charles, 1969).

Bartels, Emily Carroll, *Speaking of the Moor: from 'Alcazar' to 'Othello'* (Philadelphia: University of Pennsylvania Press, 2008).

'Too Many Blackamoors: Deportation, Discrimination, and Elizabeth I', *SEL Studies in English Literature 1500–1900*, 46:2, 2006, pp. 305–22.

Beer, Anna R., *Bess: The Life of Lady Ralegh, Wife to Sir Walter* (London: Constable, 2004).

Berlin, Ira, *Many Thousands Gone: The First Two Centuries of Slavery in North America* (Cambridge: Belknap Press of Harvard University Press, 1998).

Bernhard, Virginia, *A Tale of Two Colonies: What Really Happened in Virginia and Bermuda?* (Columbia and London: University of Missouri Press, 2011).

'Beyond the Chesapeake: The Contrasting Status of Blacks in Bermuda, 1616–1663', *Journal of Southern History*, 54:4, 1988, pp. 545–64.

Bindman David, Henry Louis Gates, and Karen C.C. Dalton, eds., *The Image of the Black in Western Art*, new ed.,. (Cambridge, Mass.: Harvard University Press, 2010), 3 vols.

Blackburn, Robin, *The Making of New World Slavery: From the Baroque to the Modern 1492–1800* (London and New York: Verso, 1997).

Blake, John W., *West Africa: Quest for God and Gold, 1454–1578: A Survey of the First Century of White Enterprise in West Africa with Particular Reference to the Achievement of the Portuguese and their Rivalries with Other European Powers*, 2nd ed. (London: Curzon Press, 1977).

'The Farm of the Guinea Trade in 1631', in H.A. Cronne, T.W. Moody, and D.B. Quinn, *Essays in British and Irish History in Honour of James Eadie Todd* (London: Frederick Muller, 1949), pp. 85–105.

'The English Guinea Company, 1618–1660', *Proceedings of the Belfast Natural History and Philosophical Society*, 2:3, 1945–6, pp. 14–27.

'English Trade with the Portuguese Empire in West Africa, 1581–

1629', in *Quarto Congresso do Mundo Portugués*, 6:1, 1940, pp. 314–33.

Blakely, Allison, *Blacks in the Dutch World: The Evolution of Racial Imagery in a Modern Society* (Bloomington: Indiana University Press, 1993).

Blumenthal, Debra, *Enemies and Familiars: Slavery and Mastery in Fifteenth-Century Valencia* (Ithaca and London: Cornell University Press, 2009).

Bolster, W. Jeffrey, *Black Jacks: African American Seamen in the Days of Sail* (Cambridge, Mass.: Harvard University Press, 1997).

Bourne, Rebecca, 'Ancestor was the first black person in the county', *Worcester News*, 23 February 2007, p. 3.

Breen, T.H. and Stephen Innes, *'Myne Owne Ground': Race and Freedom on Virginia's Eastern Shore, 1640–1676* (Oxford: Oxford University Press, 1980).

Burkhardt, Jacob, *The Civilisation of the Renaissance in Italy*, trans. S.G.C. Middlemore (London: Swan Sonnenschein, 1892).

Cairns, J.W., 'Slavery and the Roman Law of Evidence in Eighteenth-Century Scotland' in eds. Andrew Burrows and Lord Rodger of Earlsferry, *Mapping the Law: Essays in Memory of Peter Birks* (Oxford: Oxford University Press, 2006), pp. 599–618.

Chandler, Wayne B. 'The Moor: Light of Europe's Dark Age' *Journal of African Civilizations* 7:2, 1985, pp. 144–75.

Chater, Kathy, *Untold Histories: Black People in England and Wales During the Period of the Slave Trade, c.1660–1807* (Manchester: Manchester University Press, 2009).

Clifford, Barry and Paul Barry, *The Black Ship: The Quest to Recover an English Pirate Ship and Its Lost Treasure* (London: Headline, 1999).

Coldham, P.W., *The Complete Book of Emigrants, 1607–1660: A Comprehensive Listing Compiled from English Public Records of Those Who Took Ship to the Americas for Political, Religious, and Economic Reasons; of Those Who Were Deported for Vagrancy, Roguery, or Non-conformity; and of Those Who Were Sold to Labour in the New Colonies* (Baltimore: Genealogical Publishing, 1987).

Cooper, Tarnya, Ian W. Archer, and Lena Cowen Orlin, *Elizabeth I and Her People* (London: National Portrait Gallery, 2013).

Cox, Noel, 'An Act to Avoid the Excess in Apparel 1554–5', *Transactions of the Burgon Society* 13:1, 2013, pp. 39–44.

D'Amico, Jack, *The Moor in English Renaissance Drama* (Tampa: University of South Florida Press, 1991).

D'Azevedo, Pedro A., 'Os Escravos', *Archivo Historico Portuguez*, 1:9, 1903, pp. 288–307.

Dabydeen, David, *Hogarth's Blacks: Images of Blacks in Eighteenth Century English Art* (Manchester: Manchester University Press, 1985).

Dabydeen, David, John Gilmore, and Cecily Jones, eds., *The Oxford Companion to Black British History* (Oxford: Oxford University Press, 2005).

Dagbovie, Pero Gaglo, *African American History Reconsidered* (Urbana and Chicago: University of Illinois Press, 2010).

Davies, Kenneth Gordon, *The Royal African Company* (London: Longmans, Green, and Co., 1957).

Davis, Robert C., *Christian Slaves, Muslim Masters: White Slavery in the Mediterranean, the Barbary Coast and Italy, 1500–1800* (New York: Palgrave Macmillan, 2003).

Dawson, Kevin, 'History from Below: Enslaved Salvage Divers in the Atlantic World' *International Review of Social History* (forthcoming, 2018).

Undercurrents of Power: Aquatic Culture in the African Diaspora (Philadelphia: University of Pennsylvania Press: forthcoming, 2017).

'Swimming, Surfing, and Underwater Diving in Early Modern Atlantic Africa and the African Diaspora', in eds. Carina E. Ray and Jeremy McMaster Rich, *Navigating African Maritime History*, Research in Maritime History ser. (St Johns: Memorial University of Newfoundland Press, 2009), pp. 81–116.

'Enslaved Swimmers and Divers in the Atlantic World', *The Journal of American History*, 92:4, 2006, pp. 1327–55.

Debrunner, Hans Werner, *Presence and Prestige: Africans in Europe: A History of Africans in Europe before 1918* (Basel: Basler Afrika Bibliographien, 1979).

Denkinger, Emma Marshal, 'Minstrels and Musicians in the Registers of St. Botolph Aldgate', *Modern Language Notes*, 46:6, 1931, pp. 395–8.

Dimmock, Matthew, *The Ashgate Research Companion to Popular Culture in Early Modern England* (London: Routledge, 2016).

'Converting and Not Converting "Strangers" in Early Modern London', *Journal of Early Modern History*, 17: 5–6, 2013, pp. 457–78.

Drescher, Seymour, *Capitalism and Antislavery: British Mobilization in Comparative Perspective* (Oxford: Oxford University Press On Demand, 1987).

Dresser, Madge, *Slavery Obscured: The Social History of the Slave Trade in an English Provincial Port* (New York: Continuum, 2001).

Earle, T. F. and Kate J. P. Lowe, eds., *Black Africans in Renaissance Europe* (Cambridge: Cambridge University Press, 2005).

Edmondson, Joseph, *Complete Body of Heraldry* (London: Printed for the author by Joseph Edmondson, 1780), vol. 1.

Edwards, Paul G., *The Early African Presence in the British Isles: An Inaugural Lecture on the Occasion of the Establishment of the Chair in English and African Literature at Edinburgh University* (Edinburgh: Centre for African Studies, Edinburgh University, 1990).

Ekeh, Peter P., 'Benin, The Western Niger Delta, and the Development of the Atlantic World', *Umẹwaẹn: Journal of Benin and Ẹdo Studies*, 1, 2016, pp. 4–41.

Elbl, Ivana, 'The Volume of the Early Atlantic Slave Trade, 1450–1521', *Journal of African History*, 38:1, 1997, pp. 31–75.

Fabricius, Johannes, *Syphilis in Shakespeare's England* (London: Jessica Kingsley Publishers, 1994).

Fletcher, Catherine, *The Black Prince of Florence: The Spectacular Life and Treacherous World of Alessandro De' Medici* (Oxford: Oxford University Press, 2016).

Fox, James, '"For Good and Sufficient Reasons": An Examination of Early Dutch East India Company Ordinances on Slaves and Slavery', in eds. Anthony Reid and Jennifer Brewster, *Slavery, Bondage and Dependency in South East Asia* (London: Palgrave Macmillan, 1983), pp. 246–62.

Fraccia, Carmen, 'The Urban Slave in Spain and New Spain', in eds. Elizabeth McGrath and Jean Michel Massing, *The Slave in European Art: From Renaissance Trophy to Abolitionist Emblem*, Warburg Institute Coloquia ser., 20, (London: Warburg Institute, 2012), pp. 195–215.

Frick, Adrianna E., 'Sexual and Political Impotence in Imperfect Enjoyment Poetry', *Portals*, 5, 2007, http://userwww.sfsu.edu/clsa/portals/2007/frick.html

Friedman, John Block, 'The Art of the Exotic: Robinet Testard's Turbans and Turban-like Coiffure' in eds. Robin Netherton and Gale R. Owen-Crocker, *Medieval Clothing and Textiles* (Woodridge, Suff.: Boydell Press, 2008), vol. 4, pp. 173–91.

Fryer, Peter, *Aspects of British Black History* (London: Index Books, 1993).

Staying Power: the History of Black People in Britain (London: Pluto Press: 1984).

Fryer, Peter and Julia Bush, *The Politics of British Black History* (Wellingborough: Wellingborough District Racial Equality Council, 1991).

Gerzina, Gretchen, *Black England: Life Before Emancipation* (New Brunswick, N.J.: Rutgers University Press, 1995).

Gowing, Laura, *Domestic Dangers: Women, Words and Sex in Early Modern London* (Oxford: Oxford University Press, 1996).

'Language, Power and the Law: Women's Slander Litigation in Early Modern London', in eds. Jennifer Kermode and Garthine Walker, *Women, Crime and the Courts in Early Modern England* (London: UCL Press, 1994), pp. 26–47.

Gragg, L.D., *Englishmen Transplanted: The English Colonization of Barbados, 1627–1660* (Oxford: Oxford University Press On Demand, 2003).

Green, Dominic, *The Double Life of Doctor Lopez: Spies, Shakespeare, and the Plot to Poison Elizabeth I*, (London: Century, 2003).

Guasco, Michael J., *Slaves and Englishmen: Human Bondage in the Early Modern Atlantic World* (Philadelphia: University of Pennsylvania Press, 2014).

'Free from the tyrannous Spanyard: Englishmen and Africans in Spain's Atlantic World', *Slavery & Abolition*, 29:1, 2008, pp. 1–22.

Habib, Imtiaz H., *Black Lives in the English Archives, 1500–1677: Imprints of the Invisible* (Aldershot: Ashgate, 2008).

'"Hel's Perfect Character"; or the Blackamoor Maid in Early Modern English Drama: the Postcolonial Cultural History of a Dramatic Type', *Lit: Literature Interpretation Theory*, 11:3, 2000, pp. 277–304.

Shakespeare and Race: Postcolonial Praxis in the Early Modern Period (Lanham: University Press of America, 2000).

Habib, Imtiaz H. and Duncan Salkeld, 'The Resonables of Boroughside, Southwark: An Elizabethan Black Family Near the Rose Theatre/ Alienating Laughter In the Merchant of Venice: a Reply to Imtiaz Habib', *Shakespeare*, 2013, pp. 1–22.

Hall, Kim F. '"These bastard signs of fair": Literary Whiteness in Shakespeare's Sonnets', in eds. Ania Loomba and Martin Orkin, *Post-Colonial Shakespeares*, New Accent ser. (London and New York: Routledge, 2013), pp. 64–83.

Things of Darkness: Economies of Race and Gender in Early Modern England (Ithaca: Cornell University Press, 1995).

Hanks, Patrick, Richard Coates, and Peter McClure, eds., *The Oxford Dictionary of Family Names in Britain and Ireland* (Oxford: Oxford University Press, 2016), vol. 1.

Harris, Bernard, 'A Portrait of a Moor', *Shakespeare Survey*, 11, 1958, pp. 89–97.

Hatfield, April Lee, 'A "very wary people in the bargaining" or "very good merchandise": English Traders' Views of Free and Enslaved Africans, 1550–1650', *Slavery and Abolition*, 25:3, 2004, pp. 1–17.

Haynes, Alan, *Sex in Elizabethan England* (Stroud: The History Press, 2011).

Hayward, Maria, *Rich Apparel: Clothing and the Law in Henry VIII's England* (Farnham: Ashgate, 2009).
Dress at the Court of King Henry VIII (London: David Brown Book Company, 2007).

Hazlewood, Nick, *The Queen's Slave Trader: John Hawkyns, Elizabeth I, and the Trafficking in Human Souls* (New York: Harper Perennial, 2005).

Herbert, Trevor, "'. . . Men of Great Perfection in Their Science . . .": The Trumpeter as Musician and Diplomat in England in the Later Fifteenth and Sixteenth Centuries', *Historic Brass Society Journal*, 23, 2011, pp. 1–23.

Higginbotham, A. Leon, Jr., *In the Matter of Color: Race and the American Legal Process: The Colonial Period* (Oxford: Oxford University Press, 1978).

Hondius, Dienke, *Blackness in Western Europe* (New Brunswick, N.J.: Transaction Publishers, 2014).
'Blacks in Early Modern Europe: New Research from the Netherlands' in eds. Darlene Clark Hine, Tricia Danielle Keato, and Stephen Small, *Black Europe and the African Diaspora* (Urbana and Chicago: University of Illinois Press, 2009), pp. 29–47.
'Black Africans in Seventeenth Century Amsterdam', *Renaissance and Reformation*, 31:2, 2008, pp. 87–105.

Hunt, Marvin, 'Be Dark but Not Too Dark: Shakespeare's Dark Lady as a Sign of Color', in ed. James Schiffer, *Shakespeare's Sonnets: Critical Essays* (New York: Garland, 1999), pp. 368–89.

Hunter, George Kirkpatrick, 'Othello and Colour Prejudice', *Proceedings of the British Academy*, 53, 1967, pp. 139–63.

Inikori, Joseph E., *Africans and the Industrial Revolution in England: A Study in International Trade and Economic Development* (Cambridge: Cambridge University Press, 2002).

Iyengar, Sujata, *Shades of Difference: Mythologies of Skin Color in Early Modern England* (Philadelphia: University of Pennsylvania Press, 2005).

Jayasuriya, Shihan de S., 'South Asia's Africans: A Forgotten People',

History Workshop Online, 2011, http://www.historyworkshop.org.uk/south-asias-africans/.

The African Diaspora in Asian Trade Routes and Cultural Memories (Lampeter: Edwin Mellen Press, 2010).

Johnson, Catherine, *The Curious Tale of the Lady Caraboo* (London: Corgi Books, 2015).

Jones, Eldred, 'Racial Terms for Africans in Elizabethan Usage', *Review of National Literatures*, 3:2, 1972, pp. 54–89.

The Elizabethan Image of Africa (Charlottesville: University of Virginia Press, 1971).

Othello's Countrymen: The African in English Renaissance Drama (London: Oxford University Press, 1965).

Jones, R., and R. Youseph, *The Black Population of Bristol in the Eighteenth Century* (Bristol: Bristol Branch of the Historical Association, reprint, 1994).

Jordan, Winthrop D., *White over Black: American Attitudes Towards the Negro 1550–1812* (Chapel Hill: University of North Carolina Press, 1968).

Kaplan, P.H.D., 'Black Africans in Hohenstaufen Iconography', *Gesta*, 26:1, 1987, pp. 29–36.

The Rise of the Black Magus in Western Art (Ann Arbor: UMI Research Press, 1985).

Kaufmann, Miranda, '"Blanke, John (fl. 1507–1512)', *Oxford Dictionary of National Biography* (Oxford: Oxford University Press, online ed., September 2014).

'Africans in Britain, 1500–1640'. unpublished D.Phil thesis, University of Oxford, 2012.

'Blacks at Early Modern European Aristocratic Courts', in ed. E. Martone, *Encyclopedia of Blacks in European History and Culture*, (Westport, Conn.: Greenwood, 2008), vol. 1, pp. 163–6.

'English Common Law, Slavery and', in Martone, *Encyclopedia of Blacks in European History and Culture*, vol. 1, pp. 200–3.

'Prester John', in Martone, *Encyclopedia of Blacks in European History and Culture*, vol. 2, pp. 423–4.

'Somerset Case', in Martone, *Encyclopaedia of Blacks in European History and Culture*, vol. 2, pp. 504–5.

'Caspar Van Senden, Sir Thomas Sherley and the "Blackamoor" project', *Historical Research*, 81:212, 2008, pp. 366–71.

'Sir Pedro Negro: What Colour Was His Skin?', *Notes and Queries*, 253:2, 2008, pp. 142–6.

Kinkor, Kenneth J., 'Black Men under the Black Flag', in ed. C. Richard

Pennell, *Bandits at Sea: A Pirate Reader* (New York: New York University Press, 2001), pp. 195–210.

King, Turi E., Emma J. Parkin, Geoff Swinfield, *et. al*, 'Africans in Yorkshire? The Deepest-rooting Clade of the Y Phylogeny within an English Genealogy', *European Journal of Human Genetics*, 15:3, 2007, pp. 288–93.

Kleist, Alice M., 'The English African Trade Under the Tudors', *Transactions of the Historical Society of Ghana*, 3:2, 1957, pp. 137–52.

Knutson, Roslyn L., 'What's a Guy like John Davies Doing in a Seminar on Theater History?', Theater History Seminar, Shakespeare Association of America Annual Meeting (Minneapolis, Minn., March 2002), nn.1–2, notes online at: http://ualr.edu/rlknutson/davies.html.

'A Caliban in St. Mildred Poultry', in eds. Tetsuo Kishi, Roger Pringle, and Stanley W. Wells, *Shakespeare and Cultural Traditions: The Selected Proceedings of the International Shakespeare Association World Congress, Tokyo, 1991* (Newark, Del.: University of Deleware Press, 1994), pp. 110–26.

Kolfin, Elmer and Esther Schreuder, *Black is Beautiful: Rubens to Dumas* (Amsterdam: Waanders, 2008).

Landers, Jane and Barry Robinson, *Slaves, Subjects, and Subversives: Blacks in Colonial Latin America* (Albuquerque: University of New Mexico Press, 2006).

Leadam, I. S., 'Blakman, Blakeman, or Blackman, John (fl. 1436–1448)', *The Dictionary of National Biography, 1901 Supplement*, vol. 1, pp. 215–6.

Lee, Sidney, 'Caliban's Visits to England', *Cornhill Magazine*, 34, 1913, pp. 333–45.

Lessa, William A., 'Drake in the South Seas', in ed. Norman J.W. Thrower, *Sir Francis Drake and the Famous Voyage, 1577–1580* (Berkeley: University of California Press, 1984), pp. 60–77.

Little, Kenneth L., *Negroes in Britain: A Study of Racial Relations in English Society* (London: Kegan Paul, Trench, Trubner, 1948).

Lowe, Kate J.P., 'The Lives of African Slaves and People of African Descent in Renaissance Europe', in ed. Joneath Ann Spicer, *Revealing the African Presence in Renaissance Europe* (Baltimore: Walters Art Museum, 2013), pp. 13–33.

'Visible Lives: Black Gondoliers and Other Black Africans in Renaissance Venice', *Renaissance Quarterly*, 66:2, 2013, pp. 412–52.

Luu, Lien, *Immigrants and the Industries of London, 1500–1700* (London: Routledge, 2017).

'Immigrants and the Diffusion of Skills in Early Modern London: The Case of Silk Weaving', *Documents pour l'histoire des techniques*, nouvelle série, 15, 2008, pp. 32–42.

MacGaffey, Wyatt, 'Dialogues of the Deaf: Europeans on the Atlantic Coast of Africa', in ed. Stuart B. Schwartz, *Implicit Understandings: Observing, Reporting and Reflecting on the Encounters Between Europeans and Other Peoples in the Early Modern Era* (Cambridge: Cambridge University Press, 1994), vol. 3, pp. 249–67.

Maltby, William S., *The Black Legend in England: The Development of Anti-Spanish Sentiment, 1558–1660*, (Durham, N.C.: Duke University Press, 1971).

Martin, Paula, *Spanish Armada Prisoners: The Story of the Nuestra Señora del Rosario and Her Crew, and of Other Prisoners in England, 1587–97* (Exeter: University of Exeter Press, 1988).

Martone, E., ed., *Encyclopaedia of Blacks in European History and Culture* (Westport, CT: Greenwood, 2009), 2 vols.

Massing, Andreas, 'Mapping The Malagueta Coast: A History of the Lower Guinea Coast, 1460–1510 Through Portuguese Maps and Accounts', *History in Africa*, 36, 2009, pp. 331–65.

'The Mane, the Decline of Mali, and Mandinka Expansion Towards the South Windward Coast', *Cahiers d'études africaines*, 1985, pp. 21–55.

Matar, Nabil I., *Europe through Arab Eyes, 1578–1727* (New York: Columbia University Press, 2009).

Britain and Barbary, 1589–1689 (Gainesville: University Press of Florida, 2005).

Turks, Moors, and Englishmen in the Age of Discovery (New York: Columbia University Press, 1999).

Islam in Britain, 1558–1685 (Cambridge: Cambridge University Press, 1998).

McCullough, Norman V., *The Negro in English Literature, A Critical Introduction* (Ilfracombe: Arthur H. Stockwell, 1962).

Merians, Lindi E., *Envisioning the Worst: Representations of 'Hottentots' in Early Modern England* (Newark, Del.: University of Deleware Press, 2001).

Meyers, Charles, 'Lawsuits in Elizabethan Courts of Law: The Adventures of Dr. Hector Nunes, 1566–1591: A Precis', *Journal of European Economic History*, 25:1, 1996, pp. 157–8.

Milton, Giles, *White Gold: The Forgotten Story of North Africa's European Slaves* (London: Hodder & Stoughton, 2004).

Morgan, Edmund S., *American Slavery, American Freedom: The Ordeal of Colonial Virginia* (New York: W.W. Norton, 1975).

Morgan, Kenneth, *Slavery and the British Empire: From Africa to America* (Oxford: Oxford University Press, 2007).

Morgan, Philip D., 'British Encounters with Africans and African Americans, c.1600–1780', in eds. Bernard Bailyn and Philip D. Morgan, *Strangers within the Realm: Cultural Margins of the First British Empire* (Chapel Hill: University of North Carolina Press, 1991), pp. 157–219.

Newman, Karen, '"And wash the Ethiop white": Feminity and the Monstrous in *Othello*', in eds. Jean E. Howard and Marion F. O'Connor, *Shakespeare Reproduced: The Text in History and Ideology*. (New York: Methuen, 1987), pp. 143–62.

Northrup, David, 'Africans, Early European Contacts and the Emergent Disapora', in eds. Nicholas Canny and Philip Morgan, *The Oxford Handbook of the Atlantic World: 1450–1850* (Oxford: Oxford University Press, 2011).

  Africa's Discovery of Europe, 1450–1850 (Oxford: Oxford University Press, 2002).

O'Connell, John, *The Book of Spice: From Anise to Zedoary* (London: Pegasus Books, 2017).

Onyeka, *Blackamoores: Africans in Tudor England, Their Presence, Status and Origins* (London: Narrative Eye, 2013).

Peabody, Sue, *'There are No Slaves in France': The Political Culture of Race and Slavery in the Ancien Régime* (New York and Oxford: Oxford University Press, 1996).

Pechter, Edward, ed., *Othello: Authoritative Text, Sources and Contexts, Criticism*, Norton Critical ed. (New York: W.W. Norton, 2004).

Pettigrew, William A., *Freedom's Debt: The Royal African Company and the Politics of the Atlantic Slave Trade, 1672–1752* (Chapel Hill: University of North Carolina Press, 2013).

Phillips, William D., Jr., *Slavery in Medieval and Early Modern Iberia* (Philadelphia: University of Pennsylvania Press, 2014).

Pike, Ruth, 'Black Rebels: The Cimarrons of Sixteenth-Century Panama', *The Americas*, 64:2, 2007, pp. 243–66.

Quinn, David B., 'Turks, Moors, Blacks and Others in Drake's West Indian Voyage', in David B. Quinn, *Explorers and Colonies: America 1500–1625* (London: Hambledon Press, 1990), pp. 197–204.

Robbins, Mary E., 'Black Africans at the Court of James IV', *Review of Scottish Culture*, 12, 1999, pp. 34–45.

Rodney, Walter, *A History of the Upper Guinea Coast: 1545 –1800* (New York: New York University Press, 1970).

Ronald, Susan, *Pirate Queen: Queen Elizabeth I, Her Pirate Adventurers, and the Dawn of Empire* (New York: Harper Perennial, 2009).

Rockwood, C., ed., *Brewer's Dictionary of Phrase and Fable*, 18th ed. (London: Chambers Harrap, 2005).

Ruddock, Alwyn A., *Italian Merchants and Shipping in Southampton, 1270–1600*, Southampton Records Series, new ser., 1 (Southampton: University College, 1951).

'Alien Merchants in Southampton in the Later Middle Ages', *The English Historical Review*, 61: 239, 1946, pp. 1–17.

Samuel, Edgar, *At the Ends of the Earth: Essays on the History of the Jews of England and Portugal* (London: Jewish Historical Society of England, 2004).

'Portuguese Jews in Jacobean London', *Transactions of the Jewish Historical Society of England*, 18, 1953–55, pp. 171–230.

Saunders, A.C. de C.M., *A Social History of Black Slaves and Freedmen in Portugal, 1441–1555* (Cambridge: Cambridge University Press, 1982).

Scobie, Edward, *Black Britannia: a History of Blacks in Britain* (Chicago: Johnson Publishing, 1972).

Sherwood, M., 'Blacks in Tudor England', *BASA Newsletter*, Pt. 1–3, 38–40, 2004.

'Black People in Tudor England', *History Today*, 53:10, 2003, pp. 40–2.

Shore, Laurence, 'The Enduring Power of Racism: A Reconsideration of Winthrop Jordan's *White over Black*', *History and Theory*, 44:2, 2005, pp. 195–226.

Shugg, Wallace, 'Prostitution in Shakespeare's London', *Shakespeare Studies*, 10, 1977, pp. 291–313.

Shyllon, Folarin Olawale, *Black People in Britain 1555–1833* (Oxford: Oxford University Press, 1977).

Black Slaves in Britain (Oxford: Oxford University Press, 1974).

Slack, Paul, *The Impact of Plague in Tudor and Stuart England* (London: Routledge & Kegan Paul, 1985).

Sluiter, Engel, 'New Light on the "20 and Odd Negroes" Arriving in Virginia, August 1619', *William and Mary Quarterly*, 54:2, 1997, pp. 396–8.

Smith, Cassander L., *Black Africans in the British Imagination: English Narratives of the Early Atlantic World* (Baton Rouge: Louisiana State University Press, 2016).

'Washing the Ethiop Red: Sir Francis Drake and the Cimarrons of Panama', in eds. Maha Simmons and Merinda Marouan, *Race and Displacement: Nation, Migration, and Identity in the Twenty-First Century* (Tuscaloosa: University of Alabama Press, 2013), pp. 113–26.

Sollors, Werner, ed., *An Anthology of Interracial Literature: Black-White Contacts in the Old World and the New* (New York: New York University Press, 2004).

Spicer, Joneath, ed., *Revealing the African Presence in Renaissance Europe* (Baltimore: Walters Art Museum, 2013).

Steggle, Matthew, 'New Directions: Othello, the Moor of London: Shakespeare's Black Britons', in ed. Robert C. Evans, *Othello: A Critical Reader* (London: Bloomsbury, 2015), pp. 103–24.

Sweet, James H., *Recreating Africa: Culture, Kinship, and Religion in the African-Portuguese World, 1441–1770* (Chapel Hill: University of North Carolina Press, 2003).

Thomas, Hugh, *The Slave Trade: The History of the Atlantic Slave Trade, 1440–1870* (New York: Simon & Schuster Paperbacks, 1997).

Thomas, Keith, *Man and the Natural World: Changing Attitudes in England, 1500–1800* (London: Allen Lane, 1983).
Religion and the Decline of Magic: Studies in Popular Beliefs in Sixteenth and Seventeenth Century England (Oxford: Oxford University Press, 1971).

Thornton, John K., *Africa and Africans in the Making of the Atlantic World, 1400–1800*, 2nd ed. (Cambridge: Cambridge University Press, 1998).
'The African Experience of the "20 and Odd Negroes" Arriving in Virginia in 1619', *William and Mary Quarterly*, 55:3, 1998, pp. 421–34.

Thornton, John K. and Linda M. Heywood, eds., *Central Africans, Atlantic Creoles, and the Foundation of the Americas, 1585–1660* (Cambridge: Cambridge University Press, 2007).

Tokson, Elliot H., *The Popular Image of the Black Man in English Drama, 1550–1688* (Boston: G.K. Hall, 1982).

Ungerer, Gustav, *The Mediterranean Apprenticeship of British Slavery* (Madrid: Editorial Verbum, 2008).
'The Presence of Africans in Elizabethan England and the Performance of "Titus Andronicus" at Burley-on-the-Hill, 1595/96', *Medieval and Renaissance Drama in England*, 21, 2008, pp. 19–55.
'Recovering a Black African's Voice in an English Lawsuit: Jacques Francis and the Salvage Operations of the "Mary Rose" and the

"Sancta Maria and Sanctus Edwardus", 1545–ca 1550', *Medieval and Renaissance Drama in England*, 17, 2005, pp. 255–71.

Vaughan, Alden T., *Transatlantic Encounters: American Indians in Britain, 1500–1776* (Cambridge: Cambridge University Press, 2006).

'Blacks in Virginia: A Note on the First Decade', *The William and Mary Quarterly*, 3rd ser., 29:3, 1972, pp. 469–78.

Vitkus, Daniel J., ed., *Piracy, Slavery and Redemption: Barbary Captivity Narratives From Early Modern England*, Intro. by Nabil Matar (New York: Columbia University Press, 2001).

Walker, Alison Tara, 'The Westminster Tournament Challenge (Harley 83 H 1) and Thomas Wriothesley's Workshop', *The Electronic British Library Journal*, 2011, pp. 1–13.

Walker, Roy S., *The Book of Almondsbury* (Buckingham: Barracuda Books, 1987).

Walvin, James, *Black and White: The Negro and English Society 1555–1945* (London: Alden Lane, 1973).

The Black Presence: A Documentary History of the Negro in England, 1555–1860, Documentary history ser. (London: Orbach and Chambers, 1971), vol. 1.

Weissbourd, Emily, '"Those in Their Possession": Race, Slavery, and Queen Elizabeth's "Edicts of Expulsion"', *Huntington Library Quarterly* 78:1, 2015, pp. 1–19.

Wheat, David, *Atlantic Africa and the Spanish Caribbean, 1570–1640* (Chapel Hill: University of North Carolina Press, 2016).

Yungblut, Laura Hunt, *Strangers Settled Here Among Us: Policies, Perceptions and Presence of Aliens in Elizabethan England* (London and New York: Routledge, 1996).

Zemon Davis, Natalie, *Trickster Travels: A Sixteenth Century Muslim Between Worlds* (New York: Hill and Wang, 2007).

Unpublished theses and online sources

Please see the full bibliography online for the details of the unpublished theses, primary online sources and secondary online sources consulted.

Works of art

Anon., 'A rare and important French Renaissance tapestry of Le Camp du Drap d'Or, the meeting of Kings Henry VIII and François Ier', c.1520, probably Tournai, sold at Sothebys, New York, 11 December 2014: http://www.artnet.com/artists/a-rare- and-important-french-renaissance-tapestry-c-hogwYhya5ohsiEo_WqRmig2

Anon., 'The Drake Jewel', 1588, Collection of Sir George Meyrick, on loan to Victoria and Albert Museum, London.

Anon., 'The Engagement of St Ursula and Prince Etherius', 1522, St Auta altarpiece, Convent of Madre de Deus, Lisbon.

Anon., 'Portrait of Peregrine Bertie, Lord Willoughby de Eresby (1555–1601)', Grimsthorpe Castle, Lincolnshire.

Anon., 'Westminster Tournament Roll', painted vellum, 1511 College of Arms, London; repro. in ed. Sydney Anglo, *The Great Tournament Roll of Westminster* (Oxford: Clarendon Press, 1968), vol. 2, plate 3, membranes 3–5; plate 18, membranes 28–9.

Bellini, Gentile, 'Miracle of the True Cross at the Bridge of San Lorenzo', 1500, Gallerie dell'Accademia, Venice.

Blake, William, 'Flagellation of a Female Samboe Slave', repro. in Capt. J. G. Stedman, *Narrative of a Five Years' Expedition Against the Revolted Slaves of Surinam*, (London: Printed for J. Johnson and J. Edwards, 1796), vol. 1, plate facing p. 326.

Carpaccio, Vittore, 'Miracle of the Relic of the Cross at the Ponte di Rialto', c. 1496, Gallerie dell'Accademia, Venice.

'Hunting on the Lagoon' (c.1490–5), The J. Paul Getty Museum, Los Angeles.

Dürer, Albrecht, 'Study of Katharina', 1521, Uffizi Gallery, Florence.

English School, unknown, 'Sir Thomas Love, c. 1571–1627', c. 1620, National Maritime Museum, Greenwich, London.

Flemish/German?, unknown, 'Portrait of a Wealthy African', 1530–40, Private Collection, Antwerp.

Gheeraerts, Marcus, the younger, 'Sir Francis Drake, 1540–1596', National Maritime Museum, Greenwich, London, Caird Collection, BHC2662.

Hogarth, William, 'A Rake's Progress, 3: The Orgy', 1733 painting, Sir John Soane's Museum, London, and 1735 print, plate 3.

Mignard, Pierre, 'Louise de Kéroualle, Duchess of Portsmouth' (1682), National Portrait Gallery, London, NPG 497.

Mostaert, Jan Jansz, 'Portrait of an African Man', c. 1525–30, The Rijksmuseum, Amsterdam.

Mytens, Daniel, 'Charles I and Henrietta Maria Departing for the Chase' (c.1630–2), Royal Collection Trust, RCIN 404771.

Rowlandson, Thomas, 'Sea Stores', 1812, Royal Collection Trust, RCIN 810882.

van Dyck, Anthony, 'Portrait of George Gage with Two Attendants', ca. 1622–3, The National Gallery, London, NG49.

'The Continence of Scipio', 1620–1, Christ Church Picture Gallery, Oxford.

van Somer, Paul, 'Anne of Denmark', 1617, Royal Collection Trust, RCIN 405887.

List of Illustrations

Albrecht Dürer's portraits of Katherina and an unknown African male. Courtesy of Wikimedia Commons.

Detail from the 'Agas' map of London, c. 1561, showing Hart Street. Courtesy of London Metropolitan Archives, City of London.

Detail from the 'Agas' map of London, c. 1561, showing St Botolph Aldgate. Courtesy of London Metropolitan Archives, City of London.

Jean Barbot's map of River Cestos, c. 1681. Originally published by Barbot and reproduced in *Barbot on Guinea: The Writings of Jean Barbot on West Africa 1678–1712*.

Detail from the 'Agas' map of London, c. 1561, showing St Mildred. Courtesy of London Metropolitan Archives, City of London.

Jean Barbot's meeting with the king of River Cestos, c. 1681. Originally published by Barbot in *A Description of the coasts of North and South-Guinea*.

Vlissingen by Andries Schoemaker. Courtesy of Wikimedia Commons/Koninklijke Bibliotheek, the Dutch National Library.

Dover castle by Wenceslas Hollar. Courtesy of Wikimedia Commons.

'An English Sailor' from *Habiti Antichi et Moderni di tutto il Mondo*, Cesare Vecelio, 1598. Courtesy of World History Archive/Alamy Stock Photo.

The Peacham Drawing, showing a 'black' man playing Aaron in Shakespeare's *Titus Andronicus* © reproduced by permission of the Marquess of Bath, Longleat House, Warminster, Wiltshire, Great Britain.

Detail from the 'Agas' map of London, c. 1561, showing St Clement. Courtesy of London Metropolitan Archives, City of London.

Almondsbury Church by Samuel Lysons. Originally published in *A collection of Gloucestershire antiquities* by Samuel Lysons, F.R.S. & F.A.S. (London: T. Cadell and W. Davies, 1804).

Plate section images

Images of John Blanke from the College of Arms MS Westminster Tournament Roll. Reproduced by permission of the Kings, Heralds and Pursuivants of Arms.

Abd el-Ouahed ben Messaoud ben Mohammed Anoun, Moorish Ambassador to Queen Elizabeth I, 1600. Courtesy of Wikimedia Commons.

A Village Festival by Marcus Gheeraerts the Elder. Courtesy of Wikimedia Commons.

Portrait of an African Woman holding a clock, c. 1583–85, by Annibale Carracci. Courtesy of Wikimedia Commons.

Notes to Text

Abbreviations

APC: *Acts of the Privy Council of England*, ed. J.R. Dasent, (46 vols., 1890–1964).

BCB: Bridewell Court Books, Minutes of the Court of Governors (37 vols., 1559–1971), *Bethlem Royal Hospital Archives*, http://archives.museumofthemind.org.uk/BCB.htm (accessed 30 March 2017).

CSPC: *Calendar of State Papers, Colonial series* ed. W.N. Sainsbury (10 vols, 1860).

CSPD: *Calendar of State Papers, Domestic series, of the reigns of Edward VI, Mary, Elizabeth and James I, 1547–1625*, ed. R. Lemon, M.A.E. Green (12 vols., 1856–72).

Calendar of State Papers, Domestic series, of the reign of James I, ed. M.A.E. Green (5 vols., 1857–1872).

Calendar of State Papers, Domestic series, of the reign of Charles I, ed. J. Bruce (23 vols., 1858–1897).

CSPS: *Calendar of Letters and State Papers relating to English Affairs preserved in or originally belonging to the Archives of Simancas*, ed. M.A.S Hume (4 vols.,1892–9).

Hakluyt: R. Hakluyt, *The Principall Navigations, Voyages, Traffiques and Discoveries of the English Nation* (12 vols., Glasgow, 1903–5).

The History of Parliament: The History of Parliament Online, Member Biographies, http://www.historyofparliamentonline.org/ (accessed 30 March 2017).

L&P, Henry VIII: Letters and Papers, Foreign and Domestic, Henry VIII, ed. J.S. Brewer, R.H. Brodie and J. Gairdner (21 vols., 1810–1920).

LMA: London Metropolitan Archives, 40 Northampton Rd, Clerkenwell, London EC1R 0HB.

TNA: The National Archives, Kew Richmond, Surrey, TW9 4DU.

Introduction

1   Bennett, G., 'Black history: the timeline', *Guardian*; Kaufmann, M., 'Elizabeth I and the 'Blackamoores', http://www.mirandakaufmann.com.

2   Bartels, 'Too Many Blackamoors: Deportation, Discrimination, and Elizabeth I'; Kaufmann, 'Caspar van Senden, Sir Thomas Sherley and the 'Blackamoor' Project'; Weissbourd, "Those in Their Possession": Race, Slavery, and Queen Elizabeth's "Edicts of Expulsion". This episode is discussed in Chapter 4 and Chapter 6.

3   This was reinforced by the range of exhibitions, programming and other materials widely circulated during the 2007 commemoration of the Bicentenary of the Abolition of the British Slave Trade.

4   The Oxford English Dictionary, "slave, n.1 (and adj.)", OED Online.

5   Milton, White Gold, p. 304. See also Davis, Christian Slaves, Muslim Masters.

6   235 Africans were sold in Lagos, Portugal; in 1444. Saunders, A Social History of Black Slaves and Freedmen in Portugal, pp. 5–11.

7   Voyages: The Trans-Atlantic Slave Trade Database calculates that 378,734 slaves disembarked from 1,328 voyages between 1514–1619.

8   Wrigley and Schofield, The Population History of England 1541–1871, p. 528. Life expectancy markedly improved for those who survived their childhoods.

9   Hobbes, Leviathan, ed. Oakeshott, p. 94.

10   Hargrave, An Argument in the Case of James Sommersett a Negro, p. 50–1, citing the 1569 Cartwright case: Rushworth, Historical Collections of Private Passages of State, II, p. 468; see also: Paley, 'Somerset, James (b. c.1741, d. in or after 1772)', Oxford Dictionary of National Biography, and Kaufmann, 'Somerset Case', pp. 504–505.

11   Cambridge University Library, G.R.G Conway Collection, Add. MSS, 7231, ff. 2, 157–8, 339–40.

Chapter 1

1   Westminster Tournament Roll, painted vellum, 1511 College of Arms, London; repro. in The Great Tournament Roll of Westminster, ed. Anglo, II, plate 3, membranes 3–5; plate 18, membranes 28–9.

2   Kleist, 'The English African Trade Under the Tudors', p. 137; Blake, West Africa, pp. 60–62; Blake, Europeans in West Africa, p. 266; Calendar of State Papers, Venice, ed. Brown, 1202–1509, p. 142; Penn, Winter King, p. 32.

3   Boorde, The Fyrst Boke of the Introduction of Knowledge, ed. Furnivall, p. 56.

4   Personal correspondence with Matthew Dimmock. See also Friedman, 'The Art of the Exotic: Robinet Testard's Turbans and Turban–like Coiffure', pp. 173–191. Henry VIII and the Earl of Essex appeared in Turkish costume during Shrovetide 1510: Johnson, So Great A Prince, p. 203.

5   Kisby, 'Royal Minstrels in the City and Suburbs of Early Tudor London', p. 201; Stevens, Music and Poetry, p. 307.

6   TNA, E 36/214, f. 109. The document can be viewed online at: http://www.national archives.gov.uk/pathways/blackhistory/early_times/docs/blanke_payment.htm

7   Lowe and Earle, Black Africans in Renaissance Europe, pp. 12, 252.

8   Records of English Court Music, ed. Ashbee, VII, pp. 185–188.

9   Thirsk, Chapters from the Agrarian History of England and Wales, I, p. 18; Woodward, Men at Work, p. 172.

10 *The Household of Edward IV*, ed. Myers, p. 131.

11 Stevens, *Music and Poetry*, pp. 235–7, 313. Shakespeare, *All's Well That Ends Well*, Act 5, Scene 2; 'Parishes: Richmond (anciently Sheen)', in *A History of the County of Surrey: Volume 3*, ed. H.E. Malden (London, 1911), pp. 533–546, n. 50. *British History Online* http://www.british-history.ac.uk/vch/surrey/vol3/pp533-546 [accessed 30 March 2017].

12 Stevens, *Music and Poetry* p. 313; G. R. Rastall, 'Secular musicians in late medieval England', pp. 149–50.

13 'Introduction', in *Memorials of London and London Life in the 13th, 14th and 15th Centuries*, ed. H.T. Riley (London, 1868), pp. vii–li, n. 94. *British History Online* http://www.british-history.ac.uk/no-series/memorials-london-life/vii-li [accessed 30 March 2017].

14 Numbers 29:1; Leviticus 23:24.

15 Sarkissian and Tarr, 'Trumpet' *Grove Music Online*.

16 Herbert, '". . . men of great perfection in their science . . .": the trumpeter as musician and diplomat in England in the later fifteenth and sixteenth centuries', pp. 1–2, 10.

17 *Records of English Court Music*, ed. Ashbee, VII, p. 234.

18 *Records of English Court Music*, ed. Ashbee, VII, p. 184.

19 Penn, *Winter King*, pp. 4–5.

20 Kaplan, 'Introduction to the New Edition', in *The Image of the Black in Western Art*, ed. Bindman, Gates & Dalton, II, 1, pp. 13–14; Kaplan, 'Black Africans in Hohenstaufen Iconography', pp. 29–36.

21 Lowe & Earle, *Black Africans in Renaissance Europe*, pp. 39, 118; Kaufmann, 'Courts, Blacks at Early Modern European Aristocratic', pp. 163–166.

22 *The Accounts of the Lord High Treasurer of Scotland*, ed. Dickson, Balfour Paul, McInnes *et al.*, II, 477 and III, 132; "Taburn(e) *n.*", and "Taburner *n.*", *The Dictionary of the Scots Language*. The last mentions of the African drummer at James IV's court suggest he died as a result of an injury sustained in the summer of 1506. The King paid his medical bills from June to August, but thereafter was supporting his wife and child. His drum was given to another musician, named Guillaume, the following summer. *The Accounts of the Lord High Treasurer of Scotland*, ed. Dickson, Balfour Paul, McInnes *et al.*, III, pp. 197, 206, 330, 335, 377, 388; Habib, *Black Lives*, p. 30; Robbins, 'Black Africans at the Court of James IV', p. 42.

23 *A rare and important French Renaissance tapestry of Le Camp du Drap d'Or, the meeting of Kings Henry VIII and François Ier*, c.1520, probably Tournai, sold at Sothebys, New York, 11 December 2014: http://www.sothebys.com/en/auctions/ecatalogue/2014/masterworks–n09209/lot.14.html

24 *The Engagement of St Ursula and Prince Etherius*, 1522, St Auta altarpiece, Convent of Madre de Deus, Lisbon.

25 Ashbee and Lasocki, eds., *A biographical dictionary of English court musicians*, I, p. 238; Dumitrescu, *The Early Tudor Court and International Musical Relations*, pp. 33, 67–8.

26 *Records Of English Court Music*, ed. Ashbee, VII, p. 174.

27 T. Knighton, 'The Spanish Court of Ferdinand and Isabella', pp. 341–343.

28 Elbl, 'The Volume of the Early Atlantic Slave Trade', pp. 31–75; Phillips, *Slavery in Medieval and Early Modern Iberia*, p. 64. Melchor de Santa Cruz, *Floresta espanola* p. 197, n. 11. See also Blumenthal, *Enemies and Familiars: Slavery and Mastery in Fifteenth-Century Valencia*.

29 T. Knighton, 'The Spanish Court of Ferdinand and Isabella', p. 349.

30 Tremlett, *Isabella of Castile*, p. 119.

31 Fraccia, 'The Urban Slave in Spain and New Spain', p. 199; Hilgarth, *The Mirror of Spain*, pp. 243–51.

32 Tremlett, *Catherine of Aragon*, pp. 40–41.

33 Crónica *Del Rey Enrico Otavo De Ingalaterra*, ed. Roca de Togores, Marquis de Molins, p. 326; *CSPS*, 1485–1509, pp. 246, 252, 254; Williams, P., *Katherine of Aragon*, p. 108.

34 Ibid., pp. 107–109.

35 BL Arundel 249, f. 85v; *The Correspondence of Sir Thomas More*, ed. Rogers, pp. 3–4; Orme, 'Holt, John (d. 1504)', *Oxford Dictionary of National Biography*; *Chronicles of London*, ed. Kingsford, p. 334 and *The Receyt of the Lady Kataryne*, ed. Kipling, p. 33; discussed by Habib, *Black Lives*, pp. 24–7 and Onyeka, *Blackamoores*, pp. 191–6. See also Johnson, *So Great a Prince*, p. 205.

36 Johnson, L., 'A Life of Catalina, Katherine of Aragon's Moorish Servant', *English Historical Fiction Authors*; Johnson, *So Great a Prince*, pp. 205–6 and p. 298, n. 2. *L&P, Henry VIII*, 1531–32, p. 169 (Holy Roman Emperor Charles V to Isabella of Portugal, 31 July 1531). As Johnson explains (p. 298, n.2), Catalina of Motril has been confused in the secondary literature with a completely different woman, Katherine of Aragon's maid of honour, Lady Catalina de Cardones. See, Crónica *del rey Enrico otavo de Ingalaterra*, ed. Roca de Togores, Marquis de Molins, pp. 325, 329; Ungerer, *The Mediterranean Apprenticeship of Slavery*, p. 97 and Onyeka, *Blackamoores*, pp. 198–9.

37 Ungerer, *The Mediterranean Apprenticeship of British Slavery*, p. 96; D'Azevedo, 'Os Escravos', p. 300, doc. III (transcription of Chancellaria de D. João II, Liv. pp. xvi, fl. 61).

38 Rushworth, *Historical Collections of Private Passages of State*, II, 468; Harrison, *Description of England*, ed. Edelen, p. 118.

39 Saunders, *Black Slaves and Freedmen in Portugal*, pp. 113–133; Fox, '"For good and sufficient reasons", pp. 246–262; Peabody, 'There Are No Slaves in France', p. 11; Taylor, *American Colonies*, pp. 155–156, 213.

40 Van Cleve, 'Somerset's Case and its antecedents in Imperial perspective', pp. 608–9.

41 Crónica *Del Rey Enrique Octavo De Inglaterra*, ed. Roca de Togores, Marquis de Molins, p. 329.

42 Fraccia, 'The Urban Slave in Spain and New Spain', p. 195.

43 MacCulloch, 'Bondmen Under the Tudors', pp. 94, 109.

44 Beier, *Masterless Men*, p. 23.

45 See n. 37 above; *Tudor Exeter Tax Assessments 1489–1599*, ed. Rowe, p. 18; For Jacques Francis, see Chapter 2; Northamptonshire Record Office, Microfiche 120p/3 (St Nicholas, Eydon, 16 December 1545); *The Diary of Henry Machyn*, ed. Nicholls, p. 74; Stow, *Annales*, ed. Howe, p. 1038.

46 *The Accounts of the Lord High Treasurer of Scotland*, ed. Dickson, Balfour Paul, McInnes *et al.*, II, pp. 465, 468, 469; III, pp. lxxxv, 94, 101, 172, 175, 182, 113, 114, 154–5, 361, 370–1, 387, 409, 336; IV: 51, 82, 59, 61, 100, 62, 116, 232, 324, 339, 401, 404, 434, 436; V, p. 328. For transcriptions see Kaufmann, 'Africans in Britain', Appendix: 5. Household Accounts, nos. 28–97.

47 Harrison, J.G., '"The Bread Book" and the Court and Household of Marie de Guise in 1549', p. 30.

48 *The Scottish Correspondence of Mary of Lorraine*, ed. Cameron, p. 296; see also Kaufmann, 'Sir Pedro Negro: What colour was his skin?', pp. 142-146.

49 Williams, P., *Katherine of Aragon*, p. 155, 158–9.

50 Penn, *Winter King*, pp. 213–225.

51 Woodfield, *The Early History of the Viol*, p. 206.

52 *L&P, Henry VIII*, 1509–1514, p. 14.

53 Easterlings were merchants of the Dutch Hanse.

54 *L&P, Henry VIII*, 1509–1514, pp. 8–24.

55 *L&P, Henry VIII*, 1509–1514, p. 43.

56 Hayward, *Rich Apparel: Clothing and the Law in Henry VIII's England*, p. 17.

57 Dillon, *Performance and Spectacle in Hall's Chronicle*, pp. 25, 28.

58 Ibid., p. 33; Johnson, *So Great A Prince*, p. 203.

59 Stevens, *Music and Poetry*, p. 301.

60 His songbook is BL, Additional MS. 31922, ff.14v–15; See also Helms, 'Henry VIII's Book: Teaching Music to Royal Children', pp. 118–135 and D. Fallows, 'Henry VIII As a Composer', pp. 27–39.

61 Stevens, *Music and Poetry*, p. 234.

62 Erasmus, *In Praise of Folly* (1509), cited in Stevens, *Music and Poetry*, p. 287, see also pp. 265–266; Hayward, *Dress at the Court of King Henry VIII*, p.266; Princess Mary demanded music from Memo: *L & P, Henry VIII, 1515–1518*, pp. 1220–1236.

63 Dumitrescu, *The Early Tudor Court and International Musical Relations*, pp. 68, 232; *Records Of English Court Music*, ed. Ashbee, VII, 22.

64 TNA, E101/217/2, no.105. A searchable database of this tranche of documents has been created by Dr. James Ross of the University of Winchester: 'Kingship, Court and Society: the Chamber Books of Henry VII and Henry VIII, 1485–1521', https://www.tudorchamberbooks.org.

65 *Records of English Court Music*, ed. Ashbee, VII, pp. 87, 100, 103, 192–201.

66 Ashbee, 'Groomed for Service: Musicians in the Privy Chamber at the English Court', p. 188. The 'More Taubronar' at the Scottish court was provided with a horse (which previously belonged to court trumpeter Pete Johne) by James IV on 13 September 1504, but the king mostly met his travel expenses. In 1504 the drummer, along with four Italian minstrels, travelled with the itinerant court to Eskdale, Dumfries, Peebles, Falkland, Strethbogy, Brechin and 'the Month': *The Accounts of the Lord High Treasurer of Scotland*, ed. Dickson, Balfour Paul, McInnes *et al.*, II, pp. 458 and 420, 435, 444, 451, 457, 458,459, 461, 462, 464.

67 Stevens, *Music and Poetry*, p. 240. For further discussion of Tudor sumptuary laws, see Chapter 5.

68 *The Great Tournament Roll of Westminster*, ed. Anglo, I, p. 1.

69 *L & P, Henry VIII*, 1509–1514, pp. 369–377.

70 Walker, 'The Westminster Tournament Challenge (Harley 83 H 1) and Thomas Wriothesley's Workshop', pp. 1–13.

71 Dillon, *Performance and Spectacle in Hall's Chronicle*, p. 42.

72 *The Great Chronicle of London*, ed. Thomas and Thornley, p. 373–4.

73 *L&P, Henry VIII*, 1515–1518, p.1450.

74 The following account of the Westminster Tournament is taken from *The Great Tournament Roll of Westminster*, ed. Anglo, *The Great Chronicle of London*, ed. Thomas and Thornley, and *Hall's Chronicle*, in Dillon, *Performance and Spectacle in Hall's Chronicle*, pp. 37–42. Despite how they are dressed in the Tournament Roll, the *Great Chronicle* says the trumpeters were 'clad in Red cloth': Anglo, I, p. 85.

75 *The Great Tournament Roll of Westminster*, ed. Anglo, I, p. 35, esp. n. 3.

76 Chaucer, *The Canterbury Tales*, ed. Wright, p. 69.

77 *The Great Chronicle of London*, ed. Thomas and Thornley, p. 371.

78 *The Great Tournament Roll of Westminster*, ed. Anglo, I, p. 55; *The Great Chronicle of London*, ed. Thomas and Thornley, p. 372.

79 *The Great Tournament Roll of Westminster*, ed. Anglo, I, p. 96.

80 *The poems of William Dunbar*, ed. Bawcutt, p. 113; Habib, *Black Lives*, p. 33, n. 40; Scott, *Dunbar*, p. 67. Bawcutt, 'The Art of Flyting', pp. 5–24; 'The Flyting of Dunbar and Kennedy', tr. Murphy, http://www.clanstrachan.org/history/Flyting_of_Dunbar_and_Kennedy.pdf (accessed 30 March 2017). *The Poems of William Dunbar*, Kinsley, p. 106.

81 *The Accounts of the Lord High Treasurer of Scotland*, ed. Dickson, Balfour Paul, McInnes *et al.*, III, p. 258; Lindsay of Pitscottie *The Historie and Cronicles of Scotland*, ed. Mackay Vol X p. 244.

82 *The Great Tournament Roll of Westminster*, ed. Anglo, I, pp. 56–7. The original source, Gibson's Revels Account, TNA, E 36/217, f. 70 refers to 1s 4d spent on 'mendyng of the floor' at the 'bechop of harforthes plas'. Presumably this was the Bishop of Hereford, who in 1511 was Richard Mayhew: Newcombe, 'Mayhew, Richard (1439/40–1516)', *Oxford Dictionary of National Biography*.

83 Dillon, *Performance and Spectacle in Hall's Chronicle*, pp. 40–41.

84 *The Great Tournament Roll of Westminster*, ed. Anglo, I p. 58; *L&P, Henry VIII*, 1509–1514, pp. 377–390.

85 Bowsher, 'The Chapel Royal at Greenwich Palace', pp. 155–161; Thurley, *The Royal Palaces of Tudor England*, pp. 196–7 and personal correspondence.

86 TNA, E 101/417/6, f. 50.

87 Hayward, *Dress at the Court of King Henry VIII*, p. 231.

88 TNA, E 101/417/6, f. 57.

89 *L & P, Henry VIII*, 1509–1514, p. 1645; TNA, E 101/417/3 f. 12; TNA, E101/420/1 no.29.

90 Ashbee and Lasocki, eds., *A biographical dictionary of English court musicians*, I, p. 151.

91 As Onyeka points out, there are various 'John Blanke''s recorded in the subsidy records as living in Tower Ward in the 1540s and 1550s, but none can be clearly

identified as the trumpeter. Onyeka, *Blackamoores*, p. 211; Kirk and Kirk, I, pp. 20, 155, 199, 252, II, 41, 81, III, 314. A Haberdasher named *Thomas* Blanke appears in the London records in 1542. His son, another Thomas Blanke, was to become Lord Mayor in 1582-3. Alfred P Beaven, 'Notes on the aldermen, 1502-1700', in *The Aldermen of the City of London Temp. Henry III–1912* (London, 1908), pp. 168–195. *British History Online* http://www.british-history.ac.uk/no-series/london-aldermen/hen3-1912/pp168-195 [accessed 31 March 2017].

92 Thurley, *The Royal Palaces of Tudor England*, p. 2.

93 Lowe and Earle, *Black Africans in Renaissance Europe*, pp. 160–161; Kaufmann, 'Courts, Blacks at Early Modern European Aristocratic', pp. 163–166. Elizabeth I bought the following outfit for her African servant to wear:

> 'Item, for making of a Gascon coate for a lytle Blackamore of white Taffata, cut and lyned under with tincel, striped down with gold and silver, and lined with buckram and bayes, poynted with poynts and ribands . . . and faced with taffata . . . with a white taffata doublet with gold and silver lace, silver buttons, faced with Taffata; a payre of Gascons, a paire of knit hose, a pair of white shoes and pantoufles, a dozen of poynts, and a paire of gaiters': TNA, LC 5/34, f. 241 (Lord Chamberlain's account); see also BL Egerton 2806, f. 70; Arnold, *Queen Elizabeth's Wardrobe Unlock'd*, p. 106. The painting identified by Sewter in 'Queen Elizabeth at Kenilworth' p. 75, in 1940 (and cited by the influential Peter Fryer, *Staying Power*, p. 9) as showing Queen Elizabeth being entertained by a group of black musicians and dancers in 1575 has been shown to be a European painting depicting Italian commedia dell' arte actors by Katrisky, *The Art of Commedia*, pp. 145–6.

94 Anthony Vause is mentioned in the burial record of 'Anne Vause a Black-more wife to Anthonie Vause, Trompetter of the said Country'. The location of the parish close to the Tower meant that various court musicians and their families appear in the register. LMA, MS 09222/1 (St Botolph Aldgate, 27 April 1618); Marshall Denkinger, 'Minstrels and Musicians in the Registers of St. Botolph Aldgate', pp. 395–398; Paul van Somer, 'Anne of Denmark', 1617, Royal Collection, RCIN 405887; Daniel Mytens, 'Charles I and Henrietta Maria Departing for the chase', c.1630–2, Royal Collection, RCIN 404771. Anne of Denmark also had an African in her Scottish household in 1590: Kaufmann, 'Africans in Britain', pp. 172–4; *Papers Relative to the Marriage of King James the Sixth of Scotland with the Princess Anna of Denmark*, ed. Gibson Craig, pp. 21, 28, 36; D. Stevenson, *Scotland's Last Royal Wedding: the Marriage of James VI and Anne of Denmark with a Danish Account of the Marriage Translated by Peter Graves* (Edinburgh, 1997), p. 109.

95 Potter, *Henry VIII and Francis I*, p. 12.

Chapter 2

1 Thomas Beckingham, mayor of Southampton, had known him for about ten years in 1549: TNA, HCA 13/93, f. 273v (High Court of Admiralty Deposition, 14 May 1549).

2 'Woolsack', Glossary, *UK Parliament Website*, http://www.parliament.uk/site-information/glossary/woolsack/ (accessed 31 March 2017); Hentschell, *The Culture of*

Cloth in Early Modern England, p. 2; Ruddock, *Italian Merchants and Shipping in Southampton*, pp. 256–272.

3   Kaplan, 'Italy, 1490–1700' in *The Image of the Black in Western Art*, ed. Bindman and Gates, III, 1, pp.93–125; Shakespeare, *The Merchant of Venice*, Act 4, Scene 1; black gondoliers appear in Vittore Carpaccio, *Miracle of the Relic of the Cross at the Ponte di Rialto*, c. 1496, Gallerie dell'Accademia, Venice, and his *Hunting on the Lagoon* (c.1490–5), The J. Paul Getty Museum, Los Angeles; Lowe, 'Visible lives: black gondoliers and other black Africans in Renaissance Venice', pp. 412–452; Lowe and Earle, *Black Africans in Renaissance Europe*, pp. 303–325; Fletcher, *The Black Prince of Florence*.

4   Ruddock, 'Alien Merchants in Southampton in the Later Middle Ages', p. 12. Another possible African in late 15th-century Southampton was Maria Moriana (discussed later in this chapter see n. 41 below), but her ethnicity is never explicitly stated in the records.

5   The following account is largely drawn from McKee, *King Henry VIII's Mary Rose* and Knighton & Loades, *Letters from the Mary Rose*. Peter Paulo Corsi appears in the former, p. 89 and the latter, pp. 132–3.

6   Knighton and Loades, *Letters from the Mary Rose*, p. 122 had it as £1.75M in 2002.

7   Ibid.; Mortimer, *The Time Travellers Guide to Elizabethan England*, pp. 262–3. The bill was for 22 tons of beer. There are 204 gallons in a ton of beer, so 22 tons is 4,488 gallons. There are 8 pints in a gallon. Hence 4,488 x 8= 35,904. I have then divided this figure by 91 men and again by 28 days (a month) to get the figure of 14 pints a day each.

8   TNA, HCA 13/5, f. 192. (Deposition by Domenico Erizzo, 14 December 1547)

9   Knighton & Loades, *Letters from the Mary Rose*, pp. 132–33, items 77–9, 81; Ungerer, 'Recovering a Black African's Voice in an English Lawsuit', p. 258; Carter, 'Carew, Sir Wymond (1498–1549)', *Oxford Dictionary of National Biography*; First fruits' were the first year's income for a new appointee to an ecclesiastical benefice, the 'tenths' an annual tax thereafter: *Encyclopaedia of Tudor England*, ed. Wagner and Schmid, I, 447–8.

10   The following account is drawn from the ensuing case between Domenico Erizzo and Peter Paulo Corsi in the High Court of Admiralty. The surviving papers comprise: deposition by Domenico Erizzo, 14 December 1547 HCA 13/5, ff. 191–195; various depositions in HCA 13/93: f. 192v (John Westcott, 29 January 1548); f. 193v-4r (William Mussen, 30 January 1548); f. 202 (Jacques Francis, 8 Feb 1548); f. 241v-2 (Domenico Paza, 16 July 1548); f. 242–3, Domenico Milanes (18 July 1548); f. 246v (Antonio de Nicolao, 1 September 1548); f. 271 (Niccolo de Marini, 7 May 1549); f. 272 (Thomas Beckingham, 14 May 1549); f. 275v (Antonio de Nicolao, 23 May 1549); f. 277v (Niccolo de Marini, 5 June 1549); f. 278 (Domenico Milanes, 5 June 1549); f. 294 (Bartolomeo Fortini, 11 September 1549); f. 303 (Giacomo Ragazzoni, 25 October 1549); and HCA 24/17/130 (objection against validity of evidence of John Westcott, William Mussen, John Ito and George Blake by an agent of Domenico Erizzo; 19 March 1549).

11   Ruddock, *Italian Merchants in Southampton*, pp. 95, 138, 240–253.

12   Dawson, 'Enslaved Swimmers and Divers in the Atlantic World', p. 1348.

13 Other testimonies concur: Bartholomew Fortini agreed that he did not 'remain in prison any while', while the Venetian Giacomo Ragazzoni believed he had been arrested for one or two days at the most. Another Venetian, Antonio de Nicolao, said that he was discharged within an hour and a half. Indeed, he said that while he was in Southampton, he 'everyday, or every other day' saw Corsi 'at his free liberty in the street there'.

14 TNA, HCA 13/5, f. 195. (Deposition by Domenico Erizzo, 14 December 1547)

15 TNA, HCA 13/93, ff. 203–4, 275–6.

16 Ungerer, 'Recovering a Black African's Voice in an English Lawsuit', n. 25.

17 TNA, C 1/1386/70 (Court of Chancery, Six Clerks Office, John Tyrart of London, vintner, v. the sheriffs of London, 7 September 1554).

18 Gallagher, 'Vernacular language-learning in early modern England', pp. 119, 192 and personal correspondence.

19 Ungerer, 'Recovering a Black African's Voice in an English Lawsuit', p. 261, n. 26; Dawson, 'History from Below: Enslaved Salvage Divers in the Atlantic World', p. 20.

20 Ungerer, 'Recovering a Black African's Voice in an English Lawsuit', p. 261, n. 29; Costello, *Black Salt*, pp. 4–5. Though the complaint in HCA 24/17/130 suggests the other divers also gave evidence, I have not been able to locate their testimonies.

21 Dawson, 'Enslaved Swimmers and Divers in the Atlantic World', pp. 1346–1347; Dawson, 'Swimming, Surfing, and Underwater Diving in Early Modern Atlantic Africa and the African Diaspora', p. 108.

22 In 1455, the Venetian Alvise de Cadamosto, wrote that Africans living along the Senegal River 'are the most expert swimmers in the world': Dawson, 'Swimming, Surfing, and Underwater Diving in Early Modern Atlantic Africa and the African Diaspora', pp. 84–86, 94–95; Dawson, 'Enslaved Swimmers and Divers in the Atlantic World', p. 1337–8; Baker, *Travails in Guinea: Robert Baker's 'Briefe Dyscourse' (?1568)*, ed. Hair. Klein, '"To pot straight way we goe": Robert Baker in Guinea, 1563–4', pp. 243–256.

23 Orme, *Early British Swimming*, pp. 63–4.

24 Boorde, *A Dyetary of Health*, ed. Furnivall, pp. 51–3.

25 Gentile Bellini, 'Miracle of the Cross at the Bridge of San Lorenzo', 1500, Gallerie dell'Accademia, Venice; Debrunner, *Presence and Prestige*, p. 22 mistakenly places the instructor in Naples, not Genoa; Burkhardt, *The Civilisation of the Period of the Renaissance in Italy*, p. 19; Jovius, *De Piscibus Romanis*, Chapter 3.

26 'Elizabeth: February 1588, 1–15', in *Calendar of State Papers Foreign: Elizabeth, Volume 21, Part 1, 1586–1588*, ed. Sophie Crawford Lomas (London, 1927), pp. 500–517. *British History Online* http://www.british-history.ac.uk/cal-state-papers/foreign/vol21/no1/pp500-517 [accessed 2 April 2017].

27 Dawson, 'Swimming, Surfing, and Underwater Diving in Early Modern Atlantic Africa and the African Diaspora', pp. 81, 109. De Marees, Description and historical account of the Gold Kingdom of Guinea, ed. Van Dantzig and Jones, p. 186.

28 Dawson, 'Swimming, Surfing, and Underwater Diving in Early Modern Atlantic Africa and the African Diaspora', p. 111; Dawson, 'Enslaved Swimmers and Divers in the Atlantic World', p. 1350; Morgan, 'British Encounters with Africans and

African–Americans, c.1600–1780', p. 170; *The Troublesome Voyage of Captain Edward Fenton, 1582–1583*, ed. Taylor, p. 107; *The Comedies of George Chapman*, ed. Parrott, p. 4.

29 Donkin, *Beyond Price*, p. 320; Dawson, *Undercurrents of Power*, Chapter 5.

30 Marx, *The History of Underwater Exploration*, pp. 40–41.

31 McKee, *King Henry VIII's Mary Rose*, pp. 93–99; Braithwaite and Bevan, 'Deane, Charles Anthony (1796–1848)', *Oxford Dictionary of National Biography*.

32 Eliav, 'Guglielmo's Secret', pp. 60–69.

33 Dawson, *Undercurrents of Power*, Chapter 5; Donkin, *Beyond Price*, p. 322.

34 HCA 13/93, f. 241v–242 (Domenico Paza, 16 July 1548).

35 'gynno' does not appear in the OED and was possibly an Italian term. All three men stated that they had known the diver for about two years.

36 Elyot, *The Boke Named the Governour*, I. p. xviii. sig. p. Jvii.

37 BL, Lansdowne MS 10, ff. 16–60, no. 5; *Returns of Aliens*, ed. Kirk & Kirk, I, p. 336. Tego is likely to be the one of the two 'Blackmores' recorded in Edmund Grindal, Bishop of London's survey of strangers of 15 December 1567: Haynes, *A Collection of State Papers, Relating to Affairs . . . from the Year 1542 to 1570*, I, pp. 455, 457, 460, 461. The other is Francis Fran, listed as a servant to Peter Fanall in Bishopsgate Ward, in *Returns of Aliens*, ed. Kirk & Kirk, I, p. 323. See also Habib Index no. 129.

38 Acts, 8: 26–40; Zemon Davis, *Trickster's Travels*, p. 65; Leo Africanus, *The History and Description of Africa*, trans. Pory, III, p. 1021. For more on Leo Africanus, see Chapter 4 and Chapter 6.

39 *Encyclopaedia of Tudor England*, ed. Wagner and Schmid, I, pp. 45–6.

40 Lowe, 'Visible lives: black gondoliers and other black Africans in Renaissance Venice', p. 425.

41 TNA, C1/148/67; her ethnic identity remains uncertain, as it is not specified in the original document. Ruddock describes her as 'an Italian servant': Ruddock, *Italian merchants and shipping in Southampton*, p. 127. Ungerer describes her as 'Moorish': Ungerer, 'Recovering a Black African's Voice in an English Lawsuit', p. 261; TNA, REQ 2/164/117 For more on Hector Nunes and the Ethiopian Negar see Chapter 4, Chapter 6 and also Kaufmann, M., 'African freedom in Tudor England: Dr Hector Nunes' petition', *Our Migration Story*, http://www.ourmigration story. org.uk/oms/african-freedom-in-tudor-england-dr-hector-nuness-request

42 *London Consistory Court Wills, 1492–1547*, ed. Darlington, p. 62.

43 TNA, HCA, 13/93, f. 275v.

44 TNA, HCA 13/5, f. 192.

45 Lewis and Short, *A Latin Dictionary*, p. 725; Latham, *Dictionary of Medieval Latin from British Sources*, I, 905. That *famulus* was used in this way in sixteenth–century English courts is proven by the fact that mariners John Tonnes and Humphrey Ffones are both described as 'famulus Johannes Hawkins' [*sic*] when they give evidence in a case of 1568: TNA, SP 12/53. Ungerer, 'Recovering a Black African's Voice in an English Lawsuit', p. 260, confuses the issue by translating *famulus* as 'slave member of a household'.

46 MacCulloch, 'Bondmen Under the Tudors', p. 98; Cairns, 'Slavery and the Roman

Law of Evidence', p. 608 and pp. 600–602. *Black Africans in Renaissance Europe*, ed. Lowe & Earle, p. 35; Schwarz, *Twice Condemned: Slaves and the Criminal Laws of Virginia, 1705–1865*, pp. 19–20. *The Statutes at Large: Being a Collection of all the Laws of Virginia*, ed. Henning, IV, 326–7.

47 Senior, 'An Investigation of the Activities and Importance of English Pirates, 1603–1640', pp. 411–12; *The Westward Enterprise: English Activities in Ireland, the Atlantic and America, 1480–1650*, ed. Andrews, Canny, Hair and Quinn, pp. 132–3; Appleby, 'Thomas Mun's West Indies Venture, 1602–5', pp. 101–110. 'The Lives, Apprehensions, Arraignments, and Executions, of the 19. Late Pyrates', sig. E2r; Weatherford, *Crime and Punishment in the England of Shakespeare and Milton*, pp. 100–1; depositions relating to this case are to be found in TNA, HCA 1/47, ff. 4–5 (William Hill 1 May 1609), f. 56 (William Longcastle), ff. 56–57 (William Tavernor), f. 59 (John Moore, 20 November 1609).

48 TNA, HCA, 24/17/130 (objection against the validity of the evidence of John Westcott, William Mussen, John Ito and George Blake by an agent of Domenico Erizzo, 19 March 1549.

49 TNA, SP 10/9 f. 93 (Report on the prisoners in the Tower of London, 22 October 1549); *CSPD*, 1547–1553, p. 151; MacMahon, 'Wotton, Sir Edward (1489?–1551)', *Oxford Dictionary of National Biography*, Lock, 'Fitzalan, Henry, twelfth earl of Arundel (1512–1580)', *Oxford Dictionary of National Biography*; TNA, PC 2/3 f. 129 (Privy Council meeting at Westminster, 26 March 1550).

50 Ireton, "They are of the caste of black Christians;" Old Christian black blood in the sixteenth century Iberian Atlantic," *Hispanic American Historical Review*, forthcoming.

51 Africans appear in the following tax returns: TNA, E179/174/415 (10 September 1594), E179/174/432 (26 September 1598), E179/174/446 (24 September 1599), E179/174/444 (8 September 1600), and E179/175/488 (4 March 1611); *Central Hampshire Lay Subsidy Assessments, 1558–1603*, ed. Vick, pp. vi, 32–38; The parish registers do not survive for most of Southampton's churches in this period, but I have found one African buried there, a servant to Laurence Groce, who also appears in the tax returns, and whose wife Mary leaves a legacy to her African servant, Joane, in 1612 (discussed in Chapter 10): Southampton Record Office, PR 7/1/1, St Michael CMB 1552–1651 6/14 (St Michael, 23 August 1598), Hampshire Record Office, 1612B/036 (Will of Mary Groce, 14 October 1612); *Third Book of Remembrance of Southampton*, ed. James, IV, 6; *Southampton in the 1620s and the 'Mayflower'*, ed. Thompson, pp. 44, 51; 'Jeffery, Sir John (1611), of High Street, Southampton, Hants and Catherston-Leweston, Dorset' *The History of Parliament*.

Chapter 3

1 Price, *Maroon Societies*, p. 1.

2 Hakluyt, II, 700; *The Hawkins' Voyages During the Reigns of Henry VIII, Queen Elizabeth, and James I*, ed. Markham, p. 5; Morgan, 'Hawkins, William (b. before 1490, d. 1554/5)', *Oxford Dictionary of National Biography*. For more on African

trade and meleguetta pepper see Chapter 7. *Voyages: The Trans–Atlantic Slave Trade Database* Much has been written on John Hawkins. See sources listed in: Morgan, 'Hawkins, Sir John (1532–1595)', *Oxford Dictionary of National Biography* and Williamson, *Hawkins of Plymouth*; Kelsey *Sir John Hawkins*; Hazlewood, *The Queen's Slave Trader*.

3   Kelsey, 'Drake, Sir Francis (1540–1596)', *Oxford Dictionary of National Biography*; Sugden, *Sir Francis Drake*, pp. 20–23; Turner, M. 'The Need to Know the Year of Drake's Birth with reference to the Early Hawkins Slaving Voyages', http://www. indrakeswake.co.uk

4   Maltby, *The Black Legend in England*, p. 15. Bartholemé de Las Casas's *Brevissima Relación de la Destructión de las Indias* was written in 1542, printed in 1552, and the English version, entitled *The Spanish Colonie*, came out in 1583. Old World diseases, particularly smallpox and measles, to which European arrivals were largely resistant or immune, combined with warfare, forced migrations and enslavement to reduce the population of some 40–70 million indigenous Amerindians in 1492 by c. 90–95% by 1650: Day, 'Disease and World History: A Dark Side of Interaction', p. 10; McNeill, *Mosquito Empires*, p. 16.

5   *Voyages: The Trans–Atlantic Slave Trade Database* calculates that 378,734 slaves disembarked from 1,328 voyages between 1514 and 1619.

6   Morgan cites 3.3 million transported between 1662 and 1807: Morgan, X., *Slavery and the British Empire*, p. 12; *Voyages: The Trans–Atlantic Slave Trade Database* has 2.9 million from 1640–1807.

7   The English resumed the slave trade c.1641 in which year the *Star* delivered a cargo of Africans to Barbados: Gragg, *Englishmen Transplanted*, p. 119; *Voyages: The Trans–Atlantic Slave Trade Database*: Voyage number 21876.

8   Kelsey, *Sir John Hawkins*, p. 93, 331, n. 60. The Inquisition records for Hawkins's abandoned crew are in Cambridge University Library, Additional Manuscripts, 7226–7306 (GRG Conway Collection, Mexican Inquisition) and listed in Street, 'The GRG Conway Collection in Cambridge University Library: A Checklist', pp. 60–81. Conway also deposited copies of his transcripts in the Library of Congress and Aberdeen University Library.

9   *Documents Concerning English Voyages to the Spanish Main 1569–1580*, ed. Wright, pp. 253–4.

10   *New Light on Drake*, ed. Nuttall, p. 171; Fernández de Navarrete, *Biblioteca Maritima Española*, I, 596. Gonzalo de Palma went on to become Governor of Costa Rica in the 1590s: Fernández Guardia, *Cartilla Histórica de Costa Rica*, p. 152.

11   *Voyages: The Trans–Atlantic Slave Trade Database*; Wheat, *Atlantic Africa and the Spanish Caribbean*, pp. 5, 12. See also Thornton, *Africa and Africans in the Making of the Atlantic World*, pp. 162–182.

12   Kelsey, *Sir Francis Drake*, p. 53.

13   Much of the following account is taken from the 1628 edition of Nichols, *Sir Francis Drake Revived* reproduced in *Documents Concerning English Voyages to the Spanish Main 1569–1580*, ed. Wright, p. 246–326.

14   Wright, *Documents Concerning English Voyages to the Spanish Main, 1569–1580*, Wright, (ed.) p. 265, n. 1

15 Ibid., pp. 258–9, 264–5; Kelsey, *Sir Francis Drake*, pp. 51, 55. See also Smith, *Black Africans in the British Imagination*, p. 66–8.

16 *New Light on Drake*, ed. Nuttall, p. 302. For a brief biography of Nichols, see Quinn, *Explorers and Colonies*, pp. 193–4. For discussion of Drake's personal input into the text, see Smith, *Black Africans in the British Imagination*, pp. 61–3.

17 Cambridge University Library, G.R.G Conway Collection, Add. MSS, 7231, ff. 2, 157–8, 339–40.

18 *Further English Voyages to Spanish America, 1583–1594*, ed. Wright, pp. 188–9; Sweet, *Recreating Africa*, pp. 94–5; ANTT, Inquisição de Lisboa, Processos, no. 5964: http://digitarq.dgarq.gov.pt/viewer?id=2306003 In around 1565 Pedro Menendez de Aviles, the first Governor of Florida, had warned Philip II that because neither England nor France then allowed slavery, any corsair might, with a few thousand men, take over all Spain's possessions by freeing and arming the grateful slaves, who would then slay their Spanish masters: Landers, *Black Society in Spanish Florida*, p. 17.

19 *Documents Concerning English Voyages to the Spanish Main 1569–1580*, ed. Wright, pp. 260–267.

20 Pike, 'Black Rebels', p.254. The original source says 16 leagues; I have converted it to miles. 1 league =3 miles, so 48 miles.

21 Price, *Maroon Societies*, p. xviii.

22 Wright, *Documents concerning English Voyages to the Spanish Main 1569–1580*, Wright, (ed.) pp. xix, 10, 72; Andrews, *The Spanish Caribbean*, p. 20. The first Cimarron attacks in Panama were in 1525: Pike, '*Black Rebels*', p. 245.

23 Wright, *Documents concerning English Voyages to the Spanish Main 1569–1580*, Wright, (ed.) p. 269.

24 In 1773, David Henry had it that Drake targeted Cartagena on Diego's advice: Henry, *An historical account of all the voyages round the world, performed by English navigators*, I, 18: 'But Drake, not to be diverted from his purpose, after being cured of his wound, inquired of a negroe, whom he took on board at Nombre de Dios, the most wealthy settlements, and weakest parts of the coast. This man recommended Carthagena as the most wealthy, and, being the most powerful, the least upon its guard. The Admiral seemed to approve the man's notion.'

25 *Documents concerning English Voyages to the Spanish Main 1569–1580*, ed. Wright, pp. 278–281. For a discussion of Diego's negotiating strategy see Smith, *Black Africans in the British Imagination*, p. 70.

26 Sugden, *Sir Francis Drake*, p. 63; Henry *An historical account of all the voyages round the world, performed by English navigators*, I, p. 24.

27 *Documents concerning English Voyages to the Spanish Main 1569–1580*, ed. Wright, p. 283.

28 Ibid, p. 297 and Smith, *Black Africans in the British Imagination*, pp. 3–7 for discussion of significance of this moment.

29 *Documents concerning English Voyages to the Spanish Main 1569–1580*, ed. Wright, p. 298.

30 Ibid., pp. 303–4.

31   Ibid., pp. 305–310; Sugden, *Sir Francis Drake*, pp. 68–70; Kelsey, *Sir Francis Drake*, pp. 62–3.

32   *Documents concerning English Voyages to the Spanish Main 1569–1580*, ed. Wright, p. 311.

33   'Le Testu, Guillaume (c. 1509–1573)' in *The Oxford Companion to World Exploration*, ed. Buisseret, I, p. 469. Pike, 'Black Rebels', p. 258, Smith, *Black Africans in the British Imagination*, pp. 73–4.

34   *Documents concerning English Voyages to the Spanish Main 1569–1580*, ed. Wright, pp. 73, 318–319.

35   Ibid., pp. 316, 324. Smith, 'Washing the Ethiop Red: Sir Francis Drake and the Cimarrons of Panama', pp. 17–18 and *Black Africans in the British Imagination*, pp. 72–3.

36   The Drake Jewel, 1588, Collection of Sir George Meyrick, on loan to Victoria and Albert Museum, London; Scarisbrick, *Tudor and Jacobean Jewellery*, pp. 84–86; Marcus Gheeraerts, 'Sir Francis Drake, 1540–1596', National Maritime Museum, Greenwich, London, Caird Collection, BHC2662.

37   Fumerton, *Cultural Aesthetics*, p. 75; Dalton, 'Art for the Sake of Dynasty', pp. 178–214; Hall, *Things of Darkness*, p. 222; Shields, D.S., 'The Drake Jewel' *Uncommon Sense*.

38   Baskerville's was a draft letter to Burghley: BL Harley MS 4762, ff. 10–11, quoted in Andrews, *The Last Voyage of Drake and Hawkins*, Andrews, (ed.) p. 256. See also ibid., p. 212 and Pike, 'Black Rebels' pp. 265–6. Not all English encounters with the Cimarrons went well; when John Oxenham, one of Drake's crew in 1573, returned to Panama in 1575, they fell out and the English were captured and executed by the Spanish: *Documents concerning English Voyages to the Spanish Main 1569–1580*, ed. Wright, pp. 327–331. Smith, *Black Africans in the British Imagination*, pp. 82–3.

39   Ibid., pp. 85–90; Boyer, 'Gage, Thomas (1603?–1656)', *Oxford Dictionary of National Biography*; Davenant, *The History of Sir Francis Drake* (1659), p. 12.

40   *Documents concerning English Voyages to the Spanish Main 1569–1580*, ed. Wright, p. 326; Worth, *The History of Plymouth*, pp. 39–62.

41   *Hawkins in Guinea, 1567–1568*, ed. Hair, pp. 16–17; Kelsey, *Sir John Hawkins*, p. 320, n. 11 citing testimonies of Robert Barrett, 8 October 1569; Michael Sole, 26 November 1569; Walter Jones, 6 December 1569; Juan Truslon, 6 December 1569 in AGI Patronato 265, ramo 11, f. 16; AGI Justicia, 902, pp. 343, 984, 1006.

42   TNA, SP 12/53 (Testimony of John Tonnes, July 1569); Kelsey, *Sir John Hawkins*, p. 99; Hair, 'Protestants as Pirates, Slavers and Proto-missionaries', p. 220; PWDRO 358/6 MF1; *St Andrews's Parish Register*, ed. Cruwys, p. 292; Bastien may also have come to Plymouth as a result of William Hawkins's voyage of 1582–3 on the *Primrose* to the Caribbean, which seems to have captured some Africans on the Cape Verde islands: *Voyages: The Trans–Atlantic Slave Trade Database*, Voyage 98853; *Further English Voyages to Spanish America, 1583–1594*, ed. Wright, pp. 1–7; Kelsey, *Sir John Hawkins*, pp. 163–4.

43   Gill, 'Drake and Plymouth', p.84; Kelsey, *Sir Francis Drake*, pp. 44, 68; Sugden, *Sir Francis Drake*, pp. 43–44, 162.

44 Essex to Burghley, 23 June 1574: Lee, 'Devereux, Walter (1541?–1576)', *The Dictionary of National Biography*, XIV, p. 444.

45 Kelsey, *Sir Francis Drake*, pp. 7–74; Sugden, *Sir Francis Drake*, pp. 84–6; Ronald, *Pirate Queen*, pp. 190–196.

46 John Wynter was the nephew of Sir William Wynter, and cousin of Sir Edward Wynter, who we will meet in the next chapter. Kelsey, *Sir Francis Drake*, p. 445, n. 62.

47 Ibid., p. 141. For the language skills of English sailors at this time see Blakemore, 'Orality and Mutiny', pp. 257–8.

48 *The Troublesome Voyage of Sir Edward Fenton*, ed. Taylor, p. 147; *An Elizabethan in 1582: The Diary of Richard Madox*, ed. Donno, pp. 201, 250, 319, 330.

49 Ralegh, *The Discoverie of the Large, Rich, and Beautiful Empire of Guiana*, p. 48. Some, unaware perhaps of the wider evidence for African sailors aboard Tudor ships, have questioned whether this passage refers to a real African or a literary trope: Smith, *Black Africans in the British Imagination* pp. 158, 211, n. 40. 40–42.

50 Guasco, 'Free from the tyrannous Spanyard', pp. 8–9.

51 *Drake's West Indian Voyage, 1585–6*, ed. Frear Keeler, p. 189.

52 Hakluyt, XI, p. 222; Purchas, *Hakluytus Posthumus, or Purchas his Pilgrims*, XVI, p. 102–3.

53 Kelsey, *Sir Francis Drake*, pp. 93–97.

54 *New Light on Drake*, ed. Nuttall, p. 302.

55 Kelsey, *Sir Francis Drake*, pp. 137–8 and pp. 113–115 on re-naming of the ship.

56 *The World Encompassed by Sir Francis Drake*, ed. Vaux, pp. 93–95, 97–99, 179.

57 Ibid., p. 95, 98.

58 *The observations of Sir Richard Hawkins, Knt. in his voyage into the South Sea in the year 1593*, ed. Drinkwater Bethune, p. 144.

59 *New Light on Drake*, ed. Nuttall, p. 44.

60 BL, Harley MS 280, f. 83 (anonymous contemporary narrative of Drake's voyage, see n. 85 below).

61 *The World Encompassed by Sir Francis Drake*, ed. Vaux, pp. 95, 98–99.

62 Clowes, *A profitable and necessarie booke of obseruations*, pp. 22–28; Murray, 'Clowes, William (1543/4–1604)', *Oxford Dictionary of National Biography*, Childs, *Tudor Sea Power: The Foundation of Greatness*, pp. 124–5; Dunglison, *Medical Lexicon*, p. 25.

63 *The World Encompassed by Sir Francis Drake*, ed. Vaux, p. 99.

64 Morgan, 'Hawkins, Sir John (1532–1595)', *Oxford Dictionary of National Biography*.

65 BL, Harley MS 280, f. 83. The marginal note is not published in the transcription in *The World Encompassed by Sir Francis Drake*, ed. Vaux, p. 179, which may have misled some scholars.

66 Price, *The Vitamin Complex*, pp. 3–4; Bown, *Scurvy*, pp. 3, 5, 34.

67 The ship left Guatulco on 16 April 1579. *New Light on Drake*, ed. Nuttall, pp. 31, 302.

68 McKee, *The Queen's Corsair*, p. 232.

69 *New Light on Drake*, ed. Nuttall, p. 199–210; *The World Encompassed by Sir Francis Drake*, ed. Vaux, pp. 182–3; BL, Harley MS 280, ff. 86–86v.

70 Giraldez, *The Age of Trade*, pp. 120, 145.

71 Camden, *Annales*, tr. Darcie, p. 424; BL, Harley MS 280, ff. 86–86v; *New Light on Drake*, ed. Nuttall, p. 31 (John Drake) and p. 250, 269 (de Silva). In 1553, the viceroy Luis de Velasco estimated Mexico's African population at more than 20,000, including about 2,000 Maroons. Maria was likely to have been from Cape Verde or Senegambia, like 90 per cent of slaves entering Mexico in the mid–sixteenth century. *Landers and Robinson, Slaves, Subjects, and Subversives*, pp. 118–9.

72 *New Light on Drake*, ed. Nuttall, pp. 29, 138–40, 171, 174, 262; *The World Encompassed by Sir Francis Drake*, ed. Vaux, p. 265. Kelsey, *Sir Francis Drake*, p. 153–6.

73 *New Light on Drake*, ed. Nuttall, p. 338, 325, 336, 354–5.

74 Hanmer, *The Baptizing of a Turke*, sig. E3r–3v. See also Dimmock, 'Converting and not converting "Strangers" in Early Modern London', pp. 457–478, and further discussion in Chapter 6.

75 *New Light on Drake*, ed. Nuttall, pp. 105–106.

76 Kelsey, 'Drake, Sir Francis (1540–1596)', *Oxford Dictionary of National Biography*.

77 McKee, *The Queen's Corsair*, pp. 198–212.

78 *New Light on Drake*, ed. Nuttall, pp. 100–2, 124.

79 The Cimarrons of Portobello and Cerro de Cabra surrendered in 1579; those of the Vallano in 1582, so Valverde may be exaggerating. Pike, 'Black Rebels', pp. 262–4.

80 *New Light on Drake*, ed. Nuttall, pp. 253, 317–9.

81 *The World Encompassed by Sir Francis Drake*, ed. Vaux, p. 243, 183.

82 According to John Drake: *New Light on Drake*, ed. Nuttall, p. 31. He is contradicted by the author of the anonymous voyage account who says the two men (besides Diego) were from Guatulco: BL, Harley MS 280, ff. 87v.

83 BL, Harley MS 280, f. 86v.

84 Kelsey, p.167; The anonymous narrative is BL, *Harley MS 280, ff.* 83–90. J.S. Corbett attributed this account to the ship's steward William Legge in 1898 because it includes details of a falling out between Legge and Drake, but this cannot be certainly proven: *Drake and the Tudor Navy*, II, p. 407.

85 Sudgen, *Sir Francis Drake*, pp. 129, 141; BL, Harley MS 280, f. 87v.

86 *British Medical Association Family Health Guide*, pp. 732–733.

87 *The World Encompassed by Sir Francis Drake*, ed. Vaux, p. 213.

88 Ibid., pp. 14–15.

89 Kelsey, *Sir Francis Drake*, p. 170.

90 Huntington Library, California, HM 1648, f. 20v.

91 Woodes Rogers, *A Cruising Voyage Round the World*, pp. 278–279.

92 Henry R. Wagner took Hawkins's remarks to mean that Diego, like Brewer, made it back to England: Wagner, *Sir Francis Drake's Voyage Around the World*, pp. 265, 364.

93 Kelsey, *The First Circumnavigators*, pp. 13, 21; Sugden, *Sir Francis Drake*, p. 61 refers to Diego as 'possibly the first black circumnavigator'.

94 Camden, *Annales*, tr. Darcie, p. 426.

95 BL, Harley MS 280, f. 86v.

96 Lessa, 'Drake in the South Seas', pp. 71, 73.

97 BL, Harley MS 280, f. 87v. The printed version of the account transcribes the amended version – it has the island named after one of the two African men: *The World Encompassed by Sir Francis Drake*, ed. Vaux, p. 184.

98 BL, Harley MS 280, f. 86v, *New Light on Drake*, ed. Nuttall, p. 31.

99 Kelsey, *Sir Francis Drake*, p. 201.

100 *New Light on Drake*, ed. Nuttall, pp. 18–21; McDermott, 'Fenton, Edward (d. 1603)', *Oxford Dictionary of National Biography*.

101 *New Light on Drake*, ed. Nuttall, p. 32.

102 *The World Encompassed by Sir Francis Drake*, ed. Vaux, pp. 148–50.

103 *New Light on Drake*, ed. Nuttall, pp. 32, 53.

104 Shakespeare, *The Tempest*, Act 1, Scene 2.

105 Kelsey, *Sir Francis Drake*, p. 201, comments on the tendency to 'gloss over or skip entirely' this episode. Sudgen, *Sir Francis Drake*, p. 141, certainly tries to put as positive a spin on it as possible, writing: 'the island had been pleasing and it is possible that the Negroes elected to remain there'.

106 *Corbett, Drake and the Tudor Navy*, II, p. 407. The dissatisfied seaman he had in mind was the ship's steward William Legge, see n. 85 above.

Chapter 4

1 William Blake, 'Flagellation of a Female Samboe Slave': a plate facing p. 326 of the first volume of J. G. Stedman's *Narrative of a five years' expedition against the revolted slaves of Surinam* (London 1796) – discussed and reproduced in Wood, *Blind Memory*, pp. 234–239 (Fig 5.6, p. 237); Klein, C., 'This viral photo changed America in 1863', *The Boston Globe*.

2 Much of the following account is taken from the papers relating to the 1597 Court of Star Chamber case of Bucke v. Wynter, kept at The National Archives, Kew, refs: TNA: STAC 5 B11/13; STAC 5/B38/11; STAC 5/B20/36; STAC 5/B37/4; STAC 5/B22/33; STAC 5 B35/22; STAC 5 B45/4.

3 A. P. Baggs and A. R. J. Jurica, 'Lydney', in *A History of the County of Gloucester: Volume 5, Bledisloe Hundred, St. Briavels Hundred, the Forest of Dean*, ed. C. R. J. Currie and N. M. Herbert (London, 1996), pp. 46–84. *British History Online* http://www.british-history.ac.uk/vch/glos/vol5/pp46-84 [accessed 31 March 2017].

4 There is now a secondary school on the site, The Dean Academy (known as Whitecross School until 2012).

5 Loades, 'Winter, Sir William (c.1525–1589)', *Oxford Dictionary of National Biography*; Waters, *The Forest of Dean* (1951); *Calendar of State Papers, Scotland*, ed. Bain, I, p. 435 (William Cecil, Lord Burghley, to the Privy Council, 26 June 1560). John Wynter was the son of George Wynter, Sir William Wynter's brother, and so cousin of Sir Edward Wynter. Kelsey, *Sir Francis Drake*, p. 445, n. 62.

6 Simpson, *Burning to Read*, p. 268. See also Childs, *God's Traitors*.

7 'Middlesex Sessions Rolls: 1615', in *Middlesex county records: Volume 2: 1603–25* John Cordy (ed.) Jeafrreson (London, 1887), pp. 107–119. *British History Online* http://www.british–history.ac.uk/middx-county-records/vol2/pp107-119

(Accessed 11 April 2017) Heal and Holmes, *The Gentry in England and Wales*, pp. 146–150.

8 Payne, 'Hakluyt, Richard (1552?–1616)', *Oxford Dictionary of National Biography*. Hakluyt described his lectures in the Dedicatory Epistle to Walsingham which prefaced the first edition of his *Principal Navigations* (1589), sig *2r; Richard Hakluyt the elder, 'Inducements to the Liking of the Voyage Intended Towards Virginia' (1585), in *The Original Writings and Correspondence of the Two Richard Hakluyts*, ed. Taylor, II, p. 332. For a vivid account of Hakluyt's visit to Middle Temple in 1568, see Mancall, *Hakluyt's Promise*, Chapter 2. The Bible passage was from Psalm 107, verses 23 and 24.

9 *A Report of the Kingdome of Congo drawen out of the writinges and discourses of O. Lopez*, tr. A. Hartwell, 'The Translator to the Reader'. Samuel, 'Lopez, Roderigo (c.1517–1594)', *Oxford Dictionary of National Biography*; see also Green, *The Double Life of Doctor Lopez*.

10 Pliny the Elder, *Natural History*, VIII:17:42. That he had 'seen above twenty men at one time together with heads like dogs' was the boast of John James, a nephew of William Sanderson, who sent him to deliver a map of the West Indies, and a 'terrestrial globe', with an instruction book in Latin to Sir Robert Cecil in September 1595: Skelton, and Summerson, *A Description of Maps and Architectural Drawings in the Collection Made by William Cecil*, p. 6; Shakespeare, *Othello*, Act 1, Scene 3. Kaufmann, 'Prester John' pp. 423–424, Alvarez, *The Prester John of the Indies*, tr. Lord Stanley, ed. Beckingham and Huntingford; Silverberg, *The Realm of Prester John*; Gumilev, *Searches for an Imaginary Kingdom: The Legend of the Kingdom of Prester John*; Relaño, *The Shaping of Africa: cosmographic discourse and cartographic science in late medieval and early modern Europe*; Braude, 'The sons of Noah and the construction of ethnic and geographical identities in the medieval and early modern periods', pp. 103–42. Ohajuru, M., 'The Black Magus [King, Magi] (c 1350–)', *BlackPast.org*, http://www.blackpast.org/gah/black-magus-c-1350; Kaplan, *The Rise of the Black Magus in Western Art*; Devisse, 'The Black and his Color', in *The Image of the Black in Western Art*, ed. Bindman, Gates & Dalton, II, 1, pp. 119–128; Koerner, 'The Epiphany of the Black Magus Circa 1500' in *The Image of the Black in Western Art*, ed. Bindman and Gates, III, 1, pp. 7–92.

11 For a detailed account of the voyage see Kelsey, *Sir Francis Drake*, pp. 240–279; for the original sources see: *Sir Francis Drake's West Indian Voyage, 1585–6*, ed. Frear Keeler. These two books furnish much of the detail in the following account.

12 *Sir Francis Drake's West Indian Voyage, 1585–6*, ed. Frear Keeler, p.215, n.1; Greville, *The Life of the Renowned Sir Philip Sidney*, p. 105. It was Sidney's friend Hubert Languet, reporting on a visit to Venice, who warned that young men might 'soften their manly virtue' by pursuing the arts of 'courtly flattery': Norbrook, *Poetry and Politics in the English Renaissance*, p. 87.

13 Kelsey, *Sir Francis Drake*, 245–249; Sugden, *Sir Francis Drake*, pp. 180–1; *Calendar of State Papers, Venice*, ed. Brown, *1581–1591*, pp. 124–5.

14 Edward Wynter to Sir Francis Walsingham, 24 October 1585: TNA, SP 12/183/49; *CSPD*, 1547–1625, II, 278.

15 Quinn, 'Turks, Moors, Blacks and Others in Drake's West Indian Voyage', pp.

197–204; *Further English Voyages to Spanish America, 1583–1594*, ed. Wright, p. 159; *Calendar of State Papers, Venice*, ed. Brown, *1581–1591*, pp. 155, 168.

16   *Drake's West Indian Voyage, 1585-6*, ed. Frear Keeler, p. 169.

17   *Drake's West Indian Voyage, 1585-6*, ed. Frear Keeler, pp. 32, 196, 242-3, 308.

18   Captain William Cecil was assigned command of the soldiers on the *Aid*: *Drake's West Indian Voyage, 1585-6*, ed. Frear Keeler, p. 253.

19   *Further English Voyages to Spanish America, 1583–1594*, ed. Wright, xlvi–lvi; *Drake's West Indian Voyage, 1585-6*, ed. Frear Keeler , pp. 33–37; Kelsey, *Sir Francis Drake*, pp. 264–269; Lemaitre, *Historia General de Cartagena*, II, p. 11. Don Juan de Castellanos mentions the African fishermen in a poem written as part of his history of Cartagena in 1586-7: '*En la bahia apresaron los ingleses a dos negros que andaban pescando, quienes les informaron de las entradas de la ciudad y de estar sembradas las playas de puas venenosas. Sondearon el puerto donde esta la punta de las Hicascis, desguarnecida imprevisormente.*': *Discurso del Capitan Francisco Draque*, XLV.

20   110,000 ducats was the price Giacomo Boncompagni, illegitimate son of Pope Gregory XIII, paid the Duke of Urbino for the Neapolitan dukedom of Sora and Arce in the Terra de Lavoro in 1579: Williams, G. L., *Papal Genealogy: The Families and Descendants of the Popes*, p. 90.

21   *Further English voyages to Spanish America, 1583–1594*, Wright, (ed.) p. 159.

22   *Drake's West Indian Voyage, 1585-6*, ed. Frear Keeler, pp. 209–210.

23   Edward Stafford to Sir Francis Walsingham, 20 August 1586: TNA, SP 78/16 f. 9. See also McDermott, 'Stafford, Sir Edward (1552–1605)', *Oxford Dictionary of National Biography*, online edition.

24   De Belleforest, *L'Histoire Universelle du Monde* (1570), p. 550, cited in S. Peabody, *There are no Slaves in France*, pp. 12, 29. As we saw in Chapter Three, sailor William Collins also asserted in 1572 that neither in England nor in France were there any slaves. Collins's cellmate Pedro de Trejo reported the following exchange between them to the Mexican Inquisition: "If you think you can deprive us of our dominion over the people of the new world you are welcome to try!" at which the said Guillermo [William] laughed much and said: "if the Queen cared to send a fleet to this land that the King of Castile would be hard put to it because if nothing else happened . . . the negroes and Indians would turn it over to us" because when the said Calens [Collins] told the negroes that neither in England nor in France were there any slaves they would answer that they were better Christians than the Spaniards. Cambridge University Library, G.R.G Conway Collection, Add. 7231, ff. 339–340.

25   TNA, REQ 2/164/117 For more on Hector Nunes and the Ethopian Negar see Chapter 2, Chapter 6 and also Kaufmann, M. 'African freedom in Tudor England: Dr Hector Nunes' petition', in *Our Migration Story* http://www.ourmigrationstory.org.uk/oms/african-freedon-in-tudor-england-dr-hector-nuness-request.

26   *The Household Papers of Henry Percy, 9th Earl of Northumberland*, ed. Batho, p. 74. For Robert Crosse, Captain of the *Bond*, see: McDermott, 'Crosse, Sir Robert (c.1547–1611)', *Oxford Dictionary of National Biography*; *Drake's West Indian Voyage, 1585-6*, ed. Frear Keeler, pp. 69, 292; Andrews, *Elizabethan Privateering*, pp. 90, 94, 255.

27 Edward Wynter to Sir Francis Walsingham, 18 August 1587: *Calendar of State Papers, Foreign, Elizabeth, 1558–1589*, ed. Stevenson, Crosby, Butler, *et. al,,* XXI, part 3: pp. 250–1; Gloucestershire Record Office, D421/9; Strype, *Annals*, III, 2, pp. 38–40; 'Wynter, Edward (c.1560–1619), of Lydney, Glos.', *The History of Parliament.*

28 No baptism record has yet been found for Edward Swarthye. The Lydney parish registers do not survive before 1678.

29 Anonymous, *Sir Thomas More*, Act III, Scene 1, 132–135.

30 Anthony Maria Browne, Viscount Montague's Household Book of 1595 contained a section on 'The Porter and his office': St. John Hope, *Cowdray and Easebourne Priory*, p. 128. His household would have been far grander than Wynter's, with maybe four times as many servants. Elzinga, 'Browne, Anthony, first Viscount Montagu (1528–1592)', *Oxford Dictionary of National Biography*.

31 Kaufmann, 'Africans in Britain', p. 161; Leicester: *Household Accounts and Disbursement Books of Robert Dudley, Earl of Leicester*, ed. Adams, p. 178, n. 364; Percy: *The Household Papers of Henry Percy, 9th Earl of Northumberland*, ed. Batho, p. 74; Cecils: Hertfordshire Archives & Local Studies, DP/29/1/1 (Baptism of Fortunatus, St Mary the Virgin, Cheshunt, 16 April 1570); City of Westminster Archives Centre, St Clements Danes Parish Registers, vol.1 (Burial of Fortunatus, servant to Robert Cecil, 21 January, 1602) Ralegh: *Household Accounts and Disbursement Books of Robert Dudley, Earl of Leicester*, ed. Adams, p. 210, n. 444; TNA, SP 12/262/104 (declaration of John Hill of Stonehouse, Plymouth, 1597); CSPD, 1595–1597, p. 381; Throckmorton: Canterbury Cathedral Archives, U85/38/14 (Sir Arthur Throckmorton's Diary, 18 July 1589); Porter: City of Westminster Archives Centre, St Martin's in the Fields Parish Registers, vol. 2 (Baptism of Maria, servant to Endymion Porter, 8 February 1621); Arundel: TNA, SP 14/148/99 (John Chamberlain to Dudley Carleton, 12 July 1623); *The Letters of John Chamberlain*, ed. McClure, II, 506–7; *CSPD*, 1623–1625, p. 13.

32 TNA, STAC 5/S14/26 (Court of Star Chamber, Hugh Smyth v Sir John Younge, Sir George Norton et. al., Interrogatory 3, and testimony of Anne White, 11th April 1580); Portrait of Peregrine Bertie, Lord Willoughby de Eresby (d.1601), Grimsthorpe Hall, Lincolnshire: Hall, *Things of Darkness*, p. 5; *The Diary of the Lady Anne Clifford*, ed. Sackville–West, lxi; *Devon Household Accounts 1627–59, Part II*, ed. Gray, pp. 33, 52, 65, 117, 173, 178, 206, 248, 297; Domingo's burial: LMA, MS 09222/1, MS 09221, MS 09234/1, f. 127v (St Botolph Aldgate, 27 August 1587).

33 Pierre Mignard, 'Louise de Kéroualle, Duchess of Portsmouth' (1682), National Portrait Gallery, London. NPG 497. See Hall, *Things of Darkness*, pp. 242–252 and Amussen, *Caribbean Exchanges*, pp. 197–214 for further examples.

34 This was the method recommended by a book of advice in 1583: Sim, *The Tudor Housewife*, p. 55.

35 A. P. Baggs and A. R. J. Jurica, 'Lydney', in *A History of the County of Gloucester: Volume 5, Bledisloe Hundred, St. Briavels Hundred, the Forest of Dean*, ed. C. R. J. Currie and N. M. Herbert (London, 1996), pp. 46–84. *British History Online* http://www.british-history.ac.uk/vch/glos/vol5/pp46-84 [accessed 31 March 2017].

36 Dimmock, *The Ashgate Research Companion to Popular Culture in Early Modern England*, pp.273–5; Wordie, 'The Chronology of English Enclosure, 1500–1914', pp. 483–505.

37 A. P. Baggs and A. R. J. Jurica, 'Lydney', in *A History of the County of Gloucester: Volume 5, Bledisloe Hundred, St. Briavels Hundred, the Forest of Dean*, ed. C. R. J. Currie and N. M. Herbert (London, 1996), pp. 46–84. *British History Online* http://www.british-history.ac.uk/vch/glos/vol5/pp46-84 [accessed 31 March 2017].

38 Ibid.; for the Earls of Rutland, see: Sim, *Masters and Servants in Tudor England*, p. 122, and for the Earl of Leicester: Adams, *Leicester and the court*, p. 362, n. 122.

39 Sir Edward Wynter to the Lord Admiral and Sir Robert Cecil, 5 February 1596: *Calendar of the Manuscripts of the Most Honourable the Marquess of Salisbury* Cecil, Roberts, Salisbury, et al (eds) VI, pp. 43–58.

40 There are no explicit records of Guy's childhood, besides the references to his education in the Wynter household in the 1597 Bucke vs. Wynter case in Star Chamber. Accounts of his early life quickly skip from his birth to Bristol shoemaker, as revealed in his baptism record, to his mercantile career post 1597: English, 'Guy, John (c.1575–1628)', *Oxford Dictionary of National Biography*; 'Guy, John (d.1629), of Small Street, Bristol, Glos.', *The History of Parliament*; Williams, A.F., *John Guy of Bristol and Newfoundland*, pp. 25–27.

41 Bridgen, *New Worlds, Lost Worlds*, pp. 242–245; Andrews, *Trade, Plunder and Settlement*, p. 242; Canny, *Making Ireland British*, pp. 121–164.

42 The Star Chamber case does not yield any further information about where in Ireland Guye intended to go, or what he intended to do once he got there. One possibility is that he was scouted by Percival Willoughby, who he certainly knew by 1610, through the Newfoundland Company: Williams, A. F., *John Guy of Bristol and Newfoundland*, pp. 52–3; University of Nottingham, Manuscripts and Special Collections, Middleton Collection, Mi X 1/2 and Mi X 1/7 (letters for John Guye to Percival Willoughby, 6 October 1610 and 17 June 1612). In 1594, Percival Willoughby had taken on the management of the iron works established by his father–in–law, Sir Francis Willoughby, in Warwickshire, Staffordshire and Derbyshire: R.S. Smith, 'Willoughby, Sir Francis (1546/7–1596)', *Oxford Dictionary of National Biography*; R. S. Smith, 'Sir Francis Willoughby's ironworks,1570–1610', pp. 90–140. Short of money, Percival may have been seeking to revive the attempts Sir Francis had made a decade earlier at iron working in Ireland. Sir Francis had acquired woodlands in Munster in 1586 in the hope of developing an iron manufactory at Kinalmeaky, West Cork, in association with the undertakers Phane Beecher and Robert Payne. Payne wrote to his co–investors, extolling the virtues of the project, and describing Kinalmeaky as the ideal location, rich in iron stone, lead ore and with enough wood to maintain 'divers Iron and lead works (with good husbandry) forever': Payne, *A Brief Description of Ireland*, p. 6. Sir Francis's attempt had failed when the local Irish chief, Donal Graney O'Mahoney, attacked and laid waste to the land at Kinalmeaky in 1589: Horning, *Ireland in the Virginian Sea: Colonialism in the British Atlantic* (2013), p. 87. If Percival wanted an up-to-date assessment of the viability of establishing a new iron works in Ireland, and a manager on the ground to oversee it if he decided to go ahead, then John Guye,

who he could easily have met through the small world of English iron-working, would have been the perfect man for the job.

43 Sharpe, *Crime in Early Modern England 1550–1750*, p. 51.

44 The full list or Privy Council members in 1597: John Whitgift, Archbishop of Canterbury, Sir Thomas Egerton, Keeper of the Privy Seal, William Cecil, Lord Burghley, Lord Treasurer; Robert, Earl of Essex; Charles, Earl of Nottingham, Lord High Admiral; Sir George Carey, Lord Hunsdon, Lord Chamberlain; Sir Roger North, Lord North, Treasurer of Her Majesty's Household; Sir Thomas Sackville, Lord Buckhurst; Sir William Knollys, Comptroller of Her Majesty's Household; Sir Robert Cecil, Principal Secretary and Sir John Fortescue, Chancellor of the Exchequer.

45 There are no fines recorded in the Star Chamber records for Bucke or Wynter before the end of Elizabeth's reign, i.e. between 1597 and 1603: TNA, Barnes Index, 'Fines handed down by Star Chamber'(unpublished finding aid).

46 Gloucestershire Record Office, D 421/T 31; 'Wynter, Edward (c.1560–1619), of Lydney, Glos', *The History of Parliament*.

47 Historical Manuscripts Commission, *Calendar of the manuscripts of the Most Honourable the Marquess of Salisbury*, XIV, p. 143: Hatfield, Petitions p. 151. A pursuivant was 'a royal or state messenger, esp. one with the power to execute warrants; a warrant officer. "pursuivant, n. and adj."'. OED Online. December 2016. Oxford University Press. http://www.oed.com/view/Entry/155082?redirected From=Pursivant (accessed January 11, 2017).

48 Bartels, 'Too Many Blackamoors: Deportation, Discrimination, and Elizabeth I'; Kaufmann, 'Caspar van Senden, Sir Thomas Sherley and the 'Blackamoor' Project'; Weissbourd, "Those in Their Possession": Race, Slavery, and Queen Elizabeth's "Edicts of Expulsion". See also Chapter 6, pp. 183–4.

49 Pepys wrote that he found John Wynter 'a very worthy man; and good discourse.' They discussed the iron works of the Forest of Dean, 'with their great antiquity': *The Diary of Samuel Pepys*, 14 August 1662; Warmington, 'Winter, Sir John (*b.* c.1600, *d.* in or after 1676)', *Oxford Dictionary of National Biography*; A. P. Baggs and A. R. J. Jurica, 'Lydney', in *A History of the County of Gloucester: Volume 5, Bledisloe Hundred, St. Briavels Hundred, the Forest of Dean*, ed. C. R. J. Currie and N. M. Herbert (London, 1996), pp. 46–84. *British History Online* http://www.british-history.ac.uk/vch/glos/vol5/pp46-84 [accessed 31 March 2017].

50 Henry Anthony Jetto was baptised aged around 26 at St Martin's, Holt on 21 March 1596 and buried there on 30 August 1627. His will, dated 20 September 1626, executed 13 September 1638, left goods to the value of £17 15s 8d. His wife was named Persida (d.1640) and his five children were Sarah, Margaret, John, Helena and Richard, all baptised in Holt between 1598–1608. Bourne, R., 'Ancestor was the first black person in the county', *Worcester News*, 23 February 2007, p. 3; Onyeka, Blackamoores, pp. 149, 342–247; personal correspondence with Peter Bluck, Jetto's nine-times great-grandson; Worcester Archive and Archaeology Service, BA4286 (i) (St Martin's Holt Parish Register), BA3583 1638 102 (Will of Henry Jetto, 1638), BA3585 box 231b 1640 126 (Will of Persida Jetto, 1640).

51 English, 'Guy, John (c.1575–1628)', *Oxford Dictionary of National Biography*; 'Guy, John (d.1629), of Small Street, Bristol, Glos.', *The History of Parliament*; Williams, A.F, *John Guy of Bristol and Newfoundland*, p. 26.

52 Williams, A. F., *John Guy of Bristol and Newfoundland*, pp. 52–3; University of Nottingham, Manuscripts and Special Collections, Middleton Collection, Mi X 1/2 and Mi X 1/7 (letters for John Guye to Percival Willoughby, 6 October 1610 and 17 June 1612); Bacon, 'Of Plantations', *The essays, or councils, civil and moral*, p. 93.

53 Williams, A. F., *John Guy of Bristol and Newfoundland*, pp. 118–126.

54 Aubrey, *Brief Lives* ed. Clark, I, 277; Williams, A. F., *John Guy of Bristol and Newfoundland*, pp. 225–30, 316–321; John Guye's will, 6 May 1629: TNA, PROB 11/155, f. 387.

Chapter 5

1   Slack, *The Impact of Plague in Tudor and Stuart England*, p. 296; LMA, MS 04887 (St Dunstan's in the East, Vestry Minutes), p. 278.

2   Indeed, some Africans had the surname 'White'. Such as John Blanke (blanco=white) and 'Phillip White alias Haumath, a barbarian Moore', baptised in Temple Church, Bristol on 17 February 1619: Bristol Record Office, FCP/Tem/R/1(a).

3   Hanks and Hodges, *A Dictionary of Surnames*, p. 54. Hanks, Coates, and McClure, *The Oxford Dictionary of Family Names in Britain and Ireland*, I, p. 243 (Black); p. 246 (Blackman and Blackmore), III, 1872 (Moore), pp. 1880–1 (Morris); Reaney, *A Dictionary of British Surnames*, p. 35. Other medieval examples include 'Elias le Blakeman' and 'Henry Blacman': Bardsley, *English Surnames*, p. 444.

4   Hitching, *References to English Surnames in 1601*, xxiii; Hughes, 'Blacman , John (1407/8–1485?)', *Oxford Dictionary of National Biography*; Leadam, 'Blakman, Blakeman, or Blackman, John (fl. 1436–1448)', *The Dictionary of National Biography, 1901 supplement*, I, 215.

5   Camden, *Remaines concerning Britain*, ed. Dunn, p. 92.

6   Reaney, *A Dictionary of English Surnames*, p. 46.

7   Bardsley, *English Surnames*, pp. 125, 161, 444; Reaney, *A Dictionary of British Surnames*, p. 34; Hanks and Hodges, *A Dictionary of Surnames*, pp. 54, 374; McKinley, *A History of British surnames*, pp. 11, 156–7; Reaney, *A Dictionary of English Surnames*, pp. 46–7, 313.

8   Black, *The Surnames of Scotland*, p. 617.

9   He is listed as 'Resonablackmore' in the St Saviour's Token Book in 1579: LMA, P92/SAV/183, f. 7, line 33, and as 'Resonable blackmor' and 'Resonabell blackmor' on 13th and 16th October 1592 in the parish register of St Olave, Tooley Street: LMA, X097/233; P71/OLA/009 p. 000126.

10 Variants found in archival sources include blackamoor, blackamore, blackamoore, blackmoor, blackmore, blakemore, blackemore and blak moir. William Dunbar's 1507 poem 'Ane Blak Moir' is the first known British text to use the word. This term was used in 158 (40%) of the entries in my database of Africans in Britain 1500–1640, compared with 93 instances of 'Moor', 47 of 'Negro', 24 of 'Negar' and

6 of 'Ethiop'. See Kaufmann, 'Africans in Britain', pp. 56–71; Oxford English Dictionary, 'blackamoor, n.' *OED Online*.

11 Haigh, *Elizabeth I*, p.113. Simon Healy suggested to me that 'Reasonable' might refer to the light of reason in a religious sense.

12 Thomas More's coat of arms also had a blackamoor crest: Chapelle Wojciehowski, *Group Identity in the Renaissance World*, p. 175, n. 98; Read., *Mr Secretary Walsingham*, II, p. 60; BL, Harley MS 6265, ff. 71v–72r.

13 Smith–Bannister, *Names and Naming Patterns in England, 1538–1700*, pp. 18–19; *The Herald and Genealogist*, ed. Gough Nichols, V, 379.

14 Blackman's entry in the token book (LMA, P92/SAV/183, f. 7, line 33) does not yield a lot of information about his household. His name was a last-minute addition, written in over another name, which has been crossed out. The man whose name was erased, Thomas Bonit, was thought to have two adults in his household. This estimation was not crossed out when Blackman's name was added, but we cannot be sure whether this indicates that there were also two adults in his household. Certainly, he did not purchase any tokens that year. See William Ingram and Alan H. Nelson, *The Token Books of St Saviour Southwark: an interim search site*: http://tokenbooks.lsa.umich.edu/. Imtiaz Habib has conflated Reasonable Blackman with a different individual mentioned in the Token Books, named John Reason: Habib and Salkeld, 'The Resonables of Boroughside, Southwark', 1–22. I do not believe Reasonable Blackman and John Reason can be the same person because the token books have only one reference to 'Resonablakmore' and half a dozen more to 'John Reason'. Moreover in the same year (1579) that 'Resonablakmore' is recorded as living on the West Side (P92/SAV/183, f. 7, line 33), 'John Reason' appears 4 pages later on the Counter/East Side (P92/SAV/183, f. 11, line 24).

15 Boulton, *Neighbourhood and Society*, p. 9. The church was demolished in 1928, and the art deco St Olaf's House built on the site is now used by the London Bridge Private Hospital as consulting and administration rooms. Edward Walford, 'Bermondsey: Tooley Street', in *Old and New London: Volume 6* (London, 1878), pp. 100–117. *British History Online* http://www.british-history.ac.uk/old-new-london/vol6/pp100-117 [accessed 31 March 2017]; Coltman, R., 'St Olaf House, London', *Modernist Britain*.

16 Boulton, *Neighbourhood and Society*, pp. 19–20, 64.

17 'Clink' in *Brewer's Dictionary of Phrase and Fable*, ed. Rockwood, p. 272.

18 Browner, 'Wrong Side of the River', Essays in History.

19 Whitelock, *Elizabeth's Bedfellows*, p. 26; Nichols, *Progresses of Queen Elizabeth*, II, p. xlii; Luu, *Immigrants and Industry*, p. 181.

20 Mikhaila and Malcolm–Davies, *The Tudor Tailor*, p. 37.

21 Beer, *Bess: The life of Lady Ralegh*, p. 123.

22 Luu, 'Immigrants and the diffusion of skills in early modern London: the case of silk weaving' *Documents pour l'histoire des techniques*.

23 Dekker *et al.*, Patient Grissill, Act 2, Scene 1.

24 Shakespeare, *The Taming of the Shrew*, Act 4, Scene 3; *Othello*, Act 3, Scene. 4.

25 Luu, *Immigrants & Industries*, p. 180, citing *The Anatomy of Abuses* (1583), p. 10.

26 Mortimer, *The Time Traveller's Guide to Elizabethan England*, p. 158; Cox, 'An Act

to avoid the excess in apparel 1554–5', p. 41. In 1559, Elizabeth I had issued a proclamation declaring that the sumptuary laws issued by her father in 1533 and her sister Mary in 1554 were still to be obeyed.

27 Habib and Salkeld, 'The Resonables of Boroughside, Southwark', p. 6.

28 Ingram, *The Business of Playing*, p. 39.

29 Luu, *Immigrants & Industries*, p. 183. 12,000lbs were imported in 1559–60, growing almost fivefold to 52,000 in 1592–3. 12,000lbs = £9,920; 52,000lbs = £40,000. Stevenson, *Praise and Paradox*, p. 33; Coates, *The Impact of the Civil War on the Economy of London*, pp. 3–4; Stern, 'The Trade, Art or Mystery of Silkthrowers in the City of London', pp. 25–8; Millard 'Import trade of London', pp. 234–235.

30 Steggle, 'New Directions: Othello, the Moor of London: Shakespeare's Black Britons', p. 113.

31 Schoeser, *Silk*, pp. 17–48.

32 Luu, 'Immigrants and the diffusion of skills in early modern London: the case of silk weaving' *Documents pour l'histoire des techniques*; Luu, *Immigrants & Industries*, p. 179.

33 My thanks to Dr Howard Bailes for bringing this subject to life for me from 1998–2000. For a thorough account see Israel, *The Dutch Republic*, pp. 9–587. See also Kamen, *Philip II* and Parker, *The Dutch Revolt* and *The Grand Strategy of Philip II*.

34 Luu, 'Immigrants and the diffusion of skills in early modern London: the case of silk weaving' *Documents pour l'histoire des techniques*.

35 Stow *Survey of London*, ed. Strype, V, p. 233. See also 1583 complaint of the Company of Weavers that 'Since the Flight of Strangers into these Parts', certain freemen of the City had 'learned of these Strangers . . . the Art of Silk–weaving; namely, making of Silk–lace, and such like things in the Loom': Ibid., V, p. 219.

36 Luu, 'Immigrants and the diffusion of skills in early modern London: the case of silk weaving' *Documents pour l'histoire des techniques*; Luu, *Immigrants & Industries*, pp. 184–5, 194.

37 A. Blakely, *Blacks in the Dutch World: The Evolution of Racial Imagery in a Modern Society* (1994), p. 226; Debrunner, *Presence and Prestige*, p. 57; Wojciehowski, *Group Identity in the Renaissance World*; pp. 161–3. There was no explicit slavery legislation in the Netherlands, and there are a couple of examples of courts asserting the freedom of Africans. More research is needed to ascertain exactly what the legal and practical status of Africans was and how it was affected when the northern Netherlands became the independent United Provinces, or Dutch Republic, under William of Orange from 1581, before the Dutch East India Ordinances were issued in 1622. See Huussen, 'The Dutch Constitution of 1798 and the Problem of Slavery', p. 104; Hondius, 'Black Africans in Seventeenth–Century Amsterdam', pp. 89–108; Hondius, 'Blacks in Early Modern Europe', pp. 29–47; Hondius, *Blackness in Western Europe*, pp. 134–142; and Lowe, 'The Lives of African Slaves and People of African Descent in Renaissance Europe', pp. 16, 26.

38 Albrecht Dürer, 'Study of Katharina', 1521, Uffizi Gallery, Florence; Jan Mostaert, 'Portrait of an African Man', c. 1525–30, The Rijksmuseum, Amsterdam; Bate and

Thornton, *Shakespeare: Staging the World*, pp. 170, 180–181. Another image from the Netherlands of a high status but as yet unidentified African is: Flemish/German?, 'Portrait of a Wealthy African', 1530–40, Private Collection, Antwerp. See *Revealing the African Presence in Renaissance Europe*, ed. Spicer, pp. 16–17, 87–88.

39 Hondius, 'Black Africans in Seventeenth-Century Amsterdam', p. 88. *Revealing the Black Presence in Renaissance Europe*, ed. Spicer, pp. 82–3; see also Blakely, *Blacks in the Dutch World*, pp. 78–170; Boele, Kolfin and Schreuder, *Black is Beautiful: Rubens to Dumas*; Kolfin. 'Rembrandt's Africans' in *The Image of the Black in Western Art*, ed. Bindman and Gates, III, part 1, pp. 271–306.

40 Stow, *Annales*, ed. Howe, p. 1038. Imtiaz Habib suggests that his behaviour would have provoked 'resentment and animosity', but this is unsubstantiated: Habib, *Black Lives*, p. 45; see also Onyeka, *Blackamoores*, pp. 235–8.

41 *A Relation, or Rather a True Account, of the Island of England*, ed. Sneyd, pp. 42–43.

42 Reddaway, 'Elizabethan London – Goldsmith's Row in Cheapside 1558–1645', p. 199.

43 BCB, III, f. 221v.

44 Bromley, *The armorial bearings of the guilds of London*, p.182; Edmondson, *Complete Body of Heraldry*, I, p. 339; Price, The Worshipful Company of Needlemakers of the City of London, p. 10.

45 LMA, MS 09221; MS9222/1 (St Botolph Aldgate, 20 August 1593).

46 At her burial 'Suzanna Pearis a blackamoore' was described as servant to a hatband maker named John De Spinosa. LMA, MS 09221; MS 09222/1 (St Botolph Aldgate, 8 August 1593). He was born in Spain, but with a French wife, and previously resident in France. In 1583, he was listed as a denizen of ten years, resident in East Smithfield, where he was still living, near the sign of the Fleur de Lys, at his death in July 1594: *Returns of Aliens*, ed. Kirk and Kirk, II, 361; LMA, MS 09234/4 (parish clerk's memorandum book, St Botolph Aldgate, 7 July 1594); in September 1602, a 'blackamoore' woman in the household of hatmaker Thomas Browne 'committed the abominable sin of whoredome' with fellow servant Roger Holgate and conceived a child as a result of their continuing affair: BCB, IV, f. 344r (5 January 1603); Griffiths, *Lost Londons*, p. 74, n. 25. See also BCB, V, f. 7v (9 January 1605) for possible further reference to the same case.

47 None of the Blackman children were described as bastards in the church records, so it follows that their parents were married. If John was their son, then we can date their marriage to early 1579.

48 Wrigley, Davies, Oeppen and Schofield, *English Population History from Family Reconstitution*, p. 123.

49 This was still the case in 1837: *Annual Report of the Poor Law Commissioners for England and Wales*, III, p. 143.

50 LMA, St Olave, Tooley Street: X097/233 P71/OLA/009 Edward's baptism: 19 February 1587: p. 00052, Jane and Edmund's burials, 13 and 16 October 1592: p. 000126; St Saviour's, Southwark, John Blakemore baptism, 26 October 1579: LMA, P92/SAV/3001.

51 Shakespeare, *The Merchant of Venice*, Act 3, Scene 5.

52 Prayger, 'The Negro Allusion in the Merchant of Venice', pp. 50–52; *The Merchant of Venice*, ed. Russell Brown, p. 99n.

53 Habib and Salkeld, 'The Resonables of Boroughside, Southwark', pp. 19–20.

54 *The Marriage Registers of St. Dunstan's, Stepney*, ed. Colyer Fergusson, I, pp. 70, 72, 78. These 'three marriages . . . between Negroes' were noted by the East London History Group in 1982, but without further elucidation or comment: French *et. al.*, 'The Population of Stepney in the Early Seventeenth Century: a report on an analysis of the parish registers of Stepney, 1606–1610', p. 173. Another possible Stepney example is Helen and Thomas Jeronimo, both 'moors', though, as discussed in Chapter 8, they could have been of east Asian origin.

55 Burial of 'Anne Vause a Black-more wife to Anthonie Vause, Trompetter of the said Country': LMA, MS 09222/1 (St Botolph Aldgate, 27 April 1618). See Chapter 1, n. 100.

56 *The Book of Common Prayer*, ed. Cummings, p. 164, 157; Baptism of Samuel Munsur: LMA, P78/NIC/001, (St Nicholas Greenwich, 28 November 1613); Marriages of Samuel Munsur: LMA, P78/NIC/001(St Nicholas Greenwich, 26 December 1613) and James Curres: LMA, MS 09155 (Holy Trinity the Less, 24 December 1617).

57 Hakluyt, VII, p. 262.

58 Another possible example is Anthony Ffageamy, described ass 'Mauri' (the Moor) in the baptism record of his son Michael (his wife was named Phyllis): City of Westminster Archives Centre, St Martin in the Fields Parish Registers, vol. 2. (15 March 1620)

59 Cornwall Record Office, St Mary's Truro, FP236/1/1: Richard's baptism, 1 October 1612; Maria's burial 18 August 1611; Emmanuel's burial 9 August 1623. The parish registers of St Mary's were written in Latin. In the three entries relating to the family, Emmanuel is described variously as 'Emmanueli Mauris Anglice (the Moore)'; 'Emmanuelis Maurus anglice the Moore' and 'Emanuelius Mauri al[ia]s Emanuel the Moore'. 'anglice' was short for *vocat in anglice* (called in English), which means that the scribe wasn't sure what the Latin for Moor was. The only other African I have found described in this way was 'Christiana Niger anglice a blackamoore' baptised at St Peter's, Sibton, Suffolk on 25 December 1634. Suffolk Record Office, FC 61/D1/1.

60 Centre Kentish Studies, All Saints Church, Staplehurst, P347/1/1, f. 108 (marriage 25 October 1616), f. 115 (George baptised 13 February 1620) and f. 119 (Elizabeth baptised 19 May 1622).

61 Steggle, 'New Directions: Othello, the Moor of London: Shakespeare's Black Britons', pp. 118–120. For Jetto, see Chapter 4, p. 126, n. 50.

62 *The Book of Common Prayer*, ed. Cummings, p. 145.

63 LMA, P71/OLA/009 (St Olave's Tooley Street, 14 July 1592). See also Habib and Salkeld, 'The Resonables of Boroughside, Southwark', p. 19.

64 *APC*, 1592, pp. 118, 183.

65 Ibid., p. 221.

66 'Accounts: December 1591 – December 1593', in *St Martin-in-The-Fields: the Accounts of the Churchwardens, 1525–1603*, ed. J V Kitto ([s.l.], 1901), pp. 435–456.

British History Online http://www.british-history.ac.uk/no-series/churchward-ens-st-martin-fields/1525-1603/pp435-456 [accessed 1 April 2017].

67 Slack, *The Impact of Plague in Tudor and Stuart England*, p.11. Balmford, *A Short Dialogue Concerning the Plagues Infection*, pp. 13–15 has a section on 'how the plague may be in a garment'.

68 Sager, *The Aesthetics of Spectacle in Early Modern Drama and Modern Cinema*, p. 129.

69 *APC*, 1592, pp. 221, 230, 273.

70 Balmford, *A Short Dialogue Concerning the Plagues Infection*, pp. 33, 43–4. It is not clear when he started work at St Olave's. He may have been working in Newcastle at the time of the 1592 plague, as in 1594 he dedicated *A Short and Plaine Dialogue Concerning the Unlawfulness of Playing at Cards* to his patrons, the mayor, aldermen, and burgesses of Newcastle upon Tyne: Jenkins, 'Balmford, James (*b. c.*1556, *d.* after 1623)', *Oxford Dictionary of National Biography*.

71 Shakespeare, *Romeo and Juliet*, Act 5, Scene 2; Mabillard, 'Worst Diseases in Shakespeare's London', *Shakespeare Online*. The plague is also mentioned in his other plays: including *The Tempest*, Act 1, Scene 2; *Timon of Athens*, Act 4, Scene 3; and *King Lear*, Act 2, Scene 4.

72 Balmford, *A Short Dialogue Concerning the Plagues Infection*, p. 10.

73 Mabillard, 'Worst Diseases in Shakespeare's London', *Shakespeare Online*.

74 Dekker, *The Wonderfull Yeare*, sig. D1r.

75 Slack, *The Impact of Plague in Tudor and Stuart England*, p. 23.

76 Browner, 'Wrong Side of the River', *Essays in History*.

77 *APC*, 1592, p. 204. Slack, *The Impact of Plague in Tudor and Stuart England*, p. 209. *Orders, thought Meete by her Maiestie, and her Priuie Councell*, sig C2v.

78 Kohn, *Encyclopaedia of plague and pestilence*, p. 231; Floyd–Wilson, *Occult Knowledge, Science, and Gender on the Shakespearean Stage*, p. 31–2.

79 Balmford, *A Short Dialogue Concerning the Plagues Infection*, pp. 39–40.

80 Harrison, G. B., *The Elizabethan Journals*, p. 175.

81 For example silk weaver Simon Brinkard lost his daughter Rachel on 14th July 1592, Hugh Van Aker's daughter Elizabeth was buried on 26th July and William, son of William Powler, was interred on 24th October. LMA, P71/OLA/009 (St Olave's Tooley Street Parish Register). LMA, MS 09221; MS 09222/1; MS 09223; MS 09234/4 (St Botolph Aldgate, 20 August, 8 October and 29 November 1593).

82 Stow, *A Summary of the Chronicles of England*, p. 438–439.

83 Kohn, *Encyclopaedia of plague and pestilence*, p. 231; Slack, *The Impact of Plague in Tudor and Stuart England*, pp. 19, 26, 151, 228–235, 438–439; *Orders, thought Meete by her Maiestie, and her Priuie Councell*, sig. B2v.

84 Slack, *The Impact of Plague in Tudor and Stuart England*, p. 292.

85 I. Archer, *The Pursuit of Stability*, p. 7; Strype, *Annals*, IV, pp. 234–6; for the full text of the Austin Friars verse see: Freeman, 'Marlowe, Kyd, and the Dutch Church Libel', pp. 44–52.

86 *APC*, 1592–1593, pp. 187, 200–201, 222.

87 An estimated 658,000 died of plague in England 1570–1670 (433,000 in London). Outbreaks occurred on average every 14 years. The so-called 'Great Plague' of

1665 resulted in 68,596 deaths (12% of the population), while the plagues of 1563 killed 20% of London's population, and that of 1603 killed 18%. In comparison, the plague that killed the Blackman children in 1592 was, with its 8.5% mortality rate, a relatively minor outbreak. Kohn, *Encyclopaedia of plague and pestilence*, p. 231; Slack, *The Impact of Plague in Tudor and Stuart England*, pp. 62, 85, 151, 174.

88 Slack, *The Impact of Plague in Tudor and Stuart England*, p. 210, 297; Balmford, *A Short Dialogue Concerning the Plagues Infection*, p. 32.

89 *Florentine Chronicle of Marchionne di Coppo di Stefano Buonaiuti*, tr. Usher, *Rubric 634a*.

90 Harding, 'Burial of the plague dead in early modern London', pp. 53–64.

91 LMA, MS 03572/1 (St Mary the Virgin, Aldermanbury, 10 and 23 May 1565).

92 LMA, MS 028867, St Olave, Hart Street, 26 and 28 January 1617).

93 Plymouth and West Devon Record Office, W132, f. 99v (Widey Court Book, 1593-4); Worth, *Calendar of the Plymouth Municipal Records*, p. 136. Another example is the burial of 'a blakmore belonging to Mr John Davies, died in White Chappel parishe, was laied in the ground in this church yarde *sine frequentia populi et sine ceremoniis quia utrum christianus esset necne nesciebamus* (without any company of people and without ceremony, because we did not know whether he was a Christian or not)' LMA, MS 07644 (St Mary Woolchurch Haw, undated, between entries for 24 April and 20 May 1597). Strangely John Davies seems to have been unable to tell the church what the African's religious status was. For more on Davies and discussion of this entry see Chapter 7, p. 199.

94 Duffy, *Saints, Sacrilege and Sedition*, p. 125.

95 LMA, MS 09222/1, MS 09221, MS 09223, MS 09234/4, 6 (St Botolph Aldgate, 27 August 1587, 8 October 1593, 29 November 1593, 3 March 1596).

96 *The Marriage Registers of St. Dunstan's, Stepney*, ed. Colyer-Fergusson, I, p. 90.

97 LMA, P71/OLA/009 (St Olave, Tooley Street, 30 August 1590).

98 Jane baptised 14 December 1614; Mary baptised 27 April 1617, buried 19 May 1620; William baptised 2 January 1619, buried 13 May 1621: LMA, P93/DUN/256 (St Dunstan's and All Saints, Stepney).

Chapter 6

1 Dimmock, 'Converting and not converting "Strangers" in Early Modern London', pp. 457–478.

2 Thomas Harridance was an ironmonger who kept memorandum books detailing the life of the parish during his time as parish clerk, 1583–1600. Adlington, 'Being no parishioner with us', p. 21. Much of the detail of the lives of the inhabitants of the parish of St Botolph's Aldgate, where Mary Fillis was baptised in 1597, comes from the parish's registers of baptisms, marriages and deaths, 1558–1665 (LMA, MS 09920, 09221, MS 09222/1 MS 09222/2 MS 09223), and crucially, the eight volumes of parish clerk's memorandum books, kept by Harridance and his two successors, which cover much of the period 1583–1625 (LMA, MS 09234/ 1-8). These have been transcribed by the Centre for Metropolitan History at the Institute of Historical Research, as part of their 'Life in the Suburbs: health, domesticity

and status in early modern London' project. The dataset will be published as Elizabeth Adlington and Mark Merry, *Parish Clerks' Memorandum Books, St Botolph Aldgate, 1583–1625*. Fillis's baptism, on 3 June 1597, was recorded thrice: in the main register: MS 09220, f. 90r; the paper burial register: MS 09223; and by Harridance: MS 09234/6, ff. 257r–258r.

3   The Oxford English Dictionary, "fillis, n." *OED Online*.

4   Henry A. Harben, 'Blakegate – Blind Chapel Court', in *A Dictionary of London* (London, 1918), *British History Online* http://british-history.ac.uk/no-series/dictionary-of-london/blakegate-blind-chapel-court (Accessed 11 April 2017).

5   Plummer, *Roads to Ruin*, p. 49; Leo Africanus, *The History and Description of Africa*, trans. Pory, II, p. 594; Zemon–Davis, *Trickster's Travels*, p. 20; Messier, *The Almoravids and the Meanings of Jihad*, p. 45.

6   Brotton, *This Orient Isle*, p. 129; Leo Africanus, *The History and Description of Africa*, trans. Pory, II, p. 262.

7   Plummer, *Roads to Ruin*, pp. 3, 83, see also his Figure 1: Morocco Under Siege, p. xxii.

8   Willan, *Studies in Elizabethan Foreign Trade*, p. 93.

9   Plummer, *Roads to Ruin*, pp. 97, 107; Andrews, *Trade, plunder and Settlement*, pp. 101–2.

10 Brotton, *This Orient Isle*, p. 30.

11 Plummer, *Roads to Ruin*, p. 82.

12 For a family tree of the Sa'adian dynasty at this time see *The Stukeley Plays*, ed. Edelman, p. 11.

13 Plummer, *Roads to Ruin*, pp. 315, 332, 334.

14 Ibid., pp. 323, 364–366, 368–9, 379, 383.

15 Brotton, *This Orient Isle*, p. 175; Kaba, 'Archers, Musketeers, and Mosquitoes: The Moroccan Invasion of the Sudan and the Songhay Resistance', pp. 457–475.

16 Plummer, *Roads to Ruin*, p. 391.

17 Ibid., pp. 139–144; Johnson, *Dois Estudos Polemicos*, pp. 85–99; Johnson, 'A Pedophile in the Palace'; Johnson, 'Through a glass darkly: A Disappointing New Biography of King Sebastian of Portugal'; *Sebastian, King of Portugal: Four Essays*; Johnson's theory has been called 'extravagant' by Sebastian's Portuguese biographer Maria Augusta Lima Cruz, though it is given credence by Plummer.

18 Plummer, *Roads to Ruin*, pp. 287, 375.

19 Barker was a director of the Spanish Company in 1577: Rabb, *Enterprise and Empire*, p. 240.

20 *Registers of St Olave, Hart St.*, ed. Bannerman, pp. 11, 122; *Two Tudor Subsidy Rolls For the City of London 1541 and 1582*, ed. Lang, pp. 278–289; 'Barker, John, I (c. 1532–1589) of Ipswich, Suff', *The History of Parliament*.

21 TNA, SP 46/185 (Papers of George Stoddard, Grocer, 1553–1568) See also Hall, *Society in the Elizabethan Age*, pp. 48–57, 159.

22 TNA, PROB 11/116/270 (Will of Anne Barker, Widow, of Saint Catherine Coleman, City of London, 28 August 1610).

23 *Returns of Strangers in the Metropolis*, ed. Scoloudi, p. 197.

24 LMA, MS 028867 (St Olave, Hart Street, 23 January 1595).

25 *Household Accounts and Disbursement Books of Robert Dudley, Earl of Leicester,* ed. Adams, p. 478; 'Barker, John, I (c. 1532–1589) of Ipswich, Suff.', *The History of Parliament*; *Queen Elizabeth and Her Times: A Series of Original Letters,* ed. Wright, II, pp. 83–85, 295, 336. The original letter of 10th April 1578 is BL, Cotton MS, Vespasian C VII, f. 371. The collection also includes two other letters from Barker to Leicester, at ff. 362 (28th April 1578) & 373 (12th April 1578). All three are written from St Lucar de Barrameda, a port to the north of Cadiz.

26 *Household Accounts and Disbursement Books of Robert Dudley, Earl of Leicester,* ed. Adams, p. 178, n. 364.

27 Willan, *Studies in Elizabethan Foreign Trade,* p. 185; Hakluyt, VI, 419–425.

28 *Household Accounts and Disbursement Books of Robert Dudley, Earl of Leicester,* ed. Adams, p. 280; TNA, SP 102/4, 54; Moore, 'Roberts, Henry (*fl.* 1585–1617)', *Oxford Dictionary of National Biography*; Willan, *Studies in Elizabethan Foreign Trade,* p. 225.

29 Hakluyt, VI, pp. 136–137. This was not the first contact. The *Trinity* of Bristol had voyaged to Morocco in 1480–1, and Roger Barlow went to Agadir early in his career: Sacks, *The Widening Gate: Bristol and the Atlantic Economy,* p. 34; Reddaway and Ruddock, *The Accounts of John Balsall,* Reddaway and Ruddock (eds) pp. 1–29; Dalton, 'Barlow, Roger (*c.*1483–1553)', *Oxford Dictionary of National Biography*. The merchant investors included William Chester, William Garrard, Thomas Lodge, Sir John Yorke, Sir Thomas Wroth, Francis Lambert and Alexander Cole: Alsop, 'Chester, Sir William (*c.*1509–1595?)', Miller, 'Garrard, Sir William (*c.*1510–1571)', McConnell, 'Lodge, Sir Thomas (1509/10–1585)', Elzinga, 'York, Sir John (*d.* 1569)', Lehmberg, 'Wroth, Sir Thomas (1518?–1573)', *Oxford Dictionary of National Biography*.

30 Willan, *Studies in Elizabethan Foreign Trade,* p. 99; Tong, 'Captain Thomas Wyndham', p. 224; Hakluyt, VI, 138–40.

31 Read, 'English Foreign Trade Under Elizabeth', p. 518.

32 Willan, *Studies in Elizabethan Foreign Trade,* p. 95; Andrews, *Trade, plunder and Settlement,* pp. 7–9; Brenner, *Merchants and Revolution,* pp. 12–13.

33 Willan, *Studies in Elizabethan Foreign Trade,* pp. 101–104, 133–5; Shepard, 'White, Sir Thomas (1495?–1567)', *Oxford Dictionary of National Biography*. The first two ventures to Barbary are recorded by Hakluyt, but as he was concerned with voyages of discovery, once the trade became established, it disappeared from his pages.

34 Plummer, *Roads to Ruin,* p. 267; Ronald, *The Pirate Queen,* p.199.

35 Willan, *Studies in Elizabethan Foreign Trade,* pp. 93–4; 'Spain: August 1551', in *Calendar of State Papers, Spain, Volume 10, 1550–1552,* ed. Royall Tyler (London, 1914), pp. 341–348. *British History Online* http://www.british-history.ac.uk/cal-state-papers/spain/vol10/pp341-348 [accessed 1 April 2017].

36 'Simancas: June 1574', in *Calendar of State Papers, Spain (Simancas), Volume 2, 1568–1579,* ed. Martin A. S. Hume (London, 1894), pp. 482–483. *British History Online* http://www.british-history.ac.uk/cal-state-papers/simancas/vol2/pp482-483 [accessed 1 April 2017].

37 Plummer, *Roads to Ruin,* p. 390.

38 Henry Roberts writing to James I in 1603, quoted in Matar, *Britain and Barbary*, p. 40.

39 Hakluyt, VI, 285–293; Brotton, *This Orient Isle*, pp. 71–76, 118–9.

40 BL, Lansdowne MS 115, f. 196. One of Barker's ships, laden with rye, was taken by the Spanish near Dunkirk that December: 'Elizabeth: December 1586, 26–31', in *Calendar of State Papers Foreign: Elizabeth, Volume 21, Part 2, June 1586–March 1587*, ed. Sophie Crawford Lomas and Allen B. Hinds (London, 1927), pp. 287–305. *British History Online* http://www.british-history.ac.uk/cal-state-papers/foreign/vol21/no2/pp287-305 [accessed 1 April 2017].

41 Rabb, *Enterprise and Empire*, p. 66.

42 Andrews, *Elizabethan Privateering*, pp. 4, 32.

43 This observation was made in the draft proclamation probably authored by Caspar Van Senden and Sir Thomas Sherley: Hatfield, Cecil Papers 91/15; *Calendar of the Manuscripts of the Most Honourable the Marquess of Salisbury*, ed. Owen, XI, p. 569; *Tudor Royal Proclamations*, ed. Hughes and Larkin, III, pp. 221–222; see also Chapter 4, p. 125 and discussion later in this chapter pp. 183–184; for statistics showing numbers of Africans recorded in England did indeed peak 1588–1604 see Kaufmann, 'Africans in Britain', p. 121.

44 TNA, SP 12/218/14, f. 25; *CSPD*, 1581–1590, p. 558.

45 TNA, HCA 13/29, ff. 40–1 (13 March 1591).

46 Letter from Antonio Fogaza to the Prince Ruy Gomez De Silva: *CSPS*, 1568–1579, p. 352. The *Castle of Comfort* was a prolific privateering ship, of 200 tons' burden. Sir Henry Compton had acquired it in 1569. In 1571, she had set out for Morocco under the command of John Garrett of Plymouth. In 1574, she was bought by William Hawkins and Richard Grenville. Andrews, *Elizabethan Privateering*, p.17; Andrews, *Trade, Plunder and Settlement*, p.110.

47 The ship's captain, Jonas Bradbury, had captained the *Disdain* during the Armada battle and was Vice-Admiral of Ireland in 1601: Corbett, *Drake and the Tudor Navy*, II, p. 150; Marsden, 'The Vice Admirals of the Coast', p. 754.

48 BL, Lansdowne MS 115, no. 82, ff. 234–238, and no. 83, f. 239. The Mayor William Hopkins reports the figures at 30 and 100, but the figures of 32 and 135 given by Nicholas Thorne, the chamberlain, seem more precise. No doubt the barn was the only lodging large enough to accommodate the group at such short notice. When Francis Drake captured the *Nuestra Senora del Rosario* in August 1588 the 397 prisoners were kept in an old barn in the grounds of Torre Abbey, near Torquay: Martin, *Spanish Armada Prisoners*, p. 44.

49 Andrews, *Elizabethan Privateering*, p. 154.

50 TNA, SP 12/262/104 (Declaration of John Hill of Stonehouse, Plymouth, 1597); *CSPD*, 1595–1597, p. 381. This may have been one of two brothers, John and William Clements, who were promoters of the privateering ship *Archangel* in 1600, which took two prizes near Cuba in 1602: Andrews, 'English Voyages to the Caribbean', p. 250.

51 Kaufmann, 'Africans in Britain', pp. 153–158.

52 Andrews, *Elizabethan Privateering*, pp. 109–111; Andrews, 'English Voyages to the Caribbean', p. 248; Archer, 'Bayning, Paul (c.1539–1616)', *Oxford Dictionary of National Biography*.

53 *Returns of Strangers in the Metropolis*, ed. Scoloudi, p. 149; LMA, MS 04310 (St Mary Bothaw, 29 March 1602); BCB, V, f. 337v (1 April 1609); TNA, PROB 11/128, f. 256v (Will of Paul Bayning, 12 October 1616). If Julyane was one of the three maids noted in 1593, then there were four Africans in the Bayning household. If she was not, then there were five (though they were not necessarily all there at the same time).

54 LMA, MS 028867 (St Olave, Hart Street); *Registers of St Olave, Hart St.*, ed. Bannerman; and St Botolph, Aldgate Registers as referenced above, n.2. Details of African entries in Kaufmann, 'Africans in Britain' Appendix, 1: Baptism Records and 2: Burial Records, see also Habib, *Black Lives*, Index and notes in Onyeka's *Blackamoores*, pp. 355–361. Robert, who worked for William Matthew, was buried at St Botolph Aldgate on 29 November 1593, Francis, who worked for Peter Miller the beer brewer, died of scurvy and was buried there on 3 March 1596; for Francis Pinto see: Samuel, 'Portuguese Jews in Jacobean London', pp. 181, 185–7.

55 Samuel, 'Nunes, Hector (1520–1591)', *Oxford Dictionary of National Biography.*

56 Skelton and Summerson, *A Description of Maps and Architectural Drawings in the Collection made by William Cecil*, pp. 6, 65.

57 For the Ethiopian Negar, see Chapter 2, p. 58 and Chapter 4, p. 113 and Kaufmann, M., 'African freedom in Tudor England: Dr Hector Nunes' petition', *Our Migration Story*, http://www.ourmigrationstory.org.uk/oms/african-freedom-in-tudor-england-dr-hector-nuness-request. In 1576, 'Elizabeth a neger' was listed amongst eight 'servants to Mr Farnando' in Tower Ward. By 1582–3, Alvarez himself was listed as part of Nunes's household, as was Elizabeth and a second black woman, 'Gratia', or Grace. This was probably the 'Grace a nigro out of Doctor Hector's' buried at St Olave Hart Street in July 1590. 'Mary a blackamore from Doctor Hector's' had been buried in the same parish two years earlier in January 1588. Kirk and Kirk, *Returns of Aliens*, II, pp. 161 279; LMA, MS 028867; *Registers of St Olave, Hart St.*, ed. Bruce Bannerman, pp. 121, 123.

58 Wilson further deposed that 'they did make Saturday their Sunday' wearing their best clothes and avoiding work on Saturdays, 'but contrariwise on Sundays they would go and do as any workday.' TNA, C 24/250, no. 6, f. 6; Sisson, 'A colony of Jews in Shakespeare's London', pp. 45–7; Habib, *Black Lives*, Index, no. 169; Adelman, *Blood Relations: Christian and Jew in the Merchant of Venice*, pp.11–13, 261–2; Meyers, 'Lawsuits in Elizabethan Courts of Law: The Adventures of Dr. Hector Nunes, 1566–1591', pp. 157-8.

59 *Piracy, Slavery and Redemption*, ed. Vitkus, p. 2.

60 Brotton, *This Orient Isle*, pp. 80–81, 166–9; Holmes, 'Stucley, Thomas (c.1520–1578)', *Oxford Dictionary of National Biography*; *The Stukeley Plays*, ed. Edelman, pp. 1–49.

61 BL, Cotton MS, Vespasian C VII, ff. 362, 371.

62 This was the first official embassy from the Moroccan state. However, 'two Moores, being noble men, whereof one was of the Kings blood' returned to Morocco with Thomas Wyndham on his first voyage there in 1551: Hakluyt, VI, p. 137. They were probably the 'gentlemen from the King of Velez in Morocco' who came to the English court in July 1551: *CSPS*, 1550–1552, p. 325. Velez was Peñón de Vélez

de la Gomera, a rocky fortress off the coast of Morocco, whose ruler was in conflict with Mohammed ash Sheikh. Despite the efforts of these men to gain support from Charles V in their struggle, the King of Velez was captured and beheaded by ash Sheikh in 1554: Willan, *Studies in Elizabethan Foreign Trade*, p. 97; CSPF, 1553-1558, p. 149.

63 Matar, *Britain and Barbary*, pp. 13–14.

64 Hakluyt, VI, p. 428.

65 TNA, SP 12/132, ff. 39–42; *CSPD*, 1547–1580, p. 633.

66 *CSPS*, 1587–1603, p. 516.

67 Green, *The Double Life of Dr. Lopez*, pp. 62–65, 72–73. BL, Lansdowne MS 158/66, ff. 131–2 (A remembrance of such matters as are requested in the behalf of the King of Portugal, 1592) and 67 f. 133 (The King of Portugal his answer upon the Supplication of his creditors, 1592).

68 Matar, *Britain and Barbary*, p. 15.

69 *CSPS*, 1587–1603, p. 523.

70 For a full account of the mission see Kelsey, *Sir Francis Drake*, pp. 341–364 and *The Expedition of Sir John Norris and Sir Francis Drake to Spain and Portugal, 1589*, ed. Wernham.

71 *CSPS*, 1587–1603, p. 550.

72 LMA, MS 028867 (St Olave's, Hart Street, 6 June 1589); TNA, PROB 11/74/77 (Will of John Barker, 16 June 1589).

73 Matar, *Britain and Barbary*, p. 21. The merchant's name was Edward Holmden.

74 Matar, *Europe through Arab Eyes*, p. 159.

75 Brotton, *This Orient Isle*, p. 203; Shakespeare, *The Merchant of Venice*, Act 2, Scene 7.

76 Stow, *A Survey of London*, p. 48. Hadfield, *Edmund Spenser*, p. 23. Pettegree, *Foreign Protestant Communities*, pp. 18, 108; Luu, *Immigrants and Industries*, p. 93; Grainger, *The Royal Navy Victualling Yard* and *The Black Death Cemetery*.

77 James Crew (d.1591), Baker and Citizen of London, and his wife Elizabeth (d.1595), had four sons living in 1595, Caleb, Joshua, James and Thomas.

78 'Lucretia', *The Dictionary of Medieval Names from European Sources*, ed. Uckelman.

79 This is recorded in Harridance's memorandum book, 19 January 1584, and also commented on in Knutson, 'A Caliban in St. Mildred's Poultry', p. 124, n. 10.

80 *The Book of Common Prayer*, ed. Cummings, p. 430; Oxford English Dictionary, "catechism, n.", OED Online.

81 Owen, 'The London Parish Clergy in the Reign of Elizabeth I', p. 417, n. 2.

82 *The Book of Common Prayer*, ed. Cummings, p. 149.

83 Van Cleve, 'Somerset's case and its antecedents', p. 610; Drescher, *Capitalism and Antislavery*, p. 188, citing *Lloyds Evening Post*, 3–5 November 1760, p. 433.

84 'Sicut Dudum: Pope Eugene IV Against the Enslaving of Black Natives from the Canary Islands, January 13, 1435', *Papal Encyclidals Online*; Smith, *De Republica Anglorum*, ed. Dewar, p. 136; *Minutes of the Council and General Court of Colonial Virginia*, ed. McIlwane, p. 33; no evidence has been found, as yet, of John Phillip's baptism in the English parish registers.

85 Fryer, *Staying Power*, p. 114. See also Kaufmann, 'English Common Law, Slavery and', pp. 200–203.

86 Dimmock, 'Converting and not converting "Strangers" in Early Modern London', p. 467.

87 TNA, PROB 11/128, f. 256v.

88 Canterbury Cathedral Archives, DCb/L/R/13 and DCb/BT/1/94; Habib Index, no. 352.

89 Dimmock, 'Converting and not converting "Strangers" in Early Modern London', p. 459.

90 A.T. Vaughan, *Transatlantic Encounters*, p. 83.

91 'The Records of a Church of Christ 1640–1687', ed. Hayden, pp. 101–2; Linebaugh and Redikker, *The Many-Headed* Hydra, pp. 71–104. Nathaniel Ingelo (1621–1683) came to Bristol from Cambridge in 1646, when he was appointed to All Saints, Bristol. He was the pastor of the independent congregation for the next few years, appointed fellow of Eton in 1650, and sent on an embassy to Sweden 1653–4. McLellan, 'Ingelo, Nathaniel (1620/21–1683)', *Oxford Dictionary of National Biography*.

92 Onyeka, *Blackamoores*, pp. 275–6.

93 BRO, FCP/St P +J/R/1(a)2.

94 The spelling 'byllys' is used by Margaret Paston in 1465: 'the tenauntes havyng rusty polexis and byllys': *Paston letters and papers of the 15th century*, ed. Davis, p. 312.

95 Numbers 12:1. Although the Hebrew refers to a 'Cushite' woman, so she may have been from Northern Arabia. Sixteenth- and seventeenth-century English readers would have taken it to mean Africa, as the Latin text was 'Aethiopissam', translated as 'a woman of Ethiopia' in the *Geneva Bible* (1560, first printed in England in 1575) and 'Ethiopian woman' in the *King James's Bible* (1611). *The Oxford Handbook of the Bible in Early Modern England*, ed. Killeen, Smith and Willie, pp. 227–8. See also Iyengar, *Shades of Difference*, p. 24.

96 Bromley Historic Collections, P92/1/1, p. 1 (St Nicholas, Chislehurst, 22 April 1593); Bristol Record Office, FCP/Dy/R/1(a)1 (St Peter's, Dyrham, 15 August 1575); LMA, MS 04310 (St Mary Bothaw, 29 March 1602); Devon Record Office, MF1, (St John the Baptist, Hatherleigh, 13 May 1604 and 10 August 1606).

97 *The Book of Common Prayer*, ed. Cummings, p. 150.

98 Dimmock, 'Converting and not converting "Strangers" in Early Modern London', p. 467.

99 Hanmer, *The Baptizing of a Turke*, sigs. A4v–5r., E3r–E4r; Hanmer cites Matthew, 5:14; Babinger, Hickman and Mannheim, *Mehmed the Conqueror and his Time*, p. 281. See also Dimmock, 'Converting and not converting "Strangers" in Early Modern London', pp. 457–478.

100 'The Records of a Church of Christ 1640–1687', ed. Hayden, pp. 101–2.

101 Acts, 10: 34–5. This is the wording from the King James Bible (1611).

102 Habib, *Black Lives*, pp. 19–20; Fryer and Bush, *The Politics of British Black History*, pp. 10–11.

103 BL, Royal MS, 17 B. X (Petition of William Bragge to the Honourable Sir Thomas Smith, Knight, and all the Company of the East India and Sommer Islands).

104 *The Lives, Apprehensions, Arraignments, and Executions, of the 19 Late Pirates*, sigs. E2r, E4r.

105 Dimmock, 'Converting and not converting "Strangers" in Early Modern London', p. 467.

106 *The Book of Common Prayer*, ed. Cummings, p. 141.

107 City of Westminster Archives Centre, St Martin's in the Fields Parish Registers, vol. 2 (8 February 1621).

108 *The Book of Common Prayer*, ed. Cummings, p. 145.

109 'The Records of a Church of Christ 1640–1687', ed. Hayden, pp. 101–2.

110 See above, n. 92.

111 Hatfield, Cecil Papers 91/15; *Calendar of the Manuscripts of the Most Honourable the Marquess of Salisbury*, ed. Owen, XI, p. 569; *Tudor Royal Proclamations*, ed. Hughes and Larkin, III, pp. 221–222.

112 For Fortunatus, see Chapter 4, p. 116, n. 31. Kaufmann, 'Caspar van Senden, Sir Thomas Sherley and the 'Blackamoor' Project'. See also Bartels, 'Too Many Blackamoors: Deportation, Discrimination, and Elizabeth I' and Weissbourd, "Those in Their Possession": Race, Slavery, and Queen Elizabeth's "Edicts of Expulsion".

113 Brotton, *This Orient Isle*, p. 273–4, citing Stow, *Annales*, p. 791. There has been some confusion as to the location of Alderman Radcliffe's house in the secondary literature. Brotton, p. 4, (possibly following Harris, 'Portrait of a Moor', p. 28) says it is on The Strand, near the Royal Exchange. But the Strand ends at Temple Bar, over a mile west of the Exchange. Anthony Radcliffe was resident in the parish of St Christopher le Stocks, and so lived near the Royal Exchange, but not on the Strand: *The register book of the parish of St. Christopher le Stocks*, ed. Freshfield, pp. 7, 34, 35; Knowles, 'Moulson, Ann, Lady Moulson (1576–1661)', *Oxford Dictionary of National Biography*.

114 TNA, SP 12/275, f. 160; *CSPD*, 1598–1601, p. 481.

115 Isom–Verhaaren, *Allies with the Infidel*.

116 TNA, SP 12/275, f. 152; *CSPD*, 1598–1601, p. 478.

117 Zemon Davis, *Trickster's Travels*, p. 65.

118 Leo Africanus, *The History and Description of Africa*, trans. Pory, I, p. 3.

119 Matar, *Britain and Barbary*, pp. 27–8, 40.

120 Knutson, 'A Caliban in St. Mildred's Poultry', p. 124, n. 10 first pointed out the possibility that the former woman was Fillis.

121 Rosemary Lane (formerly Hogg Lane; the street was named Rosemary Lane in the early seventeenth century, and renamed Royal Mint Street in 1850) was situated a little to the north east of the Tower of London, about half a mile south east of St Botolph's Church. The death of an individual in the street was not unique. In the period 1583–1625 covered by the parish clerk's memorandum books 13 men and 12 other women died in the street. Fifteen of these 25 were described as poor, and eight as vagrants. Two died in Rosemary Lane itself: just a few weeks before Mary the 'Blacke Moore' was buried, on 22 October 1623, 'a poor man . . . whose name we could not learn' was found there dead, and the year before, on 13 December 1622, 'a poor woman, being a vagrant, who died in the Street in Rosemarie Lane, was buried'.

122 She may have been the same 'Mary Peter Blacamore woman', who appeared before

the London Bridewell Court on 9 June 1619, brought in by the Constable from Holborn, accused of vagrancy. She was described as 'an old guest', which suggested this was not her first stay in the prison, and as 'unruly': BCB, VI, f. 127r.

Chapter 7

1   The word *'maafa'* was used to refer to the slave trade by Marimba Ani in his 1998 book *Let the Circle Be Unbroken*. See also Dagbovie, *African American History Reconsidered*, p. 191.
2   LMA, MS 04429/1 (St Mildred Poultry, 1 January 1611). See also Knutson, 'A Caliban in St. Mildred Poultry', p. 111. These are their names as recorded in the London parish register when Jaquoah was baptised. They might well have been spelt or pronounced quite differently at home.
3   *Barbot on Guinea*, ed. Hair, Jones and Law, I, pp. 273, 290, 294–5.
4   Villault, *A relation of the coast of Africa called Guinee*, pp. 77. Towerson, noted the 'very high trees all along the shore' in 1555: Hakluyt, VI, p. 182; Jean Barbot also mentioned the large trees, adding that the eastern bank was covered with mangroves: *Barbot on Guinea*, ed. Hair, Jones and Law, I, p. 264
5   Hakluyt, VI, p. 158.
6   Zeguebos was the name recorded by Pacheco Pereira in 1507: Hair, 'Ethnolinguistic Continuity on the Guinea Coast', p. 257 and 'An Ethnolinguistic Inventory of the Upper Guinea coast before 1700: Part II', p. 227. De Marees, *Description and historical account of the Gold Kingdom of Guinea*, ed. Van Dantzig and Jones, p. 14, n. 5; Massing, 'Mapping The Malagueta Coast', p. 350; Dalby & Hair, "Le langaige de Guynee": A *Sixteenth Century* Vocabulary from the *Pepper Coast*', pp. 174–91.
7   *Barbot on Guinea*, ed. Hair, Jones and Law, I, pp. 264–9.
8   *Europeans In West Africa, 1450–1560*, ed. Blake, I, p. 167.
9   Chaucer, *The Canterbury Tales*, The Miller's Tale, lines 580–582; O'Connell, *The Book of Spice*, pp. 121–125; De Marees, *Description and historical account of the Gold Kingdom of Guinea*, ed. Van Dantzig and Jones, p. 14, n. 4.
10 Blake, *West Africa: Quest for God and Gold*, p. 9.
11 Hakluyt, VI, p. 147.
12 *Barbot on Guinea*, ed. Hair, Jones and Law, I, p. 276.
13 Northrup, *Africa's Discovery of Europe*, pp. 12–13, 20–22.
14 Blake, *West Africa: Quest for God and Gold*, pp. 85–6.
15 Ibid., pp. 2–3, 107, 125–6, 157, 169; Centers, 'Fourteenth Century Normans in West Africa'; Hakluyt, VI, p. 238. This trading contact with Guinea may explain the presence of an African servant in Sir William Wynter's London household (see Chapter 4).
16 Hakluyt, II, p. 700. Morgan, 'Hawkins, William (*b.* before 1490, *d.* 1554/5)', *Oxford Dictionary of National Biography*. This is the first known English voyage to Guinea that set out from England. English merchants resident in Spain and Portugal may have travelled to Africa earlier. See Ungerer, *The Mediterranean Apprenticeship of British Slavery*, p. 28.
17 Tong, 'Captain Thomas Wyndham', pp. 221–228; Thomas, H., *The Slave Trade*, p. 154; Hakluyt, VI, pp. 145–154.

18 Hakluyt, VI, pp. 158, 163–4; Slack, 'Judde, Sir Andrew (c.1492–1558)', *Oxford Dictionary of National Biography*.

19 Appleby, 'Towerson, William (d. 1584)', *Oxford Dictionary of National Biography*.

20 The merchants were William Brayley, Gilbert Smyth, Nicholas Spycer and John Daricott of Exeter, John Younge of Colyton, Devon, Richard Dodderidge of Barnstaple, and Anthony Dassell and Nicholas Turner of the City of London. Their remit covered the entirety of the coastline of modern–day Senegal, from St Louis to Bakau: TNA, C 66/1312, ff. 41–43 (Patent Rolls, 3 May 1588); *Calendar of Patent Rolls, 30 Elizabeth*, ed. Neal, p. 84; Willan, *Studies in Elizabethan Foreign Trade*, p. 139.

21 Gregory was also to pay Don Antonio his cut of the profits. Scott, *English, Scottish and Irish Joint–Stock Companies*, II, p. 10; *Calendar of Patent Rolls, 34 Elizabeth*, ed. Neal, p. 45.

22 McDermott, 'Howard, Charles, second Baron Howard of Effingham and first earl of Nottingham (1536–1624)' and Hicks, 'Stanhope, John, first Baron Stanhope (c.1540–1621)', *Oxford Dictionary of National Biography*.

23 Hair, 'Attitudes to Africans in English Primary Sources on Guinea up to 1650', p. 46.

24 *Pieter Van Den Broeke's Journal of Voyages to Cape Verde, Guinea and Angola*, ed. La Fleur, p. 4.

25 William Rutter called at River Cestos in the *Primrose* on 3 April 1562: Hakluyt, VI, pp. 258–261; a voyage was proposed to River Cestos for ivory and pepper in 1582: *CSPD, 1581–1590*, p. 59. TNA, SP12/154/24.

26 Jobson, *The Golden Trade*, pp. 88–9.

27 The English resumed the slave trade c.1641 in which year the *Star* delivered a cargo of Africans to Barbados: Gragg, *Englishmen Transplanted*, p. 119; *Voyages: The Trans–Atlantic Slave Trade* Database, Voyage 21876. See further discussion in Chapter 3.

28 Hakluyt's account talks of Hawkins's dealings with the king of 'Castros' in 1567. This was misidentified as Cestos by Walter Rodney, in his *A History of the Upper Guinea Coast*, p. 53. See Massing, 'The Mane, the Decline of Mali, and Mandinka Expansion towards the South Windward Coast', p. 52 and Hair 'An ethnolinguistic inventory of the Upper Guinea coast before 1700, Part I', pp. 49, 61.

29 Knutson, 'A Caliban in St. Mildred Poultry', p. 115; Knutson, 'What's a Guy like John Davies Doing in a Seminar on Theater History?', nn.1–2, notes online at: http://ualr.edu/rlknutson/davies.html (accessed 3 April 2017).

30 Andrews, *Elizabethan Privateering*, pp. 121, 266–7; Blake, 'The English Guinea Company, 1618–1660', p. 17; TNA, C2/Jas I/D10/61 (Court of Chancery, Davies vs. Kilburne, 15 October 1622).

31 Knutson, 'What's a Guy like John Davies Doing in a Seminar on Theater History?' p. 2, n. 4, notes online at: http://ualr.edu/rlknutson/davies.html (accessed 3 April 2017).

32 *Pieter Van Den Broeke's Journal of Voyages to Cape Verde, Guinea and Angola*, ed. La Fleur, p. 48.

33 Blake, 'The farm of the Guinea Trade in 1631', pp. 92–3; Porter, 'The Crispe Family and the African Trade in the Seventeenth Century', p. 58; Blake, 'The English Guinea Company, 1618–1660', p. 17.

34 Blake, 'English Trade with the Portuguese Empire in West Africa, 1581–1629', p. 324; TNA, HCA 14/39, no. 85.

35 The port books for the 1610 voyage do not survive, but it seems likely that the cargo was similar to those recorded on the *Abigail* in January 1608: Knutson, 'A Caliban in St. Mildred Poultry', p. 117; TNA, E 190/14/4 (Port book, London overseas outwards, 25 December 1607–25 December 1608).

36 McDermott, 'Hudson, Henry (*d.* 1611)', *Oxford Dictionary of National Biography*.

37 *Trinity House of Deptford Transactions*, ed. Harris, p. 151; Rediker, *Between the Devil and the Deep Blue Sea*, p.234. Scammell, 'Mutiny in British Ships, c.1500–1750', p. 349.

38 LMA, MS 30045/1, f. 9v (Corporation of Trinity House, Transactions, 1 January 1611); *Trinity House of Deptford Transactions*, ed. Harris, p. 7.

39 LMA, MS 04429/1 (St Mildred Poultry, 1 January 1611).

40 Knutson, 'A Caliban in St. Mildred Poultry', p. 122; TNA, C 2/JasI/K7/12 (Court of Chancery, Kilburne v Watts, 9 July 1622); TNA, C2/Jas I/D10/61(Court of Chancery, Davies vs. Kilburne, 15 October 1622).

41 See Towers' testimony in the High Court of Admiralty: HCA 1/47/290; Knutson, 'A Caliban in St. Mildred Poultry', p. 117.

42 Blake, 'The English Guinea Company, 1618–1660', p. 24; *Barbot on Guinea*, ed. Hair, Jones and Law, I, p. 268.

43 LMA, MS 07644 (St Mary Woolchurch Haw, undated, between entries for 24 April and 20 May 1597).

44 Shakespeare, *Twelfth Night*, Act 5, Scene 1; *Returns of Aliens*, ed. Kirk and Kirk, III, p. 385. See also The Oxford English Dictionary, 'belonging, vbl, *n.*', *OED Online*.

45 Knutson, 'A Caliban in St. Mildred Poultry', pp. 115, 124, n.14.

46 Hakluyt, VI, pp. 176, 217–8, 225, 245. Lok and Gainsh had taken the Africans in 1554, arriving with them in London in 1555. They have been cited as the 'first' Africans to come to England by: Little, *Negroes in Britain*, p. 166; Scobie, *Black Britannia*, p. 5; Shyllon, *Black People in Britain 1555–1833*, p. 6; and Walvin, *Black and White: the Negro and English society 1555–1945* (1973), p. 7.

47 Farrington, *Trading Places*, pp. 10–22. Chaudhuri, *The English East India Company*, pp. 21, 209.

48 Hakluyt, VI, pp. 205, 207.

49 TNA, HCA 24/59, ff. 29–46; TNA, REQ 2/353/44; BL Lansdowne MS 158, ff. 131–137.

50 Northrup, *Africa's Discovery of Europe*, pp. 26, 38.

51 Northrup, 'Africans, Early European Contacts and the Emergent Disapora', p. 52.

52 Northrup, *Africa's Discovery of Europe*, p. 33; Blake, *Europeans in West Africa*, p. 124; There is some confusion as to which Oba was ruling at this time and whether the war was with the Idah or the Uromi: Bradbury, 'Chronological Problems in The Study Of Benin History', pp. 263–28; Ekeh, 'Benin, The Western Niger Delta, and the Development of the Atlantic World', p. 20, n. 36.

53 *Before Van Riebeeck: Callers at South Africa from 1488 to 1652*, ed. Raven–Hart, pp. 64, 70, 84, 88.

54 Edward Blitheman to Sir Thomas Smith, 20 February 1615: *Letters Received by the East India Company* ed. Danvers and Foster, II, p. 331.

55 Hakluyt, VI, pp. 185, 187.

56 *Before Van Riebeeck: Callers at South Africa from 1488 to 1652*, ed. Raven–Hart, p. 23.

57 This Gabriel Towerson was the tenth child of William Towerson (d. 1584) who conducted some of the voyages to Guinea discussed earlier. Alsop, 'Towerson, Gabriel (*bap.* 1576, *d.* 1623)', *Oxford Dictionary Of National Biography*.

58 Ibid.; Hakluyt, VI, pp. 205, 207, 218; Alsop, 'The career of William Towerson, Guinea trader', pp. 45–82. For a detailed analysis of the Guinean merchants' interactions with Towerson, see Smith, C. L., *Black Africans in the British Imagination*, pp. 29–48. Binne had returned by June 1558; see n. 94 below. Anthony probably returned too. An African of that name is mentioned in the account of William Rutter's voyage of 1562: Hakluyt, VI, p. 260. Hair and Alsop, *English Seamen and Traders in Guinea*, p. 67, quote Archivo Nacional da Torre do Tombo, Lisbon, CC–1–106–11 in which a Portuguese agent reported in 1562 that the English vessels had carried back to Guinea two Africans who had been in London when King Philip was there. Philip had been in England from June 1554 until August 1555 and again from March to July 1557 (Loades, *The Reign of Mary Tudor*, pp. 95, 191, 207, 312).

59 *The Troublesome Voyage of Captain Edward Fenton*, ed. Taylor, p. 56.

60 Vaughan, A.T., *Transatlantic Encounters*, pp. 11–12.

61 MacGaffey, 'Dialogues of the deaf: Europeans on the Atlantic coast of Africa', p. 253.

62 Northrup, *Africa's Discovery of Europe*, pp. 20–21.

63 Vaughan, A.T., *Transatlantic Encounters*, p. 13.

64 TNA, HCA 24/59, ff. 29–46; TNA, REQ 2/353/44; BL Lansdowne MS 158, ff. 131–137. See also *APC*, 1592, pp. 128–9, 131–2.

65 Hakluyt, VI, p. 273.

66 TNA, HCA 24/59, ff 49–51; TNA, REQ 2/353/44; BL Lansdowne MS 158, ff. 131–137. Ungerer, 'The presence of Africans in Elizabethan England and the performance of Titus Andronicus at Burley-on-the-Hill, 1595/96', pp. 19–55. Richard Kelly also appears in an account of the voyage of Richard Rainolds and Thomas Dassell to Guinea in 1591 in Hakluyt, VII, pp. 90–99.

67 *Before Van Riebeeck: Callers at South Africa from 1488 to 1652*, ed. Raven–Hart, pp. 54, 83; Laughton, 'Saris, John (1580/81–1643)', rev. Trevor Dickie, *Oxford Dictionary of National Biography*.

68 Edward Blitheman to Sir Thomas Smith, 20 February 1615: *Letters Received by the East India Company* ed. Danvers and Foster, II, p. 329.

69 Isaac Kilburne referred to Davies 'not having any [children] of his own' in October 1622: TNA, C2/Jas I/D10/61(Court of Chancery, Davies vs. Kilburne, 15 October 1622). Knutson, 'What's a Guy like John Davies Doing in a Seminar on Theater History?', n.2.

70 LMA, MS 07644, (St Mary Woolchurch Haw, 29 June 1612) The next day Davies

paid £1 2s. 6d. 'for breaking the ground in the middle Ile for Mrs Davis and for the knell and peales' LMA, MS 1013 (St Mary Woolchurch Haw Churchwardens' Accounts, 30 June 1612).

71 Hakluyt, VI, p. 176.

72 BL Lansdowne MS 158, ff. 131–7.

73 Terry, *A voyage to East–India*, pp. 20–21.

74 'Smythe, Sir Thomas (c.1558–1625), of Philpott Lane, London and Bounds Place, Bidborough, Kent', *The History of Parliament*.

75 A third Virginian, named Abraham, was buried at St Dionis Backchurch in 1616. Vaughan, A. T., *Transatlantic Encounters*, pp. 52, 93.

76 *Household Accounts and Disbursement Books of Robert Dudley, Earl of Leicester,* ed. Adams, p. 210, n. 444; TNA, SP 12/262/104 (Declaration of John Hill of Stonehouse, Plymouth 1597); *CSPD*, 1595–1597, p. 381. See also Beer, *Bess: The life of Lady Ralegh,* p. 124; Vaughan, A.T., 'American Indians in England (*act.* c.1500–1615)', *Oxford Dictionary of National Biography*; Vaughan, A.T., *Transatlantic Encounters*, pp. 11–12, 22–24, pp. 30–33, 35. Lee, 'Caliban's Visits to England', pp. 337–9.

77 Von Bulow, 'Journey through England and Scotland Made by Lupold von Wedel in the Years 1584 and 1585', p. 251; Ford, 'Wedel, Lupold von (1544–1615)', *Oxford Dictionary of National Biography*.

78 Sir James Bagg to Edward Nicholas, 18 January 1628, TNA, SP 16/334/50; *CSPD*, 1636–1637, pp. 177–179; Matar *Britain and Barbary*, p. 122.

79 Vaughan, A.T., *Transatlantic Encounters*, p. 11.

80 This was what William Towerson told the Guinea traders who asked after them: Hakluyt, VI, p. 200.

81 Von Bulow, 'Journey through England and Scotland Made by Lupold von Wedel in the Years 1584 and 1585', p. 251. Von Wedel himself acquired an African servant during his stay in England – see his entries for 24 and 28 April 1585 on p. 269.

82 Salmon, 'Thomas Harriot (1560–1621) and the origins of Algonkian Linguistics', p. 149; Vaughan, A.T., *Transatlantic Encounters*, p. 23.

83 Ibid., p.22. Salmon, 'Thomas Harriot (1560–1621) and the origins of Algonkian Linguistics', pp. 151, 145; *Aubrey's Brief Lives*, ed. Barber, p. 126n. The alphabet itself survives in two copies, one at the British Library, (BL Add MS 6782, f. 337) the other in the library at Westminster School. For a reproduction, and analysis of the letters, see Stedall, 'Symbolism, Combinations, and Visual Imagery in the Mathematics of Thomas Harriot', pp. 381-4.

84 *Before Van Riebeeck: Callers at South Africa from 1488 to 1652*, ed. Raven–Hart, p. 99.

85 Knutson, 'A Caliban in St. Mildred Poultry', p. 111.

86 Hakluyt, VI, pp. 218–9.

87 Terry, *A voyage to East–India*, p. 21.

88 *Before Van Riebeeck: Callers at South Africa from 1488 to 1652*, ed. Raven–Hart, p. 64, 66.

89 An account of this voyage was included in Samuel Purchas's 1625 compendium of voyages, but it omitted events prior to the arrival at the Cape of Good Hope

in October 1614. Purchas, *Purchas His Pilgrims*, pp. 524–527; Makepeace, 'Middleton, David (*d.* 1615)', *Oxford Dictionary of National Biography*; Richard Rowe, master of the *Thomas*, to the East India Company, 21 February, 1615: *Letters Received by the East India Company* ed. Danvers and Foster, II, pp. 333–4.

90 Edward Blitheman to Sir Thomas Smith, 20 February 1615: *Letters Received by the East India Company* ed. Danvers and Foster, II, p. 329.

91 Barbot, *A Description of the coasts of North and South-Guinea*, p.132; *Barbot on Guinea*, ed. Hair, Jones and Law, I, pp. 271, 284–5, n. 22.

92 *Barbot on Guinea*, ed. Hair, Jones and Law, I, pp. 266, 268.

93 Edward Blitheman to Sir Thomas Smith, 20 February 1615: *Letters Received by the East India Company* ed. Danvers and Foster, II, p. 329.

94 Hakluyt, VI, p. 217, 225. At this point, George appears to have been left behind in Shama due to a skirmish with the Portuguese.

95 Binne had returned at some point since his absence was noted in January 1557, perhaps even with Towerson himself, who refers to 'our Negro' a little earlier in his account of the 1558 voyage: Hakluyt, VI, pp. 240, 245.

96 The sources disagree about whether Coree's armour was made of copper or brass. *Before Van Riebeeck: Callers at South Africa from 1488 to 1652*, ed. Raven–Hart, pp. 72, 75, 88, 114. L. E. Merians, *Envisioning the Worst: Representations of "Hottentots" in Early–Modern England* (2001), p. 90.

97 Villault, *A relation of the coast of Africa called Guinee*, p. 77. This defunct factory is also referenced in an 'Account of the Limits and Trade of the Royal African Company' amongst the Colonial State Papers in 1672: 'they trade to Cabe Mount and Cestos for elephants' teeth, where there was formerly a factory': *Calendar of State Papers Colonial*, ed. Noel Sainsbury, 1669–1674, pp. 412–3.

98 *Barbot on Guinea*, ed. Hair, Jones and Law, I, p. 273.

99 The Gynney and Bynney Company was a chartered company headed by Lord Rich (Earl of Warwick from 1619), Sir Robert Mansell (Treasurer of the Navy) and Sir Ferdinando Gorges: Kelsey, 'Rich, Robert, second earl of Warwick (1587–1658)', Thrush, 'Mansell, Sir Robert (1570/71–1652)', and Clark, 'Gorges, Sir Ferdinando (1568–1647)', *Oxford Dictionary of National Biography*; Scott, *English, Scottish and Irish Joint-Stock Companies*, II, pp. 11–13; Jobson, *The Discovery of River Gambra (1623)*, ed. Gamble and Hair, Introduction. For Davies' career see: Blake, 'The farm of the Guinea Trade in 1631', pp. 92–3; R. Porter, 'The Crispe Family and the African Trade in the Seventeenth Century', p. 58; Blake, 'The English Guinea Company, 1618–1660', pp. 17, 22; Hair and Law, 'The English in Western Africa', p. 252.

100 Keay, *The Honourable Compan*, p. 15; Hair, 'Africa (other than the Mediterranean and Red Sea lands) and the Atlantic Islands', p. 207.

101 These events were described when the Guinea Company complained to Parliament in 1650 regarding interlopers to the African trade: TNA, CO 1/11, no. 15 (Colonial Papers, 25 May 1650).

102 Blackburn, *The Making of New World Slavery*, pp. 222–229.

103 McFarlane, *The British in the Americas*, p. 49.

104 *Voyages: The Trans-Atlantic Slave Trade Database*.

105 Davies, *Royal African Company*, p. 41.

106 *An answer of the Company of Royal Adventurers of England trading into Africa to the petition . . . exhibited to the Honourable House of Commons by Sir Paul Painter, Ferdinando Gorges, Henry Batson, Benjamin Skutt, and Thomas Knights on the behalf of themselves and others concerned in His Majesties plantations in America* (1667), p. 11; Inikori, *Africans and the Industrial Revolution in England*, p. 220. See also Zook, *Company of Royal Adventurers* and Davies, *Royal African Company*. For a recent account of the Royal Africa Company (which succeeded the Company of Royal Adventurers Trading into Africa in 1672) see William Pettigrew, *Freedom's Debt: The Royal African Company and the Politics of the Atlantic Slave Trade, 1672–1752* (2013).

107 TNA, CO 268/1, ff 5v (Accompt of the Limits & Trade for the African Company, 1672).

Chapter 8

1   John Anthony is described in this way in the two petitions for payment of wages due to him for his service aboard the *Silver Falcon* that he sent to Lord Zouche over the winter of 1619 that form the basis of this chapter. They appear in the State Papers, held at the National Archives: TNA, SP 14/113, ff. 59–60. The summary of these two documents listed as nos. 28 and 29 in *CSPD*, 1619–1623, p. 131 is too brief to do them justice, but have nonetheless formed the basis of the limited scholarly comment on Anthony to date (e.g. Habib, *Black Lives*, p. 221, who mistakenly characterises the petitions as a legal suit). The following item in the Calendar (*CSPD*, 1619–1623, p. 131, no. 30/ TNA, SP 14/113, ff. 61–2) is also pertinent. In this letter, Sir Henry Mainwaring (whose relationship to John Anthony will become clear as this chapter unfolds) mentions to Lord Zouche that 'the black boy' has been paid, with interest.

2   Bolster, *Black Jacks*, p. 9.

3   Burial 23 November 1618: Centre for Kentish Studies, TR2451/6 (St Mary's, Dover). This was likely to be the 'Capt. Ward of Dover' whose funeral was reported by Richard Marsh to Edward Nicholas on 3rd March 1623: *CSPD*, 1619–1623, p. 509, i.e. William Warde, the Mayor of Dover who appears later in this chapter, and who was buried on 1 March 1623 at St James's, Dover: Canterbury Cathedral Archives, U3/26/1/1, p. 33.

4   No comparable names have as yet been found. LMA, MS 09222/1 (St Botolph, Aldgate, 26 November 1623); PROB 11/152 (Will of Sir Thomas Love, 1627). He also sponsored privateering voyages, and had his portrait painted: English School, 'Sir Thomas Love, c. 1571–1627', c. 1620, National Maritime Museum, Greenwich, London.

5   *The Marriage Registers of St. Dunstan's, Stepney*, ed. Colyer-Fergusson, I, p. 78; The Jeronimos appear in the Middlesex Sessions records, when Helen was accused (but exonerated) of theft by the *converso* merchant Francis Pinto in 1616: 'Sessions, 1616: 5 and 6 September', in *County of Middlesex. Calendar To the Sessions Records: New Series, Volume 3, 1615–16*, ed. William Le Hardy (London, 1937), pp. 288–312.

British History Online http://www.british-history.ac.uk/middx-sessions/vol3/ pp288-312 [accessed 2 April 2017]; LMA, MJ/SR/S53, nos. 112, 113 (Middlesex Sessions Roll); LMA: MJ/SR/2/346, 349a (Middlesex Sessions Register); LMA: GDR 2/93 (Gaol Delivery Registers). Once a widow, Helen successfully petitioned the company for financial assistance: BL, IOR, B/8, f. 280. (East India Company Court Minute Book, 26 November 1623); BL, IOR, B/9, f. 78. (Helen Jeronimo's second petition to the East India Company, 18, August 1624); BL, IOR, B/10, f. 102. (Helen Jeronimo's third petition to the East India Company, 7 July 1625). A further example of the Black presence in maritime Stepney is the February 1631 baptism record for: 'James, son of Grace a blackmore servant of Mr Bromfield of Limehouse begotten as she affirmeth by James Diego a Negro late servant to Mr Bromfield born in the house of William Ward of Limehouse mariner', LMA, P93/ DUN/256 (St Dunstan and All Saints, Stepney, 9 February 1631). This Mr. Bromfield was probably Richard Bromfield, a merchant linked to the East India Company through both his daughter Elizabeth's marriage to a Company captain, and his son Robert's apprenticeship to the Company: Habib, *Black Lives*, p. 155; 'East Indies: December 1627', in *Calendar of State Papers Colonial, East Indies, China and Persia, Volume 6, 1625-1629*, ed. W Noel Sainsbury (London, 1884), pp. 428-438. *British History Online* http://www.british-history.ac.uk/cal-state-papers/ colonial/east-indies-china-japan/vol6/pp428-438 [accessed 2 April 2017]; TNA, PROB 11/175/364 (Will of Bence Johnson, Mariner of Limehouse, 21 November 1637).

6   There were 46 English, 5 'Swarts', 15 'Japaners' and 3 'passengers' aboard the Clove when it departed Hirado, Japan on 5 December 1613. Eleven of the Japanese men returned home on the *Expedition* in 1615. *The voyage of Captain John Saris to Japan, 1613*, ed. Satow, p. 183.

7   LMA, MS 017602 (St Dionis Backchurch, 22 December 1616), MS 09659/2 (St Katharine by the Tower, 20 August 1623).

8   Jayasuriya, S. de S., 'South Asia's Africans', *History Workshop Online*, and *The African diaspora in Asian trade routes and cultural memories*.

9   Barbour, 'The *English* Nation at *Bantam*', p. 179.

10 'East Indies, China and Japan: September 1621', in *Calendar of State Papers Colonial, East Indies, China and Japan, Volume 3, 1617-1621*, ed. W. Noel Sainsbury (London, 1870), pp. 450-462. *British History Online* http://www.british-history.ac.uk/ cal-state-papers/colonial/east-indies-china-japan/vol3/pp450-462 [accessed 3 April 2017].

11 Senior, *A Nation of Pirates*, p. 7.

12 *Calendar of State Papers, Venice*, ed. Brown, 1607-10, p. 192.

13 Appleby, 'Jacobean Piracy' in *The Social History of English Seamen*, ed. Fury, pp. 277-299.

14 *The Life and Works of Sir Henry Mainwaring*, ed. G.E. Mainwaring, II, pp. 8-9, 22; 'Mainwaring, Sir Henry (1586/7-1653), of Dover Castle, Kent; later of Camberwell, Surr'., *The History of Parliament*; *The Autobiography of Phineas Pett*, ed. Perrin, p. 96; 'Venice: January 1619, 21-25', in *Calendar of State Papers Relating To English Affairs in the Archives of Venice, Volume 15, 1617-1619*, ed. Allen B.

Hinds (London, 1909), pp. 436–456. *British History Online* http://www.british-history.ac.uk/cal-state-papers/venice/vol15/pp436-456 [accessed 2 April 2017].

15 'James 1 – volume 65: July 1611', in *Calendar of State Papers Domestic: James I, 1611–18*, ed. Mary Anne Everett Green (London, 1858), pp. 51–65. *British History Online* http://www.british-history.ac.uk/cal-state-papers/domestic/jas1/1611-18/pp51-65 [accessed 2 April 2017].

16 Thomas Duffus Hardy, 'Appendix: G. Extracts from Letters relating to English Naval and Military Celebrities', in *Report to the Master of the Rolls On Documents in the Archives of Venice* (London, 1866), pp. 84–86. *British History Online* http://www.british-history.ac.uk/no-series/master-of-rolls-report/pp84-86 [accessed 2 April 2017].

17 'James 1 – volume 113: March 1620', in *Calendar of State Papers Domestic: James I, 1619–23*, ed. Mary Anne Everett Green (London, 1858), pp. 127–135. *British History Online* http://www.british-history.ac.uk/cal-state-papers/domestic/jas1/1619-23/pp127-135 [accessed 2 April 2017].

18 *Voyages: The Trans-Atlantic Slave Trade Database; The Life and Works of Sir Henry Mainwaring*, ed. G.E. Mainwaring, I, p. 42.

19 *Minutes of the Council and General Court of Colonial Virginia*, ed. McIlwaine, p. 33.

20 The figure of 30% (possibly exaggerated) comes from Clifford, *The Black Ship*, p. 165. See also *The Social History of English Seamen*, ed. Fury, p. 292; Earle, *The Pirate Wars*, pp.171–2. See also Bolster, *Black Jacks*; Costello, *Black Salt*; Linebaugh and Reddiker, *The Many Headed Hydra*, pp.165–7; Gates, 'Were There Black Pirates?', *The Root*; Kinkor, 'Black Men under the Black Flag', pp. 195–210.

21 *Newes from Mamora*, tr. William Squire.

22 Earle, *The Pirate Wars*, p. 33; *The Life and Works of Sir Henry Mainwaring*, ed. G.E. Mainwaring, I, p. 21. It is not impossible, given the black presence in Europe, that John Anthony joined Mainwaring in France.

23 Earle, *The Pirate Wars*, p. 29; Tinniswood, *Pirates of Barbary*, p. 71; 'Venice: March 1613', in *Calendar of State Papers Relating To English Affairs in the Archives of Venice, Volume 12, 1610–1613*, ed. Horatio F Brown (London, 1905), pp. 498–516. *British History Online* http://www.british-history.ac.uk/cal-state-papers/venice/vol12/pp498-516 [accessed 3 April 2017].

24 *Calendar of State Papers, Venice*, Brown (ed.) *1613–1615*, p. 509, and n. 3. *The Life and Works of Sir Henry Mainwaring*, ed. G.E. Mainwaring, II, pp. 12, 26; Horwood, *Plunder & Pillage*, p. 39. By Midsummer's Day, Mainwaring may actually mean 4th July which was the midpoint by the Julian calendar (Britain only adopted the Gregorian calendar in the eighteenth century). The Spanish ships are recorded as returning to Lisbon on 8th July.

25 *The Life and Works of Sir Henry Mainwaring*, ed. G.E. Mainwaring, II, p. 42.

26 Jowitt, *The Culture of Piracy*, p. 156; 'Venice: January 1618, 21–31', in *Calendar of State Papers Relating To English Affairs in the Archives of Venice, Volume 15, 1617-1619*, ed. Allen B. Hinds (London, 1909), pp. 108–126. *British History Online* http://www.british-history.ac.uk/cal-state-papers/venice/vol15/pp108-126 [accessed 3 April 2017].

27 Thomas Duffus Hardy, 'Appendix: G. Extracts from Letters relating to English Naval and Military Celebrities', in *Report to the Master of the Rolls On Documents in the Archives of Venice* (London, 1866), pp. 84–86. *British History Online* http://www.british-history.ac.uk/no-series/master-of-rolls-report/pp84-86 [accessed 2 April 2017].

28 The *Seaman's Dictionary* was written in 1623 while Mainwaring was at Dover Castle, though only published in 1644. It formed the basis of the Virginia governor Captain John Smith's popular and repeatedly printed maritime manual, *An Accidence, or the Path-Way to Experience, Necessary for All Young Seamen* (1626), revised and republished as *A Sea Grammar* (1627). Morgan, 'Smith, John (*bap.* 1580, *d.* 1631)', *Oxford Dictionary of National Biography*; Blakemore, 'Orality and Mutiny', p. 257, n. 21. Cruz, N., 'The Seaman's Dictionary: 'This book shall make a man understand', *Royal Museums Greenwich blog*.

29 *The Life and Works of Sir Henry Mainwaring*, ed. G.E. Mainwaring, II, p. 278.

30 Ibid., I, p. 29, II, p. 277.

31 There had been an unsuccessful English expedition against Algiers in 1620–1. The government continued to struggle with the problem of Barbary pirates throughout the 1630s and 1640s. See Matar, *Britain and Barbary*, pp. 45–75.

32 Earle, *The Pirate Wars*, p. 28.

33 *The Life and Works of Sir Henry Mainwaring*, ed. G.E. Mainwaring, II, p. 11, 26.

34 *APC*, 1615–1616, pp. 359–60.

35 Zell, *Early Modern Kent*, p. 151; Worthington, *Proposed Plan for Improving Dover Harbour*, p. 11; Hasted, 'The town and port of Dover', pp. 475–548.

36 Senior, 'An Investigation of the Activities and Importance of English Pirates, 1603–1640', pp. 411–12; *The Westward Enterprise: English Activities in Ireland, the Atlantic and America, 1480–1650*, ed. Andrews, Canny, Hair and Quinn, pp. 132–3; Appleby, 'Thomas Mun's West Indies Venture, 1602–5', pp. 101–110. *The Lives, Apprehensions, Arraignments, and Executions, of the 19. Late Pyrates*, sig. E2r; Weatherford, *Crime and Punishment in the England of Shakespeare and Milton*, pp. 100–1; Depositions relating to this case are to be found in T.N.A., HCA 1/47, ff. 4–5 [William Hill 1 May 1609], f. 56 [William Longcastle], ff. 56–57 [William Tavernor], f. 59 [John Moore, 20 November 1609].

37 Sweet, *Recreating Africa*, pp. 94–5; citing ANTT, Inquisição de Lisboa, Processos, no. 5964.

38 McCaughey, 'Pett, Phineas (1570–1647)', *Oxford Dictionary of National Biography*.

39 Knafla, 'Zouche, Edward la, eleventh Baron Zouche (1556–1625)', *Oxford Dictionary of National Biography*.

40 *The Autobiography of Phineas Pett*, ed. Perrin, pp. 116–7.

41 McCaughey, 'Pett, Phineas (1570–1647)', *Oxford Dictionary of National Biography*. The Naval establishment caught up with Pett, and his associates Sir Robert Mansell and Sir John Trevor, in the course of an official enquiry into embezzlement in the Navy in 1608–9: Rodger, *The Safeguard of the Sea*, pp. 365–8; 'TREVOR, Sir John I (1563–1630), of Oatlands Palace, Surr.; Plas Têg, Flints. and Cannon Row, Westminster', The History of Parliament; *Jacobean Commissions of Enquiry, 1608 and 1618*, ed. McGowan, pp. 260–5.

42 *The Life and Works of Sir Henry Mainwaring*, ed. G.E. Mainwaring, II, p. 42.

43 Giles Milton, *White Gold*, p.303. See also Davis, *Christian Slaves, Muslim Masters.*

44 James I, *A Counterblaste to Tobacco*, sig D2r.

45 Jones and Salmon. 'Tobacco in Colonial Virginia' *Encyclopedia Virginia*; Tilton, 'Rolfe, John (1585–1622)', *Oxford Dictionary of National Biography.*

46 Rolfe, *A True Relation of the state of Virginia Lefte by Sir Thomas Dale Knight in May Last 1616*, p. 37.

47 Their correspondence is one of the main sources for the following account of the adventures of the *Silver Falcon*. It is preserved in the British Library, BL Add MS 37818, ff. 7v–34v (Lord Zouche's letters to Warde, 27 January 1619–1 March 1620); and BL Egerton MS 2584, no. 245, f. 53, no. 255, f. 71v and no. 352, f. 240 (Warde's letters to Lord Zouche, 13 February 1619, 1 March 1619 and 17 December 1619). These letter collections also contain relevant correspondence between the other key figures in this chapter: Jacob Braems's letters to Lord Zouche, 12 Feb 1619 and 31st March 1619 (BL Egerton MS 2584, no. 243, f. 50, and no. 288, f. 133) and Lord Zouche's letters to Mainwaring, 24 February 1620 and 20 March 1620 (BL Add MS 37818, f. 34r–35r). The other source for the following events are the various legal records generated when merchant Jacob Braems ended up in court in the aftermath of the *Silver Falcon*'s voyage of 1619. This account draws on papers in The National Archives from The High Court of Admiralty: TNA, HCA 1/48, ff. 310–311 (Examination of Jacob Braems, 13 May 1620) and the Court of Exchequer: TNA, E 112/88, no. 316 (Jacob Braems's Bill of Complaint and the Answers of John Berry and Thomas Fultnetby, defendants, 1624); TNA, E 134/22Jas1/Mich38 (Interrogatories and Depositions in the case of Jacob Braems vs. John Berry and Thomas Fulnetby, 1624); TNA, E134/10Chas1/Trin6 (John Reston and his wife Susan v Jacob Braems and William Nethersole, 1634).

48 TNA, CO 1/1, no.38 (Project of the intended voyage to Virginia by Captain Andrews and Jacob Braems in the *Silver Falcon*, ? October 1618); 'America and West Indies: October 1618', in *Calendar of State Papers Colonial, America and West Indies: Volume 1, 1574–1660*, ed. W. Noel Sainsbury (London, 1860), pp. 19-20. *British History Online* http://www.british-history.ac.uk/cal-state-papers/colonial/america-west-indies/vol1/pp19-20 [accessed 4 April 2017].

49 Billings, W. M., & the *Dictionary of Virginia Biography*, 'Thomas West, twelfth baron De La Warr (1576–1618)', *Encyclopedia Virginia.*

50 Collins and Brydges, *Collins's Peerage of England*, V, 23. Camden, *Annals of King James I*, p. 32; *Calendar of State Papers Colonial*, ed. Noel Sainsbury, *1574–1660*, pp. 19–20.

51 Lord De la Warr's covenant to Lord Zouche for his adventure to Virginia, 27 December 1617: *Calendar of State Papers Colonial*, ed. W. Noel Sainsbury, *1574–1660*, p. 18.

52 Price, *The Vitamin Complex*, pp. 3–4; Bown, *Scurvy*, pp. 3, 5, 34.

53 In 1624, Daniel Braems of London, aged 43, estimated his cousin Jacob Braems had spent more than £700 on fitting out the ship. Braems himself claimed he adventured £1700 and said the ship 'did wholly or for the most part belong' to him.

54 *The visitation of Kent*, ed. Hovenden, pp. 215–6. In November 1624, Braems: TNA, E112/88/316.

55 Hariot, *A briefe and true report of the new found land of Virginia of the commodities and of the nature and manners of the naturall inhabitants*, p. 9.

56 See n.48 above.

57 Fenner adventured £115: TNA, E 44/353. (Covenant between John Fenner, Henry Bacon and Jacob Braems concerning a voyage to Virginia and north–west and south parts of America for trade, discovery and plantation, 22 February 1619).

58 TNA, CO 1/1, no 44 Warrant by Lord Zouche for John Fenner, Captain of the *Silver Falcon*, and Henry Bacon, master, to pass to Virginia, 15 February 1619. The ship then took two weeks to get as far as Dartmouth, where she spent at least seven days, finally heading into the Atlantic by the end of March, as Jacob Braems reported to Lord Zouche in a letter of 31 March 1619.

59 Bernhard, *A Tale of Two Colonies*, pp. 40, 166, 109–110, 186.

60 Berlin, *Many Thousands Gone*, p. 29; Sluiter, 'New Light on the "20 and Odd Negroes" Arriving in Virginia, August 1619', pp. 396–398; Thornton, 'The African Experience of the "20 and Odd Negroes" Arriving in Virginia in 1619', pp. 421–434.

61 He may have come from England. Thornton and Heywood, *Central Africans, Atlantic Creoles and the Foundation of the Americas*, p. 320.

62 Breen and Innes, '*Myne Owne Ground*'.

63 Higginbotham, *In the Matter of Color*, pp. 32–40.

64 *Minutes of the Council and General Court of Colonial Virginia*, ed. McIlwaine, p. 33. See Chapter 6, p. 176, n. 87.

65 Thornton and Heywood, *Central Africans, Atlantic Creoles and the Foundation of the Americas*, p. 320.

66 Coldham, *The Complete Book of Emigrants, 1607–1660*, pp. 62, 67. This 'Antonio' was actually Anthony Johnson, Breen and Innes, *Myne Owne Ground*, p. 8. These Africans could also have joined ship en route, in the same way that Angelo came to be on board the *Treasurer*.

67 The average voyage to Virginia took 11.5 weeks, with a range from 7–25 weeks, with the return voyage being 6.5 weeks ranging from 4.5–9 weeks: Steele, 'Empire of Migrants and Consumers', p. 498.

68 This was Jacob Braems's version of events, as reported to the High Court of Admiralty.

69 *A Voyage to Virginia in 1609*, ed. Wright, pp. vii, xv.

70 Morgan, P. D., 'British Encounters with Africans and African Americans', p. 169; Bernhard, 'Beyond the Chesapeake', pp. 547, 554.

71 Bernhard, *A Tale of Two Colonies*, pp. 160–1, 181; Kingsbury, *The Records of the Virginia Company of London*, I. Kingsbury (ed.) p. 367.

72 Personal correspondence with Dr. Richard Blakemore, University of Reading.

73 According to Thomas Fulnetby and John Berry. Appleby, *Women and English Piracy*, pp. 51–86 shows how pirates were able to sell their plunder in England in spite of the authorities, often with the help of female receivers.

74 Braemes, Arnold (1602–81), of Bridge, Kent', *The History of Parliament*.

75 Thomas Lawley, by then 'of London' gave evidence to the Exchequer aged 36 in

1624. 'Lawley, Thomas (1580/3–1646), of London; Twickenham, Mdx. and Spoonhill, Much Wenlock, Salop; formerly of Middelburg, Zeeland and Delft, Holland', *The History of Parliament*.

76 Daniel Braems later said he saw this tobacco stored in the cellar of Lord Zouche's house in Hackney.

77 See n. 47 above.

78 TNA, SP 14/110, f. 104 (Braems served notice to appear before Lord Zouche on 23 September, 17 September 1619); 'James 1 – volume 110: September 1619', in *Calendar of State Papers Domestic: James I, 1619–23*, ed. Mary Anne Everett Green (London, 1858), pp. 74–82. *British History Online* http://www.british-history.ac.uk/cal-state-papers/domestic/jas1/1619-23/pp74-82 [accessed 2 April 2017].

79 The friend was one Mr Broadreaux.

80 'Breeches (ensemble)', 1600–1700, Museum of London, ID no: 53.101/1b: http://collections.museumoflondon.org.uk/online/object/83032.html; *Elizabeth I and her People*, ed. Cooper, item 84, pp. 202–3; Cunnington and Lucas, *Occupational Clothing in England*, pp. 55–58.

81 Blakemore, 'Pieces of eight, pieces of eight: seamen's earnings and the venture economy of early modern seafaring', pp. 1–32.

82 For example, Vincent Lovet, groom, petitioned Lord Buckingham in March 1628 for 13l. 6s. he was owed after the last expedition to Cadiz, in which voyage he 'received many wounds' . . . Sir Thomas Love (who had an African servant – see p. 218, n. 4 above) 'in his life always put him off, saying he had no money of the King's in his hands': *CSPD, 1628–29*, p. 51. For examples from the High Court of Admiralty see Steckley, 'Litigious Mariners: Wage Cases in The Seventeenth-Century Admiralty Court', pp. 315–345.

83 See cases of Grebby and Claybrook (1561–2) and Leache (1564–5) in Hair and Alsop, *English Seamen and Traders in Guinea, 1553–1565*, pp. 116, 298, 323.

84 Harris, 'Mainwaring, Sir Henry (1586/7–1653)', *Oxford Dictionary of National Biography*.

85 'Extracts from the Accounts of the Burgh of Aberdeen', in *The Miscellany of the Spalding Club*, ed. Stuart, V, pp. 79, 85.

86 Sim, *Masters and Servants in Tudor England*, pp. 44–45; Kaufmann, 'Africans in Britain', pp. 189–201; *The Accounts of the Lord High Treasurer of Scotland*, ed. Dickson, Balfour Paul, McInnes *et al.*, XII, 97, 18, Laing, 'Notice Respecting the Monument of the Regent Earl of Murray, Now Restored, within the Church of St. Giles, Edinburgh', pp. 52–53; The 6s payment was made at Theobalds in Hertfordshire, formerly a Cecil house, but by 1622 a favourite residence of James I: Cecil Papers, Box F/8, Cash Book 1622, f. 18r; *Calendar of the Manuscripts of the Most Honourable the Marquess of Salisbury*, ed. Dyfnallt Owen, XXII, 166; Daniel Lysons, 'Theobalds', in *The Environs of London: Volume 4, Counties of Herts, Essex and Kent* (London, 1796), pp. 29–39. *British History Online* http://www.british-history.ac.uk/london-environs/vol4/pp29-39 [accessed 2 April 2017].

87 Blakemore, 'Pieces of eight, pieces of eight: seamen's earnings and the venture economy of early modern seafaring', pp. 1–32.

88 TNA, PROB 11/257/248 (Will of John Anthony, Shipwright of Dover, Kent, 16

July 1656). This man's family can be traced in the parish records of St Mary's Dover. On 4 December 1628, a John Anthony married Sybil Sparks, widow of Giles. He is described in their marriage licence as being a 'ship carpenter, a bachelor of the age of 24 years or thereabout'. She died and was buried on 5 May 1629. Soon afterwards, on 5 April 1630, John Anthony married Elizabeth Hazelwood. They had two sons and two daughters. Richard, the eldest, was born in May 1634. John arrived in February 1636, but died the following year. Martha was born in April 1638 and Sarah in September 1640. There is also a baptism record, of a 'John Anthony, son of John Anthony' on 20 January 1620. As none of these records include an ethnic descriptor, and John Anthony is not an uncommon name it's impossible to tie them definitively to the African sailor aboard the *Silver Falcon*. Canterbury Cathedral Archives, CCA-U3-30 (St Mary, Dover Parish Registers); CCA-DCb-L/R/vol 11, f. 223v (Register of General Licences, 1625–1629). Strangely, a man described as 'John Anthony of Inde, musician and moor' was bound for Helen Jeronimo to appear before the Middlesex Sessions in 1616; see n. 5 above.

Chapter 9

1 Fryer, *Staying Power*, p. 8, Sherwood, 'Blacks in Tudor England' p. 41; Scobie, *Black Britannia*, pp. 5–8; Habib, *Shakespeare and Race*, pp. 13, 30–31. See also Kaufmann, M., 'Time Traveller's Guide to Africans in Elizabethan England', http://www.miranda-kaufmann.com, which engages Ian Mortimer in debate over the proposition on his BBC2 programme *Time Traveller's Guide to Elizabethan England*, Episode 3: 'Brave New World', broadcast 14 June 2013, that 'rich men are lending out their black female servants to friends and neighbours for sexual novelty and experimentation'.

2 G.B. Harrison, *Shakespeare at Work* (1933), p. 310.

3 The details of Anne Cobbie's life and circumstances of her employment in the Bankes's bawdy house in this chapter are largely drawn from the case brought against the Bankes by Clement Edwards and Mary Hall at the Westminster Quarter Sessions in 1625–1626. The relevant documents are held at the London Metropolitan Archives and comprise: LMA, WJ/SR/NS/15/104 (Clement Edwards's indictment, Westminster Sessions Roll, 24 June 1625); WJ/SR/NS/15/24 (Solomon Carr, surgeon and Richard Watmough, cordwainer, of St Clements Danes bound for John and Jane Bankes to appear at the next Sessions, 10 February 1626); WJ/SR/NS/15/26 (John Bankes and Solomon Carr bound for Anne Edwards to appear at the next Sessions, 16 February 1626); WJ/SR/NS/15/130 (The Information of Mary Hall against John Bankes and Jane his wife for keeping a bawdy house, Westminster Sessions Roll, 23 February 1626): printed, with a commentary by Martin Ingram in *Reading Early Modern Women*, ed. Ostovich and Sauer, pp. 40–41; WJ/SR/NS/15/71(John Little, butcher, Peter Johnson, bricklayer, both of St Clements Danes and James Wright of St Martins in the Fields, gentleman, bound for Mary Hall to appear, 27 February 1626); WJ/SR/NS/15/76 (Clement Edwards and Francis Heath of London, draper, to give evidence against John and Jane Bankes, and Anne Edwards, 16 February 1626); WJ/SR/NS/16/120 (John Bankes, Thomas Caulfield of St Martin in the Fields, gentleman, and Peter Collier of London, cook, bound

for Jane Bankes to appear, 2 June 1626); WJ/SR/NS/16/121 (John Bankes and John Fuller of London gentleman, and Brian Buckley of Westminster, gentleman, bound for John Bankes to appear, 2 June 1626); WJ/SR/NS/16/41(Clement Edwards to appear to prosecute Mr and Mrs Bankes, 4 June 1626); WJ/SR/NS/16/153. (Mrs and Mrs Bankes appear on list of prisoners in the Gatehouse, 23 June 1626); WJ/SR/NS/17/56 (John and Jane Bankes, Peter Collier of St Dunstan in the West, cook, Brandon Buckley, of St Margaret's, Westminster, gentleman and William Smith of Hampstead Norris, Berks, yeoman bound for the Bankes to appear to prosecute a traverse on the indictment against them 11 July 1626).

4   In the eighteenth century, a sample of prostitutes working around the Strand were found to be aged 15–22, with a median age of 18: Stone, *The Family, Sex and Marriage in England*, p. 618.

5   The Oxford English Dictionary, 'tawny–moor, n'., *OED Online*.

6   *The Right Plesaunt and Goodly Historie of the Foure Sonnes of Aymon*, tr. Caxton, p. 565.

7   Thomas, *Principal Rvles of the Italian Grammer*, X2r.

8   Shakespeare, *Othello*, Act 1, Scene 2; *Titus Andronicus*, Act 4, Scene 2.

9   Schlueter, 'Rereading the Peacham Drawing', pp. 171–184.

10   This is Eldred Jones' conclusion in his 'Racial Terms for Africans in Elizabethan Usage', p. 85. See also Chandler, 'The Moor: Light of Europe's Dark Age', pp. 144–175. G.K. Hunter concluded in 1967 that the term 'Moor' had 'no clear racial status': Hunter, 'Othello and Colour Prejudice', p. 147.

11   Shakespeare, *The Merchant of Venice*, Act 2, Scene 1; *Antony and Cleopatra*, Act 1, Scene 1.

12   Leo Africanus, *The History and Description of Africa*, trans. Pory, I, p. 205, n.13.

13   Boling, 'Anglo–Welsh relations in Cymbeline', p.52; Owen, *Description of Pembrokeshire*, p. 46.

14   Hanks, Coates, and McClure, 'Cobby', *The Oxford Dictionary of Family Names in Britain and Ireland*, I, p. 533.

15   The eighteenth century survey of girls arrested in the streets around the Strand found the median age of first becoming a prostitute was 16½ while seven of the girls had begun at 14 or less: Stone, *The Family, Sex and Marriage in England*, p. 618.

16   Sugden, *A Topographical Dictionary to the Works of Shakespeare and his Fellow Dramatists*, p. 489. The poet was Joshua Sylvester, his surname giving rise to the epithet 'silver-tongued'. 'Sylvester, Joshua (1562/3–1618)', *Oxford Dictionary of National Biography*.

17   Merritt, *The social world of early modern Westminster*, p. 182.

18   Shugg, 'Prostitution in Shakespeare's London', p. 295; Sugden, *A Topographical Dictionary to the Works of Shakespeare and his Fellow Dramatists*, pp. 58, 488. Ben Jonson uses these terms in Bartholomew Fair, Act 2, Scene 6, and in his 'An Epistle to Sir Edward Sackville, now Earl of Dorset'.

19   Merritt, *The social world of early modern Westminster*, pp. 168, 225.

20   Shugg, 'Prostitution in Shakespeare's London', n. 33; Sugden, *A Topographical Dictionary to the Works of Shakespeare and his Fellow Dramatists*, p. 124.

21 Taylor, 'A Whore', in *All the Works of John Taylor the Water Poet*, p. 110; Shugg, 'Prostitution in Shakespeare's London', pp. 294; *Sermons by Hugh Latimer*, ed. Corrie, 133–34.

22 Archer, *The Pursuit of Stability*, p. 215; Nashe, *Christ's Tears Over Jerusalem*, p. 141; BCB, III, f. 318.

23 Westminster Archives, St Martin-in-the-Fields, vol.1 (27 Sept 1571).

24 For Fortunatus, see Chapter 4, p. 116, n. 31 and Chapter 7, p. 184, and footnote. *Issues of the Exchequer: Being Payments Made Out of His Majesty's Revenue*, ed. Devon, p. 98; 'Stallenge, William (b.c.1545), of Plymouth, Devon', *The History of Parliament*.

25 City of Westminster Archives Centre, St Martin's in the Fields Parish Registers, vol. 2 (8 February 1621).

26 Asch, 'Porter, Endymion (1587–1649)', *Oxford Dictionary of National Biography*. Neither of his recorded trips to Spain (in 1612 and 1622–3) fits perfectly with the timing of Maria's baptism. She was only born in 1616, so could not be a product of the first trip, and was already in London by the time Porter went back to Spain in 1622. So either he went there at another, unrecorded time, or one of his agents or contacts may have brought Maria to London on his behalf.

27 TNA, SP 14/148/99 (John Chamberlain to Dudley Carleton, 12 July 1623); *The Letters of John Chamberlain*, ed. McClure, II, pp. 506–7; *CSPD*, 1623–1625, p. 13.

28 DiMeo, 'Howard, Aletheia, countess of Arundel, of Surrey, and of Norfolk, and suo jure Baroness Furnivall, Baroness Talbot, and Baroness Strange of Blackmere (d. 1654)', *Oxford Dictionary of National Biography*; Howarth, 'The Patronage and Collecting of Aletheia, countess of Arundel, 1606–54', p. 130.

29 David Howarth has suggested that the 'blackamore' who came to London was the individual depicted in Van Dyck's *Portrait of George Gage with Two Attendants and The Continence of Scipio*. However, the word '*massara*' is the feminine form of '*massaro*', an Italian word meaning servant, so Lady Arundel's black servant was a woman, and therefore unrelated to the man depicted by Van Dyck. Howarth, *Lord Arundel and his Circle*, pp. 158, 196, 242. Anthony Van Dyck, 'Portrait of George Gage with Two Attendants', 1622–3, The National Gallery, London and 'The Continence of Scipio', 1620–1, Christ Church Picture Gallery, Oxford.

30 Griffiths, 'The structure of prostitution in Elizabethan London', pp. 49–50; Newman, *Cultural Capitals*, p. 137. Salkeld, *Shakespeare amongst the Courtesans*, pp. 164–5.

31 'An Act for The Reformation of Divers Abuses', in Stow, *The survey of London* (1633), p. 681.

32 BCB, V, f. 26v.

33 Varholy, 'Rich Like A Lady', p. 10.

34 Shakespeare, *Hamlet*, Act 3, Scene 2.

35 BCB, IV, ff. 352r, 373r; Salkeld, *Shakespeare amongst the Courtesans*, pp. 64, 139; LMA, WJ/SR/NS/18/73 (Westminster Sessions Roll, 5 June 1627).

36 Griffiths, 'The structure of prostitution in Elizabethan London' p. 51, Griffiths, *Lost Londons*, pp. 149–30; Newman, *Cultural Capitals*, p. 140. LMA, MJ/SR/0510/33 (Middlesex Sessions Roll: Sessions of the Peace and Gaol Delivery, March 1612).

37 Griffiths, 'The structure of prostitution in Elizabethan London' p. 44; BCB, III, f. 121r.

38 Newman, *Cultural Capitals*, p. 136. Archer, *The Pursuit of Stability*, p. 213.

39 Griffiths, 'The structure of prostitution in Elizabethan London', p. 46.

40 Nashe, *Christ's Tears Over Jerusalem*, pp. 141–2; Browner, 'Wrong Side of the River', *Essays in History*; Shugg, 'Prostitution in Shakespeare's London', p. 301. The average fee in Elizabethan England was 4s 3d: Griffiths, 'The structure of prostitution in Elizabethan London', p. 47.

41 Dekker, *The Honest Whore, Part II*, Act 5, Scene 2.

42 Griffiths, 'The structure of prostitution in Elizabethan London', p. 47. n. 67; BCB V, f. 378r.

43 Newman, *Cultural Capitals*, pp. 140–142. Varholy, 'Rich Like a Lady', pp. 11, 16: Cranley, *Amanda: or the Reformed Whore*, p. 35.

44 Griffiths, 'The structure of prostitution in Elizabethan London', p. 45; Archer, *The Pursuit of Stability*, p. 213; BCB, III, ff. 279–81.

45 The other church frequented by the gentry was St Martins in the Fields. Merritt, *The social world of early modern Westminster*, pp. 145, 147, 151,195.

46 Dekker and Webster, *Westward Ho!*, Act 4, Scene 1.

47 Griffiths, 'The structure of prostitution in Elizabethan London', p. 55.

48 Stone, *The Family, Sex and Marriage in England*, p. 616; Archer, *The Pursuit of Stability*, p. 215.

49 *A Pepysian Garland*, ed. Rollins, p. 41.

50 Nashe, *Christ's Tears Over Jerusalem*, p. 141; Griffiths, *Youth and Authority*, pp. 220–221.

51 BCB, III, ff. 218r (15 May 1577), 261v (16 December 1577), 277r– 277v (15 January 1578); Griffiths, *Lost Londons*, p. 74, n. 25; D. Salkeld, *Shakespeare amongst the Courtesans*, pp. 106, 131. Habib (*Black Lives*, p. 109), insists that Rose Brown may also have been an African, due to her surname.

52 Newman, *Cultural Capitals*, pp. 139, 145.

53 By the Restoration failed erection had become a conventional topos in erotic verse, with poems such as the Earl of Rochester's 'The Imperfect Enjoyment' and Aphra Behn's 'The Disappointment', following the classical example set by, for example, Ovid's *Amores* 3.7: Frick, 'Sexual and Political Impotence in Imperfect Enjoyment Poetry', *Portals*.

54 Nashe, *The Choice of Valentines*, lines 130–227, 257–259.

55 Lowe, *An easie, certaine, and perfect method, to cure and prevent the Spanish sickness*, sig. B2v; Dingwall, 'Lowe, Peter (*c*.1550–1610)', *Oxford Dictionary of National Biography*.

56 Brome, *The English Moor*, Act 3, Scene 3.

57 Hall, *Things of Darkness*, p.22. It seems unlikely that the character of Hermia was literally meant to be from Ethiopia. McCullough, *The Negro in English Literature*, p.24, concludes: 'certainly . . . Hermia was not as black as the raven nor as dark as an Ethiope, yet she obviously was of a darker hue than the others'.

58 Jonson, *The Characters of Two Royall Masques: The One of Blacknesse, The Other of Beautie* (1608).

59 Hall, *Things of Darkness*, p.205. For further examples, see Shakespeare, *Love's Labour's Lost*, IV, iii, 114–5, *Two Gentlemen Of Verona*, II, vi, 25–6.

60 Jonson, 'Masque of Blackness', in *Court Masques: Jacobean and Caroline Entertainments*, ed. Lindley, p. 4.

61 Hall, *Things of Darkness*, pp. 206–10.

62 Shakespeare, Sonnets 127 and 144. Crewe, *Trials of Authorship*, p. 120; De Grazia, 'The Scandal of Shakespeare's Sonnets', pp. 89–112; Hall, 'These bastard signs of fair', pp. 64–83; Hunt, 'Be dark but not too dark: Shakespeare's dark lady as a sign of color', pp. 369–91.

63 Other examples include: John Collop, 'On an Ethiopian Beauty, M.S.' (1656); Walton Poole, 'To a Black Gentlewoman: Mistress A.H.' (1656); Abraham Wright, 'On a Black Gentlewoman' (1656); Eldred Revett's One Enamour'd on a Black-Moor (1657); Edward Herbert, "Sonnet of Black Beauty" (1665). These and related poems are all printed in Hall, *Things of Darkness*, 269–290. For a broader context, see *An Anthology of Interracial Literature*, ed. Sollors.

64 Shakespeare, *Antony and Cleopatra*, Act 2, Scene 2; Anonymous, *Lust's Dominion*, Act 3, Scene 1; Beaumont and Fletcher, *The Knight of Malta*, Act 1, Scene 1.

65 Dekker, *The Honest Whore, Part II*, Act 5, Scene 2.

66 The Lord Chamberlain at this time was Thomas Howard, Earl of Suffolk. Shugg, 'Prostitution in Shakespeare's London', p. 305; 'Poor and vagrants', in *Analytical Index to the Series of Records Known as the Remembrancia 1579-1664*, ed. W. H. Overall and H. C. Overall (London, 1878), pp. 357–364. *British History Online* http://www.british-history.ac.uk/no-series/index-remembrancia/1579-1664/ pp357-364 [accessed 1 April 2017].

67 Griffiths, *Lost Londons*, pp. 11–13; Merritt, *The social world of early modern Westminster*, p. 8.

68 *A Pepysian garland*, ed. Rollins, pp. 40–43.

69 Massinger, *The City Madam*, Act 5, Scene 1.

70 *Female Transgression in Early Modern Britain*, ed. Ruberry–Blanc and Hillman, p. 81. Porter, 'Lupton, Donald (d. 1676)', *Oxford Dictionary of National Biography*.

71 Nashe, *Christ's Tears Over Jerusalem*, pp. 144–145.

72 LMA, WJ/SR/NS/13, no. 18 (Daniel Powell accuses Jane Bankes of 'misdemeanours', Westminster Sessions Roll, 22 March 1624).

73 Samuel Rowlands, *Greene's Ghost Hunting Coney Catchers* (1602), cited in Fabricius, *Syphilis in Shakespeare's England*, p.117.

74 Clement Edwards graduated from Corpus Christi, Cambridge, and was ordained as a deacon on 23rd May 1619 by Bishop Thomas Dove at Peterborough Cathedral. He was Rector of Witherley in Leicestershire from April 1619 until June 1622: Clergy of the Church of England Database, Person ID: 139450.

75 This was during the Trinity session. The Westminster Sessions were held quarterly (at Epiphany, Easter, Trinity and Michaelmas) in Westminster Hall. Merritt, *The social world of early modern Westminster*, p. 8.

76 William Camden, *Britannia* (1586), cited in Fabricius, *Syphilis in Shakespeare's England*, p. 81.

77 The indictment is in Latin. This translation is from an unpublished finding aid at the LMA.

78 'Preachers and preaching', in *Analytical Index to the Series of Records Known as*

the Remembrancia 1579–1664, ed. W. H. Overall and H. C. Overall (London, 1878), pp. 364–369. *British History Online* http://www.british-history.ac.uk/no-series/index-remembrancia/1579-1664/pp364-369 [accessed 28 March 2017].

79 'Heywood, Peter (d.1642), of King Street East, Westminster', *The History of Parliament*; Merritt, *The social world of early modern Westminster*, pp. 334, 350.

80 There is no record of what was said, but we know that the Grand Jury thought there was enough evidence to commit the case for trial at the next Quarter Session because the court clerk wrote 'a bill of vera' on the back of the indictment.

81 Lovelace, 'To Althea, from Prison', (1649).

82 LMA, WJ/SR/NS/17/127 (List of Prisoners in the Gatehouse, 3 October 1626).

83 Creighton, *A History of Epidemics*, I, p. 429, and p. 424, citing William Clowes, *A short and profitable Treatise touching the cure of the disease called Morbus Gallicus by unctions* (1579).

84 Richard Ames, *The Female Fire–Ships. A Satyr Against Whoring* (1691), p. 14.

85 Sydenham, *A New Method of Curing the French–Pox* (1690), p. 20.

86 *Aubrey's Brief Lives*, ed. Dick, (1957), p. 86; Edmond, 'Davenant, Sir William (1606–1668)', *Oxford Dictionary of National Biography*. For further discussion of the woman's ethnicity, see Habib, *Black Lives* pp. 157–9 and Kaufmann, 'Africans in Britain', pp. 187–188.

87 Shugg, 'Prostitution in Shakespeare's London', pp. 302–3. William Clowes recommended stewed prunes in his 'Treatise on Lues Venerea' included in his *A profitable and necessarie booke of obseruations.* (1596).

88 O'Connell, *The Book of Spice*, p. 124.

89 Haynes, *Sex in Elizabethan England*, p. 187.

90 *Sins of the Flesh*, ed. Siena, p. 41.

91 Taylor, 'A Whore', in *All the Works of John Taylor the Water Poet*, p. 112.

92 Nashe, *Christ's Tears Over Jerusalem*, p. 142.

93 Fabricius, *Syphilis in Shakespeare's England*, pp. 136–7.

94 Siena, *Venereal Disease, Hospitals and the Urban Poor*, pp. 62–67.

95 City of Westminster Archives Centre, St Mary Le Strand Parish Registers, vol. 1 (3 July 1626).

96 Galen, *Galen on the Usefulness of the Parts of the Body*, tr. Tallmadge May, II, 633. Samuel Purchas reported that some, including Herodotus, attributed dark skin to the 'blacknesse of the Parents sperme or seed': Purchas, *Purchas his Pilgrimage* (1613), p. 545.

97 Dorset Record Office, PE/SH: RE 1/1 (Sherborne Abbey, Sherborne, 15 January 1631).

98 Adair, *Courtship, Illegitimacy and Marriage in Early Modern England*, p. 50; McFarlane, 'Illegitimacy and Illegitimates in English History', pp. 73–4.

99 Dorset Record Office, Mayors Accounts (town and County of Poole) 1609–10, MA 10, transcript, 15. For further examples and discussion see Kaufmann '"Making the beast with two backs" – Interracial relationships in Early Modern England', pp. 22–37.

100 Dabhoiwala, *The Origins of Sex*, p. 13; Ridley, *John Knox*, p. 417; Ingram, *Church Courts, Sex and Marriage in England*, p. 238; Capp, *England's Culture Wars*, p. 134.

101 Essex Record Office, D/AEA 16, ff. 162v, 196. (Archdeacon of Essex, Act Books, 17 February 1593, 24 March 1593); Emmison, *Elizabethan Life: Morals and the Church Courts*, p. 19; West Sussex Record Office, Ep.I/17/8, ff. 139r, 140r (Diocese of Chichester Detection Books, 15 December 1593 and 19 January 1594); in April 1632 'Grace, a blackamoore' was accused by Stepney churchwardens of 'living incontinently' with Walter Church: LMA, MS 09065E/1 f. 81(London Commissary Court '*Ex Officio*' Book).

102 Personal correspondence with Peter Bluck, Jetto's nine times great-grandson. See Chapter 4, p. 126, n. 50.

103 Personal correspondence with one of Adam Ivey's descendants, Clem Lee Canipe III of Kinston, North Carolina.

104 King, Parkin, Swinfield, *et. al.*, 'Africans in Yorkshire?', pp. 288–293; Redmonds, King, and Hey, *Surnames, DNA, and Family History*, pp. 200–4.

105 Shakespeare, W. *Measure for Measure*, Act 3, Scene 2; Cranley, *Amanda: or the Reformed Whore*, p. 33.

106 Griffiths, 'The structure of prostitution in Elizabethan London', p. 52.

107 City of Westminster Archives Centre, St Clements Danes Parish Registers, vol.1 (11 June 1626); LMA, CLC/L/HA/C/007/MS15857/001, f. 209 (Worshipful Company of Haberdashers, Register of Freedom Admissions, 1629).

108 William Hogarth, 'A Rake's Progress, 3: The Orgy', 1733 painting, Sir John Soane's Museum, London, and 1735 print, plate 3; Dabydeen, *Hogarth's Blacks*, pp. 96–97 and Fig. 62, p. 92; Thomas Rowlandson, 'Sea Stores', 1812, Royal Collection.

109 M. Kaufmann, '"Making the beast with two backs" – Interracial relationships in Early Modern England', pp. 29–31.

110 *Gesta Grayorum*, ed. Bland, p. 17.

111 Archer, *The Pursuit of Stability*, p. 213; Salkeld, 'Black Luce and the "Curtizans" of Shakespeare's London' p. 5, Hotson, *Mr. W.H.*, p. 252.

112 TNA, SP 12/270/119 (Denis Edwards to Thomas Lankford, 28 May 1599); *CSPD*, 1598–1601, p. 199.

113 Sugden, *A Topographical Dictionary to the Works of Shakespeare and his Fellow Dramatists*, p. 533.

114 Shakespeare, *Henry IV Part 2*, Act 3, Scene 2. III.

115 Gowing, 'Language, power and the law: women's slander litigation in early modern London', p. 30.

Chapter 10

1 This is the conclusion drawn by Habib, *Black Lives*, p. 116.

2 I first came across Cattelena in Dresser, *Slavery Obscured*, p. 11. She was also mentioned in Jones and Youseph, *The Black Population of Bristol in the Eighteenth Century*, p. 2; Linebaugh and Redikker, *The Many Headed Hydra*, p. 78 mistakenly refer to Cattelena as the first African recorded in Bristol.

3 Thomas Gray, *An Elegy Wrote in a Country Churchyard* (1751), p. 6.

4 *When Death Do Us Part*, ed. Arkell, Evans and Goose, p. 72.

5   Bristol Record Office, FCI/1620-1632/19, frames 1–2 (Probate Inventory of Cattelena of Almondsbury, 24 May 1625).

6   Froide, *Never Married*, p. 3.

7   Martyr de Anghiera, *The Decades of the New World*, tr. R. Eden, f. 355.

8   Bristol Record Office, FCP/Xch/R/1(a)4 (Christ Church, 4 January 1612). See also Kaufmann, 'Africans in Britain', p. 65 and Appendix, 1: Baptism Records and 2: Burial Records.

9   Kelly, 'Ealhmund (784)', *Oxford Dictionary of National Biography*; Britton and Brayley, *The beauties of England and Wales*, (1810), V, 728–9; 'Almondsbury', *Open Domesday*, http://opendomesday.org/place/ST6084/almondsbury/; Walker, *The Book of Almondsbury*, p. 14.

10 Smyth, *A description of the hundred of Berkeley*, in *The Berkeley manuscripts*, ed. Maclean, III, p. 54; 'Smith (Smyth), John (1567–1641), of Warrens Court, North Nibley, Glos.', *The History of Parliament*; Warmington, 'Smyth, John (1567–1641)', *Oxford Dictionary of National Biography*.

11 Walker, *The Book of Almondsbury*, p. 37.

12 Wells, 'Baker [*née* Willcocks], Mary [*alias* Princess Caraboo] (*bap.* 1791, *d.* 1864)', *Oxford Dictionary of National Biography*. See also Catherine Johnson's 2015 novel, *The Curious Tale of the Lady Caraboo*.

13 Northamptonshire Record Office, Microfiche 120p/3 (St Nicholas, Eydon, 16 December 1545).

14 County Record Office, Huntingdon: HP5/1/1 (St Mary's, Bluntisham-cum-Earith, 16 December 1594); Mayo, 'Parish Register of Stowell, Somerset', p. 6 (St Mary Magdalene, Stowell, 12 May 1605); Suffolk Record Office, FC 61/D1/1 (St Peter's, Sibton, 25 December 1634). See also Kaufmann, 'Africans in Britain', Appendix, 1: Baptism Records and 2: Burial Records.

15 Bristol Record Office, FCP/Dy/R/1(a)1 (St Peter, Dyrham, baptisms: 28 October 1578, 25 February 1581, burial: 9 June 1583). Ivie himself was baptised in the same parish on 15 August 1575 – see Chapter 7, p. 179, n. 100 and Chapter 9, p. 264, n. 116.

16 Cornwall Record Office, P99/1/1(St Keverne, Cornwall, 14 January 1605).

17 Dresser, *Slavery Obscured*, p. 11; TNA, STAC 5/S14/26 (Court of Star Chamber, Hugh Smyth v Sir John Younge, Sir George Norton *et. al.*, Interrogatory 3, and testimony of Anne White, 11th April 1580).

18 These were in the parishes of St Philip and St Jacob (3), St Augustine the Less (3), Temple (2), St John the Baptist (2), and one each in St Nicholas, St Stephen and Christ Church. See n.19 below; Dresser, *Slavery Obscured*, p. 11 and Kaufmann, 'Africans in Britain', Appendix, 1: Baptism Records and 2: Burial Records for further details.

19 Bristol Record Office: FCP/StP+J/R/1(a)2 (St Philip and St Jacob, 18 August 1600); FCP/StP+J/R/1(a)4 (St Philip and St Jacob, 14 December 1600); FCP/Xch/R/1(a)4 (Christ Church, 4 January 1612); FCP/St.Aug/R/1(a)3 (St Augustine the Less, 12 and 28 September 1632); FCP/St. JB/R/1(a)2 (St John the Baptist, 14 August 1636); *The Oxford English Dictionary*, 'maudlin, n.' and 'maudlin, adj.', *OED Online*.

20 Idle or vagrant persons were punishable under legislation such as the 1572 Act for the Punishment of Vagabonds, and the 1576 Act for the setting of the poor

on work and for the avoiding of idleness. *Tudor Economic Documents*, ed. Power and Tawney, II, p. 331; Kussmaul, *Servants in Husbandry in Early Modern England*, p. 180, n. 6.

21 BCB, IV, f. 209v; Salkeld, *Shakespeare amongst the Courtesans*, p. 112.

22 Dorset History Centre, DC/DOB 8/1 f. 181v (Dorchester Offenders' Book, 8 July 1633).

23 Brooks and Verey, *Gloucestershire: The Vale and the Forest of Dean*, p. 142.

24 Walker, *The Book of Almondsbury*, p. 39.

25 Inwood, 'The Chesters of Bristol', p.27; *APC*, 1554–1556, p. 358.

26 TNA, STAC 5/S14/26 (Court of Star Chamber, Hugh Smyth v Sir John Younge, Sir George Norton *et. al.*, Interrogatory 3, and testimony of Anne White, 11th April 1580).

27 Chester had acquired the former Carmelite friary in 1569: Inwood, 'The Chesters of Bristol', pp. 24–5. Colston Hall is named after the slave trader and merchant Edward Colston (1636–1721), but after much public debate it is due to be renamed when it reopens in 2020.

28 Chester Waters, *Genealogical Memoirs of the Families of Chester of Bristol, Barton Regis, London and Almondsbury*, pp. 31–35; 'Caplyn, John II (d.c.1603), of Southampton', *The History of Parliament*; Southampton tax returns: TNA, E179/174/432 (26 September 1598), E179/174/446 (24 September 1599), and E179/175/488 (4 March 1611); *Central Hampshire Lay Subsidy Assessments, 1558–1603*, ed. Vick, pp. 32–38.

29 Oxford English Dictionary, 'bed, n.', *OED Online*.

30 We don't know how old Cattelena was. More women (about half) over the age of 45 headed their own households. Froide, *Never Married*, p. 19; Wall, 'Women alone in English society', p. 311.

31 Burial records of 'Suzanna Pearis a blackamoore': LMA, MS 09221; MS 09222/1 (St Botolph Aldgate, 8 August 1593) and John de Spinosa: LMA, MS 09234/4 (St Botolph Aldgate, 7 July 1594) See also Chapter 5, n. 46 above; BCB, V, f. 94v (29 March 1606); LMA, MS 09222/1 (St Botolph Aldgate, 31 September 1616).

32 Erickson, *Women and Property*, p. 191.

33 Bristol Record Office, EP/J/4/6 (Will of Richard Ford of Almondsbury 25 April 1639).

34 Karras 'Sex and the Singlewoman', p. 131.

35 Froide, *Never Married*, pp. 21, 159.

36 Forgeng, *Daily Life in Elizabethan England*, p. 118; Worsley, *If Walls Could Talk*, p. 5; TNA, PROB 1/4 (Will of William Shakespeare, 25 March 1616); Oxford English Dictionary, 'flock, n.2', and 'bolster, n.1'. *OED Online*; Gretton, L., 'Beds in Late Medieval and Tudor Times', *Old and Interesting*, http://www.oldandinteresting.com/medieval-renaissance-beds.aspx.

37 Harrison, W., *Description of England*, ed. Edelen, pp. 200–1.

38 Milward, *A glossary of household, farming, and trade terms from probate inventories*, p. 45; Buxton, *Domestic Culture in Early Modern England*, p. 192.

39 Milward, *A glossary of household, farming, and trade terms from probate inventories*, p. 44.

40 Strachan, 'Coryate, Thomas (1577?–1617)', *Oxford Dictionary of National Biography*; Coryat, *Coryat's Crudities*, I, 236–237; Jonson, *The Devil is an Ass*, Act 5, Scene 4.

41 Shakespeare, *Much Ado About Nothing*, Act 1, Scene 1; Oxford English Dictionary, 'trencher, n.1', OED Online; Milward, *A glossary of household, farming, and trade terms from probate inventories*, pp. 56–7.

42 Ransome, 'Wives for Virginia, 1621', p. 16.

43 Lodge and Greene, *A Looking Glasse for London and England*, Act 1, Scene 3.

44 Palliser, *The Age of Elizabeth*, p. 176; Digby, *A late discourse made in a solemne assembly of nobles and learned men at Montpellier in France touching the cure of wounds by the powder of sympathy*, tr. White, p. 117.

45 Peters, *Women in Early Modern Britain*, p. 33.

46 Thomas, *Man and the Natural World*, p. 96.

47 Fudge 'Farmyard Choreographies in Early Modern England', p. 159.

48 Markham, *Countrey Contentments, Or, The English Huswife*, pp. 174–190.

49 Neeson, *Commoners: Common Right, Enclosure and Social Change in England*, p. 311.

50 Markham, *Countrey Contentments, Or, The English Huswife*, pp. 179, 182.

51 Martin Parker, *The Woman to the PLOW; And the Man to the HEN-ROOST; OR, A fine way to cure a Cot-quean* (London 1629), University of Glasgow Library – Euing 397, *English Broadside Ballad Archive*, ID: 32024, http://ebba.english.ucsb.edu/ballad/32024/xml.

52 Hill, *Women Alone*, p. 19; Valenze 'The Art of Women and the Business of Men: Women's Work and the Dairy Industry c. 1740–1840', p. 145; Pinchbeck, *Women Workers in the Industrial Revolution*, pp. 22–3.

53 Walter, *The Book of Almondsbury*, p. 43. Local lore has it that Sundays Hill was so-called because Bristolians used to drive out on Sundays by horse and carriage to the escarpment for the great views across the estuary.

54 Thirsk, *Chapters from The Agrarian History of England and Wales*, III, p. 87.

55 LMA, MJ/SBR/1 ff. 479, 498 (Middlesex Sessions Registers, 1612); Griffiths, *Lost Londons*, p. 74.

56 Oxford English Dictionary, 'band, n.2' and 'pillow-bere, n.', *OED Online*; Mortimer, *The Time-Traveller's Guide to Elizabethan England*, pp. 167–8.

57 The following discussion is based on these three examples: TNA, PROB 11/98, f. 301 (Will of William Offley, 1600); Hampshire Record Office, 1612B/036 (Will of Mary Groce, 14 October 1612) and TNA, PROB 11/52, ff. 194v–195 (Will of Nicholas Witchals, 1570).

58 Habib, *Black Lives*, p. 116

59 Erickson, *Women and Property*, p. 3.

60 Devon Record Office, MFC 46/6 (St Peter's, Barnstaple, 18 June 1565).

61 Woodward, *Men at Work*, p. 172.

62 LMA, P95/MRY1/413, pp. 15, 35 (Churchwardens Accounts, St Mary's, Putney, 27 March 1625 and 20 March 1627). For Jetto, see Chapter 4, p. 126, n. 50.

63 Her third and final marriage was to John Thornborough, Bishop of Worcester, in 1627. Habib, *Black Lives*, p. 149; Collins, *The Peerage of England*, VII, p. 316.

64 Erickson, *Women and Property*, pp. 32, 204–6, 217. Froide, *Never Married*, pp. 46–49.

65 Bristol Letters of Administration do not survive earlier that 1660, but Helen Ford is named as administrator in the inventory; Erickson, *Women and Property*, p. 34.

66 Poynton 'The Family of Haynes of Westbury-on-Trym, Wick and Abson, and other places in Gloucestershire', pp. 277–297.

67 Erickson, *Women and Property*, p. 33.

68 Ibid., pp. 33–34. D. Hey (ed.), *The Oxford Companion to Local and Family History*, p. 239.

Conclusion

1 *The copie of a leter, vvryten by a Master of Arte of Cambrige, to his friend in London* (1584), p. 13.

2 Hair, 'Attitudes to Africans in English Primary Sources on Guinea up to 1650', p. 47.

3 See the Runnymede Trust website, *Our Migration Story* for examples: http://www.ourmigrationstory.org.uk/.

4 Jordan, *White Over Black*, p. 44; Shore, 'The Enduring Power of Racism: A Reconsideration of Winthrop Jordan's *White over Black*', pp. 195–226.

Index

Page numbers in italics refer to illustrations and maps. Names of nobility are indexed by their title, for example: 'Arundel, Henry Fitzalan, 19th Earl of'. Works of literature and plays are indexed under author's name.